HISTORY
OF RUSSIA

Sergei Mikhailovich Soloviev

The Academic International Press Edition of Sergei M. Soloviev's History of Russia From Earliest Times. *Peter von Wahlde, General Editor.*

Contributing Editors:

HUGH F. GRAHAM

JOHN D. WINDHAUSEN

ALEXANDER V. MULLER

K.A. PAPMEHL

RICHARD HANTULA

WALTER J. GLEASON JR.

WILLIAM H. HILL

G. EDWARD ORCHARD

LINDSEY A.J. HUGHES

NICKOLAS LUPININ

GEORGE E. MUNRO

SERGEI M. SOLOVIEV

History of Russia

Volume 16

The First Romanov

Tsar Michael, 1613–1634

Edited, Translated and With an
Introduction by

G. Edward Orchard

Academic International Press

1991

The Academic International Press Edition of S.M. Soloviev's
History of Russia from Earliest Times in fifty volumes.

Volume 16. *The First Romanov. Tsar Michael, 1613–1634.*
Unabridged translation of the text of Volume 9, Chapters 1–3, as
contained in Volume V of S.M. Soloviev's *Istoriia Rossii s
drevneishikh vremen* published in Moscow in 1959–1966, with
added annotation by G. Edward Orchard.

ISBN: 0-87569-124-2

Composition by Janice Frye

Printed in the United States of America

A list of Academic International Press publications is found at
the end of this volume.

ACADEMIC INTERNATIONAL PRESS
Box 1111 Gulf Breeze FL 32562

CONTENTS

Weights and Measures   *viii*

Preface   *ix*

Introduction   *xiii*

I TSAR MICHAEL'S EARLY YEARS IN POWER, 1613–1617   1
Delegation from the Assembly to the Newly-Elected Tsar—
Instructions to Delegates—Negotiations with Michael and his
Mother—Michael's Secure Position—Journey from Kostro-
ma to Yaroslavl—Correspondence with the Assembly and the
Boyars—Entry into Moscow—Coronation—Pitiful State of
the Realm—The Shulgin Affair—War on Zarutsky—Corre-
spondence with the Cossacks—Zarutsky Quarrels with As-
trakhan and Terek Cossacks—Khokhlov Moves Against
Zarutsky—Zarutsky's Capture—Execution of Rebel Lead-
ers—Rebel Cossacks Move Northwards—Lykov Moves
Against the Cossacks—Aladin's Embassy—Muscovites
Capture Belaia—Unsuccessful Siege of Smolensk—War on
Lisowski—Cherkassians Perish in the North—Letter of the
Polish Lords to the Boyars—Zheliabuzhsky's Mission to Po-
land—Zheliabuzhsky and Filaret Nikitich—Negotiations
Break Down at Smolensk.

II DIPLOMACY AND WAR, 1613–1617   66
Austria—Turkey—Persia—Crimea—Embassies to Holland
and England—John Merrick's Peace Mission—Great Nov-
gorod under Swedish Rule—Defense of Tikhvin—Failure of
Trubetskoy and Mezetsky—Gustavus Adolphus Captures
Gdov—Unsuccessful Siege of Pskov—English and Dutch
Mediation at Dederino—Peace of Stolbovo—Liberation of
Novgorod—Merrick Rewarded—Gustavus Adolphus Asses-
ses Stolbovo—Boriatinsky's Mission to Sweden.

III END OF THE TROUBLES, 1616–1619   124
Military Action Against Lithuania—Military Difficulties
Outside Smolensk—Suleshov and Prozorovsky—Wladyslaw

Prepares to Advance on Moscow—Primate's Speech—Capture of Dorogobuzh and Viazma—Wladyslaw's Letter to Moscow—Pozharsky in Kaluga—Unsuccessful Peace Negotiations—Unsuccessful Attack on Borisov, Mozhaisk Besieged—Pozharsky in Borovsk—Retreat to Moscow—Assembly in Moscow—Hetman Sahaidachny—Assault on Moscow—Negotiations—Wladyslaw Moves to Pereiaslavl—Deulino Conference and Truce—Exchange of Prisoners—Filaret Returns to Moscow.

IV PATRIARCH FILARET, 1619–1633   159
Dual Power—Impressions of Filaret—Fate of Maria Khlopova—Search for Danish or Swedish Bride—Khlopova's Cause Revived—Marriages of the Tsar—Relations with Crimeans and Nogay—Swedish Affairs—Relations with England—First French Ambassador to Moscow—Dutch Embassy—Danish Ambassador—Embassy to Denmark—Hungarian Embassy—Relations with Persia.

V   RELATIONS WITH POLAND, 1619–1634   199
Flaws of the Deulino Truce—Annoyance at Polish Governors—Prince Ivan Shuisky Returns to Moscow—Quarrels between Russian and Polish Governors—The Poles Threaten the Sovereign—Turks Urge War on Poland—The Assembly of 1621—Preparations for War—Crimean Raids—Foreign Mercenaries and Tactics—Precedence Dispute between Cherkassky and Lykov—Instructions to Commanders—Gathering Supplies for the Army—Successful Beginning to the War—King Wladyslaw Aids Smolensk—Wladyslaw's Triumph—Moscow During the Smolensk Disaster—The Commanders Executed—Chronograph's Verdict on Shein—Valiant Defense of Belaia—Polish-Russian Negotiations—Eternal Peace—Lykov's Mission to Poland—The Missing Treaty—Ratification Ceremony—Shuisky's Remains Returned to Moscow.

Appendix   243
Kostomarov on Ivan Susanin

Maps

   Sweden and the Baltic in the Early Seventeenth Century   91
   Poland-Lithuania in the Early Seventeenth Century   125
   Muscovy and Its Western Neighbors, 1613–1645   170

Illustrations

   Ivan Susanin   6
   Tsar Michael   13
   Gustavus Adolphus   89
   Fortress of Marienburg   149
   Patriarch Filaret   160
   Sigismund III   204
   Wladyslaw IV   216

Notes   252

Index   327

The Editor and Translator   350

WEIGHTS AND MEASURES

Linear Measure

Verst: 500 sazhen, 1166 yards and 2 feet, .663 miles, 1.0668 km.
Sazhen: 3 arshins, 7 feet, 2.133 m
Arshin: 16 vershoks, 28in. (diuims) 72.12 cm
Chetvert: 1/4 arshin
Fut: 12 diuims, 1 foot, 30.48 cm
Vershok: 1.75 in., 4.445 cm, 1/16 arshin
Diuim: 1 inch, 2.54 cm
Desiatina: 2400 square sazhens, 2.7 acres, 1.0925 hectare
Chetvert (quarter): 1/2 desiatine, 1.35 acre (sometimes 1.5 desiatinas or ca. 4.1 acres)

Liquid Measure

Stof: Kruzhka (cup), 1/10 vedro, ca. 1.3 quarts, 1.23 liters
Kufa: 30 stofy
Vedro (paid): 3.25 gallons, 12.3 liters, 10 stofy
Bochka (barrel): 40 vedros, 121 gallons, 492 liters
Chetvert (quarter): 1.4 bochka, 32.5 gallons

Weights

Berkovets: 361 olbs., 10 puds
Pud: 40 funts, 36,113 lbs. (US), 40 lbs. (Russian), 16.38 kg
Funt: 96 zolotniks, .903 lb., 14.4 ozs., 408.24 grams
Grivenka: 205 grams
Korob (basket): 7 puds, 252 lbs.
Rad: 14 puds, 505.58 lbs
Chetvert (grain measure): 1/4 rad, 3.5 puds, 126.39 lbs., ca. 8 bushels
Chetverik (grain measure dating from 16th century): 1/8 chetvert, 15.8 lbs.
Zolotnik: 1/96 lb., 4.26 grams

Money

Chervonets (chervonny): A gold coin minted in the first half of the 18th century worth
  about 3 rubles
Muscovite Denga: 200 equals 1 ruble
Novgorod Denga: 100 equals 1 ruble
Ruble: 100 copecks, 200 dengas
Altyn: 6 Muscovite dengas, 3 copecks
Grivna: 20 Muscovite dengas, 100 grivnas equals 1 ruble, 10 copecks
Poltina (Poltinnik): 50 copecks, 100 dengas
Polupoltina (-nik): 25 copecks, 50 dengas
Poltora: 1 1/2 rubles
Peniaz: 10 equals one grosh (Lithuania)
Kopa grosh: 60 groshas, one Muscovite poltina
Chetvertak: silver coin equal to 25 copecks or 1/4 rubles (18-19th centuries)
Copeck: two Muscovite dengas
Foreign Denominations: 1 efimok or 1 thaler (Joachimsthaler)-about 1 ruble, 1 chervonets
  or chervonnyi—a ducat, about 3 rubles
Levok—Dutch silver lion dollar

Note: Weights and measures often changed values over time and sometimes held more than
  one value at the same time. For details consult Sergei G. Pushkarev, *Dictionary of
  Russian Historical Terms from the Eleventh Century to 1917* (Yale, 1970).

PREFACE

This book is an unabridged translation of Volume 9, Chapters 1-3, which are pages 7-185 in Volume V of Soloviev's *Istoriia Rossii s drevneishikh vremen* (History of Russia from Earliest times, 29 vols., St. Petersburg, 1851-1879), published from 1959 through 1966 in Moscow. For the sake of convenience I have divided into two the first and third chapters of Soloviev's text. Chapter I of the translation corresponds to pages 7-55 of the Soviet edition, Chapter II to pages 56-97. Chapter III corresponds to Soloviev's second chapter, while Chapters IV-V correspond to Chapter III of the Soloviev text (pages 123-185), the division occurring on page 153. I have also included the appendix "Kostomarov on Ivan Susanin," occurring on pages 355-362 of the Soviet edition.

The present translation endeavors to render the text and Soloviev's thought as accurately as possible. No attempt has been made to reproduce his style and text word for word for this would have yielded a bizarre Russianized text. The main consideration has been to make his history as readable as possible consistent with accuracy, while retaining at least something of the flavor of the language of the era. An effort has been made to find English-language equivalents for all technical terms Soloviev employs (ranks, offices, titles, legal, administrative and so forth) in the belief that English is no less rich in such terms than other languages. This is intended to smooth the flow of the narrative for the reader and to avoid marring the pages with annoying untranslated words. The exception involves Russian words which have become common in English—boyar, tsar, cossack. In all of this the translator remains painfully aware of the inevitable shortcomings that may remain.

Soloviev's pages are featureless and interminable, one long and complex sentence marching after the last. To make the text easier to follow for today's readers, long paragraphs and sentences have been broken into shorter ones. Most of the subtitles are based on the descriptive topic headings clustered at the beginnings of the chapters in the Russian edition. These headings have been moved into the body of the text as subtitles to mark and ease for the reader the transition from one subject to another. In some cases, to even the frequency of breaks in the text or to show topics not listed by Soloviev at the beginning of chapters, new subtitles have been added. Soloviev's arrangement of the material has been followed strictly.

Brief explanatory or interpretive materials have been inserted into the text enclosed in brackets, or added as footnotes to each chapter at the end of the book. All material enclosed in brackets has been added by the present editor and all materials in parenthesis is the author's. Emphasized words or phrases in italics are the author's.

The general policy followed in annotating has been to identify prominent personalities at first mention, and to give explanation and elucidations of less common or obscure terms and passages, assuming the typical reader to have relatively little familiarity with Russian history. If brief, these have been included in the text in brackets; otherwise they appear as numbered footnotes at the back of the book by chapters. Most of the author's own notes are not included because of their highly specialized archival, documentary and bibliographic nature is of value solely to specialists who, in any case, will prefer to consult the original Russian text. In addition, most of the notes added by the editors of the edition published in the Soviet Union which also are technical in nature—fuller bibliographic citations than those in Soloviev's notes—have not been included. When the author's notes and those of the Soviet editors are included, they are so designated. All other notes are those of the present editor.

Russian personal names are preserved in their Russian form except for Alexander, Alexis, Michael, Nicholas, Catherine and Peter, which English usage has made familiar with respect to Russian historical figures, and important ecclesiastics whose names have been recast into Latin or Greek equivalents, especially for the earlier period of Russian history. This applies to prominent individuals; Russian forms usually are used for the less prominent. Certain other names and terms have been anglicized for the sake of clarity and because they are used widely—Casimir, Sophia, Dantzig, boyar, rubles, versts, Dnieper river, and others.

The editors of the edition published in the USSR frequently have added patronymics and other names, and these have been retained without brackets; patronymics appearing in the original edition also have been included. Plural forms for names and terms which might be confusing have been anglicized—Vologdians rather than Vologzhane, Voguls and not Vogulichi, the Dolgorukys not Dolgorukie, and so forth. Even so, in a few cases the Russian plural form is used when this form is common. Most Slavic surnames show gender, and this has been preserved. Since an "a" at the end of a name usually signifies a female, Golovkin would have a wife or daughter Golovkina. The final "iia" in feminine personal names has been shortened to "ia"—"Maria" and "Evdokia" instead of "Mariia" and "Evdokiia."

Non-Russian names, locations, terms, ranks and so on are spelled according to the language native to the person or particular to the city, region or culture when this can be determined. Confusion arises at times because the text is not clear about nationalities. An excruciating example is Lithuania where at least three languages intermingle. In such cases the context is the guide used and as a last resort the Russian spelling in the text is accepted. Individuals whose names were once non-Russian but had been in Russian service for generations are named by the original spelling of the family name. Turkish, Tatar, Persian and other names and terms are spelled in the original according to accepted forms in scholarly books. In some instances, if not otherwise ascertainable they are translated from the Russian as given by Soloviev. The names of geographical locations conform to commonly accepted English usage—Podolia, Moscow, Copenhagen, Saxony and so forth.

Finally, with respect to transliteration, this translation follows a modified Library of Congress system omitting diacritical marks and ligatures, and rendering the initial "ia" and "iu" as "ya" and "yu" ("Yasnaia" and "Yury"), the suffixes "ii", "skii", "skaia" and "skoe" ("Dmitry Poliansky", "Polianskaia", "Polianskoe", instead of "Dmitrii Polianskii"), and the form "oi" has been replaced by "oy" ("Donskoy" not "Donskoi"). In some cases "i" has been inserted in place of hard and soft signs, or apostrophes indicating these signs. Hence Soloviev, not Solov'ev. The soft sign is not indicated by an apostrophe, as in some transliteration systems, but is dropped completely.

All dates, as in the original, except where otherwise specified, are according to the Julian calendar ("Old Style"); that is, for the sixteenth and seventeenth centuries, ten days behind the Gregorian used in the West. A table of weights and measures is included at the front of this volume for the convenience of the reader.

In the preparation of this volume, I was particularly grateful for the help afforded by the staff of the libraries of the University of Illinois at Champaign-Urbana, where many scholars in the Slavic field foregather each summer, and the University of Alberta, Edmonton, which was particularly useful for consulting Polish and Swedish reference material. I am also grateful to Peter von Wahlde and the staff of the Academic International Press for urging me on to the completion of this, for me, third volume of the Soloviev series.

G. Edward Orchard

INTRODUCTION

As the last volume ended, Moscow had just been liberated from the Polish invader, and an Assembly of the Land had elected as tsar Michael Fedorovich, whose father Metropolitan Filaret was still languishing in Polish captivity at the fortress of Marienburg. This present volume deals with the difficult reign of Michael Romanov to the time of the death of Filaret in 1633 and the conclusion of the Truce of Polianovka in 1634. The remaining decade or so of the reign will be dealt with in Volume 17.

Our story opens as members of the Assembly, having elected Michael, are faced with the task of obtaining the successful candidate's acceptance. While by now it had become customary for a tsar-elect to put on a ritual show of unwillingness, in this instance there is good reason to believe that Michael's reluctance was unfeigned. First, there was the probability that his election might provoke Polish reprisals against his father. Secondly, the state of the country was such that nobody could be blamed for refusing the rulership. Although Moscow was again in Russian hands, there were still undisciplined bands of Polish and Swedish troops all over the country, as well as cossacks, bandits and undisbanded foreign mercenaries. Even in his secluded retreat at the Hypatian monastery near Kostroma, deep within the heartland of Russia, Michael was not secure, as the Ivan Susanin incident demonstrated. Furthermore, the fate of Michael's predecessors on the Russian throne was scarcely encouraging; Vasily Shuisky had been deposed, forcibly tonsured and handed over to the Poles, while both Fedor Godunov and False Dmitry had been murdered in palace revolts.

The delegation at length prevailed upon Michael and his mother to accept, and they set off on their journey to Moscow; but the state of the countryside through which they passed was so pitiful that Michael was dissuaded only with great difficulty from abandoning the whole venture. The treasury was empty, and even supplies for the tsar's own household could scarcely be gathered in time for the coronation.

Yet, despite this inauspicious beginning, Soloviev points out that Michael was more secure upon the Russian throne than his predecessors had been. The reason was that the Russian people, having undergone the trials caused by their disunity, "had sufficient force to turn their repentance to good advantage, to rise up, unite and purge the realm, despite the absence of material means." Great pains had been taken to ensure that, as far as was humanly possible, the electoral assembly was representative of the whole land. It was immaterial that the new tsar was immature, of frail health and obviously dimwitted. There were plenty of self-appointed counsellors willing and able to carry on the tasks of government.

This task required a number of measures which, without the manifest support of the community at large, would have caused widespread unrest. The tsar was unable to dispense the customary bounty at his coronation; instead the treasury had to be replenished, soldiers re-equipped or paid off, marauding cossacks pacified, peasant revolts suppressed, as well as the task of repelling Polish and Swedish invaders. The Assembly was kept in almost perpetual session through the opening years of the reign, and co-operated in the raising of no less than seven levies of the "fifths" (*piatinnye den'gi*), a twenty-percent tax on immoveable property.

By the summer of 1614 the rebel cossack leader Zarutsky, the last champion of Marina and her infant son, the heir to the claims of Tsarevich Dmitry, had been defeated. Acting on the principle that stone dead hath no fellow, the four-year-old pretender was hanged outside the Serpukhov gates of Moscow, while Zarutsky was impaled. The hapless Marina, a victim of her own ambition, shortly afterwards died of grief in her prison tower at Kolomna. Another band of renegade cossacks cut a swath through the northern towns, but finally were brought to heel by Lykov.

The war against the Poles continued, with an unsuccessful attempt by the Russians to recapture Smolensk. Failing in this attempt, the two sides began to exchange missives, and the Muscovites sent Afanasy Petrovich Zheliabuzhsky to initiate discussion with the Polish lords. Although he did manage to exchange a few words with Filaret, Zheliabuzhsky's mission was taken up largely with mutual recriminations, on the Polish side voiced by Chancellor Leo Sapieha and Mikolaj Olesnicki, who had been Polish ambassador in Moscow during the reign of False Dmitry. Despite the unpromising nature of the exchange, teams of negotiators met near Smolensk. The talks bogged down in an acrimonious dispute over titles and a rehashing of the entire history of the Time of Troubles. Mediation by Emperor Matthias's ambassador Erasmus Handelius likewise proved fruitless. On this inconclusive note, the first chapter ends.

The early part of the second chapter is taken up with relations with various other powers. Between 1613 and 1616 Moscow sent no less than three embassies to Vienna, hoping that Emperor Matthias would use his good offices to restrain King Sigismund III of Poland, but once again the embassies degenerated into procedural wrangles, and it became abundantly evident that Austria did not consider Muscovite friendship worth cultivating. A more promising potential ally was Turkey, but here the prospects of common action against the Poles was jeopardized by the Don Cossacks, for whose attacks on Turkish towns the vizier held the Muscovite government responsible, even though in fact these incidents were beyond its control. With regard to the Crimean khanate, the main difficulty was that, with his depleted treasury, Michael was unable to send the customary gifts to buy peace on his southern frontier. Ambassador Volkonsky was able to fend Khan Janibek-Girey off with partial payment and promises, and thereafter the tribute, disguised as goodwill gifts, resumed on a regular basis.

More serious business was done with Holland and England. The Russians needed help in the form of cash and munitions and the maritime powers were interested in commercial concessions and transit facilities for the Persian trade. Consequently both the Dutch and the English emissaries came to act as intermediaries in the peace talks between Russia and Sweden. Especially interesting is Soloviev's summary of the harrowing account of the annalist of the Dutch delegation, Anthonis Goeteeris. The English agent John Merrick played the major part in the mediation process, and personally did very well out if it, although he did not succeed in obtaining the desired advantages for the Muscovy Company. Indeed, in nearly all the diplomatic and trading negotiations related at such great length in this volume, the Russians show themselves to be very canny, far from being the simpletons their foreign counterparts expected.

At the end of Volume 15 Great Novgorod was under Swedish occupation, and the Swedish prince Karl Philipp, the younger brother of Gustavus Adolphus, was set to assume the Russian tsardom. With the election of Michael, which took the Swedes by surprise, the latter hope was dashed, but Karl Philipp's pretensions still constituted a valuable bargaining counter, and the Swedes were still hoping to improve their position. They failed to capture Tikhvin in March 1613, but a Russian attempt in September to relieve Novgorod ended in ignominious failure. The following year Gustavus Adolphus, who had succeeded to the Swedish throne in November 1611, assumed personal command of the Swedish forces in Russia. This was to be the first chapter in his brilliant career as a general, but his Russian expedition was not an unmixed success. He captured the fortified town of Gdov but in the following year, despite a six-month siege, failed to capture Pskov, and his eminent general Evert Horn was killed in the first assault. The siege was lifted in October 1615, and serious peace negotiations began. The chief Swedish negotiator was Jacob de la Gardie, the original leader of the Swedish contingent which had entered Russia in 1609 as allies of Tsar Vasily Shuisky against the Poles. When after the battle of Klushino and the deposition of Shuisky the Swedes lost their paymaster, they began to pursue their own ends, culminating in the seizure of Novgorod on the night of July 16, 1611. Naturally the first round of negotiations at Dederino were taken up with protocol wrangles and mutual accusations of perfidy. Realistically, however, Gustavus Adolphus had no desire to hold on to Novgorod, considering that, since "the sea had been taken away from the Russians," the Peace of Stolbovo was a good bargain. Besides, with storm clouds developing in western and central Europe, he would need the alliance, or at least the benevolent neutrality, of Russia.

Now that peace was secured with Sweden the Russians' primary task, which constitutes the subject matter of our third chapter, was to end the Polish intervention. After the collapse of peace talks outside Smolensk active hostilities recommenced in June 1616, but neither side seemed able to make any real progress. In 1618 Prince Wladyslaw launched his final assault. Although he penetrated deep into Muscovite territory and reached the environs of the capital, he lacked the resources to conduct a proper siege, and his lines were hopelessly extended. The Muscovites merely had to await their two powerful allies, hunger and cold. Once more, after interminable wrangling, which Soloviev insists on reproducing verbatim, a fourteen-and-a-half-year truce was concluded at Deulino, a village close to the Trinity monastery, on December 1, 1618. The exchange of prisoners took about six months to effect, and Filaret himself expressed impatience at the Muscovite diplomats' pedantry, which was holding up his release.

The fourth chapter is mostly concerned with foreign affairs; indeed there is very little on domestic affairs in this volume. These are mostly dealt with in the final chapter of Soloviev's ninth volume, which presumably will be part of Volume 17 of this series. Domestic affairs do intrude briefly at the beginning of this chapter, in the description of the dual power wielded jointly by tsar and patriarch, and the tsar's marital history. Even in the latter instance there is a foreign component since Filaret, after his return, strove for a while to obtain a Swedish or a Danish bride for his son. Filaret was undoubtedly the real ruler from 1619 until his death in 1633. Michael was such a cipher that an attempt to put together a coherent biographical sketch of him is an exercise in frustration. No doubt he had a very disturbed childhood. In his fourth year both his parents were arrested and sent to monastic confinement, and he was shunted about between various relatives. His education had been neglected during the troubled times of his childhood and adolescence; indeed, there is no evidence that he was even functionally literate. He was always dominated by a more powerful personality, whether the boyar Fedor Ivanovich Sheremetev, his mother the nun Martha, Filaret or Boris Morozov. Even in the matter of his own marriage he seems to have had very little to say. His original betrothed, Maria Khlopova, was ruled out because of the intrigues of the Saltykovs. Then Filaret returned and tried to marry him off to a foreign princess. Failing this, Michael wished to send for his original betrothed, but his mother vetoed the plan. Michael then married Princess Maria Dolgorukova, but she died within the year. Finally he married Evdokia Streshneva, who outlived him by a few months.

Relations with European powers between the Truce of Deulino and the War of Smolensk naturally took place against the background of the Thirty Years' War, of which the Russo-Polish conflict of 1632-1634 consituted a minor sideshow. War and peace in Russia at this time seems to have been anticyclical to what was happening elsewhere in Europe. Perhaps this situation was determined by the mercenary market. With the wars of religion halted and the Dutch truce holding, there were plenty of soldiers of fortune looking for employment in Russia, on one side or the other, but more remunerative prospects opened up with the Prague defenestration, providing more affluent paymasters than the indigent Russian tsar. Russia, although itching for revenge, was in no position to take on Poland single-handed, quite apart from incurring the ignominy among the international community of a unilateral breach of the truce. Soloviev in our final chapter, devoted to Russo-Polish relations, points out two opportunities, the Turkish alliance in 1621, and the alliance with Sweden in 1632. Both were frustrated by the untimely death of the respective rulers. Osman II was murdered by his janissaries, and Gustavus Adolphus was slain at Lützen. In the first instance, the Muscovites had not yet committed any forces, but in the second, they were inextricably drawn in.

Gustavus Adolphus and Filaret had decided on joint action against Poland. In June 1631, almost two years before the expiry of the truce, an Assembly decided to open hostilities immediately. In fairness it must be stated that there were so many running disputes and incidents that either side had ample pretext for accusing the other of having violated the truce. Because of a precedence dispute the original commanders Cherkassky and Lykov were removed from their posts, and the expeditionary force sent to recapture Smolensk was entrusted to Shein and Izmailov. Shein had been the siege commander at Smolensk between 1609 and 1611, and had spent the next eight years in Polish captivity. He was well aware of the formidable nature of the city's defenses, and so at first attempted to starve the garrison out. The blockade was completed by the end of January 1633. The garrison, however, held out, so Shein ordered an assault, which failed largely through the weakening of his own forces. Because of Crimean incursions, many of the service gentry from the southern regions were compelled to leave the besieging forces in order to defend their home territories. Another factor, which Soloviev does not mention here, is that the Russian effort was sapped by rebel activities. A partisan movement lead by one Ivan Balash harassed the Poles, but also was seizing the occasion to settle scores with Muscovite landlords. Following unsuccessful attempts to integrate these irregulars into the Muscovite army, Balash was arrested, and died shortly afterwards in prison. Nevertheless the social revolt continued until well after the cessation of the war, and the ranks of the rebels were swelled by cossacks and other deserters from the regular army.

Sigismund III had died on April 30, 1632 but Wladyslaw did not secure his own election until November 8, being crowned on February 5, 1633. Having secured his throne, Wladyslaw now took a personal interest in the Smolensk war since he had not abandoned his title to Muscovy conferred by the agreement with the boyar administration in 1610. By September Shein's besiegers were themselves besieged as well as being plagued by gross indiscipline, especially among the foreign mercenary officers. Since promised reinforcements from Moscow failed to materialize, Shein on his own authority negotiated a capitulation on February 15, 1634. Shein's army was permitted to march away with the honors of war, but on their return to Moscow Shein and Izmailov were made the scapegoats, and were beheaded by order of the boyar council on April 28. Peace was concluded on the banks of the Polianovka river, near Viazma, on June 3. All things considered, the military defeat was transformed into a diplomatic victory, since Wladyslaw renounced his claim to the Russian throne. He was also glad to pocket the war indemnity, which under a secret clause of the treaty was made payable to Wladyslaw personally, not to the Polish government. The Muscovites also retained Serpeisk, and further minor territorial adjustments favorable to Moscow were made between then and 1640.

There were two other unfinished items of business. Under the terms of the Treaty of Polianovka the Poles were obliged to return the original of the treaty concluded in August 1610 by Hetman Stanislaw Zolkiewski with the Moscow boyars. The royal archives were in such disarray that the document could not be found; instead the Polish plenipotentiaries were obliged to swear an oath that the treaty was null and void, and was to be consigned to oblivion. The other matter was the return to Moscow of the remains of Tsar Vasily Shuisky, his brother Prince Dmitry, and the latter's wife, Ekaterina Grigorievna, daughter of Ivan the Terrible's henchman Maliuta Skuratov. The coffins were exhumed, placed inside more sumptuous caskets, and brought back to Moscow, where they were solemnly reinterred in the Archangel cathedral. With them was buried the last spectre of the Time of Troubles, which consitutes a fitting end to this present volume.

Great literary merit cannot be claimed by Soloviev, at least for this present volume. It was evidently composed in great haste, and in essence consists of a number of undigested passages of primary source material, tenuously strung together by narrative, often without comment on the significance of the source material. Nevertheless, since it does present much material which otherwise is either unpublished or not readily accessible, this volume has considerable value.

The unpublished sources Soloviev uses are mainly diplomatic documents, which during his time were in the Foreign Ministry archives, but which are now more conveniently gathered together in the Central State Archive of Ancient Acts, grouped in *fondy* relating to the various countries: England (35), Holland (50), Holstein (51), Denmark (53), Poland (79), Turkey (89), France (93), Sweden (96) and the Crimea (123). The main printed documentary sources he used were the third volumes, respectively, of the *Collection of State Documents and Treaties* (Moscow, 1822), *Acts Collected in the Archives and Libraries of the Russian Empire by the Imperial Archeographical Commission* (St. Petersburg, 1836), *Historical Acts Collected and Edited by the Archeographical Commission* (St. Petersburg, 1841) and the fourth volume of the *Acts Pertaining to the History of Western Russia, Collected and Edited by the Archeographical Commission* (St. Petersburg, 1851). For chronicle sources Soloviev mainly relied upon the Novikov edition of the *Chronicle of Many Rebellions* and an unidentified recension of the *Chronograph*.

For Polish subject matter Soloviev relied upon the Latin chronicle by Stanislaw Kobierzycki, *History of Wladyslaw, Prince of Poland and Sweden* (Dantzig, 1655) and a secondary work by J. Bobrowicz, *Zycia slawnych polaków* (Lives of Famous Poles), 4 vols. (Lipsk, 1837-1838). In addition to archival material, for Dutch background he relied upon J. Scheltema, *Russia and the Netherlands* (Amsterdam, 1617).

The history of Michael's reign has been neglected somewhat by modern historians. English readers would do well to consult the relevant chapters of George Vernadsky, *The Tsardom of Moscow 1547-1682* (New Haven, 1969) or Paul Dukes, *The Making of Russian Absolutism* (London, 1982). V.O. Kliuchevsky's treatment of Michael's reign is contained in *A Course of Russian History. The Seventeenth Century*, translated by N. Duddington (Chicago, 1968), or the alternate translation by Lilian Archibald *The Rise of the Romanovs* (London, 1970). A discussion of the role of the Muscovite governing caste during this period is found in Robert O. Crummey, *Aristocrats and Servitors. The Boyar Elite in Russia 1613-1689* (Princeton, 1983). Three very useful articles by John L. Keep relevant to this period are "The Regime of Filaret 1619-1633," *Slavonic and East European Review*, Vol. 38, No. 91 (1960), pp. 334-360; "Bandits and the Law in Muscovy," *Slavonic Review*, Vol. 35, No. 84 (1956), pp. 201-222; and "The Decline of the Zemsky Sobor," *Slavic and East European Review*, Vol. 36 (1957), pp. 100-122.

Since the bulk of this volume concerns international relations, in order to comment intelligently I was obliged to read up extensively on the general history of early modern Europe. On the Polish background, an excellent recent work is Norman Davies, *God's Playground. A History of Poland*, 2 vols. (London, 1981). For Sweden, Michael Roberts, *Gustavus Adolphus. A History of Sweden 1611-1632*, 2 vols. (London 1953-1958), is still unsurpassed. On the general European conflict, a study of C.V. Wedgwood, *The Thirty Years' War* (London, 1937 and many subsequent reprintings), is still rewarding. More recent works on the same topic include S.H. Steinberg, *The Thirty Years' War and the Struggle for European Hegemony 1600-1660* (London, 1960), J.V. Polisensky, *The Thirty Years' War* (London, 1971) and the excellent book of essays edited by Geoffrey Parker, *The Thirty Years' War*, revised edition (New York, 1987). On the French background, Victor-L. Tapié, *France in the Age of Louis XIII and Richelieu* (Cambridge, 1984), is indispensible, as also for Holland is Pieter Geyl, *The Netherlands in the Seventeenth Century* (London, 1961). On Austria, the second chapter of Robert A. Kann, *A History of the Habsburg Empire 1526-1918* (Berkeley, 1974), is to be recommended. Perry Anderson, *Lineages of the Absolutist State* (London, 1974) provides a stimulating comparative analysis, with one chapter specifically devoted to Russia.

As far as Russia is concerned, the reign of Michael tends to be somewhat of a historiographical lacuna. It seems that even the contributors to the standard full-length history, *Ocherki po istorii SSSR. XVII v.* (Notes on the History of the USSR. The Seventeenth Century) (Moscow, 1955), find it easier to skim over the political history in favor of discussion of socio-economic trends and specialized aspects. In 1913 E.D. Stashevsky published in Kiev the first volume of *Notes on the History of the Reign of Michael Fedorovich*, but no subsequent volumes appeared. A.E. Presniakov contributed an article "The Muscovite Realm in the First Half of the Seventeenth Century" in *Tri veka* (Three Centuries), an anthology devoted to the tercentenary of the Romanov dynasty edited by V.I. Kallash (Moscow, 1912). What promised to be a formidable body of scholarly work on the early Romanov period was interrupted by war and revolution. When historical studies in Russia once again settled down to a situation at least resembling normality, scholars had very different preoccupations. The reign of Michael Romanov still awaits its definitive history. For English readers, this present volume at least partially will fill the gap.

History of Russia

Volume 16

The First Romanov

Tsar Michael, 1613–1634

I

TSAR MICHAEL'S EARLY YEARS IN POWER
1613–1617

DELEGATION FROM THE ASSEMBLY TO THE NEWLY-ELECTED TSAR
Having proclaimed the sixteen-year-old Michael Fedorovich, the
Assembly of the Land[1] appointed the following petitioners to go to
him: Archbishop Feodorit of Riazan;[2] three archimandrites, namely
those of the Miracles, New Savior[3] and Simonov[4] monasteries; the
cellarer Avraamy Palitsyn of the Trinity monastery;[5] the boyars Fedor Ivanovich Sheremetev (who was related to the young tsar)[6] and
Prince Vladimir Ivanovich Bakhtcrianov-Rostovsky;[7] and Lord-in-
waiting Fedor Vasilievich Golovin,[8] together with table attendants,
crown agents, officials, residents of the capital and elected representatives from the towns.

INSTRUCTIONS TO DELEGATES
The Assembly did not know where Michael was at the time and
therefore in the instructions to the delegates they were told to "proceed to the sovereign Tsar and Grand Prince Michael Fedorovich of
All Russia at Yaroslavl or wherever the sovereign may be." The
delegates, after doing obeisance to the newly-elected tsar and his
mother, and informing them of the election, were to say to Michael:
"All people of every rank beg of you, great sovereign, to take pity
on the remnant of the Christian race, and gather together the much-
plundered Orthodox Christian community of the Russian tsardom
and deliver it from dismemberment by the ravenous Poles and Lithuanians, taking it under your loving care, under your strong right
hand, and not disregard the tears and sighs of all the people, but according to the will of God and the election of all ranks of the people, be lord tsar and grand prince of All Russia over the Vladimir
and Muscovite realm and all the territories of the Russian tsardom.

Be so gracious, great sovereign, as to travel to your royal capital in Moscow and grant us by reason of your noble birth deliverance from all misfortunes and sorrows that are upon us. And when you, O sovereign, are seated upon your throne in Moscow, then upon hearing of your arrival, the Lithuanians and all enemies of your rule will be stricken with fear, but all the people of the Muscovite realm will rejoice. And when you make your triumphant entry into the capital the metropolitan and the archbishops with all the Holy Synod,[9] the boyars and all the people will meet you with miraculous icons and life-giving crosses, according to your royal dignity, and all people from the greatest to the least will be pleased to serve you, O sovereign, and favor you and sacrifice their lives for you."

The instructions conclude: "If the sovereign does not agree, or refuses, or reconsiders, do obeisance and plead with him in every way to take pity and be our tsar and come to Moscow as soon as possible. Such a divine matter is not achieved by men or even by his own sovereign will, but by this election God has chosen him as tsar. And if the sovereign pleads that his father Metropolitan Filaret[10] is presently in Lithuania, and so he cannot be upon the Muscovite throne lest evil befall his father, do obeisance and say that he should not be deterred for that reason. The boyars and all the land would send to the Lithuanian king and say that for his father they would exchange many eminent Lithuanians."

The delegates left Moscow on March 2 but even before this, starting February 25, documents were sent around the towns with news of Michael's election. The Assembly wrote: "You, my lords, must chant prayers for long life to the sovereign, and must be with us under one roof and under one power and under the mighty arm of a Christian sovereign, Tsar Michael Fedorovich. And we, all the people of the Muscovite realm, from the greatest to the least, and all the people of the towns, not only the elected people, but all the other townsmen as well, all will rejoice with heartfelt joy that one thought has found place in the heart of all the people, namely that Michael Fedorovich, the kinsman of our Lord Tsar Fedor Ivanovich of blessed memory, is to be our tsar. God has chosen him to sit upon the great royal throne not through any human agency, but independently of all people according to his ineffable kindness; concerning his election, God placed in the hearts of all people a single thought and resolution."

Accompanying these tidings a loyal rescript also was sent, in which there is nothing concerning penalties for violation or similar matters such as were included in the loyalty oaths to the Godunovs. The allegiance of the provinces followed rapidly. As early as March 4 the governor of Pereiaslavl-in-Riazan[11] informed Moscow that the inhabitants of his town had sworn allegiance to Michael. This news was followed by other such communications from even more distant provinces.

NEGOTIATIONS WITH MICHAEL AND HIS MOTHER
Finally there came news from the delegates sent by the Assembly, who had found Michael and his mother at Kostroma, in the St. Hypatius monastery.[12] The delegates reported to the Assembly that on March 13 they had arrived at Kostroma at vespertide, and had informed Michael of their arrival, whereupon he commanded them to attend him the following day. The delegates reported this to the governor and all the townsmen, and on the 14th, bearing icons, they went in procession to the St. Hypatius monastery. Michael and his mother met the images outside the monastery, but when the delegates told them why they had been sent, Michael replied "with great anger and weeping" that he did not wish to be sovereign and his mother Martha added that she would not bless her son with the tsardom. For a long time the couple refused to follow the cross into the cathedral church; only with difficulty were the delegates able to persuade them. Within the church the delegates handed Michael and his mother the documents from the Assembly and delivered their speeches according to their instructions, but again received the same reply. Martha said that "her son did not have it in his thoughts to be sovereign over such glorious realms, he was not of mature years, and people of all ranks of the Muscovite realm had become feeble-minded, since they had entrusted their souls to previous sovereigns, but had not served them properly."

Martha recalled how they had betrayed Godunov, murdered the False Dmitry, deposed Shuisky and handed him over to the Poles, and then continued: "Having witnessed such perfidy towards previous sovereigns, such humiliation, murder and outrage, how will it be with a sovereign who is on the throne by hereditary right? This is impossible for yet another reason. The Muscovite realm has been utterly ruined at the hands of Poles, Lithuanians and inconstant

Russians, and the previous royal regalia gathered together from ancient times have been carried off by the Lithuanians. The court villages, tax-paying districts, bytowns and town quarters have been distributed as estates to gentry, junior boyars and all manner of servicemen, and have been laid waste. The servicemen were poor, so how is whoever God ordained to be tsar to reward his servicemen? How is the royal revenue to be restored, and how is he to resist his enemies?"

Then Michael and Martha said that it would be simply ruinous for him to be ruler, and for her to bless him with the tsardom. Besides, his father Filaret was with the king in Lithuania under great oppression. The king had announced that should his son became ruler of the Muscovite realm he would order immediately some evil to be done unto him; moreover it would be impossible for Michael to be ruler of the Muscovite realm without his father's blessing. The delegates tearfully besought and petitioned Michael not to disregard the pleas and petition of the Assembly. They had chosen him according to the will of God, not according to their own desires, since God had placed this desire unanimously in the hearts of all Orthodox Christians, from the greatest to the least, in Moscow and in all the towns.

As for previous sovereigns, Tsar Boris had usurped the throne. Having done away with the sovereign stem of Tsarevich Dmitry, he committed many injustices, and God had taken revenge upon him for the blood of Tsarevich Dmitry through the apostate Grishka Otrepiev. Grishka the brigand and renegade monk had been punished by God for his deeds and died an evil death.[13] Tsar Vasily had been elected by a mere handful of men and thanks to the working of Satan many towns refused to serve him, and fell away from the Muscovite realm. All this occurred because of the will of God and the sins of all the Orthodox people, and among all the peoples of the Muscovite realm there was dissension and strife. But now the people of the Muscovite realm had done penance and had achieved unity throughout all the towns.

The delegates pleaded and did obeisance to Michael and his mother from the third hour to the ninth. They said that he should not frustrate the will of God, but become sovereign of the Muscovite realm. Michael still refused. The delegates threatened him, saying that God would visit utter ruin upon the realm. Then Michael and Martha said that they would rely in everything upon the just and unfathomable judgment of God. Martha blessed her son, Michael accepted the staff from the archbishop, allowed them all to kiss his hand and said that he would soon come to Moscow.

MICHAEL'S SECURE POSITION

Feodorit's words, that Michael need not fear to suffer the fate of his predecessors because all the people of the Muscovite realm had done penance and had achieved unity, were fully justified. By fearful experience the people of the Muscovite realm had learned how strife and dissension, which untied the hands of brigands, had arisen. The people of the land had sufficient moral resources to turn their repentance to good advantage, to rise up, unite and purge the realm, and were now in a fit state to support a new sovereign, despite the absence of material resources to which Martha had alluded. There was no treasury, nor could funds be gathered from anywhere, for the realm was ruined and the land was filled with brigand cossacks whose turbulence knew no measure. Zarutsky[14] was threatening from the southeast, the Poles and Swedes from the west. The new sovereign was inexperienced, a feeble young man, at whose side there were no people of strong mind or good will.

Despite this, Michael kept hold of his throne. As soon as danger arose, on every important occasion, we see alongside the tsar the Assembly, inspired by that impetus with which the "last remnant" of the people sought the liberation of the country. To that extent there was among the influential people of the year 1613 the strong conviction that they must sacrifice everything to support and preserve the new tsar, who was re-establishing order.

The extent to which these people were prepared to make sacrifices is exemplified best by the heroic feat of Ivan Susanin. When Michael, who had left Moscow after the surrender of the Kremlin, was living in Kostroma, a detachment of Poles (according to the document, but in all probability they were rebel cossacks since the Poles were no longer in these localities) who had heard of the new tsar's election, searched for him in order to stifle the restoration of order which they did not desire. During the searches the enemy seized the peasant Ivan Susanin from the village of Domnino, near Kostroma, and inflicted dreadful tortures on him, demanding that he show them where Michael was hidden. Susanin knew that he was in Kostroma, but he did not tell and was tortured to death.[15]

Ivan Susanin
Memorial in Kostroma

JOURNEY FROM KOSTROMA TO YAROSLAVL

On March 19 Michael left Kostroma for Yaroslavl, where he arrived on the 21st. Yet again Yaroslavl was the scene of a great national gathering, the scene of a great triumph. Not long ago its inhabitants had seen Pozharsky's militia;[16] now they saw the consummation of this militia's heroic deeds. The inhabitants of Yaroslavl and the gentry, junior boyars, leading merchants and traders, together with their wives and children, who had assembled from all over, met the new tsar, bore him icons, bread and gifts, and were speechless with joy.

CORRESPONDENCE WITH THE ASSEMBLY AND THE BOYARS

On March 23 Michael wrote to the Assembly in Moscow saying how the delegates had visited him in Kostroma, and how he had persisted in refusing the throne. "It had never even entered our thoughts that we should reign over so many great realms, for numerous reasons; namely, that we are not yet of mature age, and the Muscovite realm is presently in ruins, and the people of the Muscovite realm have become feeble-minded on account of their sins, and have not served properly their previous great sovereigns. Therefore, seeing such perfidy, humiliation and murder, how will a lawful hereditary tsar fare in Moscow, let alone myself?" In conclusion, informing them of his consent, Michael added: "Now that you, our boyars and all manner of people, have kissed the cross and entrusted your souls to us, you must stand fast in the strength of your reason, must serve us unwaveringly and favor us, not call any brigands by the tsar's name, not serve any brigands, ensure that there is no plundering or murder among you in Moscow or in other towns or along the highways, and you must be in unity and love among yourselves. On this you have entrusted your souls to us and kissed the cross, and you will stand firm on this, so will I gladly reward you for your righteousness and service."

The Assembly replied that all the people tearfully were thanking God, praying for the tsar's health and asked: "Have mercy upon us orphans, great sovereign. Hasten to the capital." The same message was sent by the Assembly to its delegates, Feodorit and his companions, requesting information as to when the sovereign would be at the Trinity monastery, and where he wanted to be met. But Prince

Troekurov[17] came from Yaroslavl and asked the Assembly: "Are there enough supplies in the palace for the tsar's arrival, and have provisions been collected from the towns, and where can we hope to obtain them? To whom have the court villages been entrusted, how are we to replenish the tsar's household, and how much of the tsar's bounty are we to give to armorers and workers? Table attendants, gentry and junior boyars make obeisance to you and state that court villages have been assigned to them, but there is a great deficiency in returns from these petitioners. What shall we say to them? That in Moscow and along the highways there has been no plundering? Gentry and junior boyars and people of all classes have dispersed from Moscow. His majesty is unaware whether they left with the Assembly's permission, or whether they left of their own accord."

The Assembly replied: "Supplies have been sent for, and it was written to collectors that they must hasten to Moscow with supplies, for there are few provisions in the tsar's storehouses. Stern orders have been given concerning plundering and brigandage. We are hunting down brigands and robbers, and we have ordered that they be punished. We have not allowed any gentry and junior boyars to depart anywhere from Moscow without the sovereign's leave. Those who have departed to their homes have been ordered to attend the sovereign's arrival in Moscow."

March came to an end. On April 1st the Assembly again wrote to its emissaries, Sheremetev[18] and his companions, to ask sovereign when he would arrive at Moscow, and where he was to be met. On April 8 the tsar answered this with the following document: "You sent a letter to us by the hand of Prince Ivan Fedorovich Troekurov requesting that we not delay our progress, and we sent a note with Prince Ivan asking how much of all kinds of provisions you had with you in the palace at Moscow. According to this note, there was little of grain or other provisions for our household, and there would be none when we arrived. Collectors whom you had sent to the towns to gather foodstuffs had not returned to Moscow, there was no money in any of the chancelleries, for the Muscovite realm is utterly ruined at the hands of the Poles and Lithuanians, many towns and districts are devastated by war, our court villages and districts have been distributed as service tenures and laid waste, and others are still being given out. No money or grain can be collected from anyone to purchase supplies for our household or to pay our servicemen. Atamans and cossacks incessantly petition and importune us concerning payment in cash, provisions for themselves and their horses, but we have nothing with which to reward them, neither have we any provisions to give them. In accordance with your petition and that of people of all ranks, we are hastening to Moscow, and we will inform you of the date on which we are leaving Yaroslavl. You, our clergy, boyars, lords-in-waiting and officials must take counsel concerning this decree with the table attendants, crown agents, Moscow gentry, provincial gentry and junior boyars, atamans, cossacks, musketeers, leading merchants, tradesmen and all residents of the capital and visiting townsmen. How are we to pay our soldiers, provision our household, give food and drink to our impoverished servicemen, and how are our armorers and rent collectors to collect supplies, and from where? Concerning this you must put together a resolution of the Assembly and inform us without delay. You yourselves know that we became tsar at your insistence, not according to our own desire, and you kissed the cross to us of your own free will. You must all, being mindful of your oath, serve us and concern yourselves with all these matters, and put together a resolution on how to deal with them. You know personally how our foes, the Poles and Lithuanians and the Swedish king, have seized many towns of our realm, and their troops are occupying these towns. According to our information, we can expect the arrival of Lithuanians and Swedes very soon, and Lithuanians are at this moment besieging Toropets, but there is no help for Toropets. Also many gentry and junior boyars are petitioning us concerning service tenures, that you are taking them away and redistributing them without due process. You are to remove this aggravation from us and order the gentry and junior boyars to conduct disputes concerning service tenures and patrimonies through the proper channels, and not petition us."

Hitherto the tsar had corresponded with the Assembly but on April 11 the boyars, Fedor Ivanovich Mstislavsky[19] and his companions, wrote to him personally that there were no governors in the towns, and towns could not remain without governors. Atamans, cossacks and musketeers petitioned for provisions, saying that previously provisions had been collected for them from court and monastic villages. Now the governors, atamans, musketeers and cossacks said that governors were being sent to the towns and collectors to the villages by the sovereign. Therefore they dared not send governors and collectors without the sovereign's decree.

Finally on April 18 the tsar informed the clergy and boyars that his progress to Moscow was delayed on account of the dismal state of the highway, which was breaking up in the spring thaw. Much ice had melted and there was a great runoff. He had left Yaroslavl on April 16 and had arrived at Rostov on the 17th. From there he intended to proceed towards Moscow on the 19th. The tsar wrote: "We are proceeding slowly because there is little transport and our servicemen are in poor condition. Musketeers, cossacks and many of our court retainers are going on foot." Yet Michael still proceeded very slowly. On April 25 he wrote from his encampment in the village of Liubtimovo that many table attendants, crown agents, and inhabitants of Moscow whose duty it was to accompany him had not yet appeared; he ordered the boyars to confiscate from these defaulters their service tenures and patrimonies. There were as many as forty-two of these defaulters.

The tsar also wrote to the boyars instructing them to prepare for him the Golden Chamber of Tsaritsa Irina, together with its workshops and reception halls. For his mother he ordered the wooden apartments which had belonged to the wife of Tsar Vasily Shuisky. The boyars replied that they had prepared for the tsar the rooms of Tsar Ivan and the Palace of Facets,[20] and for his mother apartments had been prepared in the Ascension convent,[21] where Tsaritsa Martha was living.[22] The apartments which the tsar had ordered to be prepared could not be renovated, for there was neither time nor materials. There was no money in the treasury, and there were few carpenters. The palaces and apartments were without roofs, staircases, benches, doors or lattices. Everything must be renovated but it was difficult to obtain the proper timber at short notice.

Another complication emerged, yet another vexation for the young tsar. On April 28 Feodorit and Sheremetev wrote to the Assembly: "The tsar has written to you many times, forbidding murder, plundering or any violence in Moscow, the other towns or on the highways. Yet on April 23 there appeared before the sovereign

in his encampment at the village of Svatkovo some gentry and junior boyars who had been plundered utterly and wounded, and in
questioning stated that some of them had been dispatched to the
sovereign with documents, others had been sent to the towns to recruit gentry and junior boyars and send them to service. On the
highway at Mytishi and on the Kliazma cossacks had seized them,
plundered them, slashed them with sabres and detained them in their
encampment for two days and wished to kill them. Some had managed to untie themselves at night, and had got away. Some of these
brigands were encamped at Mytishi, others on the Kliazma, about
two hundred of them altogether, both mounted and on foot. Certain
officials wrote to the sovereign from Dmitrov informing him that
some peasants had fled to them from the villages and hamlets, having been burned and tortured by fire. On April 26 these brigands
arrived at Dmitrov and would have plundered the town quarter, but
at that time there happened to be in Dmitrov gentry and junior boyars, service and trading cossacks, who fought and prevented the
brigands from plundering the town quarter. The inhabitants of
Dmitrov, leaving the town, wanted to make their way free of these
brigands, but there was even greater plundering and murder by these
brigands in the villages and hamlets. Cossacks who had been sent
to various places for service took their allotted subsistence, yet
robbed and assaulted the people passing along the highways and the
peasants in the villages and hamlets; they plundered, tortured,
burned them with fire, captured and beat them to death.

"On April 26 the sovereign and his mother spoke angrily and
tearfully to the men of all ranks assembled in the cathedral church
of the Trinity monastery that brigands were shedding Christian
blood incessantly. The entire realm had chosen him as sovereign,
they had promised to serve and respect him and to be united in love.
Yet now in Moscow, in the other towns and along the highways
there was plundering and murder. Having forgotten their oaths, they
had closed the highways to all messengers, servicemen and traders
with goods, and allowed no provisions to get through. The sovereign and his mother, seeing such brigandage, did not wish to leave
the Trinity monastery unless all the people achieved unity and
ceased to shed Christian blood. The sovereign and his mother said:
'You did obeisance and said that you had come to your senses and

had left off brigandage. You in fact did obeisance and spoke falsely.' And we, gentlemen, hearing such words and such reproaches
from the sovereign, were cast into profound grief, and by the sovereign's permission sent to you chosen people from all ranks to tell
you that, being mindful of your souls and your solemn oath, you
must seek out the brigands and make them leave off brigandage."

The tsar himself wrote to the Assembly about the same matter:
"Perhaps you yourselves know—it is written in the tsar's document—that unless brigandage is dealt with in and around Moscow
what mercy can we expect from God? No one is reaching Moscow
with either provisions or grain, the roads are all closed. If the roads
from Moscow to the towns, and from the towns to Moscow, are not
clear, how can any good come of this situation? I myself know how
many leading merchants, traders and residents fled Moscow during
the devastation of the city; but now they are ordered to return to
Moscow with their wives, children and all their possessions, and
they are bound to do so by heavy sureties. Yet they do not dare
travel to Moscow by reason of this murder and plundering."

The tsar, or rather his mother, was not satisfied with the boyars'
answer about preparation of the Kremlin palaces for their arrival.
On April 29 the tsar wrote to the the boyars: "In accordance with
the previous decree, and in accordance with this decree, see to it
that the Golden Chamber of Tsaritsa Irina is made ready, and also
the apartments of Tsaritsa Martha for our mother. If there is no
wood, use the beams from the apartments of Tsar Vasily. You wrote
to us that apartments had been prepared for our mother in the Ascension convent, but it is not suitable for our mother to live in those
apartments."

ENTRY INTO MOSCOW

On April 30 the Assembly resolved that the boyars Prince Ivan
Mikhailovich Vorotynsky[23] and Vasily Petrovich Morozov,[24] the
Lord-in-waiting Prince Danilo Ivanovich Mezetsky[25] and Crown
Secretary Ivanov, together with chosen men of all ranks, should
wait upon the sovereign, make obeisance, and implore him to take
pity upon Orthodox Christians and not delay his progress to Moscow. Concerning brigandage and all other matters the metropolitan
and the boyars had issued a stern decree. The atamans and cossacks

Tsar Michael
Seventeenth-Century Dutch Engraving

had agreed among themselves that each day two atamans would keep watch on each encampment, and wherever there was any hint of brigandage it must be reported immediately, and they would deal with it, as also cases where collectors refused to perform their duties on account of brigands. In Moscow in all the free trading areas and in the cossack encampments strict order was to be kept, captains were assigned to patrol the streets to prevent brigandage or drunkenness, and wherever brigands appeared along the highways detachments would be sent from Moscow to deal with them.

The commanders of the Militia Force, Prince Trubetskoy[26] and Prince Pozharsky, sent the tsar a petition: "We your slaves Mitka Trubetskoy and Mitka Pozharsky, who are on your service around Moscow, have endured hunger and much hardship, and during the onslaughts of the Polish hetman have endured hard sieges; we have fought against the destroyers of the Christian faith, not sparing our lives, and persuaded many people not to disregard God's grace by deserting Moscow. By the grace of God, and the steadfast service and blood of all ranks of the people, the Muscovite realm was liberated and many people were set free. Now there are many table attendants, crown agents, Muscovite gentry, officials, residents of Moscow, provincial gentry and junior boyars, who were with us outside Moscow, who come to us and petition you, O sovereign, that they may be graced with your presence. But we dare not to advance to greet you without your command. We await your favor and command, as you shall order."

The delegates from the Assembly, Prince Vorotynsky and his companions, found Michael in the villages of Bratovshchino, half way between the Trinity monastery and Moscow. The tsar and his mother, having heard their petition, spoke gracious words, saying that they would be at Taininskoe, the last stage before Moscow, on May 1, and would enter Moscow on May 2. On that day, which was a Sunday, people of all ranks in Moscow arose as one and ventured out of the city to meet the sovereign. Michael and his mother heard prayers in the Dormition cathedral,[27] after which the people of all ranks approached the tsar's hand and greeted the great sovereign.

CORONATION

The tsar's coronation took place on July 11. Before proceeding to the Dormition cathedral he sat in the Golden Scriptorium and there

two table attendants were promoted to boyar rank: Prince Ivan Borisovich Cherkassky[28] and the leader of the liberation force, Prince
Dmitry Mikhailovich Pozharsky. At the elevation of the latter the
conciliar noble Gavrilo Pushkin was ordered to stand. He had petitioned that he could not stand at the elevation for he had never had
ancestors less in rank than the Pozharsky family, and so he would
be disparaged thereby. The sovereign indicated that on the occasion
of his coronation there would be no order of precedence within
ranks, and ordered that decree of his to be inscribed in the service
records in the presence of all the boyars. The secretary Peter Tretiakov came forward and declared that the boyar Prince Mstislavsky
would sprinkle the sovereign with gold coins; boyar Ivan Nikitich
Romanov[29] would hold the Cap of Monomakh, the boyar Prince
Dmitry Timofeevich Trubetskoy would hold the orb.

Once again the familiar petition was heard. Trubetskoy brought a
petition against Ivan Romanov, saying that he would be disparaged
by serving in a lesser position. The sovereign said to Trubetskoy:
"It is true that your ancestry is superior to that of Ivan, and he may
well be inferior to you, but now he must be accorded a higher position since he is my paternal uncle. You will have to take a lesser
position."

When the matter had been resolved in this manner, the sovereign
entered the cathedral church, where he was crowned with the royal
diadem by Metropolitan Ephraim of Kazan.[30] The next day, July 12,
the tsar's name-day,[31] the Feast of St. Michael Malein,[32] was celebrated. On the occasion of this festivity the sovereign elevated
Kuzma Minin to the rank of conciliar noble.[33]

PITIFUL STATE OF THE REALM
The new sovereign was unable to give favors and tax exemptions to
the people. The treasury was empty, and at the same time circumstances were even more grave. On May 24 the tsar was compelled
to write to the Stroganovs:[34] "In Moscow, gentry and junior boyars,
cossacks, musketeers and all ranks of soldiers are petitioning us,
saying that when they were besieging Moscow they suffered great
need and hardships and shed their blood. Their service tenures and
patrimonies were devastated by reason of the long war, and they
lacked the wherewithal to perform their service. Musketeers and
cossacks had worn out their service equipment, and they could not

perform service for us on account of their great poverty. There is no money in our treasury or grain in our storehouses, and there is no way we can reward our servicemen. Deserters and spies on being interrogated by our boyars say that the Lithuanians intend to advance on Moscow, and there is no money in our treasury or any grain whatsoever in our storehouses. We do not really know how much cash dues you pay into our treasury from your estates, but presently according to our decree we have sent to you Andrei Ignatievich Veliaminov. He has been ordered to take from your estates cash dues in full for past years and for this year according to our books and rescripts, and to send them to us.

"We have also instructed that you be asked to make a loan of money, grain, fish, salt, cloth, and all kinds of goods for the sake of Christian peace and tranquillity, so that we may distribute the same to our soldiers. And we have ordered that whatever you lend, whether in money, grain or goods, shall be set down in the books, so that you may assign this debt to the archimandrites, abbots and tax collectors, since you have made this loan to our treasury. If you add provisions and pay additional soldiers insofar as you are able, and there are adequate funds in our treasury, we will order you to be reimbursed immediately. Thus you will be able constantly to pay soldiers without any complications. Better than any alms is payment to soldiers, whereby the beauty of the churches of God and the integrity of the holy faith will be restored, and Orthodox Christians will be freed from the encroachment of people of alien faith! Whatsoever you give we will order repaid immediately, and your service to us and your solicitude for the whole Muscovite realm we will commemorate in perpetuity. If you do not lend us money, grain and provisions, and the soldiers are unable to endure hunger and privation and disperse from Moscow, it will not go unnoticed by God that the Orthodox Christian faith is ruined."

The clergy, in the name of the whole Holy Synod wrote to the Stroganovs: "The soldiers are petitioning the tsar incessantly, and they come daily with loud complaints to us, the tsar's clergy, and to the boyars, saying that they are impoverished from many tours of duty and from the depredations of Poles and Lithuanians, and can no longer serve. There was nothing for them to eat while on service, and so many of them travelled along the highways and robbed and killed because of hunger, and it was impossible to redeem them without rewarding them. As long as they were not rewarded by the tsar with money and grain, they would be driven against their will into brigandage by reason of poverty. They would steal, destroy and kill. So now we, the tsar's clergy and yours, and also the boyars, lords-in-waiting and all the people of all the towns of the great Russian tsardom, speaking through an *ecumenical* council, petition the tsar to send to you in all the towns collectors for tax levies, and collections of grain and all manner of provisions. These should be senior gentry, sent personally by the tsar and by us with all dispatch, so that the great sovereign may be able to reward all his troops."

At the conclusion of the document the clergy blessed all who would fulfill the demands of the tsar and the Assembly, and threatened those who ignored it with anathema. Documents phrased in exactly the same manner were sent throughout the towns. The government urged the citizens to generosity by the example of the citizens of Moscow: "You should aid the troops incessantly without stinting, and not do as the Moscow leading merchants and traders did. At first they spared themselves. They did not give money to reward the troops, and for this reason they saw utter ruin descend upon them, and lost all their possessions."

The Nogay[35] were devastating the borderlands, crossing the Oka and making war on the regions of Kolomna, Serpukhov, Borovsk and even reaching the district of Domodedovsk, close to Moscow. Troops plundered along the roads, as they had not received any pay. Tax collectors, travelling through the districts to raise money for the troops, were also plundering, so that the government was compelled to recall them and lay upon the peasants themselves the responsibility of collecting money and taking it to Moscow. The monasteries complained of devastation by the Lithuanians, requested tax exemption, and the government, in order to strengthen trade, fulfilled their request "for the sake of the foreign community, to relieve their poverty and devastation."

In the distant towns there was open opposition to the government's financial measures. For example, it was found necessary to punish some inhabitants of Cherdyn. "Three men were beaten with rods and thrown into prison for a month, so that they should not for long persist in their disobedience." But the inhabitants of Cherdyn continued to disobey and drove away the tax collector.

At Beloozero the townsmen likewise refused to pay taxes, and when the governor ordered them to be tortured they did not submit to this, ordered the tocsin sounded and tried to assault the governors. Thereafter the tax collectors showed themselves in the settlements only when accompanied by an armed guard. The governor of Kolomna wrote to the sovereign: "It was ordered that the emissaries who were on their way to Turkey be assigned two hundred and fifty oarsmen. But at the post station there were altogether ten couriers, and it was impossible to recruit oarsmen from anyone. We wanted to take them from the townsmen, but they did not give us any oarsmen. Two of them came at us noisily and commanded that nobody obey us. From other localities there are messages saying that it is impossible to collect money, supplies or oarsmen for the emissaries from anyone, and the emissaries are still waiting."

From Riazan came this petition from the archbishop, clergy, gentry and junior boyars: "From the time that the brigand began to call himself by the tsar's name, there were dissensions and wars, our service tenures and patrimonies are utterly ruined. We have all abandoned our own homes and are living with our dependents in Pereiaslavl. Just as the land was beginning to unite, the Tatars came frequently and set fire to the remnants of our homes, seized our remaining peasants and dependants, and even took and slew some of our brothers in waste places, and now the Tatars live among us without any intention of leaving. Your government emissary came to us on his way to Constantinople. He stayed in Pereiaslavl for three weeks and tortured us in an attempt to extort transportation and supplies from us; but there was no way we could provide them."

THE SHULGIN AFFAIR

Under such circumstances the new government had to wage an unrelenting war with both domestic and foreign enemies. Within the realm there raged the cossacks, the hope of those who desired a prolongation of the Time of Troubles. Nikanor Shulgin[36] at the command of the Assembly assumed command of the Kazan levies and campaigned against Zarutsky but, hearing of Michael's election, halted at Arzamas, having written to Moscow on March 15 that he would not continue the campaign. The troops had decided on this for they had exhausted their supplies and no longer could remain on active service. At the same time Shulgin informed the Assembly that all the Kazan levies had sworn allegiance to Michael, but at the same time urged this army not to recognize the new tsar, who had been chosen without the counsel of the Kazan realm. Nikanor was relying upon the cossacks and in order to invite them he left his army in Arzamas and moved off to Kazan; but here a cossack tsardom was no longer wanted, so when Shulgin arrived in Sviyazhsk emissaries from Kazan were already awaiting him, to tell him that Kazan had sworn allegiance to Michael and that his journey was in vain. Lest he should think of disobeying, he was placed under guard. The sovereign was amazed when he heard that Nikanor was under arrest, and sent to Rostov to enquire what was the charge against him. The matter was clarified, and Shulgin was exiled to Siberia, where he died.

WAR ON ZARUTSKY

Shulgin had relied upon the cossacks and the cossacks had not yet lost hope, since they still had Zarutsky. Having devastated Mikhailov, Zarutsky withdrew to Epifan, leaving his governor in Mikhailov. But on April 2 the inhabitants of Mikhailov arrested that governor without resistance, placed him under arrest, rounded up the "free" cossacks and cast them into prison, and sent news of this to Zaraisk and Pereiaslavl-Zalessky[37] with a request for assistance. Shortly thereafter two cossacks fled from Epifan to Kashira and under interrogation stated: "Over two hundred junior boyars and cossacks had fled from Zarutsky, while about three hundred Cherkassians[38] had joined him. Zarutsky wanted to go to Persia but Marina did not want to go with him, and was calling upon him to return with her to Lithuania. The cossacks had held a council of war, and many of them wished to return to the sovereign."

Then fourteen cossacks came to Kashira and declared that Zarutsky had twenty-five hundred cossacks apart from the newly arrived Cherkassians, and that he had proposed to his army a campaign against the Ukraine. When they received these tidings the boyars, Prince Mstislavsky and his companions, decided on April 13

that Prince Ivan Nikitich Odoevsky,[39] together with the governors of
Mikhailov, Zaraisk, Vladimir, Suzdal and other towns, should leave
Moscow in pursuit of Zarutsky. But at that time the boyars had been
informed that Zarutsky had fled from Epifan, had sacked Dedilov
thoroughly, burned down Krapivna and intended to advance on
Tula. The tsar answered these reports to the boyars by saying that
they should devise every means to pursue Zarutsky and prevent him
from joining the Lithuanians.

Prince Odoevsky set out from Moscow on April 19. In May it
was learned in Moscow that Zarutsky was approaching Livny and
from there was moving on Lebedian. Accordingly an order was sent
to Prince Odoevsky in Tula to advance with all his forces against
Zarutsky to Donkov and towards Lebedian. Odoevsky moved out of
Tula and news soon came that he had made contact with Zarutsky
near Voronezh, had fought against him for two days without respite
and soundly defeated him, capturing his artillery, banners, and bag-
gage train, taking many informers and driving off his horses. Zarutsky with a handful of followers had fled into the steppe beyond
the Don, towards Medveditsa. Such was the commander's report,
but the chronicle[40] states that the commanders did nothing against
Zarutsky, that he slew many of the inhabitants of Voronezh and
went away to Astrakhan. Some cossacks did not wish to follow Zarutsky into the steppe and came to Moscow with their submission,
saying that more of their comrades would follow. The tsar pardoned
them and sent them to the siege of Smolensk.

CORRESPONDENCE WITH THE COSSACKS

Meanwhile Odoevsky and his companions wrote to the cossacks on
the Volga that by the service of their atamans and cossacks, their
solicitude and loyalty, the Muscovite realm had been cleansed and
liberated. "Presently many of your brothers, atamans and cossacks,
are struggling for the Christian faith, are pursing the foemen and
plunderers and are making war upon the Lithuanian land. Within the
great realms of our great sovereign everything is going well, people
of all kinds have come to their senses, and have established love,
good counsel and unity. Only in Astrakhan the notorious brigand,
Ivashka Zarutsky the Cherkassian, has broken away from the whole
Muscovite realm, and together with Marina is committing brigandage and disorder." The commanders urged the cossacks not to join

Zarutsky and the Lutheran heretic[41] Marina, but instead join the commanders and together settle accounts with the brigands. "And if you are impoverished, we have government supplies, wine, cash from the treasury and cloth, so you will not lack for anything."

The commanders wrote to the inhabitants of Astrakhan, urging them to abandon Zarutsky. "You yourselves know what evil he has done in Astrakhan. He has spilled much Orthodox Christian blood, he has slain without mercy the lord-in-waiting and governor Prince Ivan Dmitrevich Khvorostinin[42] and many others upon whom previously this Cherkassian unbeliever Ivashka would not dare to have looked. Furthermore the Lutheran heretic Marina cares nothing for the shedding of Christian blood as long as she can be glorified. They turn people away from truth to falsehood; they are corresponding with the Persian shah, and wish to cede to the shah the Astrakhan tsardom, which has been the patrimony of our great sovereign from time immemorial, and contains many Orthodox Christians. Thus he seeks to embroil our great sovereign and his great Russian realm with the Persian shah."

Having stirred up the Volga cossacks against Zarutsky, the Muscovite government also stirred up against him the Nogay horde, informing its prince Ishterek that in Astrakhan Zarutsky had released his enemy Jan Arslan from prison. Documents were sent to the Don Cossacks along with pay from the tsar, cloth, saltpetre, lead, powder and provisions. The clergy, in the name of Orthodoxy, urged the Don Cossacks immediately to proceed to the Severian land against the Lithuanians, for which they would receive blessing from God and praise from men. The Don Cossacks honorably received the emissaries, who informed them of the election of the new tsar, rejoiced in the tsar's name, tolled bells, sang prayers, fired salvoes and beat mercilessly with rods one of their number who declared that the Kaluga brigand[43] was alive. They promised to serve and respect Michael as they had his predecessors, but they refused to go to the Severian land to attack the Lithuanians.

Since peace was desired with the Turks, the government demanded of the Don Cossacks that they cease their attacks on Azov. The cossacks promised to remain at peace with the inhabitants of Azov, but only until the Russian ambassadors had returned from Constantinople, and they demanded from the tsar rewards, money, cloth and supplies, so that they might have the wherewithal to feed and clothe themselves during their peace with Azov. The tsar had to agree to the conditions, and promised even more, sending a banner to the Don. "Under this banner," it said in the tsar's charter, "you will resist our enemies, advance against them and, asking for God's mercy, deal with them insofar as the merciful God gives you help. As long as you begin and continue to render us service and support according to your promise, our royal word will not alter towards you."

The Don Cossacks, having received their reward from the sovereign, raised the tsar's banner, formed a circle around it, and beneath the banner there lay a man who had been condemned to death. When the tsar's emissary, Opulchin, asked what manner of man he was, they told him: "Two drunken cossacks babbled that the atamans and cossacks had changed sides frivolously, and that they should not desert Ivashka Zarutsky, but be under his command." One of these cossacks had been hanged beforehand and the other had been condemned to death and lay here under the banner. Thereupon many cossacks petitioned the emissary that in the name of the tsar he remit this young man's sentence, because he had offended without treachery, out of thoughtlessness and drunkenness.

The emissary, knowing what had happened beforehand, and seeing that many cossacks from the Volga and Yaik were present, and that hopes had been raised of the tsar's clemency, said: "You did nothing to this cossack before I arrived. Now that I have come with the tsar's pardon, there is joy among all of you, and the sovereign is merciful and just. He has pardoned all the guilty among us and has forgotten all offenses. Now you wish to pardon this offender in the name of his majesty the tsar. But God holds his majesty the tsar in his safekeeping, and his enemies can do no evil against him." As soon as the emissary had uttered these words, the cossacks cried out: "God grant the lord tsar health and long life! We ourselves know that the sovereign is merciful and just, that he is God's chosen and that nobody can do any evil against him." The condemned man was lifted up and the ataman Epikha Radilov abused him, and reproached him at length. "Now come to your senses; we ourselves know how much blood has been shed in the Muscovite realm on account of our brigandage and subversive speech, which has also led simple people astray. We are already wading up to our necks in

Christian blood. Now God has given us a gracious sovereign, so you dogs should leave off brigandage, for if you do not cease, God will destroy you all, wherever you may be."

Fearful news soon arrived in Moscow. Zarutsky was corresponding with the Volga and other neighboring cossacks, calling for them to make common cause against the realm. Successive missives were sent from Moscow to the Don and Volga, first from the tsar and then from the clergy and finally from the boyars and men of all ranks, urging them not to join Zarutsky, but to resist him. As before the documents flattered the cossacks, heralded their heroic feats and urged them all the more strongly to serve the realm. Zarutsky was depicted as the man who wrought the greatest evil against the Muscovite realm. "The conciliar noble and commander Prokopy Liapunov[44] was the first to point out the unrighteousness of King Sigismund. Zarutsky took counsel and urged his co-conspirators to kill him, in order to instill hope into the Poles and Lithuanians." Here the document directly accuses Zarutsky of complicity in Liapunov's death.[45] But we have seen that in Pozharsky's document to the inhabitants of the provinces complaining about Ivan Petrovich Sheremetev, that same Sheremetev is represented as being to blame for Liapunov's death. In letters brought to the cossacks the chief culprit in the uprising against the Poles is represented as being Liapunov, but in other documents there is no mention of Liapunov, and all the honor is ascribed to Trubetskoy. In general in documents of that time there is no concern about corroborating testimony, but they depicted events according to the circumstances.

Continuing to enumerate Zarutsky's crimes, the Moscow documents describe how after Liapunov's death Zarutsky enlisted the aid of the Poles, Eustace Waljawski, Marcin Kazanowski[46] and others, and together with them plotted the ruin of the Muscovite realm. He secretly summoned Hetman Sapieha[47] and all his forces, corresponded with the Poles under siege in the Kremlin and Kitai quarter and agreed with them to set fire to the encampment outside Moscow the very moment the Poles were effecting a sortie from the city, but his spies were captured and tortured, and Walawski and Kazanowski were slaughtered with all their army. In the documents it was also stated that even in 1612 Sigismund sent Colonel Siniawski to Zarutsky, urging him to harass the Muscovite realm until the king managed to conclude peace with the Turks and had paid his army, and then he would advance on Moscow. When he had captured it, he would give Zarutsky the town of Great Novgorod or Pskov with all its bytowns, or Smolensk, and would make him his great boyar and administrator.

In order that the documents might have greater effect upon the cossacks the tsar sent money, cloth, provisions and wines to the Volga. "And you, atamans and cossacks, seeing our royal kindness and solicitude for you, will serve us, your great sovereign, and respect us and resist our enemies, and we, the great sovereign, will see fit to hold you in our royal favor and solicitude to a greater extent than previous Russian tsars."

Finally two documents were sent directly to Zarutsky himself by the tsar and the clergy. The tsar promised pardon if he would return to his allegiance. The clergy threatened him with anathema should he ignore the tsar's document. The Don Cossacks wrote to their brethren on the Volga concerning peace and tranquillity, but in very vague terms, probably because cossacks had only a vague notion as to the meaning of peace and tranquillity. "To the great and glorious warriors of the Volga, the Terek and Yaik and all the famous rivers, to the atamans and cossacks and all the great host. The autocratic sovereign Tsar and Grand Prince Michael Fedorovich of All Russia has conveyed to us his royal documents and his gracious word, and has sent us grants in the form of money, saltpetre, cloth and supplies, and also to you at the famous river he has sent grants in the form of much cash, cloth, saltpetre and supplies. And we sent to you, my lords, his royal documents to all the host, and also to Astrakhan and to Zarutsky, and to all ranks of the Russian tsardom and the Muscovite provinces, saying that the Lord has averted His anger and has turned to mercy, so that you may receive peace and tranquillity, and you should be in unity in your hearts and souls, and should serve and respect the sovereign, and not connive at idlers. Forget what is past and turn towards the future. My lords, await the blessings that are to come, and be mindful of the scriptures of Holy God: a thousand years is like a single day, and a single day like a thousand years. And we, my lords, have written much before about love, but you have not penned a single line to us, we do not even know who are your great atamans, so do not, my lords, be angry at us." But why should the Don Cossacks think that the Volga Cossacks might be angry at them? The heading of this document is also curious: "From the great Russian realms and the Moscow provinces to their protectors, the Volga, Terek and Yaik atamans and warriors and to all the great host."

ZARUTSKY QUARRELS WITH ASTRAKHAN AND TEREK COSSACKS

Meanwhile Prince Odoevsky and his companions were receiving news from the north that bands of cossacks were pulling out of the districts of Beloozero and Poshekhonie, through the districts of Uglich, Yaroslavl and Romanov, towards the southeast in an attempt to join up with Zarutsky. The Nogay prince Ishterek at first quarrelled with Zarutsky, but then was reconciled with him, gave his sons as hostages and vowed that in the spring he would go up the Volga against the ice on rafts with artillery to besiege Samara and Kazan.

The town of Terka declared for Zarutsky but in Astrakhan the better people submitted to him against their will, and awaited with impatience the tsar's regiments. In the winter, just before the feast of St. Nicholas, Zarutsky and Marina sent to the city assembly some document or other and ordered men of all ranks to set their hands to it, but nobody was allowed to examine its contents. The clergy and all the people set their hands to it unwillingly. Marina observed the disaffection of the citizens and feared an uprising. She well remembered the fearful tolling of the Moscow bells on May 17[48] and, fearing the same would happen in Astrakhan, forbade the early call to matins under the pretext that the bells would frighten her son. Foreign merchants, from Bukhara and Gilian, who had been plundered by Zarutsky, fled. Day and night the blood of the wealthier people flowed by reason of tortures and executions.

Zarutsky travelled outside the town with the Nogay Tatars, who numbered five or six hundred, and ate and drank with them from morning to evening. He thus provided for them in order that they might be persuaded to come with him the next spring to besiege Samara and Kazan. He said: "I know the Muscovite artillery. Before anyone can come from Moscow, I will have taken Samara and will be dealing with Kazan." In Astrakhan it appears that Zarutsky was claiming to be Dmitry; at least there is extant a petition from the year 1614 addressed to Tsar Dmitry Ivanovich, Tsaritsa Marina Yurievna and Tsarevich Ivan Dmitrevich. Zarutsky also was relying upon the shah, but the Persian merchants assured the inhabitants of Astrakhan that Abbas[49] would not take Astrakhan, would not send his troops, nor would he give any of his treasure to Zarutsky, for he did not wish to quarrel with the Muscovite realm. As far as the cossacks were concerned, the encampment nearest Astrakhan under Ataman Verziga declared for the brigand, but the encampments further upriver were against Zarutsky.

Witnesses say that when the document mentioned earlier arrived from the Don the cossacks who had gathered together rejoiced when they read through it. They cursed Zarutsky, Marina and her son and mocked them despite the fact that Zarutsky, when calling upon them to make war on the realm, had promised them riches beyond their imagination. The cossacks said: "So much Christian blood has been shed on account of our rebellion, so many holy shrines and churches of God have been ruined, that we have resolved no longer to plunder, but to make our submission to our Lord Tsar Michael Fedorovich and to all the land." But the cossacks, according to their custom, wished to serve the sovereign and all the land in the manner most convenient to them. To this end they made ready to proceed to Astrakhan, fraudulently accept rewards from the brigand, and then settle accounts with him. Then they intended to put out to sea and lie in wait for the shah's vessels in order to plunder them. If they did not succeed in plundering the Persian ships, they would land near Astrakhan and plunder the Tatar encampments. It was time to deal with the snake, while it was still in the hole.

But the younger cossacks had other ideas. "It matters little to us from where we get the clothes for our backs, but why do we not go to Samara with Zarutsky?" Five hundred and sixty who were of this counsel went over to Zarutsky in Astrakhan. It is said that Zarutsky was encouraged by the arrival of the cossacks and, since he hated many citizens for their disaffection towards him, wanted to slaughter on Palm Sunday all those whom he suspected. Whether in fact Zarutsky had such intentions, or whether the citizens of Astrakhan, being warned by the arrival of the cossacks, were frightened and suspected such an aim, it is difficult to determine. Whatever the

truth of the matter, quarrels arose between the inhabitants of Astrakhan and the cossacks. Zarutsky was compelled to barricade himself
in the citadel while the citizens took up their positions in the suburbs, and on Wednesday in Holy Week of 1614 fighting broke out
between the two sides.

Meanwhile news came that Terek region had forsaken Zarutsky.
Here, as in Astrakhan, not all the inhabitants were devoted to the
brigand, the lady brigand and the baby brigand, but supported them
because they lived far from Moscow, and did not receive any news
from there. Peter Golovin, the Terek commander, was particularly
suspect to Zarutsky, who sent to the town of Terka to have the commander arrested and brought to Astrakhan. But the Terek people did
not surrender Golovin, saying to the emissaries from Astrakhan:
"Doubtless you intend to kill Peter Golovin even as you killed Ivan
Khvorostinin. We are not of your criminal counsel, nor will we
desert the Moscow miracle-workers."[50] Halfway through Lent,
Mikhail Cherny came on behalf of Zarutsky. Cherny went as far as
Kabardia[51] in order to stir up the mountain people against Moscow.
But the people of Terka were already falling out with Zarutsky,
whom they suspected of sinister designs against their town. They
arrested Cherny and brought him before the governor for questioning. At first Cherny refused to say anything concerning Zarutsky's
intentions, but finally torture loosened his tongue. He declared that
Zarutsky was beside himself in Astrakhan, where the majority of
inhabitants were against him. He was executing and drowning the
wealthier people and clergy, plundering their possessions and committing sacrilege. He had taken a silver censer out of the Trinity
monastery and had melted it down to make a stirrup for himself. He
was angered at the town of Terka and wanted to be there on Easter
Sunday to execute the governor, Golovin, and many other people.
This last piece of news prompted the commander and all the community to take decisive measures. On the spot they kissed the cross
to Tsar Michael and sent the musketeer Vasily Khokhlov to Astrakhan with seven hundred men.

KHOKHLOV MOVES AGAINST ZARUTSKY

Having arrived outside Astrakhan, Khokhlov administered to the
Nogay Tatars the oath of allegiance. Among those who switched to

the tsar was Ishterek Bey, whom we have mentioned, who had sent
a letter to Odoevsky in which the position of a dependent Tatar during the Troubles of the Muscovite realm is very naively depicted.
"His grace the tsar gave us a charter in which he undertook to protect us against all enemies, and we have undertaken to serve him all
our lives with loyalty and justice. Meanwhile the people of Astrakhan and all the Tatar horde have begun to oppress us. They say
they are serving the son of the lawful tsar. All the Christian people
have gathered together and proclaimed as their sovereign the son of
Tsar Dmitry. If you wish to be with us, give us your signature and
also send one of your sons to us as a hostage. Do not deceive us, do
not mix your words with us. Did we not stir up Jan Arslan and his
seven brothers and ourselves make war on you? To that end we
gave some of our own uhlans as hostages."

Khokhlov found the inhabitants of Astrakhan in open war against
Zarutsky. But the war had brought them no advantage, since cannon
had been aimed at them from the citadel. Two thousand men, and
six thousand women and children fled to Khokhlov's camp from
Astrakhan; but Zarutsky himself saw that he could not remain in the
citadel and await the tsar's commanders. On May 12 he fled Astrakhan by night and moved a little way upriver. Khokhlov attacked
and inflicted a heavy defeat upon him. Zarutsky, Marina and her
son managed to put out to sea, but Khokhlov sent fresh troops in
pursuit.

ZARUTSKY'S CAPTURE

Meanwhile the tsar's commanders, learning that Zarutsky was hard
pressed in Astrakhan, quickly hastened to that city. On the way they
learned that Astrakhan already was cleared of brigands. This news
was evidently unwelcome to Odoevsky, for all the honor for this
feat belonged not to him, but to Khokhlov. He wrote to the latter,
ordering him not to report to the tsar concerning the events in Astrakhan until he arrived, and that if he had sent a courier already, he
should be brought back "since it is befitting for the commander to
write to the sovereign concerning many matters of state." Even
though he had taken no part in the liberation of Astrakhan, the
commander ordered Khokhlov to compel the inhabitants to greet
him triumphantly. "You should order the inhabitants of Astrakhan

and the Terek to meet us halfway, thirty or twenty versts[52] from Astrakhan."

Learning that Zarutsky had fled to the Yaik, on June 6 Odoevsky detached two musketeer captains, Palchikov and Onuchin, to capture him. On June 23 the detachments caught up with the fugitives and fought, not actually with Zarutsky, but with his cossack hosts, Ataman Us and his companions, since this Us was in charge of everything, whereas Zarutsky and Marina had no influence at all. Palchikov and Onuchin besieged the cossacks in their fort, and when the latter saw the position was hopeless they were compelled to swear allegiance and kiss the cross to Tsar Michael, having surrendered Zarutsky and Marina. This occurred on June 25.

EXECUTION OF REBEL LEADERS

The prisoners were brought to Astrakhan, whence they were sent immediately to Kazan since, Odoevsky wrote, they did not dare keep them in Astrakhan on account of the disorder and confusion. Zarutsky was sent on separately from his woman. Marina was escorted by six hundred musketeers, Zarutsky by two hundred and thirty. Should they be attacked by a superior rebel force, the escort was ordered to kill the prisoners. From Kazan they were sent on to Moscow, where Zarutsky was impaled and Marina's son hanged. Marina herself died in prison, according to Russian accounts from grief, according to Polish accounts either drowned or strangled. The same chronicler[53] mentions the execution of Fedor Andronov.[54]

REBEL COSSACKS MOVE NORTHWARDS

Having got rid of Zarutsky, Astrakhan was pacified but there remained very many cossacks within the realm, and there was scarcely a single province which had not suffered from their depredations, of which the chronicles say that even in the most ancient times there were no such tortures.[55] The governors reported: "The cossacks stationed themselves here and there, they went somewhere or other, they devastated villages and hamlets and razed them to their foundations. We saw about seventy peasants who had been severely burned and about forty dead, both men and women, who had died from suffering and torture or had frozen to death."

Ataman Baloven was particularly distinguished among the cossacks. On September 1, 1614, which at that time was New Year's Day, the sovereign said in the Assembly with the clergy, boyars, councillors and men of all ranks: "We have received letters from cities around Moscow and in the maritime towns that renegade cossacks have come into their districts in great number, they kill Orthodox Christians, they inflict various tortures by burning, they do not allow taxes and supplies of grain to be collected, neither on account of their brigandage may any of the money or grain which has been collected be dispatched to the tsar's treasury. Gentry and junior boyars are asking whether they should deal with the brigands themselves. What should we do: should we send missives concerning these brigands, or send directly to these brigands, commanding them to leave off brigandage?" It was resolved: "To send a message to the brigands from the spiritual authorities, boyars and people of all ranks, to tell them to leave off brigandage."

For this purpose Archbishop Gerasim of Suzdal[56] with two other clergymen, the boyar Prince Boris Mikhailovich Lykov[57] and the secretary Ilyin were sent, with delegates from the gentry, leading merchants, traders and cossacks. They were to travel to Yaroslavl and from there they were to announce to the cossacks that those who wished to stand for the name of God, serve and honor the sovereign and forsake those outlaws who wished to commit acts of brigandage, would have their names inscribed in lists to be sent to the tsar, who would receive them into his service. As for those who would not serve the tsar, but preferred to betray the sovereign, plunder God's churches, desecrate icons, burn and take people captive, these would be dealt with by the atamans and cossacks who would be united in resisting them, for they were worse and baser than the Lithuanians and Swedes. Such brigands no longer would be called cossacks in order that proper atamans who agreed to serve would not be dishonored. If cossacks opened negotiations with Lykov, but came to him without pledges, let them give pledges according to how many followers they brought. They were to be persuaded through all means to leave off brigandage and be sent on government service; they should be promised pay, and debtors and serfs should receive freedom. Food and drink must be given to atamans and cossacks who came to Prince Lykov in Yaroslavl to negotiate, or on government service. Food was to be given to atamans and cossacks who left off brigandage and came to be received into the tsar's service. This was to be collected from the suburbs and the rural districts, and they were to be made as comfortable as possible. No more than necessary must be taken and no violence must be committed. As for cossacks and atamans who did not cease brigandage and report for government service, no quarter was to be given them. Prince Lykov must crush them by whatever means necessary, using levies gathered from the towns, whether gentry, junior boyars, auxiliary troops or other local levies.

Lykov informed the sovereign that he had written to the cossacks and had sent to persuade them many times, but the brigands would not desist. It was impossible to stop them, and they were committing brigandage worse than before. In his reply the sovereign commanded Lykov to deal with the cossacks. Subsequently Lykov wrote that he had moved against the cossacks and had sent out missives and had defeated the cossacks in many places. Then the cossacks sent a message to Lykov declaring that they would leave off brigandage and would report for government service against the Swedes at Tikhvin.[58] For this the tsar would reward them, and send commanders from Moscow to go with them to deal with the Swedes. Two commanders, Prince Nikita Volkonsky and Stepan Vasilievich Chemesov,[59] were sent to them from Moscow. But soon these commanders informed the sovereign that when they arrived at Tikhvin and wished to call the roll of the cossacks, the cossacks did not show up for the roll call, but dispersed through the villages and hamlets and along the highways. They were plundering and doing violence, burning villages and hamlets, taking peasants captive, and their brigandage was worse than ever before. They had visited the commanders with great clamor and threats, wishing to plunder and kill them. Then cossacks who wished to respect the sovereign fled from Tikhvin to Moscow, and under interrogation by the boyars stated that those cossacks who had halted brigandage and enrolled with the sovereign had forsaken the brigands and proceeded to the commanders, Prince Volkonsky and Chemesov, but had been overtaken by renegade cossacks who seized and plundered them and also the tsar's commanders. Many of the loyal atamans and cossacks had been slain, and now the cossacks were causing havoc

along the highways. A messenger came from the governor of Ustiuzhna relating that many cossacks were coming in the direction of
this town, reportedly proceeding towards Moscow, but their intentions were unknown. Receiving these tidings, the tsar wrote to
Prince Lykov in Yaroslavl and to Fedor Mikhailovich Boiashev,
gov-ernor of Kashin, commanding them to send out reconnaissance
patrols along the highways to locate the cossacks, and find out
where they could be expected to attack. If the brigands were proceeding towards Moscow, Lykov and Boiashev were to pursue them
as far as Moscow.

The cossacks indeed appeared near Moscow and encamped along
the Trinity road in the village of Rostokino, and sent to the tsar offering to serve him. They would no longer commit acts of brigandage and were prepared to report for service. The sovereign sent
gentry and crown secretaries to Rostokino to make a list of the cossacks and determine how many there were. The cossacks did not
submit to the roll call, and barely allowed a count to be taken, saying that the atamans knew how many cossacks there were in their
encampments. They placed guards day and night along the roads
from Rostokino to Moscow and along the road to the Trinity monastery. They sent reconnaissance expeditions and placed encampments along all the roads, all on the lookout for Prince Lykov and
his companions, and in the meantime sent another petition to the
sovereign that they be permitted to hold a market, otherwise they
would do violence and rustle livestock. In accordance with the
sovereign's decree traders were sent from Moscow to hold a market,
if only to prevent them rustling livestock. The sovereign also ordered them to be conducted from Rostokino to the Donskoy monastery.[60] From there they arrived at Moscow in battle order, saying
that they would plunder the people of Moscow. Others said that unless the sovereign rewarded them they would join Lisowski[61] in the
Severian land. Then they sent a message to Lykov and Boiashev,
demanding that they be allowed to proceed to Moscow along the
country roads stealthily and, arriving outside Moscow, halt and conceal themselves wherever it was convenient.

LYKOV MOVES AGAINST THE COSSACKS
Lykov and Boiashev finally arrived and the sovereign ordered them
to take out of the cossack encampments the atamans, lieutenants and

cossacks to interrogate and investigate them. The boyars, nobles and junior boyars complained that they, the cossacks, had plundered their estates and patrimonies. Furthermore the commanders Prince Volkonsky and Chemesov complained that the cossacks had beaten and plundered them. The cossacks were arrested and brought for interrogation, while the lord-in-waiting Artemy Vasilievich Izmailov[62] was sent from Moscow to the Simonov monastery with orders to stand guard against the cossack encampments and send a message forbidding them to leave the encampments. They might remain in their encampments without fear for he had been sent to protect them. If they broke out of the encampments, Izmailov and Lykov had orders to pursue and prevent them from reaching Moscow. But as soon as Izmailov arrived at the Simonov monastery and began blockading the cossack encampments the brigands fled precipitately from Moscow along the Serpukhov and other roads. Izmailov and Lykov pursued them, defeated their detachments several times along the way, and caught up with a large concentration of them in the Maloyaroslavets region on the Luzha river. There the cossacks were soundly defeated and the remnants, seeing themselves at the mercy of the sovereign's forces, made their submission and kissed the cross.

In accordance with the sovereign's decree Lykov and Izmailov brought all these cossacks, numbering 3256, to Moscow. They were all pardoned and sent out on service. Only Baloven was hanged, while several other atamans were distributed among the prisons. But even this did not give the government any respite from the cossacks. In 1616 news came from Vladimir, Suzdal, Murom, Balakhna and Nizhny Novgorod that there were gatherings of brigands, slaves of boyars and all kinds of destitute people who called themselves cossacks. They appeared in the districts of Vladimir and Suzdal, in Shuia and other places. Throughout the villages, hamlets and along the highways they had slaughtered nobles, junior boyars and other people, burned villages and hamlets, tortured peasants to discover their provisions, and threatened to attack the towns. The sovereign ordered Prince Dmitry Petrovich Lopata-Pozharsky[63] and Stepan Mikhailovich Ushakov, governor of Kostroma, to deal with the brigands. How they fulfilled this commission is not known.

In the same year the sovereign heard from Kazan and other places that the Tatars and Cheremiss were becoming restive, had betrayed the sovereign, were burning villages and hamlets, capturing and killing people and advancing on the towns. The roads from Kazan to Nizhny Novgorod were closed. The boyar Prince Yury Yansheevich Suleshov[64] and the table attendant Prince Alexis Mikhailovich Lvov[65] were sent to deal with them.

ALADYIN'S EMBASSY

Apart from the cossacks, Tatars and Cheremiss, the Lithuanians, Lisowski and the Ukrainian Cossacks, or Cherkassians, had to be dealt with. As soon as Michael was elected, in Moscow consideration was being given as to how to conclude the war with the Lithuanians and, principally, how to free the sovereign's father from captivity. As early as March 10, 1613 the Assembly sent the nobleman Denis Grigorievich Aladyin[66] to the king with a document which, having catalogued all Sigismund's iniquities, demanded an exchange of prisoners. Nicholas Struys,[67] in the name of all his confreres, also wrote to the king, urging him to return Filaret and his companions, and thus release his own subjects from Muscovite captivity.

In the instructions to Aladyin it was written: "If they say that they know for sure that of the Polish and Lithuanian people who were distributed among the towns after the capture of the Kremlin, all the men were slain, you are to reply that the Poles and Lithuanians were sent from Moscow to the towns for their own protection. Some were sent to Sol Galitskaia, Galich, Chukhloma, and Unzha, and these towns were attacked by brigands, your Cherkassians, and a few of these Poles and Lithuanians were killed by these wretched Cherkassians of yours. Those in the other towns are all safe."

The Assembly wished to conceal news of Michael's election from the Poles, and thereby facilitate Filaret's liberation. Thus Aladyin was instructed: "If they say that Michael Fedorovich Romanov has been chosen tsar in Moscow, you are to reply 'Somebody has told you an untruth. In Moscow men of all ranks have gathered together and are taking counsel concerning the election of a sovereign, but they are still awaiting delegates from the more distant provinces.' If they ask why we tortured the traitors Fedka Andronov and his companions, since they stood up for justice, you are to reply: 'Mikhail Glebovich Saltykov,[68] Fedka Andronov and their companions are the leading traitors and the initiators of every of evil. They summoned the royal army from before Smolensk to attack the Muscovite realm, and together with the Poles and Lithuanians conspired to ruin Moscow, sent much of the tsar's priceless treasury, assembled by previous great sovereigns, to the king or distributed it among the soldiery. Therefore these malefactors deserve not only torture but every variety of evil death.'"

Aladyin was ordered not to volunteer any information. The emissary was to forward to the king the petition from the Holy Synod, the boyars, lords-in-waiting, etc., and from men of all ranks of the great Russian tsardom. If the Polish lords say that the Russians are traitors to Wladyslaw,[69] he was to reply by expounding all the king's iniquities and among other things say: "Mikhail Saltykov and Fedka Andronov have sent to you the tsar's jewels and caps and crowns, all the inheritance of the tsars and the miraculous icons." If at the time of the embassy Mikhail Saltykov, Ivan Gramotin,[70] Vasily Yanov[71] or any other Muscovite traitors were in the king's presence, Aladyin was to complain, saying that this was unprecedented. Should these traitors nonetheless break in with unbefitting words, Aladyin was to say aloud and without fear in the presence of the Polish lords that Mikhail and his companions were the instigators of all evil and despoilers of the Muscovite realm, and that now they must be mindful of God and their Christian nature and desist from their evil designs, for if they do not desist they will soon receive punishment from God.

Aladyin was able to inform the Assembly that any powerful movement against Moscow by the king was not to be expected in the near future. A certain Pole said to him on the way: "You yourself have seen how the soldiers here are devastating the king's towns and villages, and they will sack many towns and villages until they are paid." In Wilno[72] the mayor told Aladyin: "We have soldiers billetted upon us. Because of them we have nothing to live on, they do great violence against us, they take great quantities of supplies from us, they strike their own coinage, they subject our wives and children to great oppression and violence. It would be better for us if the earth would open up and swallow them."

Thus disorder in Poland gave the Muscovite realm the chance to recover from its own disorder. In June 1613 Aladyin returned and brought the reply from the Polish lords, who naturally exculpated Sigismund on all counts and placed all the blame on Moscow. With regard to Wladyslaw they wrote: "It is well known to us that even during the reign of Prince Dmitry Ivanovich, whom you call Grishka Otrepiev, Prince Vasily Ivanovich Shuisky and his brothers and many boyars spoke through several Poles and Muscovites petitioning the king that he rid both themselves and the Muscovite realm of the renegade monk Grishka Otrepiev and give his son Wladyslaw Zhigmontovich to rule over the Muscovite realm." In conclusion the Polish lords wrote that they, and together with them Holy Roman Emperor Matthias,[73] have inclined Sigismund towards peace with Moscow. The lords demanded of the boyar council that it desist from its hostile actions against the Poles before the arrival of the imperial ambassadors, through whose mediation steps would be taken towards a peace agreement. Concerning the king, the Polish lords wrote that he could not answer the Assembly's letter personally since it was replete with insulting, false, proud and shameful words.

MUSCOVITES CAPTURE BELAIA

Meanwhile hostilities continued. In March 1613 the Assembly dispatched forces against the Lithuanians, who had advanced against the regions of Belaia, Meshchovsk, Kaluga and Kozelsk and stood with superior forces on the Bryn river. In April the boyars dispatched commanders to the Severian land, where matters were going well for the Russians, but quite different news came from outside Kozelsk. Princes Andrei Andreevich Khovansky[74] and Semeon Nikitich Gagarin[75] were drawn up about sixteen versts from Kozelsk, and Prince Ivan Andreevich Khvorostinin[76] was about six versts from them. Khovansky sent a message to the latter, bidding him to come nearer so that together they might deal with the Lithuanians, but Khvorostinin disobeyed and withdrew to Mtsensk with all his forces. There was great hostility between Khovansky and Khvorostinin, and the cause of the realm could not prevail over their quarrel. To complicate matters another commander, Artemy Izmailov, was alleged to be in communication with the Lithuanians.

The tsar bade Khovansky and Khvorostinin change their ways and conduct a strict investigation concerning Izmailov, but apparently no such investigation took place.

In July even worse news arrived. Cherkassians and Lithuanians had captured Serpeisk, Meshchovsk, Kozelsk, Bolkhov, Likhvin and Peremyshl, and at Belev they had captured the fort and within the town the commander Semeon Gagarin was being besieged by them. Izmailov wrote from Kaluga that the Cherkassians were already outside the town, and even more were expected. Nashchokin[77] wrote from Mozhaisk that the enemy were trying to approach his town. The sovereign addressed the Assembly, together with the clergy and boyars, on how to deal with the Lithuanians and Cherkassians, and decided to send against them table attendants Prince Dmitry Mamstriukovich Cherkassky[78] and Mikhail Matveevich Buturlin.[79] When these commanders arrived at Kaluga the Lithuanians and Cherkassians, hearing of their arrival, abandoned the regions of Serpeisk and Meshchovsk and retreated to Viazma and Dorogobuzh. The commanders pursued them, occupied Viazma and Dorogobuzh which had been abandoned by the Lithuanians, and arrived outside Belaia. The Lithuanians attempted a powerful sortie, but they were defeated and in August they were compelled to surrender.

UNSUCCESSFUL SIEGE OF SMOLENSK

The tsar rewarded the commanders with gold coins and ordered them before Smolensk. The commanders set out to besiege Smolensk and halted two versts from it, but they could do nothing because they lacked forces. Many Ukrainian nobles and junior boyars failed to show up outside Smolensk, while others fled. Prince Troekurov (since Buturlin had been wounded severely at the siege of Belaia) stood facing the Cherkassians and their comrades outside Smolensk without any action until June 1615, when he was replaced by the dispatch of the commanders boyar Prince Ivan Andreevich Khovansky[80] and Miron Andreevich Veliaminov.[81] When Cherkassky arrived in Moscow, the sovereign bade him sit at his table, and after the meal rewarded his service with a sable robe, a golden globe and a goblet.

WAR ON LISOWSKI

At the same time news came that Lisowski was fortifying himself in the Severian land, the Lithuanians were pressing hard on Briansk and had captured Karachev. The commanders Prince Dmitry Mikhailovich Pozharsky and Stepan Ivanovich Istlenev were dispatched against Lisowski. Knowing how the followers of Lisowski waged war, orders were given for the commanders to exercise extreme caution while on campaign or in their encampments. "Having made exhaustive enquiries about the route, send some nobles on ahead and order them to reconnoiter and survey the land around wherever they encamp, ensuring that they are secure, and also post pickets. When the pickets are established close to the encampments and well fortified, let the commanders proceed to the encampment with extreme caution, sending out patrols to scout for Lithuanians, so that they do not surprise us and thus do great harm."

Pozharsky pursued Lisowski from Belev through Bolkhov. Lisowski was fearful of being besieged in Karachev, so he burned the town and proceeded upstream to Orel. Prince Dmitry, hearing of this, also quickly approached Orel. For one whole day and one morning they clashed head on. Ivan Pushkin,[82] going ahead, opened the battle. The Russians did not hold against Lisowski. The commander Istlenev[83] turned and fled, but Pozharsky stood firm and with six hundred men who surrounded themselves with sleds and formed a circular encampment repelled three thousand of Lisowski's followers. Lisowski did not guess how few men Pozharsky had, and therefore did not dare attack him, but withdrew his encampment two versts away. Pozharsky did not dare leave his encampment. "Better for us to die on this spot," he replied to some of his soldiers who urged him to withdraw to Bolkhov. In the evening the fugitive commander Istlenev returned, and during the night various other fugitives rallied.

On the following day, seeing himself surrounded by a strong force, Pozharsky opened offensive operations against Lisowski, who quickly retreated and stood before Kromy. Seeing that the pursuit was not letting up, in a couple of days he covered a hundred and fifty versts and appeared before Bolkhov. Repelled there by the commander Stepan Volynsky,[84] he burned Belev. He then wished to advance on Likhvin, but here he suffered a reverse and halted at

Peremyshl, whence the commander and all his forces had fled to Kaluga.

Pozharsky stood fast in Likhvin. Here, having fortified himself with levies from Kazan, he set off again in pursuit of Lisowski, who as before retreated, burning Peremyshl and making a dash between Viazma and Mozhaisk. Pozharsky sent his commanders but he himself, exhausted by the incredibly rapid pursuit after his own indefatigable horsemen, was laid low by a serious illness and was carried off to Kaluga. With Pozharsky removed from the scene the pursuit ended. The soldiers did not pursue Lisowski, since the levies from Kazan fled homewards. Lisowski freely could attack Rzhev Volodimerov, where he was barely kept out by the boyar Fedor Ivanovich Sheremetev, who had come to the aid of Pskov. Withdrawing from Rzhev, Lisowski attacked Kashin and Uglich, which barely held out against him. After this Lisowski no longer attacked towns, but instead skirted them like a shadow, devastating everything on the way. He stole between Yaroslavl and Kostroma to the Suzdal countryside, then between Vladimir and Murom, between Kolomna and Pereiaslavl-in-Riazan, and between Serpukhov and Aleksin. Several commanders were sent in pursuit of Lisowski, but they fruitlessly turned from one place to another. Only once in the Aleksin district did Prince Ivan Semeonovich Kurakin[85] make contact with him, but was not able to inflict any significant damage or bar the way back to Lithuania, where finally Lisowski appeared after his amazing epic in military chronicles, long remembered in the Muscovite realm.

CHERKASSIANS PERISH IN THE NORTH

The Little Russian cossacks were moving with the same miraculous rapidity in the far North. Such warfare, says the chronicler,[86] had not been known since the beginning of the world. The Russian people did not understand where and how the Cherkassians made their way. From the Vologda region they went to the maritime towns, harried the Vaga basin and the districts of Totma and Ustiug, then proceeded by way of the Dvina lands towards the sea. They passed through impenetrable places, and God only knows where they did not go, emerging in the Novgorod district in the direction of the Suma fort.[87] Nowhere was anyone able to stop them. Only in the trading settlements beyond the Onega were many of them slain, and it was the inhabitants of Olonets who caught up with them. They had harried the Muscovite land through and through, states the chronicler. Around the towns and districts there was nowhere they had not been, much land was devastated, but they perished themselves all the same.

LETTER OF THE POLISH LORDS TO THE BOYARS

While these military exploits were going on in various places protracted but unfruitful peace negotiations were being conducted. In November 1614 the Polish Senate sent the Muscovite boyars a document in which it accused them of betraying Wladyslaw, and pointing out that at first the boyars themselves had wished to entrust their case to the decision of the Holy Roman emperor, but then haughtily had rejected his mediation, continued the war and were holding Polish captives under harsh conditions. Despite this they, the Polish lords, once again, proposed to conduct peace negotiations on the frontier.

The boyars replied that it was not befitting to accept this piece of paper from the Polish lords, nor could they accept it as a basis for conducting affairs of state, for it had not been written according to previous custom. The great sovereign's name was not inscribed on it, and it was written throughout in a haughty manner not in keeping with previous custom. Notwithstanding, the boyars, in accordance with their love of peace, had decided to accept the document from the Polish lords and reply to it. They justified themselves in all the matters raised against them by the Polish lords. "God knows, and also all neighboring rulers, both Christian and Muslim, that we are innocent of all the charges that you write against us. All these injustices were committed by your sovereign and by your side, and our consciences are quite clear on these matters. You, our brothers and lords of the council, should not now or at any time in the future bring up the matter of Prince Wladyslaw, your king's son, being the ruler of the Muscovite realm. That matter is closed."

Concerning the matter of the emperor's mediation they replied that even when the Second Militia Force stood before Moscow the commander had sent the translator Yeremey Yeremeev to the emperor with the request that he urge Sigismund to desist from injustices. "And concerning this we did not sit in judgment between us and your sovereign. There is no way we can go to judgment with your sovereign. The wrongs committed by the king against the Russian realms are well known to Almighty God, to his imperial majesty and all neighboring sovereigns." The boyars wrote that the emperor had sent the translator back with a promise to write to Sigismund that Tsar Michael, as soon as he had ascended the throne, had sent ambassadors to the emperor, and they had fulfilled their mission. Subsequently it appeared strange to the boyars that within the Polish realm there had appeared the imperial herald Singel, who had been sent, not to the tsar, but to the boyars. It was not befitting the boyars to enter into any relations with Singel; but the sovereign, out of respect for the previous strong love of the Muscovite tsars towards the Holy Roman emperors, had ordered the boyars to receive Singel. The necessary preparations were therefore made, but for some reason or other neither the German herald nor the Polish ambassador appeared before the boyars, and the Polish government hitherto had not issued letters of safe conduct for the tsar's ambassador to Sigismund. Then the boyars replied with reproaches concerning the ill treatment of prisoners. "Our people whom you are holding," they wrote, "are not prisoners but ambassadors; Metropolitan Filaret and Prince Golitsyn,[88] who have been separated and are imprisoned in various places. Your people whom we hold captive, Struys and his companions, live in Moscow. They have been given fine houses and receive sufficient food and drink. Their servants are free to go about their masters' business, neither do they suffer any want or oppression."

The boyars concluded the document with notification that the tsar had authorized them to send *their own ambassadors* to the frontier to hold sessions with the Polish ambassadors. It is interesting to glance at the boyars' signatures on the document: first of all we see the name of the ranking boyars, Princes Mstislavsky, I.V. Golitsyn, I.N. Romanov, Sheremetev, Kurakin and others. In tenth place there is the signature of Prince D.T. Trubetskoy, in eleventh place Prince D.M. Pozharsky, in nineteenth place Minin, and among the crown secretaries Sydavny Vasiliev.

ZHELIABUZHSKY'S MISSION TO POLAND
The bearer of this document was one Afanasy Petrovich Zheliabuzhsky,[89] who received the following instructions: if the Poles say

that men of all ranks of the Muscovite realm have kissed the cross to Prince Wladyslaw, he was to reply: "Men of all ranks of the Muscovite realm are blameless in this respect before your great sovereign Sigismund and his son. All injustice and shedding of innocent Christian blood has originated from your great sovereign, but the souls of the people of all the Muscovite realm are clear of it. And on account of the iniquity of your sovereign it is not befitting, either at this time or in the future, to mention the matter of your sovereign's son, Prince Wladyslaw, being ruler of the Muscovite realm. This matter is now closed, and we have long since firmly rejected this proposal to your sovereign and to you on behalf of the entire Muscovite realm." Concerning Zarutsky, Zheliabuzhsky was to say: "The brigand Ivan Zarutsky, the brigand Marina and her son have been brought to Moscow to answer for their brigandage. For his evil deeds Ivashka and Marina's son have been executed, while Marina has died of illness and melancholy at her loss of freedom, even though the sovereign and the boyars would have wished her to live and bear witness to your injustices. So now the patrimony of his majesty the tsar has been cleared of rebellious brigandage, which is now a thing of the past."

ZHELIABUZHSKY AND FILARET NIKITICH

Zheliabuzhsky was to call upon Filaret, make obeisance to him on behalf of his son and say: "O great sovereign, your son has ordered me to enquire after your health, and concerning his own health he has ordered me to say 'Through your fatherly and priestly prayers and those of my mother the sovereign lady the nun Martha Ivanovna on behalf of our great and sovereign realms, we are in good health. We are only grieved that it is not vouchsafed to us to see your fatherly and priestly eyes. We pray to our merciful God and will entreat, urge and wish that God release your holiness from such hardship.'"

The tsar's missive to his father began thus: "To the most venerable and exalted metropolitan, father of fathers, Great Sovereign Filaret Nikitich, glorified by our great and all-merciful God in the Trinity, worthy of sacred and divinely adorned rank, venerated and beautified, true teacher of the Christian race, blamelessly and diligently interceding and praying to the Lord, pastor of the Christian flock, diligent seeker of the lost sheep, counsellor of the bewildered and spiritually troubled and sufferer on behalf of the holy illustrious Christian churches, firm pillar of Orthodoxy, for the sake of Christ living a life of virtue in hope of attaining heavenly paradise. By the grace of God and His strong right arm, hold the sceptre of the great Russian tsardom. Chastise its enemies and reward its benefactors. Your son, scion of your eminently illustrious stem, Michael, by the grace of God tsar and grand prince, autocrat of All Russia, bows his head zealously to the ground, touching your sacred and honorable feet with tears to you, great sovereign, imploring your sacred prayers and blessing."

Zheliabuzhsky also was to convey to Filaret the petition from the nun Martha Ivanovna, then from the spiritual authorities, the boyars and all the Council. Zheliabuzhsky was also to enquire after the health of Prince Vasily Vasilievich Golitsyn and his companions, and deliver them this speech: "Your service, your devotion and your suffering are known to us and we, the great sovereign, will do our utmost to see that you are delivered speedily from such grievous hardship." He was to deliver the same speech on behalf of the tsar to Shein,[90] should he see him. The former tsar, Vasily Ivanovich Shuisky, and his brother Dmitry were no longer alive. Concerning their brother Ivan Ivanovich the ambassador had no instructions.[91] If it were possible to see Filaret alone, Zheliabuzhsky was to tell him that in Moscow all was going well, and that all great sovereigns were sending gifts and great tokens, requesting the tsar's love and friendship.

In Warsaw the Polish lords received Zheliabuzhsky in the customary manner, asking after the health of the boyars. Zheliabuzhsky replied that all the boyars were in good health *under the great sovereign*. When he uttered the words, *under the great sovereign*, of all the senators only Leo Sapieha[92] answered ungraciously: "You do not yet have a genuine sovereign!"

Filaret was living in the house of Leo Sapieha, who was his jailer. Zheliabuzhsky was allowed to visit him there. Accepting the sovereign's missive, Filaret asked: "How is God favoring my son?" Zheliabuzhsky gave the response he was bound to give. Thereafter Filaret said to the ambassador and his companions: "You did not act properly when you sent me from the Muscovite Russian realm with instructions to King Sigismund to ask his son Prince Wladyslaw to be sovereign over the Muscovite realm. I have until now acted in everything in good faith, but subsequently my own son Michael Fedorovich has been elected sovereign of the Muscovite realm. In doing this you have committed an injustice against me. If you really wished to choose a sovereign for the Muscovite realm, you could have elected someone other than my son, but now you have done this without my knowledge."

The ambassador replied: "The business of the tsardom cannot be held up. Even if you, great lord, had been there, you could have done nothing to change it, for this was achieved through the will of God and not through the wish of your son." Filaret replied to this: "You speak truly when you say that my son became sovereign not through his own wish, but by the permission of God and by compulsion on your part." Turning to Sapieha, he added: "What was my son to do? When I left him he was young, no more than sixteen years old and without family, since there only remains myself here and only one brother, Ivan Nikitich, in Moscow." Sapieha answered him rudely, tearing at his hair: "It was merely the Don Cossacks who placed your son upon the Muscovite throne." Zheliabuzhsky contradicted him, saying: "How can you, chancellor, utter such words? This was done by God's permission and will. God sent His Holy Spirit into the hearts of all our people." Sapieha fell silent. Zheliabuzhsky delivered his petitions and Filaret, having read the documents, handed them to Sapieha. Concerning Prince Golitsyn, Sapieha said that he still remained in Marienburg.[93] Shein and his wife and daughter were on Sapieha's estate in the region of Slonim, and his son in Warsaw. Filaret remarked on hearing this: "I do not know whether the boyar Prince Vasily Vasilievich Golitsyn is still alive, since I have been separated from him for a long time."

Apart from Sapieha, there was yet another jailer present, Lord Olesnicki.[94] Filaret turned to him and said: "Tsar Boris got rid of us all. He had me tonsured, he killed three of my brothers and ordered them to be suffocated. I now have only one brother, Ivan Nikitich, left." Olesnicki asked Sapieha: "Why did Tsar Boris deal thus with them?" Sapieha replied: "The reason why Tsar Boris ordered them to be dealt with thus was that he was apprehensive of them, and did not want any of these brothers to rule over the Muscovite realm, because they were eminent men and close to Tsar Fedor."

Lord Olesnicki once again spoke, addressing the ambassador: "In spring Prince Wladyslaw will go to Moscow, and all of us of the Polish Commonwealth will come with him. Wladyslaw will make your metropolitan a patriarch and his son a boyar." Filaret replied: "I do not want the patriarchate," and Zheliabuzhsky said: "You, my lord, speak boastful words, but we rely upon the mercy of God and upon our great sovereign Michael Fedorovich, upon his sovereign good fortune, nobility and bravery, and upon wisdom and reason. Now in all his realms there is peace, quiet and tranquillity. All the people serve the great sovereign and unanimously favor him, and will resist Wladyslaw your prince and all of you. Even before now your king and your prince and all of you came to gain the Muscovite realm and came before Volokolamsk, which in terms of the great realm of Moscow is but a little hamlet. Yet there your king's troops were defeated, and your king retreated from Volokolamsk with only a few forces." Olesnicki made no reply to this, but asked Zheliabuzhsky: "Do you remember me from the time I was in Moscow?" "I remember," replied Zheliabuzhsky, "that you were in Moscow during the reign of Tsar Vasily, and when you took you leave in the palace you kissed the cross to keep the truce for a number of years, and not do any harm to the Muscovite realm." Olesnicki fell silent.

Then the wife of Struys entered and asked Filaret to write to Tsar Michael to take pity upon her husband. Zheliabuzhsky told her: "Our great sovereign is merciful and just. He has taken pity not only upon your husband, who is a famous man, but also upon those who are inferior to your husband, and has been gracious to them all." To this Leo Sapieha retorted: "What is this you are saying, that your tsar is merciful and does not thirst after Christian blood? We have seen how your sovereign sent bribes to the Turkish tsar, in order that he might ally with him against the Polish and Lithuanian realm, and your sovereign's documents to that effect are in our possession." Zheliabuzhsky replied that he knew nothing of the matter. With this the visit ended.

At the farewell audience with the lords of the Council Leo Sapieha again spoke ungraciously: "You do not yet have a proper sovereign. You have two sovereigns. One is with you in Moscow, and the other is here, Prince Wladyslaw, to whom you have all kissed the cross." Zheliabuzhsky responded according to his instructions that the matter was now closed, and it was not befitting to discuss it further. He demanded that in the reply the name of Tsar Michael should be inscribed properly. Sapieha replied: "Now we, the lords of Council, send you back with good news to those who sent you, your brother boyars, but we cannot write the sovereign title, concerning which there will be more ambassadors from both sides who will speak and judge before God on all great matters, and when the prime affairs of state are resolved favorably, we will inscribe the sovereign's name and title."

Zheliabuzhsky made a speech saying that all the Lithuanian senators wanted peace with Moscow except for Leo Sapieha, who alone was deceiving the king. The king himself and the Polish senators were great encroachers upon the Christian faith, worst of all the chancellor Lord Krzycki and the Lithuanian marshal Lord Dorohostajski.[95] In the Sejm[96] the king would request a subsidy in order to advance on Moscow with the army of the Commonwealth. But in Lithuania it had been resolved that thenceforth no subsidies would be voted, nor would the Lithuanian army go to Moscow with the prince. The venture had already failed, there was no purpose in the prince going to Moscow, and they would look after their own affairs. In fact, in the Sejm the Lithuanian senators did not agree to war.

On the way home, on Leo Sapieha's estates, Zheliabuzhsky visited Shein, who urged the sovereign and the boyars: "When an exchange with the Lithuanians takes place, the sovereign and the boyars should urge the ambassadors strongly to beware of deception on the part of the Lithuanians. The ambassadors should meet somewhere between Smolensk and Orsha, on the old border. In Lithuania there is great disaffection against Poland, and there is no peace with the Turks. If the sovereign's troops are assembled, they should make war constantly on the Lithuanian land, and exert pressure upon it, since for them time is running out." He also urged that there should be no partial exchange of prisoners. Zheliabuzhsky also learned that the king had ordered Filaret to send his son letters at the king's dictation, but the metropolitan had stood firm and refused to obey the king, saying that henceforth he would not write any such letters. Accordingly Zheliabuzhsky was not permitted to take his leave of the metropolitan. Lord Grydycz, whom the king and Sapieha had sent to Filaret, himself said to the ambassadors: "When Filaret learned that his son had become sovereign he began to place hope in his son, became firm and took heart, refused to receive visits and ceased writing letters."

NEGOTIATIONS BREAK DOWN AT SMOLENSK

Zheliabuzhsky brought the boyars the document in which the Polish lords proposed a meeting of plenipotentiaries on the border between Smolensk and Viazma. In the document the lords also wrote: "As long as you are ruled by your slaves and not by one coming from the true blood of great sovereigns, you will feel the wrath of God upon you, for they cannot govern the realm as it ought to be governed, neither can they pacify it. Our king has received nothing from the Muscovite treasury, it has been dissipated by lawless people, because it was collected unjustly and by deceiving the people."

Notwithstanding such discourtesies the proposal was accepted, and in September 1615, by a resolution of the Assembly, high ambassadors with plenipotentiary powers were sent to the Lithuanian frontier, including the boyars Ivan Vorotynsky and Alexis Yurievich Sitsky[97] and the lord-in-waiting Artemy Izmailov. On the Polish side the plenipotentiaries were Prince Kazimierzski, bishop of Kiev; Jan Chodkiewicz, hetman of Lithuania,[98] Chancellor Leo Sapieha and Alexander Gasiewski, governor of Velizh.[99] The intermediary was Erasmus Handelius, the imperial ambassador. The talks were to take place between Smolensk and Ostorozhki.

Vorotynsky and his companions were at first to expound the king's injustices, beginning with the breach of the truce during the reign of Tsar Boris at the instigation of the False Dmitry. If the Polish lords said that, even during the reign of the brigand, Prince Vasily Ivanovich Shuisky, his brothers and many boyars had petitioned the king to defend them from the renegade monk and give them the king's son as their tsar, Prince Vorotynsky was to answer: "I, Prince Ivan Mikhailovich, at that time was highly honored by my brother boyars, and my brethren had great affection for me. I was friendly with the Shuiskys, neither did they conceal anything from me. You say this because Prince Vasily Ivanovich and his brother are no more, and you wish to make mock of the dead, but we never did so, nor would we think of doing so." If the Polish lords said that the boyars declared concerning this to the king through Ivan Bezobrazov and Mikhail Tolochanov,[100] the reply was to be: "Ivan Bezobrazov and Mikhail Tolochanov were the first of the renegade monk's friends and confidants among the Russians. Even when the renegade monk arrived at Monastyrevsky, Mikhail Tolochanov was considered his confidant. On account of Mikhail's treason Tsar Boris had dispersed his wife and children among the towns and prisons. According to the brigand Fedka Andronov, Ivan Bezobrazov grew close to the renegade monk in Moscow, and when the renegade monk was killed he fled from Moscow and was in Tushino[101] with the brigand. How can any reliance be placed on such people?" If Alexander Gasiewski says that after the renegade monk was killed he was with Prince Dmitry Shuisky and bade him remember concerning what he had urged the king, and Prince Dmitry did not deny it, then answer: "Prince Dmitry is no more, do you wish to make mock of him?"

Vorotynsky also was to complain thus concerning the conduct of Gasiewski and the Poles in Moscow: "Several of our brother boyars lived in our own homes but many boyars and boyars' wives were evicted from their houses, and Poles and Lithuanians occupied them, appropriating our possessions and supplies. When the hetman left for Smolensk you, Alexander Gasiewski, moved into the house of Tsar Boris, Mikhail Saltykov left his modest dwelling and took residence in the home of Ivan Vasilievich Godunov, and Fedka Andronov in the office of the archpriest of the Annunciation cathedral, where previously nobody ever had stayed or dwelt. I, Prince Ivan, and Prince Andrei Golitsyn and the lord-in-waiting Prince Alexander Zasekin[102] were placed under arrest. Guards were placed on all the gates, barricades on all the streets and none of the Muscovites were allowed to go about with sabres on their thighs or merchants with their wares or carpenters with their axes and nobody was allowed to wear a dagger on his thigh, peasants were not allowed to bring kindling wood for sale. Wives and daughters were taken for debauchery and at night people passing through the streets from house to house were assaulted so that by matins not only the people but even priests were not allowed to move about. Your sovereign ordered Fedka Andronov to be our treasurer, the conciliar noble

Stepan Solovetsky to be the conciliar noble in charge of the Chancellery for Nizhny Novgorod, Vasilka Yuriev in charge of tax collections, Evdokim Vitovtov first conciliar secretary in the Chancellery for Military Appointments, Ivan Gramotin as keeper of the seal and also local secretary in charge of the Chancellery of Foreign Affairs. The Chancellery of Crown Revenues was placed under Fedor Andreevich Meshchersky,[103] the Chancellery for Artillery under Yury Khvorostinin,[104] the chancellery dealing with the Polish lords under the brigand Mikhail Tolochanov and the Kazan chancellery under Ivan Saltykov.[105] "You, Alexander Gasiewski, according to the king's charter were granted the title of boyar and placed in charge of the Chancellery for Musketeers. You personally saw what harm we, the boyars, suffered from our own councillors, from base people, from Fedka Andronov and his companions. Nobody had so dishonored us under previous sovereigns as did this lout, and you allowed him full license. Were it not for you, how could he have acted thus, speaking against us and dishonoring us? The ruin of the Muscovite realm originates with your sovereign and you. God will avenge this upon you and your wives and children, as you yourself will see. Your sovereign's son by his own doing alienated himself from the Muscovite realm by his many injustices and bloodshed. When the hetman came with his army you, Karol Chodkiewicz, then you, Alexander Gasiewski, told us all that we should be under the king's hand, and then you sent to us the traitors Prince Yury Trubetskoy, Ivan Gramotin and Vasily Yanov."

They may say: "The boyars themselves sent to the king saying that in Moscow you had stirred up trouble. The brigand had sent the priest Khariton to Moscow with letters, and others had corresponded with the brigand. The boyars themselves investigated the matter, and as a result he, Prince Ivan Mikhailovich, Prince Andrei Golitsyn and Zasekin had been implicated, and the boyars themselves had placed them under arrest. If therefore there was treason even among your most eminent people, how could the king possibly give his son to rule over the realms?" Or if they place on the table boyar documents in which this matter is written about, you are to reply: "You were making a mockery of me, Prince Ivan (Vorotynsky), and my companions, and you instructed the brigand priest and the boyars.

Whatever you commanded, they performed. Because of you there has been much unrest, dissension and bloodshed. If only you, sovereign, had relied on us nobly-born boyars, and you, Alexander, had not sent these brigand traitors, base people, one after another to take charge of the chancelleries, nothing evil would have happened and all would have gone better. We suffered disgrace from previous sovereigns, but at the same time in all the realm the administration was in our hands, and we did not suffer dishonor from base people, neither did anyone take from us our hereditary dignities. And when we chose your sovereign's son as our ruler he was not even there, but he dishonored us all. He sent you, and ordered you to take charge of all matters pertaining to the crown and to the land in such a great realm, even though hitherto you had not appeared before your sovereign in the Council. Furthermore traitors to the Muscovite realm were sent with you, the basest of men, common tradesmen and the most lowly of junior boyars, whom you appointed as lords-in-waiting, treasurers and conciliar secretaries. There was not one of the lower orders who was not appointed to the Council by your sovereign. If anyone gave Leo Sapieha a pair of sables he became a conciliar secretary. For forty he became a boyar or lord-in-waiting. That was the kind of respect we could anticipate from your sovereign while matters thus stood."

They may say: "Even while Hetman Zolkiewski[106] was in Moscow Vasily Ivanovich Buturlin was sent by the boyars to Riazan, and there he held discussions with Prokopy Liapunov, and Liapunov advanced upon the capital, and Vasily Buturlin turned back to Moscow and persuaded the foreign infantry to betray the king, as he himself admitted under torture." You are to reply: "Even if Vasily Buturlin had contemplated such a design from his youth the boyars ordered him to be interrogated, and even under torture Vasily admitted to no such design. Prokopy Liapunov sent someone to him to enquire as to what was going on in Moscow. You, Alexander Gasiewski, together with your counsellor the common tradesman Fedka Andronov, your sovereign's treasurer, went into the treasury of our sovereigns, surveyed the tsar's regalia, and you were seized with envy, since you have never inherited such wealth. The boyars sealed the treasury but when they returned to the treasury the boyars' seal was no longer there, only that of Fedka Andronov. Fedka was questioned many times by the boyars concerning this and he said that you, Alexander Gasiewski, had ordered it to be re-sealed." The ambassadors were ordered to show the Polish lords a list of things which had been sent to the king, and say: "This is what we know about, and this is very little. In addition to this many artifacts were removed from the treasury and sent secretly to the king. You, Alexander Gasiewski, took other items for yourself and sent them to your friends."

If they say to you that the king did not wish to take Moscow for himself, but wished to send his son, then place on the table the documents written to Prince Ivan Kurakin, Mikhail Saltykov and Andronov. If Gasiewski says that in Moscow he governed only the Polish people and did not interfere in the Muscovite administration, and that when he approached the boyars to discuss a matter the Russians handed him many petitions, and he took all these petitions and conveyed them to the boyars, and all the boyars acted upon and disposed of all these petitions, and the petitions were signed by Russian crown secretaries, and these same boyars wrote letters to the king and he, Gasiewski, did not alter these documents, you are to reply: "This, Lord Alexander, is exactly how it was: you used to go to the boyars and hand them the petitions. Only, after you had arrived, you sat down, and alongside you sat your counsellors Mikhail Saltykov, Prince Vasily Mosalsky, Fedka Andronov, Ivan Gramotin and their companions. We did not hear what you were saying or deciding with your counsellors, and whatever you ordered them to do concerning any petition, this was done. It was your counsellors Ivan Gramotin, Evdokim Vitovtov, Ivan Chicherin and Stepanka Solovetsky, one of the common traders, who signed these petitions, but you drove away the more senior crown secretaries. And what most of all inspired us boyars with deadly hatred was that this unworthy common tradesman Fedka Andronov came and sat down with us, with Mstislavsky, with me, Vorotynsky, and with our other brother boyars and gave us orders and settled matters without consulting us. God sees into our hearts: it was as though we were dead. Documents from the boyars were written entirely according to your wishes, we were all equally your prisoners, you ordered us to sign documents, and we signed."

If the Polish lords say that they, the boyars, had sold much of the treasury of previous sovereigns, had melted down many silver vessels for money and had given it to the Poles and Lithuanians who were stationed in Moscow to protect them from the brigand, and concerning this had drawn up a boyar document, which they dispatched with Ivan Bezobrazov on January 19, they were to reply: "The boyars had no say in the treasury. Andronov was in charge of the entire treasury, and over him was Gasiewski. They sold the treasury and small pieces of jewellry and clothing. Boyars and crown secretaries were ordered to be present at the sale, but they only sat and looked on." At the end of the instructions it was written: "Speak calmly, and do not be embittered, so that we do not break with them because of harsh words."

But it was difficult to speak of such things calmly, and it was especially difficult to fulfill this instruction for Prince Vorotynsky, to whom Gasiewski had taken a dislike even in Moscow. In November, when the sessions opened and the Muscovite ambassadors in accordance with their instructions began talks by reading off the many wrongs committed by King Sigismund, the Lithuanian ambassadors began to get annoyed, to cry out and quarrel. "We cannot put up with this abuse of our sovereign!" they cried. The intermediary, the imperial ambassador, was present, but did not intervene in the proceedings, and with this the first session concluded.

At the second session the bishop of Kiev delivered a speech about past events and from Polish chronicles concerning oathbreaking under previous Israelite and Roman rulers, leading up to the fact that the Muscovite ambassadors in the first session had read out a list of the wrongs committed by the king. Then Jan Grydycz read a prepared text concerning the renegade monk, exculpating his sovereign king. Finally Alexander Gasiewski read a prepared text listing the wrongs committed by the sovereigns Boris and Vasily, and their relations with foreign powers directed against the king.

Among other things, Gasiewski read: "A long time ago, during the reign of Dmitry, whom you call Grishka Otrepiev, the boyar Prince Vasily Ivanovich Shuisky and his brother and many other Muscovite boyars and prominent men secretly expressed their sentiment to several lords of the Council that they would like to see Prince Wladyslaw as their sovereign. Then Prince Vasily Golitsyn, forgetting his allegiance to the prince, and wishing to obtain the Muscovite realm for himself, set off from Moscow for Smolensk, but on the way corresponded with the Kaluga brigand, and conspired with his advisors how to set the Kaluga brigand on the Muscovite throne and then kill him, as they previously had killed Dmitry the renegade monk, so that he himself might become sovereign, as Shuisky had done before him. I, Alexander Gasiewski, remained together with the hetman and the army. I never commanded any Muscovite troops or interfered in the domestic affairs of Moscow but, being only the hetman's deputy, took charge of my own army and soldiers, for my sins, strictly and severely, according to the het-man's articles of war. Remember how, soon after the hetman's departure, my companion in arms Tarnowiecki, while drinking with a Russian priest, picked a quarrel with him, and he struck the priest with his fist in the face, drawing blood. I sentenced him to death but the patriarch and boyars sent to me, and Prince Mstislavsky and many other boyars and the priest himself came to me in the antechamber, begging me to release Tarnowiecki from prison and lift the death sentence. Having assured the patriarch and boyars, I was obliged to do so, but in order that henceforth other licentious persons would not be allowed to plunder simple and undiscerning Muscovites, and alienate them from the sovereign, I ordered Tarnowiecki's right hand to be cut off, and this was done in the Kitai quarter, close by the Frolov gates, before all the community. The boyars and all the Russians were amazed at this, and the patriarch himself afterwards reproached me, saying that it was unbefitting to punish such a trivial offense so severely.

"Then some haiduks caused a disturbance, making a noise next to the church where the patriarch was officiating. I sentenced them to death. The same night two squires stole some apples and nuts that were for sale in the Kitai quarter, and I sentenced them to death, but the patriarch summoned me and would not let me go until I lifted the death sentence, which was commuted to knouting. I ordered some foreign troops executed for plundering churches and struck such fear into the others that they did not dare utter another harsh word to any Russian. Remember also how a Pole of the Arian faith in a fit of drunkenness fired at the image of Our Lady of Vladimir at the St. Nicholas gates. I ordered his arms and legs to be severed, his body to be burned alive, and his severed arms to be nailed to the

wall beneath the image. Not only in the capital, but also in the provinces, no crime went unpunished. Prince Boris Mikhailovich Lykov
is alive to bear witness. I sentenced to death a captain who had
plundered his hamlets, and Boris himself was barely able to get me
to commute the sentence. And to render judgment in petty cases in-
volving disputes between Lithuanians and Muscovites, Prince Grigory Petrovich Romodanovsky was appointed, and as my deputies
from the army Colonel Dunikowski and Lieutenant Wojtkowski.

"Thus on our part no pretext was given for discontent or rebellion. But on your part there were such injustices as we cannot
express in bare words, but only in writing. First, when Hetman Zolkiewski entered Moscow the table attendant Vasily Ivanovich Buturlin, who had been given leave by the boyars to see his estate,
took counsel with Prokopy Liapunov in Riazan, conspired and secretly devised between themselves how to raise up disorder anew
within the Muscovite realm, how to kill the Poles and Lithuanians
in Moscow and raise up armed rebellion against the king and the
prince. Liapunov himself wanted to make himself tsar, saying to his
fellow-conspirators: 'Boris Godunov, Vasily Shuisky and Grishka
Otrepiev were no better than I, yet they sat upon the throne.'

"Returning to Moscow, Buturlin deceived us, saying that he
served Tsar Wladyslaw, but was corresponding with Liapunov in
Riazan, was inciting the foreign mercenaries against us and was
bribing people against us. One of Liapunov's emissaries was caught
with seditious documents and under torture incriminated Buturlin,
and was impaled. All the boyars, gentry, elders and hundredmen
ordered Buturlin to be interrogated and he incriminated himself,
saying that together with Liapunov and the foreign mercenaries he
intended one night to strike at us and kill us.

"Then shortly after the hetman's departure spies began to dissem-
inate documents from the Kaluga brigand. One of the spies, a priest,
was arrested and interrogated in front of the gentry, leading merchants, elders and hundredmen, and he said that Prince Vasily Golitsyn, while proceeding towards Smolensk, had written secretly to
the Kaluga brigand, calling upon him to seize the Muscovite throne.
Prince Andrei Golitsyn also knew of this. The same priest said that
the brigand, in collaboration with many Muscovites, was planning
to descend on Moscow at night, kill us, the boyars and gentry from

leading families who had not been with him in his brigand council, and give our wives, sisters and possessions to the slave-cossacks who wished him well.

"Patriarch Hermogen also showed me, Alexander, his kindness and love, sent me gifts of food and drink and kissed me on the lips, but in his heart he bore malice without cause against his sovereign Wladyslaw and against us. Having invited us into the city for his own protection, he immediately incited disorder and bloodshed. He ordered the priests to incite you, his spiritual sons, to malice and anger against us. This is evident from a letter of one of your Muscovite priests, which warned me and described many of the patriarch's previous actions; how he had been with the Don Cossacks and later had been a parish priest in Kazan. According to that priest's letter there had been found in the Chancellery for Kazan many denunciations against Hermogen brought against him under previous sovereigns by Russians living in Kazan. When the brigand died in Kaluga the patriarch secretly sent many seditious documents around the towns. Then Fedor Pogozhy was caught in Moscow in treasonous dealings. Under interrogation he related all the evil machinations and counsel of Metropolitan Filaret; how he, as he left Moscow, agreed with the patriarch that the prince should not rule the Muscovite realm, and the patriarch bound himself to urge everyone to place Filaret's son Michael upon the throne. From outside Smolensk Filaret wrote subversive letters to Yaroslavl and other towns, alleging that the king did not wish to give his son to reign over the Muscovite realm.

"Following such urging from the patriarch and Filaret, how were your Muscovites expected to behave towards our people? Everywhere our men were enticed into the suburbs or into the Wooden City or other crowded places, or invited as guests into houses, where they were smothered and killed. Cab drivers gathered up drunks, smothered and drowned them. Traders in the market sold provisions, fish and meat to our people at ten times the normal price, and also berated and abused our servants. When Liapunov and his companions were hastening towards Moscow we took counsel on Sunday with the boyars in the place, while in the White quarter on Kulishki street common, base people attacked our men without cause, wounded up to fifty of them, took ten of our sleds and horses and plundered them, abused police officers and emissaries from the boyars and wanted to kill them.

"All this we bore with patience. On Monday artillery was placed around the gates. Early on Tuesday Captain Kozakowski took a cannon towards the Water gate in the Kitai quarter, while I and my colonels and captains were hearing mass in the Kremlin. Lord Zborowski was doing the same in the Kitai quarter. We had no thought of any untoward event and no wish to start any bloodshed. At that time in the Kitai quarter, alongside that cannon, a Muscovite fellow struck Lord Gruszecki with a club, so that he fell dead to the ground, while others rang bells. On the Zhivoy bridge in many places new banners were unfurled. Halfway through mass I ran into the Kitai quarter and I had scarcely passed through the Frolov gates when they caught up with me and grabbed my horse. I immediately began to calm the bloodshed and wounded several Polish squires with my broadsword. But at that moment the Muscovites began shooting even at me with their crossbows.

"At this our army became angered and charged straight into the fray. The Muscovites overcame us by force of numbers. At night Fedor Kirillovich Pleshcheev[107] arrived with his companions from Liapunov with a large army into the Wooden City by the Kolomna highway, and together with all the traitors fought against us. On the next day, Wednesday, the senior boyars all went to the White quarter to plead for cessation of bloodshed, but the Muscovites did not heed them and began to fire upon them. Then we joined in cruel battle." The Muscovite ambassadors responded to all this according to their instructions. They did not rise when the king's name was mentioned, neither did they remove their hats. With this the second session ended.

Meanwhile the Muscovite ambassadors visited Handelius, who spoke with them in the Old Slavic language without an interpreter. He said: "You have named your sovereign, the Polish ambassadors call the prince your sovereign, so one realm has two sovereigns. Here between you there is fire and water. How can water be reconciled with fire?" When the nobles of the Muscovite embassy enquired of the Austrian nobility on what basis the Poles would make peace, the Germans replied: "Lithuania wishes you harm. This is what you need to make peace with them." (indicating a crossbow).

When news of all this reached Moscow, the ambassadors were sent a document. "You will not send to the imperial ambassador to speak concerning anything, and you yourselves will not speak at the sessions, you will not send to him or propose anything to him or consult with him alone. And should he propose that you speak with him, be on your guard in all matters and do not trust him in anything."

Thereafter Handelius sent to tell Vorotynsky that he would like to pay him a visit. The ambassadors received him in their own quarters in the encampment and arranged with him to meet again with the Polish ambassadors. But when they informed Moscow of this, they received this document: "We are astounded. Following what custom did you do this? We wrote to you that the imperial ambassador favors the king. In everything, in the manner of his arrival and in the letters he wrote to the boyars and to you, and from his conversation with you, it is plain that he favors the king. Yet you allowed him into your encampment, and showed him everything and gave orders to write to him. It is obvious that he wrote not only concerning how the next session with the Polish ambassadors was to take place, but also what he observed and noted in the encampment. In future you will not allow the imperial ambassador into the encampment. You will not discuss with him the next session or anything else. You will confine your conversations with him to the matter at hand, but speak smoothly and not harshly, so as not to annoy him."

At the third session Jan Grydycz read again from a prepared text, lasting almost to the very evening. The whole speech was written with many and extensive incidences of perfidy, copied from Polish and Lithuanian chronicles, amplified by many sermons and philosophical instructions. The entire speech was directed at justifying the king and Polish lords in everything, and ended by urging that the prince take the rulership. Among other things, Grydycz read: "You frequently speak of Fedor Andronov, saying that it was not befitting for a member of the Merchants' Hundred[108] to be put in charge of the treasury. Yet this occurred with the confirmation of your own most prominent people, who stated that such persons had performed such duties under previous sovereigns. Kuzma Minin, a butcher from Nizhny Novgorod, who is no better than Andronov, is now your treasurer and great administrator, and lords it over all of you, and there are many such others who preside over affairs in the chancelleries."

The ambassadors reported: "We did not wish to hear these speeches of theirs, for they querulously and noisily spoke against your sovereign decree, saying that we should not obey it, and that it was unbefitting to speak about it, thus calling down God's judgment upon ourselves. This matter is closed. The Lithuanian ambassadors said noisily: 'We have listened to all your speeches, so we cannot sit down with you. When you have heard out our speeches, then you may speak.' When the Lithuanian ambassadors drew apart from us and delivered us those speeches of theirs in written form, we did not accept them for in them were written many unbefitting words concerning you, great sovereign, all aimed at placing the prince upon the Muscovite throne. We firmly stood our ground with them on the matter of your sovereign name and rebuffed them, saying that henceforth we did not wish to hear anything concerning the prince, and so they dispersed." The sovereign answered the ambassadors: "You have done well in standing your ground on the matter of our royal name, and in not accepting the text of their speeches. You have acted as though God has inspired you with regard to their speeches."

The fourth session took place on December 1st. The Muscovite ambassadors gave a written reply to the speeches of the Polish ambassadors delivered at the third session. The bishop justified Gasiewski in everything, saying the Gasiewski was a lord of the Council and an honorable man and therefore it was not befitting to utter such speeches concerning him. "And we," Vorotynsky reported to the sovereign, "said that we had known Alexander Gasiewski when he was in Moscow with Leo Sapieha as an undersecretary, but he had obtained honor from his sovereign through callousness and the ruin of Moscow. But for that he would still be an undersecretary as before. In reply Alexander Gasiewski spoke angry, reproachful and unbefitting words concerning you, great sovereign, saying that you had been chosen solely by the cossacks, and Krzystof Radziwill[109] said that all had kissed the cross to the prince, now the prince was ready to assume the rulership of Muscovy, and if he is not accepted as ruler they are all ready without delay to lay down their lives to avenge his dishonor. And in reply to these speeches we answered in irritation that we wished to hear nothing further in this matter. Alexander Gasiewski began to justify himself and boasted that when he was in Moscow he had taken the tsar's treasury and sent it to the king and the prince inasmuch as all the people had kissed the cross to the prince, so all the treasury was his, and he might do with it as he pleased. When the Muscovites betrayed the prince he, Gasiewski, resisted them, thus gaining honor for the king and fame for himself. But Filaret Nikitich, just before he left Moscow, had agreed with Patriarch Hermogen that you, great sovereign, should be ruler, but Prince Vasily Vasilievich Golitsyn apparently wanted the throne for himself. The Polish ambassadors all supported Gasiewski. The tumult did not let up, and they dispersed. On the way out Gasiewski said threateningly: 'May the blood pour from my throat if, when I arrive before Moscow I do not set fire to your capital!' We replied: 'By the grace of God you will end up where your confrere Fedka Andronov is!'"

Meanwhile it was reported to Moscow that Poland was entering a complex situation. The Turks were attacking, the gentry were angry at the king on account of his Muscovite adventures and did not wish to aid him. On the basis of these rumors the tsar wrote to the ambassadors: "If the ambassadors speak to you loudly and angrily, you are to speak with them regarding their speeches boldly and angrily, according to the subject in question. And if the Lithuanians speak to you from a prepared text, you also will speak to them smoothly from a prepared text."

Finally Handelius intervened in the proceedings. Apologizing for their injudicious dealings with him, the ambassadors wrote to the tsar: "We prevailed upon him to honor your name, that of the great sovereign, and rise when it is mentioned and remove his hat, and so we expected much good from him. When he was in the encampment with us everything was in good order, neither could he see anything within the encampment since he travelled on a sledge and there were musketeers standing on either side of him, and he could not see past the crowd." Thereafter Vorotynsky conferred once again with Handelius, who began by saying that the emperor had ordered him to visit the Russians again, and asked why the Muscovite ambassadors would not confer with the Lithuanians. Vorotynsky replied that the Lithuanian ambassadors were at fault in that they insisted on talking about the prince. In all realms it is the custom that subjects are raised to royal rank to preserve life, to defend and protect the realm, whereas with the prince we suffered utter ruin.

Handelius With such speeches there will be no peace. The Lithuanian ambassadors must stand up for their prince; but if you desist from mentioning your sovereign by name, the Lithuanian ambassadors will cease to talk about the prince.

Vorotynsky We cannot do as you ask. Since the Lithuanian ambassadors will not cease talking about the prince, no good can come of further dealings with them.

Handelius Could we not do thus: leave aside the sovereigns' names on both sides and make peace between your countries?

Vorotynsky This can be done if we have no sovereign, but God now has granted us a sovereign. We are not a lawless land, without the sovereign's command we can do nothing.

Handelius You kissed the cross to the prince, but now you do not wish to accept him as your sovereign, so now how are you going to pacify him, and on what will he live?

Vorotynsky Long ago we renounced that allegiance, henceforth we do not wish to speak or hear of it, and there is no place for him anywhere within the Muscovite realm, for in his name the Muscovite realm was ruined.

Handelius I have heard from the Lithuanian ambassadors that they will not continue to speak of the prince, but wish to discuss how to induce the prince to leave the Muscovite realm.

Vorotynsky The prince has been rejected and we will not have any dealings with him. The Polish lords are speaking against God's judgment. God did not wish him to rule over us and be our sovereign, and who can withstand the will of God? And why should we compensate him for having ruined and incinerated the Muscovite realm and for having spilled much Christian blood? God has entrusted the Muscovite realm to our great sovereign Michael Fedorovich on behalf of his forefathers. He is not obliged to give anything in exchange for this gift or purchase it from anyone, for the tsardom is a gift from God.

Thereupon Handelius proposed once more that peace be made between the two countries without naming sovereigns. The ambassadors gave the same answer. Handelius continued: "There will be no war between your sovereign and the king because the king is in

Lithuania without the lords of the Council, and nothing can be done without the consent of all the estates of the Sejm." The ambassadors replied: "This has no precedent in the Muscovite state; the land can do nothing without the sovereign's decree. From the beginning it has been the practice that only the sovereign may act on behalf of all the realm, but the boyars and the whole land can do nothing without the tsar's command."

The fifth session of the Muscovite ambassadors with the Lithuanians on December 26 also began noisily. A quarrel arose over the fact that while the talks were going on the war was continuing on both sides. "For this reason," reported Vorotynsky, "there was a furious quarrel with them, and on both sides sabers were drawn. Alexander Gasiewski threatened violence, and the imperial ambassador had to separate us." When peace was restored temporarily, the Lithuanian ambassadors proposed peace between the countries. There would be no mention of the prince on the part of the lords of the Council or the Polish Commonwealth. The Muscovite title could be left out and the boyars could send from Moscow ambassadors to the Sejm so that the prince might renounce his title. In this way the boyars would save the prince's dignity. Vorotynsky gave the same answer as previously. The Lithuanian ambassadors replied that in that case they could reach no agreement and would end the negotiations because they had to leave to attend the Sejm. With that the session ended. When news of this reached Moscow Vorotynsky was sent a last instruction to conclude a truce conceding everything in Lithuanian hands and that Wladyslaw during the truce would undertake not to allow any hostile actions or designs against the Muscovite realm.

Meanwhile there was correspondence between the boyars and the lords of the Polish Council, and also between the boyars and the ambassadors who happened to be near Smolensk. The boyars wrote to the Polish councillors complaining about the Lithuanian ambassadors and, among other things, wrote the following: "You did not look upon those who wrought all kinds of evil matters and quarrels between our realms for the sake of their own vanity. Neither their fathers nor their grandfathers enjoyed such high position, and so they did not bring about any good matters between our realms." The boyars were referring to Gasiewski. The Lithuanian ambassadors, having heard of this document, were offended and sent to the boyars in Moscow a document of their own in which they complained about the conduct of the Muscovite ambassadors, and declared their terms for making peace. The truce was to be concluded between realms and not between sovereigns, with the condition that Smolensk and all the towns and districts ascribed to it in true documents be ceded to the Polish Commonwealth. Concerning the boyars' remarks about Gasiewski, the ambassadors declared: "We are very surprised at your words, that you write so discourteously, so insultingly and so unseemingly. Among our ambassadors all are men of mature years, honorable and of old established noble families. It is not the custom in our nation to admit to such great matters of state unworthy persons as, for your sins, you do presently in Moscow. Simple people, base persons, priests' sons and common butchers, are admitted unbefittingly to the business of the state, of the land and the conduct of foreign affairs, in place of many princely and boyar families. And you, our brothers, should yourselves beware, not giving liberties to such unworthy men, who have learned to live by brigandage and malice and who by their own insistence lead you, great and honorable men, to support the shedding of the people's blood. If you persist in your stubbornness, we and all our realm will stand firmly together. The king and the prince, taking counsel with all great sovereigns, in the presence of the ambassadors will pronounce judgment on Metropolitan Filaret and, confronting him with the patriarch's documents, Shein in person and much other evidence, both witnesses and documents, prove that he committed injustice and plain treason against all the Muscovite realm and his true legitimate sovereign Wladyslaw, and in place of him unjustly sought the Muscovite rulership for his son Michael. We will punish him for his misdeeds and Prince Wladyslaw will hasten towards the capital with an army against his son."

"If Metropolitan Filaret," the boyars responded, "had been seeking the throne for his son at the time when we, the boyars, were negotiating with Hetman Zolkiewski, he would have broken off negotiations and not allowed it, for at that time he was the most senior authority in Moscow next to the patriarch, and his brothers and kinsmen were likewise great boyars; neither would he have gone with the embassy to your sovereign, leaving his son with your people in Moscow. And while our great sovereign Michael Fedorovich was being held captive by your people in Moscow, and were things really as you now write concerning Metropolitan Filaret, would the great sovereign have held his peace? Those of whom you had suspicion you arrested and tortured, and some you even put to death. You, Alexander Gasiewski, personally told us boyars that Prokopy Liapunov was seeking the rulership of Moscow. Then the lords of the Council wrote to us that Prince Vasily Vasilievich Golitsyn was seeking it in collusion with Metropolitan Filaret; but now you write that the metropolitan was seeking the rulership for his son! You incriminate yourselves by your own letters for you do not know what fault to lay upon anyone. You write that we admit unworthy men to the conduct of affairs of state. The great sovereign has in his council and in all offices and chancelleries men who are their fathers' sons, who are worthy of their office by reason of their ancestry, their prudence or their service, but your sovereign and his son through kissing of the cross sent to Moscow as treasurer the base tanner Fedka Andronov, and as conciliar secretaries the sheepskin vendor Stepanka Solovetsky, the steward Bazhenko, the cloth merchant Kirilka Skorbovitsky and the priest's son Vaska Yuriev. So, brothers, enough has been written on this subject."

At the sixth session, when the Lithuanian ambassadors heard from the Muscovites that no business could be transacted without mention of the sovereigns' names, they dispersed in a noisy and quarrelsome manner, saying they would sit no longer and return to Poland. The authorities in Moscow were alarmed and wrote to Vorotynsky: "You should now speak in the sessions with the Lithuanian ambassadors politely and formally, and not angrily, so that you in no manner cause a breach with them." The Lithuanian ambassadors declared through Handelius that they would not return to the session until the Muscovites declared that they would agree to a truce "between realms." Vorotynsky informed Moscow and received permission to agree to such a truce. "At first," wrote the tsar, "you must speak of practical matters; at the beginning you must not speak with them about how to write our name and thereby protract negotiations. But when you have reached agreement on all matters and it comes to writing it down and confirming it, you should speak concerning our name and the king's; the term of the session will be

prolonged, allowing you to drag out the negotiations with the Lithuanian ambassadors until our ambassadors have concluded and
confirmed an agreement with the Swedish ambassadors."

Thereafter the Muscovite ambassadors conferred several times
with Handelius, who demanded that they inform him of their final
offer. But they insisted on a session with the Lithuanian ambassadors themselves, with whom they might negotiate. Finally Handelius said that the ambassadors must take their final leave of him,
for he would not attend any more sessions. He would proceed to his
sovereign and tell him of all the wrongs and slights shown by them,
the ambassadors, to his imperial majesty and to him personally, in
that they had detained and thus dishonored him, and his sovereign
would take all this into account. The Lithuanian ambassadors had
acted properly in all things towards the Muscovites, and had sent
their ambassador to interview him *personally* and learn through him
from the Muscovite ambassadors on what basis they would make
peace, but they would declare nothing to him. Vorotynsky replied
that they were prepared to discuss peace terms, but Handelius replied: "It will be time to talk of that when you confirm the prince in
your missives and the prince's rights under the hetman's treaty,[110]
and your oath of allegiance remains unbroken. During the years of
the truce the king and the prince confirm that they will not open
hostilities, and that after the years of the truce the right of the prince
will remain completely inviolate. You will cede all the Severian
towns to the Polish side, and to Smolensk all the towns of the Smolensk principality—Belaia, Dorogobuzh, Toropets and all their districts—as was defined between King Casimir and Grand Prince
Vasily Vasilievich.[111] You will also pay money to the Polish army.
On these conditions, you may conclude truce for eighteen months."

"We have agreed to conclude a truce between realms," Vorotynsky answered, "but now you tell us that the Lithuanian ambassadors want to write about the inviolability of the hetman's treaty?
Once again they make inordinate demands." Handelius departed angrily. When the tsar received the report of this he sent the ambassadors protocol documents instructing how to conclude a truce. "By
the grace of God, the ambassadors (names follow) of the great sovereign (here follows the title), the boyars and all the councillors and

all the great Russian realms sat down with such-and-such ambassadors and talked." There followed an indictment against the Poles.
"We have concluded a truce between the great Russian realms of
the great sovereign Michael Fedorovich and the great realms of the
crown of Poland and the grand principality of Lithuania." Naturally
the Polish ambassadors in no way could agree to this in such a
form, since for them it was a precondition that the name of the new
Muscovite tsar not be mentioned. Vorotynsky sent to Moscow for
resolution of yet another complication. Gasiewski stated that
Michael Fedorovich had kissed the cross to Prince Wladyslaw, but
the ambassadors had denied this. The tsar replied: "You must con-
tradict Gasiewski without hesitation. Should the Lithuanian ambassadors write alleging that our great lord and father sought the
Muscovite throne for us and helped us obtain it, you are merely to
say that God watched over us, and we did not kiss the cross to the
prince. If the Lithuanian ambassadors insist upon this and other
things, and make allegations against our father, saying that he was
seeking the throne for us, and so prevented us from kissing the
cross to the prince, you are to say to the ambassadors in conference
that we kissed the cross to the prince, and this was done by the
judgement of God."

The last session took place on January 28. The Lithuanian ambassadors came not alone, but with Handelius, and demanded a
truce on the conditions already pronounced by the latter. The Muscovite ambassadors did not agree and declared that they would correspond with the sovereign concerning Smolensk. When in fact
Vorotynsky sent to Moscow to enquire concerning Smolensk, he
received the following reply: "You did this out of weakness, not
strength. You declared you would send for instructions about Smolensk without awaiting further concessions from them and you made
two moves towards them as though you were doing obeisance to
them. You should have stood firm over the matter of Smolensk and
not have requested a session from the Lithuanian ambassadors, but
waited for them to send to you." But in Moscow they were gravely
mistaken. Handelius visited the ambassadors to apologize, and then
made excuses: "Do not take to heart that I did not speak properly and from the heart to you in the session. I also suffered great

dishonor from the Lithuanian ambassadors. I shall tell my sovereign of your honesty and good faith, and of the stubbornness of the Lithuanian ambassadors." Then Handelius informed them that the Lithuanian ambassadors were insisting on their previous terms, and were leaving. Vorotynsky, despite his instructions, sent to demand another session, but he received the reply that the Lithuanian ambassadors had already departed.

In Moscow the news of the collapse of negotiations was entrusted to Crown Secretary Peter Tretiakov, who delayed sending the tsar's instructions to the ambassadors outside Smolensk. But in any case it was difficult to propose that a truce be concluded under the existing circumstances. The Poles were demanding too much because the preceding events had raised their hopes; and Moscow had no need to concede everything in exchange for a short truce which would guarantee nothing. Handelius could do nothing, and it is apparent that he did not even wish to do so. In general, relations with the Austrian court under Tsar Michael did not have their previous amicable character. The Austrian court did not consider it necessary to alter its tone in relations with a realm unable even to send precious furs to Vienna. The court was not convinced that the new tsar could maintain himself on the throne after such disorders, and therefore did not hold him in the same regard as his predecessors.

II

DIPLOMACY AND WAR
1613–1617

AUSTRIA

As early as June 1613 the sovereign had ordered the noble Stepan Ushakov[1] and the crown secretary, Semeon Zaborovsky, to go to Matthias, the Holy Roman emperor, as emissaries. The journey was long; because of the war with Lithuania and Sweden they had to travel by way of Archangel. The emissaries received these instructions: they were to say that Emperor Matthias, being mindful of the fraternal love and friendship of his predecessors for the forbears of the great sovereign, should be in fraternal love, friendship and correspondence with him, and might demonstrate his love primarily by sending his ambassador or personal emissary to the Polish king to confront him with his injustices and admonish him to set right the wrongs he had committed against the great sovereign Michael Fedorovich and the Russian realms, to desist from the shedding of Christian blood and bring about peace and tranquillity lest the enemies of the cross of Christ—the Turks and other rulers of the Muslim dispensation—rejoice at dissension among Christians. Should the emperor's councillors enquire as to the sovereign's age, let the answer be that the tsar is eighteen years old, although God has endowed his royal majesty with maturity, handsomeness, bravery, reason and fortune.[2] He is gracious and good-humored to all people, God has endowed him with everything above all people, with all blessings, cheerful disposition and good deeds.

Finally the emissaries were instructed: "If you are in the presence of the emperor's councillors perhaps they may say that in the past year, in 1612, there was a subject of the emperor, one Joseph Grigoriev, who together with the shah's ambassador was having a farewell audience in Yaroslavl with Prince Dmitry Mikhailovich Pozharsky, and he said to the prince: 'If it is desired to have the emperor's brother Maximilian on the Muscovite throne, the emperor will give his brother and reconcile him with the Polish king by a perpetual peace,' and that Prince Dmitry replied: 'If the emperor gives his brother to be ruler over Moscow they would do much obeisance to the emperor and accept his brother with great rejoicing,' and that Joseph returned and spoke to the emperor of this. The emperor was pleased and informed his brother Maximilian, who wrote back that on account of his advanced age he wished to remain in peace in order to pray to God. Then the emperor sent a message by Joseph to Prince Dmitry, saying that he had a cousin named Piliusz, and if they wanted him to be ruler over the Muscovite realm, he would give him. For this purpose the emperor sent to the Muscovite realm his own ambassador, a privy councillor named Razmysl, and sent Grot as ambassador to the Polish king. Did they, Ushakov and Zaborovsky, have any instructions with regard to this matter?"

They were to reply: "We know that the emperor's emissary Joseph Grigoriev came into the Muscovite realm and was with the boyars, but concerning the matter about which Prince Dmitry Pozharsky communicated to the emperor concerning his brother, we have heard nothing. Indeed it was not even in the minds of our boyars, governors and all Russian people to choose a sovereign from a foreign land who was not of the Greek faith. In any case Prince Dmitry Pozharsky was discussing this with Joseph without the authorization of the whole land of the Muscovite realm, or otherwise Joseph or the translator Yeremey was making all this up with the intention of obtaining by deceit some sort of favor from his imperial highness. You, councillors, can well appreciate how such a great matter cannot be decided without the counsel of the whole land. It is not befitting for you to speak of it, and we did not send ambassadors to your sovereign for this purpose. This is an unworthy matter, causing dissension between sovereigns."

The emissaries brought to Moscow a document from the emperor but it contained no mention of Tsar Michael. There was mention only that the emperor had taken to heart the dire position of the Muscovite realm, and that hopefully the Polish king would respect his wishes and make peace. The emissaries were asked to explain how it was that the emperor's document was not addressed to the sovereign, neither was the sovereign's name mentioned in it. Ushakov and Zaborovsky replied that the emperor had received them and had asked amicably after the sovereign's health. The councillors always had spoken with them about everything using the tsar's name, and the tsar's name was respected in every way. At the farewell audience the emperor amicably ordered a bow to the sovereign, and said that he rejoiced at the sovereign's accession to the throne, and wished to be in brotherhood, love and correspondence with the great sovereign, and would send his ambassador to him. They, the emissaries, believed him and accepted that paper as his document, and naively omitted to read the signatures on it, being convinced that the emperor had received them as emissaries of the sovereign, and was sending them back to the sovereign. They questioned the interpreter, who said that truly in the emperor's speeches the tsar's name was mentioned in reply to many articles and both the emperor and the councillors had treated the emissaries with respect. They referred to the sovereign as "tsar and grand prince" but did not mention Michael Fedorovich by name. The emperor had bowed or raised his hat only a few times at the sovereign's name, and had ordered obeisance to the sovereign while sitting, but the emissaries had said nothing to him about it. He, the interpreter, had translated the paper which the emissaries brought to the sovereign and the signatures on it, and had told them that the sovereign's name was nowhere to be found. Yet when they had been in Holland and had received a document from the Dutch prince and the States General with the full name and title of the tsar he, the interpreter, had pointed out to the emissaries the difference between the imperial and the Dutch documents, but they replied: "That matter is already finished."

The emissaries were summoned once again for questioning. They replied: "The emperor while receiving the ambassadors and at leavetaking did not stand, and did not mention the sovereign by name. The emissaries had not spoken about this to the emperor or his councillors, omitting to do so out of simplicity, and not out of any guile, for this was not their custom. They thought that among Austrians things were done in this manner, in the conduct of affairs of state and in diplomatic dealings, as of old. This unintentional offense of theirs against the sovereign had been punished, and for these unintentional offenses God and the sovereign must do as they pleased. They had done this by reason of their simplicity, but had no treasonable intentions. As for the fact that they had accepted from the emperor in place of an official document a reply to their speeches written without naming the tsar, and that not only the documents but also the reply lacked the tsar's name, they had hoped that in response to their speeches both the official document and the speeches would be compiled together, since they were unaware of the proper custom. They had not participated in embassies before. They had done this without guile, but wished they had done better. For their sins they had been misled on account of their simplicity, and in this they were to blame, for on the day before they concluded their business without letting the interpreter read the signature or translate the text, only taking it upon trust for the emperor had left Linz already. Even had they inquired, nothing could have been done without the emperor. For these offenses God and the sovereign shall judge, and these unintentional offenses should not be concealed or covered."

The boyars said to Crown Secretary Zaborovsky: "Stepan Ushakov is a man who has seen much service, and you have sat in the Chancellery for Foreign Affairs, and also as an undersecretary in the Chancellery for Military Appointments, so you are well acquainted with proper procedures. How could you have dared act in this way? Even if you were threatened with death you should not have accepted a response not containing the tsar's name." The interpreter once again was summoned for questioning, and he testified that the emissaries had no secret relations with the emperor's followers, and there had been no unbefitting speeches about the sovereign, although the emissaries and their party had conducted themselves badly. A maiden had passed by Stepan's residence and Stepan's followers had seized and molested her, which caused a scuffle between them and the Germans. Then one of Stepan's servants in the house where he resided tried to dishonor the wife of the doorkeeper, who chased after him with a battle axe and wished to kill him yet Stepan, although he knew of his followers' lawlessness, did nothing to restrain them. Stepan's servants almost caused a conflagration while drunk. He, the interpreter, tried to restrain them, telling them that they were in a foreign country and should not insult people in this way, but they beat him for his pains. Even Ushakov and Zaborovsky drank and quarrelled between themselves. In Hamburg one of Ushakov's servants dishonored the daughter of an English officer, in Holland he had laid violent hands upon the daughter of a treasurer in whose house the emissaries were lodged. Indeed in many places Stepan and Semeon feasted, drank and spoke many foolish words, which in the countries in question were not conducive to the dignity of the tsar's name. At first the emperor desired to give them chains with his portrait, but then he ordered the portraits to be removed, saying: "I have heard about them, that they are simple men, unlearned, good for nothing but mischief. Previous ambassadors and emissaries coming from the Muscovite sovereign did not act in such an unseemly way, and it is unbefitting to give my portraits out to such idle dogs."

In order to rectify the matter, in August 1614 a messenger, the translator Ivan Fomin,[3] was sent to the emperor with a document in which it was stated that the emissaries Ushakov and Zaborovsky had brought a paper with an answer, but it was not known from whom or to whom. Before the arrival of the emissaries Ushakov and Zaborovsky the imperial herald Singel had announced that he was preceding the imperial ambassador who had been sent to the boyars, commanders, and all the people. "And we, the great sovereign," the document continued, "are amazed at the way you are doing things not according to previous custom. Hitherto we have exchanged messages of brotherhood and love. There was no hostility between us, sovereign accorded sovereign honor according to his rank and one praised the other, and between themselves they sought friendship and love on either side. We have placed our disfavor upon our ambassadors because they did not safeguard our royal honor, and have ordered them to be punished."

When Fomin bowed to the emperor in the name of the sovereign the emperor remained seated, slightly touched the hat on his head and did not stand when the tsar's name was mentioned. Fomin remarked that by this action the emperor was showing his brother enmity. The chancellor replied that the emperor did not recall that previously Holy Roman emperors stood when the Russian tsars' names were mentioned. Fomin in turn, when he took leave of the emperor, merely bowed to the waist, not down low. The emperor was offended at the emissary's behavior, sent to him his conciliar secretaries with a reproach and ordered a guard placed on his lodging so that no one could visit him without the knowledge of the councillors. The bailiff Jakob Bauer said to the messenger: "When the tsar's emissaries Ushakov and Zaborovsky were here, he, Jakob, was among the bailiffs and they placed him in the seat where the emperor normally sits in state, and made them practice bowing for three days so that when they were in his imperial majesty's presence they bowed down to the ground." Fomin answered: "The emissaries did wrong in that they did not safeguard the sovereign's honor. Moreover I shall not bow to the ground before the emperor, since in all the world it is not the practice for emissaries and heralds to bow to the ground, but only subjects." Bauer replied: "Now his imperial majesty is assured that your great sovereign is established upon the Muscovite throne; but before you, Fomin, arrived, there was news that the great sovereign was not established upon the

Muscovite throne, and that the Muscovite people were still not yet
in unity."

Thereafter the guard was withdrawn but the bailiff once again
reproached the emissary, asking how he dared demand of the emperor that he rise at mention of the tsar's name. "You have dishonored his imperial highness, and the emperor wishes to write concerning this to all sovereigns and electors, so that they may give
their ruling on it. They have heard that during the reign of Ivan
Vasilievich there was an ambassador who entered the audience
chamber without taking off his hat, whereupon Tsar Ivan immediately ordered that it be nailed to his head. Also, if you had spoken
thus before Emperor Rudolph[4] and had ordered him to rise at the
tsar's name, immediately he would have ordered you thrown out of
the window or raised on halberd points." Fomin answered "What I
have said, I uttered on the tsar's instructions. No such thing as you
relate ever happened under Tsar Ivan Vasilievich. Furthermore our
great sovereign has something to write to all rulers concerning the
emperor's enmity. Among great Christian sovereigns it was not the
custom to treat emissaries and heralds in this manner." The emissary's sternness had its effect. The conduct of Ushakov and Zaborovsky led them to judge the weakness of the sovereign who had
sent them, but after Fomin's answers they changed their minds, and
in accordance with the Austrian watchword (you, happy Austria,
marry)[5] addressed the question to the herald: "Would his majesty
the tsar consider a marriage alliance with the emperor?" Fomin replied that the tsar's intentions were in the hand of God. Apart from
God, who could know?

Fomin lived for more than eighteen months in Vienna, nobody
knows why, as he himself expressed it. He was not given leave to
depart since everyone was awaiting the conclusion in Moscow of
matters concerning Poland and Sweden, and whether Michael would
become established on the throne. Finally he was given a document,
but not with the sovereign's full name and style. Fomin refused to
accept the document, and departed. Without waiting for Fomin, the
sovereign sent to Vienna in June 1616 the well-known Lukian Miasnoy,[6] who was entrusted to find out secretly by any means the following: what was the relationship between the emperor and the king
of Poland; why had the emperor sent his ambassador Handelius to

the talks outside Smolensk, to ensure fair play or as a favor to the Polish king; was the emperor planning to ally with the Polish king against the Muscovite realm, and what had Handelius reported to the emperor and his councillors about the negotiations outside Smolensk? In his letter to the emperor which he sent with Miasnoy the tsar wrote that peace had not been concluded outside Smolensk because of the intransigence of the Polish ambassadors, and he asked that the emperor refrain from aiding the Polish king with money or men, and that imperial troops be forbidden to hire themselves out to the Poles.

The new emissary was greeted with complaints about Fomin. Concerning his journey he did not write beforehand that he was coming from his majesty the tsar. The emperor had ordered a cardinal to make inquiries of Fomin; by whom was he sent, by the tsar or by the land, and on what matter? But Fomin did not meet with the cardinal, but said: "I was sent from his majesty the tsar to his imperial majesty, not to some priest or other, and since I have not yet had audience with the emperor I cannot converse with any of his subjects." When Fomin appeared before the emperor he spoke discourteously, and even threateningly; the emperor could not rise at the mention of the tsar's name because he had severe gout. Lastly, Fomin refused to accept the emperor's document.

But Miasnoy gave the same answer. His imperial majesty's councillors were beginning new practices which were unprecedented and were not practical anywhere else. Emissaries who had not attended his imperial majesty and not presented their credentials properly could not confer with his subjects ahead of time should they do this unilaterally, through these new and unprecedented policies they will overturn love and friendship between great sovereigns, and if this is done at the emperor's behest, the emperor is taking unprecedented steps and displaying hostility towards his majesty the tsar. Miasnoy was told on behalf of Cardinal Melchior Klesl:[7] "If you, the tsar's emissary, do not appear before me, you will not be summoned to the emperor's presence, and there will be no favorable dealings between our great sovereigns. No matter from whom you have come, are you to speak discourteously before the emperor and dishonor us as Ivan Fomin did?" Lukian made a concession and visited the cardinal, who also began with complaints against Fomin: "Fomin

angered the emperor in everything. He spoke discourteously before
the emperor and dishonored me. We also know that in the Muscovite realm persons close to the throne and ecclesiastical dignitaries
are held in great honor, but this base fellow Ivan did everything according to his own stupid reasoning, frustrated all business of state,
and because of him friendship and love did not flourish between
two great sovereigns. If you are sent by the same people as Ivan
Fomin, who spoke disrespectfully before the emperor and dishonored us, your mission to his imperial highness will fail also, and if
his majesty the tsar does not acknowledge you as his emissary, you
will not be honored as such."

Then Miasnoy was told that after being presented to the emper-
or he was to visit the empress. Miasnoy replied: "The sovereign sent
us to his imperial highness and did not order us to call upon the
empress, and we do not know what to say to the great sovereign
lady. Previous ambassadors and emissaries did not call upon em-
presses." The cardinal sent the following reply: "The previous emperor, Rudolph, was not married, but now the emperor and empress,
showing favor to you, have invited you. This is their sovereign
will." The cardinal also sent the title by which the empress was to
be addressed. The day for the presentation was set. The emperor received the emissaries standing and when they bowed to the emperor
he raised his hat. The empress also received them standing. Miasnoy
presented to the emperor a lynx fur and forty sables,[8] to the empress forty sables, and to the cardinal he also sent forty sables. The
cardinal, accepting the gifts, said that he would favor his majesty
the tsar in everything. This favor led him to say that his imperial
highness was seeking nothing from the Polish king and had no wish
to aid the Polish king with money or men against the Muscovite
realm, and he had forbidden soldiers within his realms to hire
themselves out as mercenaries. It was well known to his imperial
highness that war with the Turks and Swedes was a cause for concern for the Polish king rather than for the Muscovite realm. Should
the Polish king not conclude peace, the emperor would send the
king an ambassador, in order to put right the injustices committed
against his majesty the tsar.

With this reply Miasnoy returned to Moscow, where he was subjected to reproach. Why had he stayed in Prague in the same lodging as other ambassadors, why had he visited the cardinal before the

emperor, etc.? But the sovereign was gracious to Lukian Miasnoy and his companion the undersecretary Posnikov, and did not place his disfavor upon them, since they were not accustomed to such duties. Lukian had seen much service, but had not performed such diplomatic tasks. The undersecretary also had not before performed such duties, he had not occupied any important posts, and he was simple and lowly.

TURKEY

At the same time as Ushakov and Zaborovsky, emissaries were sent in June 1613 to the sultan in Constantinople. These were the nobleman Solovoy Ivanovich Protasiev[9] and the secretary Danilov. They were to declare to the sultan that the new tsar wished to be in friendship and love with him, and to stand together against all enemies. He should send his ambassadors to Moscow with plenipotentiary powers and, seeing the injustice of the Polish king and lords of the council, should avenge their injustices and send his command to the Crimean tsar to descend with his whole horde upon the Polish and Lithuanian land, but order him not to attack the Russian land. The grand vizier replied: "The sultan wishes to be in brotherhood, friendship and love with the great sovereign. He wishes to oppose the Lithuanian king and has sent an order to the Crimean tsar to attack Lithuania from Belgorod (Akkerman), and also from Constantinople; he will send ten thousand soldiers including Wallachians and Moldavians against Lithuania, and on the Black Sea he has ordered two towns to be established at the estuary of the Dnieper as a defense against the Cherkassians of the Dnieper and to repel the cossacks from the Dnieper. He has ordered you emissaries to take your leave, and is sending with you his herald." The vizier added that the sultan was gratified by the amicable proposal on the part of the Muscovite sovereign. "You all know," he said, "that under the sun there are two great sovereigns. Among the Christian countries there is your great sovereign, and among the Muslim countries Sultan Ahmed,[10] and who can resist them?"

In August 1615 new emissaries, Peter Mansurov and the secretary Semeon Samsonov,[11] were sent from Moscow to Constantinople to persuade the sultan to order the Crimean khan to attack Lithuania because the Polish king, hearing of the amicable correspondence between tsar and sultan, was corresponding continuously with the Holy Roman emperor, the pope, the Swedish king and other sovereigns, designing every evil against Russia and Turkey. The emissaries also were to complain about raids by the inhabitants of Azov[12] on the Russian borderlands. The emissaries found the Don Cossacks making war on Azov. The pasha of Azov said with annoyance to Mansurov and Samsonov: "You would do well to bring about peace between the Don Cossacks and the inhabitants of Azov. Presently the cossacks are causing the inhabitants of Azov great oppression and harm; they are worse to us than the Jews, and if the cossacks do not make peace with the inhabitants of Azov we will write to the sultan on behalf of the whole city, and you will not be received honorably by him."

At that time the people of Azov brought prisoners from the Dead Donets,[13] namely Matvey Lisishnikov, the Don ataman, and twenty cossacks. They tortured the ataman dreadfully, tore strips from his spine and hanged him on the very ship which had been prepared for the emissaries. Under torture the cossacks said that the tsar had sent Mansurov to them with gifts—money, cloth, grain and military supplies. The emissaries declared to the pasha that they would not travel on a vessel where a common rebel was hanging. The pasha replied: "Here there live free and lawless men just like the cossacks on the Don. They captured the brigand cossacks and hanged them on the ship not according to my orders but on their own initiative. I will give you another ship." Finally the Don Cossacks, Ataman Smaga Chertensky and his companions, sent to Azov three atamans who concluded peace with the inhabitants of Azov. Thereafter the tsar's emissaries set off for Constantinople.

In Constantinople an honorable welcome awaited them. The grand vizier said to them: "You are welcome guests with us, you come to us with fair and amicable business, and our sovereign has ordered us to show you honor greater than the ambassadors of all other great sovereigns and to think of your great sovereign as a true friend and ally." But the cossacks did not delay in complicating matters. The vizier sent word to the emissaries that the Don Cossacks had been attacking Azov for twelve days, were threatening many ships on the Mius[14] and now were besieging Kaffa on seventeen rafts. "And you, emissaries," the vizier ordered them to be told, "have not come to our sovereign in good faith, but for purposes of deceit." The emissaries were obliged to chant the old refrain, that on the Don there dwelt brigands, fugitive dependents of boyars, who had fled execution in the Muscovite realm and who lived on the Don, moving from place to place in outlaw fashion. But the vizier's emissary argued: "You say that brigands live on the Don; but why did your sovereign send you with supplies for them—money, cloth, sulphur, lead and provisions? The vizier has instructed me to tell you this: if the Don Cossacks cause such harm upon the sea or at Kaffa you will come to no good here, and we may even execute you here for your deceitfulness. Write to the cossacks, telling them to desist from their brigandage." The emissaries replied: "We were sent concerning our common good. When we are with the vizier let us speak of these great matters, then we can come to an agreement over the Don Cossacks."

But soon more news came. The Don Cossacks went by sea on many rafts, took the cities of Trebizond and Sinope, burned them, killed many people and took captives. The vizier for a long time refrained from sending for the emissaries, who resorted to the treasurer, the vizier's son-in-law. They made him a gift of forty sables in order that he might induce the vizier to consider their case. The vizier sent word to them that they should not worry about anything, that all their business would be done, and in fact shortly thereafter he sent for them. The conversation did not open very pleasantly for the emissaries. The vizier said to them: "It is impossible not to inform my sovereign about the cossack brigandage, but as soon as I tell him it will not be good for you, I tell you straight. My sovereign will order the Tatars be sent to make war on your land, and what profit will there be to your sovereign in that?" The emissaries gave their previous answer, that "on the Don there dwell brigands, who had inflicted great harm on the Muscovite realm also, since they allied first to Grishka Otrepiev and then to the Poles, and thereafter proclaimed many brigands as sons of sovereigns. His majesty the tsar has ordered them to quit the Don for the sake of friendship with the sultan. It is not surprising that outlaws commit brigandage. Yet the Azov people are not cossacks but live in towns and come every year to defend our sovereign's borderlands." The vizier replied: "But surely the Crimeans do not attack your borderlands." The emissaries replied: "We are not speaking of the Crimeans. We are asking that the sultan call off the inhabitants of Azov."

The vizier fell silent, and after this silence spoke again: "Tell me, how many soldiers accompanied you to Azov and how many rafts carried you and your soldiers, and where are these soldiers and rafts now? Rumor has reached us that you left these soldiers and rafts with the cossacks on the Don, and now on these rafts the cossacks are committing piracy on the sea, threaten ships and lay waste coastal districts and hamlets." The emissaries replied that no soldiers or rafts had been left on the Don. The vizier replied: "If your sovereign does not now pacify the cossacks, neither can our sovereign pacify his own troops, and there will be no friendship between our sovereigns, and you will be detained here. But enough of this matter; we will speak of favorable matters."

The favorable matters consisted of the emissaries' declaration to the vizier: "If you soon send your army against the Polish king, fulfill all the desires of our great sovereign and dismiss us quickly with a favorable message, we will make obeisance to you with seven times forty sables." The vizier was greatly swayed and said: "The sultan will immediately send his army against Poland and will order you to be dismissed immediately with a favorable message. He will write to your sovereign with his full name and title. On this I give my assurance, and until my old age I shall work for and serve the interests of your great sovereign." The emissaries for their part demonstrated their sovereign's friendship for the sultan, declaring that the Persian and Austrian emissaries were being detained in Moscow because the emperor, the Persian shah, and the Polish king were corresponding with each other.

But friendly relations purchased by the sables were short-lived. The cossacks overcame the sables. The vizier declared to the emissaries that the sultan would send his army against Lithuania, but they, the emissaries, must undertake that the Don Cossacks inflict no harm upon Turkish territories during the Turkish army's campaign in Lithuania. The emissaries refused to give this undertaking, saying that there was nothing concerning this in their instructions, and that for a definitive agreement about the cossacks they must send their own ambassador to Moscow. The vizier replied: "It would be good for you to take the Don Cossacks to heart, for if you do not, how can you expect anything good from our sovereign? You will not be given your leave, there will be no love between our sovereigns, our sovereign will not help yours against the Polish king, and our sovereign will send his commanders against the Don Cossacks, our soldiers will kill all the cossacks, will lay waste all their yurts,[15] and this will not redound to the honor of your sovereign." The emissaries replied: "Even though the Turks destroy the Don Cossacks to the last man, our great sovereign will not hold it against yours. Our great sovereign intends that there shall be no more cossacks on the Don whose brigandage hinders good relations between the two realms."

Vizier You call the Don Cossacks brigands and outlaws but why did your sovereign send them plenty of supplies? With these supplies they take to the sea and cause much harm to our sovereign.

Emissaries Our sovereign sent the Don Cossacks supplies because they were undertaking a campaign against the Nogay, and wanted to rescue a Russian prisoner from them. Besides, the Don Cossacks honorably met with our emissaries Solovoy Protasiev and his companions, and entertained your emissary for a whole winter. On the Don there are brigands who live like outlaws; they move from place to place. But the people of Azov who are subjects of your sovereign live in the town, yet they commit brigandage against our borderlands!

The vizier replied that the sultan had ordered the people of Azov to be called off. At the same time the vizier was visited by the Polish emissary Jan Kochanowski, whom the vizier seated lower than the Muscovite emissaries. Kochanowski informed the vizier that the cossacks who were committing piracy on the Black Sea were not Zaporozhian,[16] but Don Cossacks.[17] The Muscovite emissaries said to the vizier: "You yourself know that it is the Cherkassians who are committing piracy."

This was the last conversation of the Russian emissaries with Vizier Ahmed Pasha. The sultan ordered him replaced for concealing bad news about the Persian war, and in his place appointed Khalid Pasha. The emissaries inquired of Patriarch Timothy whether he could help them with the new vizier. The patriarch replied: "You know very well that the old vizier was a great persecutor and destroyer of us Orthodox Christian Greeks, and almost brought me to my death, and there was no way I could help you with him. I think the new vizier is well disposed towards me, and therefore I will concern myself with political affairs. Tomorrow you should send the vizier a present of two or three times forty good sables, and with your people I will send my deacon Manuel, in order that on my behalf he might do obeisance to the vizier and his majordomo. The vizier's majordomo knows this deacon Manuel and loves him very much, and the majordomo is the vizier's uncle, so you should also send him forty sables."

The emissaries followed the patriarch's advice and the vizier promised to promote their cause, but declared that he was completely hampered because of the Don Cossacks, in that the tsar had sent gifts to the cossacks. The Polish king had promised to call off the Cherkassians, and if he did so the sultan would make peace with him and send his army against the Don Cossacks. If the Polish king did not send his army against the Cherkassians, but the Don Cossacks ceased their piracy on the sea, the sultan was willing to ally against the Polish king and they, the emissaries, would be sent back to Moscow. Again the emissaries sent the vizier a sable robe with the request that he be of service to the great sovereign and complete all transactions of state. The vizier replied that one of the emissaries would be dispatched to the tsar with the sultan's document, while the other was to remain in Constantinople since the emissaries did not wish to deal with the matter of the Don Cossacks, who were committing piracy and attacking Turkish coastal towns and districts. "Go to the mufti and do obeisance to him," added the vizier.

The emissaries visited the mufti and from him heard the same speeches, namely that one emissary was to travel to Moscow as was the case with the imperial ambassadors, one of whom, the senior, had remained in Constantinople to rectify certain amicable state matters. The old demand also appeared, that the tsar cede Kazan and Astrakhan to the sultan. Khalid Pasha left on campaign against Persia. His place was taken by Mahomet Pasha, from whom the emissaries were to hear the previous speeches. "If you do not write to the cossacks and call them off, your sovereign will have to wait for such friendship from ours, and on account of the cossacks you will not be given leave to depart from Constantinople."

The emissaries unofficially sent the Greeks to the son and majordomo of the mufti, who sent the following word to them: "We have raised your matter with the mufti, but in order that we may not be forgotten we would appreciate any gifts from overseas which you might have." The mufti in fact sent for the emissaries, but declared: "If your sovereign cedes to us our ancient Muslim towns of Kazan and Astrakhan, our sovereign will aid him immediately against the Polish king. According to our Muslim faith we are forbidden to aid Christians without anything in return." With that he dismissed them. The emissaries went to Vizier Mahomet Pasha and told him that if the sultan attacked Poland with his army the sovereign would send him, the vizier, soft furnishings to the value of three thousand gold pieces, and gave him a promissory note in the same amount. The vizier held the note in his hands and then gave it back, saying: "I do not need your note, but I will raise the matter of your sovereign's affairs immediately and favorably with the sultan."

Thereafter a secretary from the chancellery of foreign affairs informed the emissaries that he had been instructed to draw up a letter from the sultan to the tsar saying that the emissaries soon would be given leave to depart, and then sent the following word to them: "The emissaries are now here for a second year, many people have received gifts from them, only I have not received anything from them. Therefore they should also seek the sovereign's favor for me. The sovereign's generosity will not be wasted, as I will work on the sovereign's behalf as far as it is in my power." The vizier's majordomo also sent word to them: "I constantly discuss state affairs with the vizier, and these matters are now approaching a conclusion. The emissaries therefore should give some token of esteem to the vizier, neither should they forget me." The emissaries sent fur robes to all of them. The mufti and his son sent to them asking them not to forget their promises, and so they also sent sable robes to them. Thanks to these robes, the emissaries after a thirteen-month stay were given leave to depart for Moscow with the information that the Turkish army was standing against the Polish king at Khotin, and as soon as Vizier Khalid Pasha returned from Persia the sultan would send all his troops against Poland.

PERSIA
Emissaries were sent to Persia as well, namely the nobleman Tikhonov and the undersecretary Bukharov. Shah Abbas declared that he wished to be in firm friendship with Tsar Michael and wished to

help him with troops and money if only the tsar would assist him in certain matters. Gazing up to the sky, the shah said: "May God destroy me if I commit any injustice against my brother Tsar Michael Fedorovich." The shah sought the sovereign's forgiveness for having promised at first, in answer to the request of Marina and Zarutsky, to help them with troops, money and grain supplies. They had assured him that the Muscovite tsar, Ivan Dmitrevich, was with them, and Moscow was occupied by Lithuanians, from whom they wanted to deliver it. As soon as he, the shah, learned of the brigandage of Marina and Zarutsky he gave them no aid. The tsar sent the nobleman Leontiev to request from the shah money and assistance against the Lithuanians, and at the end of 1617 some slight monetary aid was sent, silver ingots to the value of seven thousand rubles.

CRIMEA

The new tsar naturally had to open relations with the Crimea, where Janibek-Girey was the ruler. These relations bore the previous character, which is well known to us. The chief matter under discussion, as before, was trade. The Crimeans overcharged, wanted to take as much as possible, while the Russians tried to give as little as possible, pleading the devastation of the country and the plundering of the treasury. These ruffians were unmoved by such pleas. In June 1614 at Livny, where according to custom the exchange of emissaries took place, the Crimean ambassador Akhmat Pasha Suleshov declared: "Unless the sovereign sends ten thousand rubles annually, besides trade goods, I cannot conclude a favorable understanding. I have two offers, a good one and a bad one. Choose! The Lesser Nogay make war on you without respite, and if we also descend on you with all our forces, what will be the result? You say that six thousand rubles is too much and that you cannot gather it from anywhere; but if I make a sweep just through Livny and capture a thousand prisoners and charge fifty rubles ransom for each prisoner, I will have fifty thousand rubles." Finally Akhmet Pasha agreed to accept a gift of four thousand rubles for the khan and in exchange made an agreement when the Muscovite ambassador gave his word that early in the spring the sovereign would send more gifts to the khan.

But when the ambassador, Prince Grigory Volkonsky, visited the Crimea to accept the agreement, Khan Janibek-Girey declared: "We will not give the agreement because the gifts to us and to our consort were too small. You made presents to too few of our privy councillors, and they were too meagre, and so our privy councillors are displeased with us. They do not wish to give an agreement, and have dissuaded us from giving one." Finally the khan gave the agreement on condition that should the sovereign not send gifts early in the spring the agreement would be invalid. After that gifts were sent annually to the Crimea in order to restrain the Crimeans from attacking the Muscovite borderlands, and to induce them to attacks on Lithuania. The last aim was poorly achieved, for the khan was preoccupied with the war against Persia, internal dissensions and fear of the Zaporozhians, who were energetically laying waste his territories. As previously the Muscovite ambassadors resided permanently in the Crimea under restriction, almost under duress. As before the interests of the Muscovite sovereign were championed by the family of Prince Suleshov—at first Akhmet Pasha and later his brother Ibrahim Pasha.

EMBASSIES TO HOLLAND AND ENGLAND
More than anywhere else the new sovereign found sympathy in the distant West, with the maritime powers Holland and England. Naturally this sympathy was sincere. The internal troubles of the Muscovite realm and the devastation caused by the Polish and Swedish wars had hurt their trade; therefore it was in their interest to promote order in the Muscovite realm and for their pains receive even more favorable trading conditions. Our old friends Ushakov and Zaborovsky, having completed their mission to the Holy Roman emperor, were to travel to Holland and there request assistance against our enemies. On May 1, 1614 Ushakov and Zaborovsky arrived at The Hague. They arrived in such an impoverished condition that the Dutch government immediately furnished them with all necessities, ordering them to be given a single grant of one thousand guilders. The ambassadors, according to the Dutch, amazed everybody by their modesty and courtesy, and were very timoros. They asked the States General to assist the tsar with troops and money. The States replied that they only recently had emerged from war and they

could not afford the tsar any help, but they would exert all their efforts to incline the Swedish king towards peace.

In June 1613 the nobleman Alexis Ziuzin[18] was sent to England. Describing the injustices of the Poles in Moscow, Ziuzin was to tell the king: "At the time of the ruin of Muscovy the Lithuanians seized your merchants and traders, the Englishman Mark and his companions, took all their goods away and kept them under close guard and later killed them." Ziuzin was to tell the king's ministers that the tsar had ordered him to request monetary aid in order to pay his troops, but that our sovereign needed no mercenaries because presently he had no money to pay them. Ziuzin was to request the king to grant aid in the form of money, provisions, powder, lead, sulphur and other munitions, and the sovereign would make recompense with his loving and fraternal friendship. Above all they must press the king to send the sovereign assistance in the form of money and artillery supplies to the value of one hundred thousand rubles, or at least eighty or seventy thousand, or at the very least fifty thou-sand. If the king's advisers said they were certain that the Englishman Mark was killed by Russian cossacks when the Kitai quarter was captured from the Poles and Lithuanians, that these same cossacks took their possessions, and that the sovereign had ordered these possessions be returned to the English traders, they were to reply that Mark was seized by the Poles and was kept under close guard in the English compound in the Kitai quarter until the very time it was recaptured from the Poles, and that thereafter there was no trace of him. It was not known whether he was killed by the Poles and Lithuanians or possibly by the rabble, because at the time many Russians held captive by the Poles were killed. Ziuzin was further to inquire concerning Grigory Grigoriev and his three companions who were sent to England to study during the reign of Boris Godunov. He was to ask for their return, for the sovereign needed them for diplomatic functions.

In England the Muscovite emissary was not received as in Austria. King James answered that he would bear friendship towards Tsar Michael more than any previous kings. "We know," he said, "what evils the Poles wrought in Moscow, and we reproach King Sigismund concerning this, and do not correspond with him on any matter, and the injustices of the Swedish king are known to us as

well." The king told the emissaries to put on their hats, twice and
three times mentioned it to them, and by his royal word compelled
them and begged them to put on their hats. But the king himself and
his son, Prince Charles, did not once put on their hats but held them
in their hands, and the queen stood right there according to her
queenly rank and custom. In reply to the king's request to put on
their hats, the ambassadors replied: "We see your brotherly love
and firm friendship towards our sovereign, we hear your sovereign
speeches, the name of our great sovereign is lauded, and we are admitted into your close royal presence, and so we slaves at this time
may put on our hats." The king, queen and princes bowed to the
ambassadors, for which reason they were praised, rewarded and politely esteemed.

JOHN MERRICK'S PEACE MISSION

As a result of this mission, in August 1614 the English merchant
John Merrick,[19] long well known to readers of this history, arrived
in Moscow, but with new significance. In the king's document he
was called a prince, a knight and a nobleman of the privy chamber.
Merrick declared the king's wish that the sovereign grant the English merchants free trade and open the route to Persia along the Volga. The Russians answered that the sovereign had given permission
for English merchants to come to the Kholmogory mooring and to
other places to trade freely in all goods without paying duty, and a
charter had been granted them under the tsar's seal. But it was perilous at present for English merchants to travel through the Muscovite realm by way of the Volga to Persia and other oriental realms.
"Prince Ivan" (Merrick) himself knew that there had been disorder,
Zarutsky and Marinka had been in Astrakhan. Now the commanders
had captured Astrakhan and had sent Zarutsky to Moscow, but
many brigands who had been with Zarutsky had fled to the Volga,
and there they were committing brigandage, had plundered many
Russian traders, and the shah of Persia had invaded the Georgian
land, which is subject to Muscovy, and there is correspondance with
him about that now, but presently Russian traders do not go to
Persia. And when God grants that the way to Astrakhan is cleared
and there is an agreement with the Persian shah concerning the
Georgian land, then the sovereign will correspond with King James
concerning this.

Subsequently, a conversation took place between Merrick and Prince Ivan Semeonovich Kurakin on the subject of making peace between the sovereign and the Swedish king.

Merrick The Swedish king personally has written to our sovereign seeking him to facilitate peace between himself and your great sovereign, and the Swedish king has entrusted the matter to our sovereign and has given me instructions ordering me to deal with the Swedish ambassadors according to the decree of the lord tsar.

Kurakin You know how matters have stood between the great sovereign tsars and the Swedish kings: how the Swedish kings have had dealings with the Novgorod lords lieutenant, so how it is unbefitting for his majesty the tsar to send concerning peace to the Swedish sovereign? So do you propose to go to the Swedes without our ambassador or emissary?

Merrick I am prepared to go, or I will send a nobleman ahead of me, and then I will go myself.

Kurakin Do you guarantee that the Swedes will make peace on the sovereign's terms?

Merrick The Swedish king is relying on our king, so how can he not reconcile him with the lord tsar?

Kurakin But if the Swedish king does not heed your King James and does not make peace with the great sovereign on his terms, will King James then ally himself with the great sovereign against the Swedes, and will he aid his majesty the tsar?

Merrick If the Swedish king does not heed and forgets the love of our king, who made peace between him and the Danish king,[20] he will be the enemy of our king, and *I think* our king will help against him.

Kurakin Tell me frankly, do you have with you an instruction from King James saying that your sovereign wishes to aid our sovereign against his enemies, when and how, and are you empowered to conclude any agreements?

Merrick Our sovereign, King James, son of Andrew,[21] not only wishes to help his majesty the tsar with money and all means and to do him every favor. He wished to send money with the tsar's ambassador Ziuzin, but he had to make many disbursements from his treasury. After the ambassador left our King James summoned a parliament with his boyars and all the people of the land concerning the collection of funds for the king's expenses and to aid his majesty the tsar, and as I departed from my sovereign the parliament had not come to any conclusion on this matter, and I was not given authority to give any confirmation. But if his majesty the tsar has any request to make of our sovereign concerning this matter, our sovereign has requested me to write to him about it.

Kurakin Can you guarantee that your sovereign will be able to afford help this spring?

Merrick How can I give such a guarantee? The way is distant, and apart from the Swedish land, there is no other way.

Kurakin Can you guarantee that he will send aid?

Merrick I think he will.

Even though he merely had held out hope of aid, Merrick hastened to mention his king's request. James requested that Englishmen be permitted to travel the Volga to Persia and along the Ob to the East Indies. "We think," said Merrick, "that the way along the Ob river has been explored and both English and Russians will travel to India, and there will be such income for the tsar's treasury as there never has been before. A way to India has been discovered, but it has not been anywhere nearly fully explored for three years, and that is a long time! Another request: the English have discovered a new land, apparently called Girlyan (Novaia Zemlia). It is a wilderness, unpopulated and its resources are the hunting of whales and walruses, the taking of blubber and fish teeth, and there are many other resources, and many reindeer. If the sovereign wishes, he may give leave to go from his patrimony, Lappland, people who know how to handle reindeer and the crafts which are practised in Lappland. It could be established by treaty how many men are needed according to the Englishmen's specifications. It can be determined how they are to be there and how they will be treated by the English, and when the Lapps are to be repatriated to the sovereign's land. I will undertake this. Then there are in his majesty the tsar's land iron and tin on the Sukhona river, so perhaps the sovereign will allow assayers and metallurgists to be brought from England. They would find the ore and work it, and the sovereign would receive income from it, and Russians would learn to assay and work ore, and could come to live there. Also close to Vologda there is much uninhabited land which is marshy and not suitable for anything. The sovereign could grant it and allow the English to bring their people there for trade. They will hire Russians, bring land under cultivation, sow flax and also manufacture linen which also can be exported overseas." The boyars replied that before everything else it was necessary to conclude the Swedish matter, so Merrick proceeded to Novgorod for negotiations.

GREAT NOVGOROD UNDER SWEDISH RULE

We left Novgorod in Swedish hands. Even as early as December 25, 1611, according to the decision of Metropolitan Isidore,[22] the governor Odoevsky[23] (who several months previously had received a rich service tenure from the king) and all the people, ambassadors had been sent to King Karl in Stockholm—Archimandrite Nikandor of St. George's monastery, Abbot Anthony of the Annunciation monastery, and from the laity, the nobles Kolychev and Boborykin, and the secretary Konshin. They were to petition the king that he grant as their sovereign one of his sons, "for our previous sovereigns and their imperial stem came from their Varangian principality, from Rurik, and they lasted until the great sovereign Fedor Ivanovich." How little the Novgorod ambassadors were assured of full and general agreement by their fellow citizens to the election of a prince and how they feared change is shown by the fact that the metropolitan, the governor, and the leading men had to swear the following oath to them: "We, the metropolitan, archimandrites and abbots will pray to God for them, and we the boyars, noblemen and all the people will protect their homes, help them and not hand them over, as far as merciful God will give help."

The citizens of Novgorod sent these ambassadors on behalf of the entire Muscovite realm but we have seen how the talks between Obolensky and Pozharsky concluded. When Moscow was liberated from the Poles, and the inhabitants of Novgorod once again reminded the leaders of the Militia Force about the Swedish prince, they answered: "We cannot now decide by ourselves such a great matter concerning the realm and the land without sending around and taking counsel and coming to agreement with the realms of Kazan, Astrakhan, Siberia and Nizhny Novgorod and with all the towns of

Gustavus Adolphus
c. 1624
Jacob Hoefnagel

the Russian tsardom and with all the people, from the greatest to the least. We have now written to all the towns concerning the election of a sovereign and sought advice as to who is to be ruler of the Muscovite realm, so that all the towns may send the delegates to us in Moscow." The towns chose Michael Fedorovich and the unfortunate inhabitants of Novgorod found themselves between two fires: to separate from Moscow meant to tear themselves loose from all lifegiving principles; to rupture the link with Sweden was not within the realm of possibility, for they were in the hands of De la Gardie.[24]

Karl IX[25] had died and in June 1613 his successor Gustavus Adolphus[26] had sent to Novgorod a document in which he informed them of the dispatch of his brother Karl Philipp[27] to Vyborg, where plenipotentiaries from Novgorod and from the entire Russian tsardom were to appear in order to resolve the matter. The inhabitants of Novgorod made excuses and sent ambassadors to Vyborg to petition the prince, urging him to come immediately to Novgorod. As soon as he arrived at Vyborg the leader of the embassy, Archimandrite Cyprian[28] of the Khutyn monastery,[29] wrote to Novgorod saying that the lord prince and his boyars who were ambassadors with plenipotentiary powers were very annoyed that many people from Great Novgorod were going over to the brigands. "We have done everything we were instructed to do," continued Cyprian. "We did obeisance concerning everything to the prince and the great plenipotentiary ambassadors. But our sovereign Prince Karl Philipp, son of Karl, and his plenipotentiary ambassadors reject us, saying that the sovereign prince will not come to the Novgorod realm alone, not until the realms of Vladimir and Moscow unite with Novgorod. Concerning this you have long been aware that the sovereign did not come to rule solely over the Novgorod realm, so you should write to us in your documents telling us what to do, given the present circumstances. By these documents of yours you are causing a cooling of relations between us and the prince and his boyars, and are bringing trouble upon your own heads. How are we to act, given the circumstances here, regardless of your instruction and your letters?"

Sweden and the Baltic in the Early Seventeenth Century

If the position of Cyprian and his companions in Vyborg was complicated, even more complicated was the position of the inhabitants of Novgorod. De la Gardie left Novgorod and his successor, Field Marshal Evert Horn,[30] in January 1614 declared to the inhabitants of Novgorod: "His princely highness wishes all the people of the Novgorod realm, without any flattering delay or evasion, fully, definitively, and sincerely to declare their opinion. Do you wish to have and respect his princely highness and his direct heirs as your direct sovereigns and kings, and show him direct and sincere loyalty and obedience, and unite with the Swedish crown, not as people subjugated, but as a special realm, similar to the manner in which Lithuania was united to the Polish kingdom? His princely highness has expressed the wish that you immediately kiss the cross to him and his successors as grand prince of the Novgorod realm, and if Almighty God gives his princely highness more than one son, one of them will be sovereign and grand prince of the Novgorod realm. If God only gives the prince one successor, you will kiss the cross to him and his successors in the same manner as you are now kissing the cross to the present king. And if you remain in your present obstinacy and do not obey the king, then know this: even as his royal majesty took Novgorod with the sword when you were not under any proper sovereign or authority, and protected you against your enemies, so now he has the right to keep the Novgorod realm for himself and his descendants." After this Archimandrite Cyprian informed the inhabitants of Novgorod that Prince Karl Philipp[31] had left Vyborg for Stockholm.

For a long time the leading men of Novgorod did not reply to this dreadful question. Finally, after it had been repeated a number of times, they obtained a postponement, so that in such a matter concerning the great tsardom they could consult with the leading merchants and men of the land and obtain from all the people letters signed by them and by their spiritual fathers. At the same time the leaders of the Five Wards[32] were ordered immediately to make enquiry in all the streets and trading settlements of the merchants, the street elders, townsmen, residents and all manner of people. But the question was worded craftily and not directly, asking: "Do you want to kiss the cross to King Gustavus Adolphus, or do you wish to remain with your previous allegiance to Prince Karl Philipp?"

Naturally all replied that they wished to remain with their previous allegiance, and the leading men presented their petition to Gustavus Adolphus that all the people of the Muscovite realm were mindful of their oath to Prince Karl Philipp and would be glad everywhere to sacrifice their lives for his most illustrious highness, "for the defense, O sovereign, against our enemies, that your royal highness may defend the Novgorod realm as God and our great sovereign prince will, as it was agreed and confirmed by his most illustrious highness with your royal majesty. We, subjects and slaves of his most illustrious highness, may not agree on or confirm any such great matter without the consent of our great sovereign the prince because the Novgorod realm and we, his slaves, are subject to the great sovereign prince's will. We do obeisance and implore your royal majesty that according to your noble lineage and benevolence you will be gracious and merciful towards us, and act towards us, men of all ranks of the Novgorod realm, according to the confirmatory documents agreed and confirmed with the Novgorod realm by your royal majesty's boyar and commander Jacob Pontus de la Gardie on the holy gospel with an oath and confirmation, signatures and seals, that the Novgorod realm and its towns and districts not be brought into subjection to the Swedish crown. As for those inconstant and simple-minded people, O sovereign, who have left Novgorod and gone over to the enemy, do not place any disfavor or anger upon us, who according to our solemn oath are serving you loyally. These people left Great Novgorod without our knowledge or counsel. Your royal highness well knows that in other neighboring countries there are also traitors, but there are also true and righteous people who do not forsake their sovereigns, and serve them loyally. Also the people of Vladimir and Moscow did thus without our counsel. We have not corresponded with them about this inconstancy of theirs, neither will we correspond with them about so contentious a matter, but will remain loyal to our own sovereign prince the most illustrious and high-born Grand Prince Karl Philipp, son of Karl."

But the inhabitants of Novgorod did not reply with such submissiveness to Evert Horn when he insisted on their oath of allegiance to the king, asserting that Prince Karl Philipp had renounced the Novgorod throne. Reminding him of the treaty concluded between them and De la Gardie, the inhabitants of Novgorod continued: "After this treaty was confirmed, the honorable shrines and the churches of God were ruined and plundered by foreign soldiers, sacred items were desecrated, broken up and burned, many relics of saints were exhumed and desecrated, bells from many monasteries and churches, the great municipal artillery and all manner of things were carried off to the Swedish realm, and close to Novgorod some Lithuanians, who here are serving his royal majesty, burn, torture and beat to death many of the rural inhabitants and peasants. Your officials extort taxes from them without any proper investigation and almost beat them to death, others have been hanged or drowned, while yet others have been mutilated and until now have been bedridden. And we, men of all ranks of the Novgorod realm, according to our solemn oath and confirmatory documents, have stood firmly and wish to stand unshakeably for our sovereign the prince, and have given to our last penny for the support of the foreigners, whence utter destitution has arisen, and people are scattering in all directions. Because of our sins our sovereign prince has not seen fit to make his progress to Novgorod. He has not done so, and that is according to his most illustrious highness's will. But wherever he, our great sovereign, will deign to be within his his patrimony we his slaves, in accordance with our solemn oath, will hold to and serve his most illustrious highness loyally. You say that we will be reputed and persecuted as perfidious and ungrateful cuckoos by the king's majesty and by neighboring sovereigns. But we are comforted by Christ's words, 'Blessed are they who are persecuted for righteousness' sake, for theirs is the kingdom of heaven.' And now we cannot kiss the cross without the authority of our sovereign prince and in violation of our previous confirmatory documents to the mighty king and to his successors the Swedish kings. We do not wish to be under the Swedish crown. Even if we have to die for our solemn oath, we do not wish to be known as oathbreakers, and if you do anything to us for direct observance of our oath, then our common judge will avenge us."

At the same time Prince Nikofor Meshchersky,[33] who had agreed with several people, arrived at the Khutyn monastery, called upon Archimandrite Cyprian and declared that it was necessary to die for the Orthodox faith and not kiss the cross to the king. Cyprian blessed them to suffer for the faith. Then Meshchersky and his companions went to Horn and openly defied him: "You wish to destroy our souls, but we will not be separated from the Muscovite realm by kissing the cross to the king." Horn ordered them to be imprisoned, under a strong guard, and then addressed the rest of the inhabitants of Novgorod, demanding a definite answer. To delay matters they petitioned to be allowed to correspond with the Muscovite realm to remind the boyars of their previous undertaking, and if they did not heed them, then the inhabitants of Novgorod would kiss the cross to the king.

Horn agreed and Archimandrite Cyprian of the Khutyn monastery, and the nobles Yakov Boborykin and Matvey Muraviev were sent to Moscow. The ambassadors appeared before the boyars and begged forgiveness in that they had kissed the cross to the king under duress, but now they wished to beg the sovereign to come to the aid of the Novgorod realm and not leave the rest of the unfortunate people to perish. The boyars reported to the tsar concerning the Novgorod petition. Michael admitted the ambassadors to his presence and ordered them to be given two documents. One was openly addressed to the metropolitan and all the Novgorod realm. In it the boyars severely replied to the inhabitants of Novgorod, calling them traitors for their intention to submit to the Swedish prince. The other document was secret. In it the tsar wrote to the metropolitan and all the people telling them that he had forgiven all their offenses. The ambassadors returned and proclaimed the boyars' response but secretly distributed copies of the sovereign's pardon. Horn took vengeance upon the ambassadors, and Cyprian especially suffered greatly. He was beaten in the marketplace and then done to death by starvation and cold.

DEFENSE OF TIKHVIN

Meanwhile warlike activities went on. As early as March 1613 the Assembly wrote to the newly-elected tsar that the Pskov governors, Prince Ivan Fedorovich Khovansky[34] and Veliaminov, were requesting aid against the Swedes who were threatening constantly to advance on Pskov from Novgorod. The Assembly dispatched to them several cossack atamans. But the Swedes besieged, not Pskov, but Tikhvin, and defeated a Russian detachment sent to aid the town under the leadership Isaac Sumbulov. The sovereign sent to the rescue another detachment under the leadership of Fedor Pleshcheev, but at Ustiuzhna Pleshcheev learned that the inhabitants of Tikhvin and their governors Semeon Prozorovsky and Leonty Vorontsov-Veliaminov[35] had repulsed the Swedes and captured their artillery.

FAILURE OF TRUBETSKOY AND MEZETSKY

In September 1613 it was decided to launch an offensive against Novgorod, and towards it were dispatched the boyar Dmitry Timofeevich Trubetskoy and the lord-in-waiting Daniel Ivanovich Mezetsky. The table attendant Vasily Ivanovich Buturlin[36] was ordered to join them, together with the regiments gathered in Yaroslavl. The commanders halted at Bronnitsy, but did not know how to assign positions. Also in Trubetskoy's camp there occurred the same phenomena as we have seen in his camp outside Moscow. In the army there was great disorder among them, says the chronicler, plundering by the cossacks and by all kinds of people. De la Gardie besieged the commanders, and hunger set in. Trubetskoy and his companions sent to the sovereign with a petition saying that they were suffering great oppression from the Swedes. The sovereign ordered them to withdraw from Bronnitsy to Torzhok. During this retreat many were lost, and the commanders barely made it on foot.

GUSTAVUS ADOLPHUS CAPTURES GDOV

Gustavus Adolphus himself appeared on Russian soil and in the autumn of 1614 captured Gdov after two assaults, but returned to Sweden with the intention of commencing hostilities in the following year with a siege of Pskov, if before then the Russians had not concluded a peace advantageous to Sweden. The king really wanted that peace, not seeing any advantage for Sweden in making new conquests in Russia, or even holding onto the conquests already made. Thus he did not wish to hold on to Novgorod, the dislike of whose inhabitants for subjection to Sweden was well known to him. "This is a proud people," he wrote concerning the Russians, "they feel a deep rooted hatred towards all foreign peoples." De la Gardie received an order from him; in case of need, if the Russians grew stronger, he should abandon Novgorod after laying it waste. "I am more concerned about you," wrote the king, "and about our good soldiers than the inhabitants of Novgorod."

The reasons which inclined the Swedish government towards peace with Moscow are expressed in a letter from Chancellor Oxenstierna[37] to Horn. "Although up to now," wrote Oxenstierna, "there has not appeared among us any internal strife or disorder, there nevertheless exist the seeds from which much of this could arise. Of our neighbours most are open enemies, the rest are false friends. We have many debts, but little money. During wartime we cannot make ends meet. Except in extreme necessity the Polish king will not renounce his rights to the Swedish throne, and our sovereign cannot conclude peace until Sigismund recognizes him as king of Sweden. Consequently we cannot expect a firm peace or even a truce with Poland. Waging war simultaneously with Poland and Moscow not only makes no sense, but is simply impossible; first, because of the power of these enemies if they should combine, secondly because of the Danes who are constantly on our necks. Thus in my opinion it is necessary to strive with all our might to conclude peace, friendship and alliance with Moscow on favorable terms. We must attract Moscow to peace partly by words and letters, partly by force of arms, insofar as our financial resources allow." This is how in fact Gustavus Adolphus acted. On one hand, he importuned the Muscovite government concerning peace and other states concerning mediation; on the other hand he continued warlike activities.

UNSUCCESSFUL SIEGE OF PSKOV

On June 30, 1615 Gustavus Adolphus besieged Pskov, where the governors were the boyars Vasily Petrovich Morozov[38] and Fedor Vasilievich Buturlin.[39] The king had sixteen thousand troops, in which there were even Russian Cherkassians. The first clash with the besieged ended for the Swedes in a major failure; they lost Evert Horn among the slain. On August 15 the enemy approached the Varlaam gates and after conducting a religious service began to dig ditches, erect gabions, hurdles, buildings and small blockhouses, and further off built a big turf town where the king himself stayed. There were more than ten of these strongholds, and two bridges were thrown across the Velikaia river. The Swedes attacked the town for three days in three places and discharged seven hundred cannon balls and countless other pieces of iron, but Pskov did not surrender. On October 9 the Swedes carried out an assault, but it was unsuccessful.

ENGLISH AND DUTCH MEDIATION AT DEDERINO
Meanwhile John Merrick was working for a peace settlement. It was resolved to decide the matter by a meeting of plenipotentiaries from both sides. From the Swedish side, Klaus Fleming, Henrik Horn, Jacob de la Gardie and Mons Martensson were appointed; from the Russian side, Prince Daniel Mezetsky and Alexis Ziuzin. While they were at Ostashkovo they received news from Merrick in Novgorod that Gustavus Adolphus was besieging Pskov. Merrick wrote: "The king in his letter to me gave me a true and firm promise that he would not commit any oppression against the city of Pskov until he heard that the business had aborted in the meeting concerning present matters because of you, the high ambassadors. But now he, the king, has to his dishonor and to the detriment of his credibility broken his promise, for this sheet of paper is in my hand under his signature and seal, and for as long as I have been with the Swedes, I have found little justice among them."

The Russian ambassadors strove to anger Merrick even more against the Swedes and told him that the Swedes in their documents did not give him due credit. Merrick replied to this: "You, my lords and high ambassadors, declare to me that the Swedish ambassadors do not write of me according to my dignity. I do not take any account of this; the honor was given me by my own great sovereign and they cannot take it away from me. I am not surprised, my lords, that they write thus of me, since they are not friendly towards me. When they have occasion to speak of his majesty the tsar and about you, high ambassadors, or about the present matter in an unbefitting manner, I encounter them with the plain truth, and I have not been silent even before the king himself, as he also has become unfriendly towards me. But I know from whom I am sent, and am not ashamed to speak the truth. He shows a countenance as if he favors the successful conclusion of this present matter. When God brings us to the meeting place, this favor will be manifest. God also sees my favor and my labors. In this light I want nothing more than that this present matter come to a favorable conclusion."

The preliminary correspondence between the plenipotentiaries began. The Russian plenipotentiaries were residing at Ostashkovo, the Swedish in Novgorod, and a dispute over titles ensued. The Swedes described Michael merely as grand prince and were angry that he called himself ruler of Livonia and Novgorod. They wrote to Mezetsky and Ziuzin: "We wish to inform you that you are full of your former arrogance and do not consider how the ancestry of our king compares to that of your grand prince. Our king is the authentic son of a king, while your grand prince is not the son of a tsar and not the lawful successor to the Russian throne. He was not seated upon the throne immediately after the death of Tsar Fedor, and after Dmitry's death you accepted Vasily Ivanovich Shuisky, and then some Polish prince."

To this the Russian ambassadors replied querulously, cited examples from biblical and Roman history, and said that God had chosen famous rulers not from a ruling stem. They stated that all the Russian people, from the greatest to the least, were all prepared to defend and avenge the honor of their realm against the Swedes. "It is not with us as it is with you in Sweden. Half the people support the sovereign, the other half King Sigismund of Poland, while others support Duke Johan. You should cease to utter such unbefitting words against God's anointed."

The Swedish ambassadors, who received this document when they were already on their way from Novgorod to the meeting place, became angry and declared to Merrick that they would travel no further. Merrick wrote to Mezetsky that he could not move them by any means or discourse. Finally he moved them and persuaded them that the meeting should take place on the Khvostov estate in the village of Dederino, where the English ambassador would lodge. The Russian ambassadors would stay at Peski and the Swedish ambassadors at Selishchi, and they would meet at the lodging of the English ambassador.

There appeared yet more mediators, the Dutch ambassadors Reinhold van Brederode, Dirk Bass, Albrecht Joachim and Anton Goeteeris. The latter has left us a description of this embassy, remarkable for us in that it gives a description of the current state of the Muscovite realm.[40] On the way from Reval to Novgorod the ambassadors had to travel through country which had been devastated by the cossacks. Nowhere did they find any habitation, almost always they had to camp in the forest except where by good luck they found somewhere or other a half-ruined monastery. From Novgorod they proceeded to Staraia Rusa, which they found in a most pitiful state. But all the privations they had suffered hitherto were as nothing compared to what they had to endure on the way from Staraia Rusa. Several times the ice broke under them on the river (this was in November), men and goods fell into the water, and in order to dry out they had to make a bonfire out of ruined huts on the shore. They spent the night in ruined hamlets. Before entering a hut they first had to drag out of it the corpses of its previous inhabitants who had been slain by cossacks, but the overpowering stench drove the Dutchmen from the hut, and they had to spend the night in the frost.

Merrick was not very pleased by the arrival of these new mediators. At first he urged the Russian ambassadors and the tsar that the Dutch had not come to do Moscow a favor, but then declared that they would sit with him and be subordinate to him in all matters. The tsar in his letter to Merrick insisted that Gustavus Adolphus, by not keeping his promise and not heeding his representations, had dishonored King James. The tsar requested "Ivan Ulianovich" (Merrick) to reproach the Swedes for their injustices and persuade them to negotiate in good faith.

The negotiations at Dederino began on January 4, 1616. They opened with a dispute, since the Swedish ambassadors called Gustavus Adolphus ruler of Korela, and asserted that Korela[41] had been ceded to the Swedes back in Shuisky's reign. This naturally led to a dispute over whether the Swedes had the right to hold on to what Shuisky had ceded, after the way they had behaved at Klushino.[42] The Swedes complained against Shuisky, saying that he had not paid them the money agreed upon, and expounded all the services they had rendered in the battles against the Lithuanians and Tushinites.

The Russians argued that De la Gardie and the foreign troops had not fought alone against the Lithuanians; there were even more Russians with Prince Mikhail Vasilievich Skopin-Shuisky[43] and the enterprise as a whole had been led by Prince Mikhail Vasilievich. To which De la Gardie replied: "You say that I and the Swedes were not the only ones to liberate towns and fight the Poles, but there were also many Russian troops with Prince Mikhail Vasilievich. So tell me, from what towns did the gentry and junior boyars come who were with Prince Mikhail Vasilievich?"

Mezetsky There were enough people with Prince Mikhail Vasilie-vich to liberate the towns, and gentry from the towns; gentry from Novgorod, Smolensk, Dorogobuzh, Viazma and other towns.

De la Gardie There were altogether fifteen gentry with Prince Mik-hail. When those of Smolensk came to Tver, and I began to fight against the Lithuanians, the gentry from Smolensk and other towns fled. The Swedes alone went on to Kaliazin, defeated the Lithuani-ans, captured Alexandrovskaia Sloboda, and thereby relieved Mos-cow.

Mezetsky There were only a few Swedes at Kaliazin, and Prince Mikhail Vasilievich paid them very well, and the brigand fled be-cause Tsar Vasily sent his own commanders and boyars after him.

De la Gardie Can you name anyone among the Russians who was wounded in these battles? For my service Tsar Vasily not only should have paid me for my services as agreed, but also should have showered me with gifts, for I served him as truly as I would have my own natural sovereign.

Mezetsky The boyars Prince Fedor Ivanovich Mstislavsky and his companions were in the fighting; as for who was killed or wounded, how can one recall offhand? Our wages were paid in full; the tsar also rewarded you, Jacob, and the captains, troop commanders and the secretary Mons Martensson over and above your wages, with expensive sables, ornaments, plate and clothing, and also sent ex-pensive gifts to your sovereign, King Karl of Sweden. And when the tsar sent his brother, Prince Dmitry, and you against the Poles before Smolensk, you were paid fully two months in advance, but you did not distribute it to your soldiers, but wished to give it out after the battle. You would help yourself to the money of those who were killed. Evert Horn betrayed us and you, Jacob, committed an injustice in that you went over to Zolkiewski and fought against the boyar Prince Dmitry Ivanovich Shuisky.

De la Gardie It was not the Swedes who betrayed you, but the Germans. You call us foreigners traitors, yet where is your justice? You deposed your sovereign from the rulership, tonsured him and handed him over to the Lithuanians! When we set out against the Poles, Tsar Vasily summoned me to his chamber and I told him that if he paid the troops in full it would keep them in service, but if he did not pay them their wages he could expect every misfortune from them. The tsar said that he would send the money to me at Moz-haisk, but he did not send it. The crown secretary Telepnev was in the same room as Tsar Vasily at the time, and he is a witness.

Mezetsky The treasury was given to you in my presence before the battle in the village of Myshkino. And even if only the Germans betrayed us, it is still all your fault because Tsar Vasily trusted you completely. As for your saying that we deposed our sovereign, we wish to point out that Tsar Vasily abdicated the throne voluntarily and then Zolkiewski tonsured him.[44] And if only Germans betrayed us, and you were not party to it, you should have gone to Tsar Vasily in Moscow and not to Novgorod.

De la Gardie I know that the treasury was sent with many crown secretaries to Prince Dmitry Shuisky and to me, and it was delivered to me, but I did not embezzle it. I myself was completely plundered, and this was not because of Horn's treachery or because of my in-justice, but because Prince Dmitry advanced from Mozhaisk on the hottest of days and proceeded by a forced march forty versts to Klushino. The soldiers and the horses under them were collapsing and others remained behind. Prince Dmitry, without waiting for the rest of the men, halted and did not fortify his encampment even though he knew the enemy was in front of him. The Germans, who had not been given their wages, wavered; if they had not been angry at the non-payment of their wages they would not have betrayed you. I did not return to Tsar Vasily after this rout because I had been plundered and remained with only seven followers, and it was impossible to reach Prince Dmitry. But on the way I sent to Tsar Vasily two Germans, saying that I would regroup my forces and re-turn to help him. Tsar Vasily sent a message by the hand of these same Germans that I should regroup in the Novgorod region; there I should gather provisions and fodder and, having done so, come to his aid. But I was unable to obtain provisions and fodder.

De la Gardie greatly angered the Russian ambassadors by saying: "Prince Ivan Nikitch Odoevsky and men of all ranks kissed the cross to Prince Karl. You should now stand by your own resolution and accept Prince Karl Philipp as ruler of the Muscovite realm." Mezetsky answered him: "Why are your trifling with this futile matter? We do not want the prince. Moreover your sovereign him-self wrote to the boyars that, apart from the Muscovite clans, no foreigners should be chosen to rule over the Muscovite realm, and the king would be in friendship and love with whomsoever is chosen sovereign. And you yourselves have declared the same to us. We warn you even before you speak of this, that we will not listen." *De la Gardie* Did not the boyars and commanders petition concerning the prince in Yaroslavl?

Mezetsky It is unbefitting to speak of that. This was done without the authority of the whole land.

The Russian ambassadors rose angrily from the table. The *mediators*, namely the English and Dutch ambassadors, said: "You have not achieved anything useful at the outset so you should leave off these immoderate matters and unreasonable words." The Russians and the Swedes, because they were acclimatized and because of the heat generated by their quarrel, did not feel the cold, sitting in a tent in the month of January. But the mediators felt it severely and declared that henceforth they were unable to sit in a tent, and proposed to meet in the English ambassador's lodging. The house was partitioned and it was decided that the Russian ambassadors should come in by the front door, the Swedish by the back. The tables and benches were placed the same way as in the tent; in the large courtyard, near the entrance, benches for the sovereign's ambassadors, and by the back wall opposite them benches for the Swedish ambassadors, and for the mediators tables and benches at the end of the high table, next to the doors to the room.

At the January 5 session the Russian ambassadors got down to business, demanding that the Swedes state the instructions their sovereign had given with regard to the centuries-old patrimony of the great sovereign tsar, Novgorod, Staraia Rusa, Porkhov, Ladoga, Ivangorod, Yama, Koporie and Gdov. De la Gardie replied that talks were not yet concluded on the principal matter. Not only did Novgorod and all its bytowns belong to Prince Karl Philipp, he also had been chosen as ruler over all the Vladimir and Muscovite realms. Mezetsky replied that they did not wish to speak or even hear of this. "We now have Michael Fedorovich as tsar, he has brought us peace, tranquillity, and unity, all great sovereigns seek his friendship and love. You should should leave off unbefitting words concerning Prince Karl Philipp, for we do not wish to hear anything about him. You captured Novgorod by deceit. You, Jacob, have not fulfilled anything on which you kissed the cross to Novgorod. The boyars did not choose the prince, and even if there was a letter to you from somebody without the counsel of the whole land, that letter is not to be believed."

The ambassadors spoke to each other angrily and querulously and wanted to leave the meeting, but the mediators dissuaded them. The mediators persuaded them not to be angry, and said to the Russian ambassadors: "We have persuaded the Swedish ambassadors not to mention the prince, for that matter is already closed, and we have persuaded them not to be so obstinate." Mezetsky replied to them: "Is it not tedious for them to speak of Karl Philipp, son of Karl, and is it not tedious for you to hear about him? You were sent to the great sovereign Michael Fedorovich to make peace, not to talk about Prince Karl Philipp. Hearing such undignified words, and being mindful of the instructions of our sovereign, you should not be silent towards the Swedish ambassadors for they are abandoning important matters and speak frivolously."

Mezetsky said this to the Dutch ambassadors with cool and calculated anger. Having spoken a moment with the Swedes, the mediators declared to the Russians that De la Gardie and his companions would cease to mention Prince Karl Philipp and that the Russians would cede to the king Novgorod and its bytowns, which had kissed the cross to the prince. Mezetsky replied that he could not yield an inch of the sovereign's patrimony. The mediators continued: "We shall speak to the Swedish emissaries, urging them to abandon many of their demands, and we will seek ways to bring the matter to a favorable conclusion, and you should do likewise."

Just as the speeches of the Swedish ambassadors about Prince Karl Philipp had angered the Russians, the Swedish ambassadors were angered by the Russian demand that the king cede Livonia to the tsar. At the session on January 7, having heard this demand, the Swedes rose from the table and said: "If we had known that you were going to bring up the matter of the Livonian towns, we would not have come to this session, since this would mean breaking off negotiations." The mediators calmed them down. The Swedes sat down and once again spoke about Prince Karl Philipp. The Russians as before became angry. Finally the Swedes agreed not to talk about the prince, and discussions began about the cession of territory. The

Russians demanded the return of the Livonian towns and Novgorod because they had been the patrimony of the Russian great sovereigns since the beginning. The Swedes replied: "Not only is the Livonian land not your sovereign's patrimony, but also you only recently have begun to rule over Novgorod, and the Muscovite sovereigns ruled over the Livonian land unlawfully, for which God has taken revenge upon them...."

The Russians The Livonian land has belonged to us since the forefathers of our great sovereigns, from the sovereign Yury Yaroslav Vladimirovich, who built the town of Yuriev-in-Livonia[45] and named it after himself. And the Novgorod realm was under the Russian sovereigns since the time of Rurik, and has never been under anyone except the Russian tsars.

The Swedes Have you ever set eyes upon Yuriev-in-Livonia? The Livonian towns have never been known to be under your sovereigns, only in your imagination.

The Russians You speak thus scorning the help of God. But we, asking God's mercy, will seek out what is ours. If you do not give it without bloodshed, you will give it with bloodshed.

The Swedes Stop speaking such haughty words. God doesn't know who Lisowski is, a commonplace person, but he was able with only a handful of followers to range at will all over the Muscovite realm. What armies, Russian and Tatar, you have, we do not know.

The Russians You know our armies, and remember how your sovereign surrendered the towns of Ivangorod, Koporie and others to our sovereign Fedor Ivanovich.[46] Remember also how when our sovereign gave the order to open fire on Narva your Germans immediately raised their hats within the town and petitioned our sovereign not to shed their blood, and when the sovereign sent Prince Fedor Ivanovich Mstislavsky, then remember what warfare and taking prisoners was wrought in that land by our men! Nowhere was there any resistance by your people to our troops. Your sovereign should therefore beware. God helps all those whose cause is just, but the unjust he will destroy.

The mediators put an end to this quarrel. "On both sides," they said, "we must be seeking a favorable outcome to this matter and come closer to peace and tranquillity, but in such great and contentious words there will be no favorable outcome...." But the quarrel did not cease. De la Gardie asserted that Tsar Vasily did not pay any money to the Swedes. The Russian ambassadors contradicted them, saying that the money was paid, and that if De la Gardie had not turned traitor at Klushino the Poles would not have got hold of the tsar's treasury. De la Gardie replied: "You brought this upon yourselves. And now, since you are so friendly with the Poles that you have hired against us ten or twelve thousand Lithuanians,[47] why don't they take Moscow back from you?" The Russians said: "Why do you think we are friendly with the Poles?" They called De la Gardie a traitor, and asked why after the battle of Klushino he did not return to Tsar Vasily in Moscow. De la Gardie replied: "Because they would have tonsured me also along with him."

Finally they got down to the matter of ceding towns. The Russian ambassadors spoke to Merrick, asking whether he could persuade Jacob de la Gardie to give back all the towns to the sovereign and quickly evacuate them. Afterwards, if he wished to come over to the sovereign's allegiance, the sovereign would reward him and order him to be given a city or some large estate, and would allow him to live in peace and tranquillity however he pleased, and above and beyond that would reward him to a greater extent than he could imagine. Merrick declined this mission, saying that he would not dare make such a proposition to Jacob. The Swedes ceded all the places they were occupying except for Korela, and in exchange for this concession demanded forty barrels of gold, each barrel being valued at one hundred thousand reichsthalers. If the sovereign did not wish to give the money, then let him cede Ivangorod, Oreshek, Yama, Koporie and the Suma district. The Russians offered to yield Korela and seventy thousand rubles, which they later topped up to one hundred thousand. Negotiations dragged on to mid-February and the time of the spring break-up was approaching. The Swedes declared that they had run out of food and were leaving. On February 22 they concluded a truce from that date until May 31, stating that during that time there would be no warfare or damage inflicted by either realm, and that towards May 31 the high ambassadors would meet somewhere between Tikhvin and Ladoga.

As the truce ran out the Muscovite ambassadors, the same who had been at Dederino, set out for Tikhvin. The Swedish ambassadors were living in Ladoga. This time the only mediator was Merrick, since the Dutch had not appeared. The ambassadors exchanged letters and messengers between June 12 and September 18. The Russians invited the Swedes to a session, but they did not come, and declared to Merrick that if they did not receive a definite reply to the articles they had presented at Dederino, they would not come to the session. On September 25 Merrick travelled to Ladoga to call on the Swedish ambassadors. According to his instructions, he was to yield Ivangorod, Yama, Koporie and an indemnity of one hundred thousand cash, but strongly hold on to Oreshek and the trading settlements beyond the Neva and the Suma region. If the Swedes would in no wise give up Oreshek, then in exchange they could yield Koporie and three trading settlements on this side of the Neva, and the Suma region. As a last resort, he should demand only the Suma region and four trading settlements, and strive for peace so that the Swedes would not carry out their threats and plunder the Holy Wisdom cathedral.[48] The inhabitants of Novgorod should not be forced to kiss the cross to the king because of their great destitution. Finally Merrick was authorized to give one hundred thousand rubles in exchange for the Suma region and the four trading settlements.

The Swedes did not agree, and meanwhile the tsar wrote to his ambassadors: "Do not break with the Swedish ambassadors in any manner or for any reason. Correspond with them secretly, hold out to them hope of the tsar's reward, make promises and do anything to keep them happy. On account of the Lithuanian business and because of the exhaustion of our troops, do not break with them in any fashion." On the other hand, news came that the Russian attack on the Swedish fortress outside Pskov had failed. In Novgorod there was much oppression from the interpreter Irik Andreev, from Grishka Sobakin and from Tomitka Pristaltsov, and many people were being tortured. Those who could not endure the torture kissed the cross to the king and nothing happened to them, and they corresponded with their wives and children in Ivangorod. The inhabitants of Ivangorod straight away kissed the cross to the king, and nothing happened to them. All the inhabitants of Novgorod, unable to bear the torment, were to kiss the cross to the king.

Merrick urged the Swedes to compromise. They were to have two of the trading settlements on the near side of the Neva, and the other two would go to the Russians, who would pay ten thousand rubles for them. But the Swedes required all of the Neva, and therefore they did not agree or demanded the impossible, one hundred thousand rubles for the two trading settlements. Finally Merrick came to an agreement: on the tsar's side Novgorod, Rusa, Porkhov, Gdov, Ladoga and the whole Suma region; on the king's side Ivangorod, Yama, Koporie, Oreshek with its whole region and two hundred thousand rubles cash. Gdov, Ladoga, and the Suma region would remain in Swedish hands until the towns were surveyed and the sovereigns confirmed the treaty by kissing the cross.

PEACE OF STOLBOVO

Having resolved upon this with Merrick, the Swedish ambassadors at the end of December came to the session at the designated place, this time Stolbovo. But here also disputes began. The Russian ambassadors demanded that the Swedes not hold the towns in pledge with the confirmation of the peace, but the Swedes did not agree. At this time the elders of the Five Wards appeared secretly before the ambassadors and did obeisance to them with tears, saying that in Novgorod foreigners were beating the inhabitants of all ranks to death in forcing them to provision the troops and perform cartage duties, and they had no means of buying them off. If things continued as they were, they thought that the Swedes would lay hands on the treasury of the Holy Wisdom and destroy the cathedral building. Therefore the ambassadors must bring the peace negotiations to a speedy conclusion and, until the treaty was concluded, the ambassadors would give them money from the tsar's treasury to deliver themselves from extortion even for half a month, and when God had delivered Great Novgorod to his majesty the tsar they would repay the sovereign the money. But if the sovereign's ambassadors prolonged the Swedish matter they would be forced against their will to go over to the king's side.

The ambassadors replied that they were mindful of God and their souls. Although they were suffering oppression from the foreigners on account of provisioning the soldiers and other imposts, they would only have to endure a little longer, so that not one hour of their many years of privation and torments would have been in vain. Meanwhile they, the ambassadors, would speak to the English ambassador, urging him to dissuade the Swedes from subjecting Novgorod to any further oppression.

The dispute over the towns held in pledge ended. The Russian ambassadors demanded that the clergy be allowed to leave the towns ceded to the Swedes. The Swedes agreed to let go only the monks, but not parish priests, for in that case there would remain to them only the walls. How could the Russian people exist without their spiritual fathers? The Russian ambassadors insisted that one condition be inserted, that Moscow and Sweden be allied against the Polish king, but the Swedes did not agree.

There remained two other complications. The Swedes demanded that their king be styled ruler of Izhora, and that for the final confirmation of the treaty the tsar should send his ambassadors to the English king, who was to sign the treaty and affix his seal. The Russians in no wise would agree to this, and without this the Swedes did not wish to sit down to negotiations and threatened to depart for Ladoga.

Finally, on February 19, 1617, the Swedes agreed not to demand the signature of the English king and to write the treaty with abbreviated titles, on condition that if the sovereigns wished to insert into the text of the treaty their full titles, in the Swedish king's title the style of ruler of Izhora should be included. On February 27 the treaty of perpetual peace was written. The Swedes undertook to surrender and evacuate Great Novgorod, Staraia Rusa, Porkhov and their districts and the Suma region in the presence of Merrick or any noblemen designated by him, two weeks after the confirmation of the treaty by the high ambassadors. Three weeks after, Ladoga and its district would be surrendered and evacuated. In addition, the Swedes were obliged not to deport any Russians, nor subject them to any violence or plunder, nor remove any artillery. Gdov and its district would remain for a while on the side of Gustavus Adolphus, until confirmation of the treaty by the king's oath and the tsar's kissing of the cross, the marking of the boundaries and proper delineation of everything, and after the ambassadors from both sovereigns had carried everything out satisfactorily and gone back to the frontier.

All monks and their possessions, also all gentry, junior boyars and townsmen, together with their wives, children, domestic servants and all their possessions were free to depart for his majesty the tsar's side within two weeks from the confirmation of the treaty in Stolbovo, but all parish priests and cultivators of the land in the towns and regions ceded to the king must remain and live under the Swedish crown, as must all the gentry, junior boyars and townsmen who did not leave during these two weeks.

King Gustavus Adolphus would accept from Tsar Michael Fedorovich twenty thousand rubles in ready, good, current and undefaced coinage of Novgorod silver. As soon as the peace agreement was concluded between the ambassadors, John Merrick, ambassador of the English king, would give this money to the Swedish ambassadors.

Cannon, munitions, bells and all other material from Russian towns taken by the king before November 20 were to remain with the Swedes, but artillery currently in the towns was to be returned to the tsar and remain there. For the delineation of the frontier, around June 1, 1617 plenipotentiary ambassadors were to meet, three men from each side, between Oreshek and Ladoga, at the estuary of the Lavuia river on Lake Ladoga, on that river in the middle of the bridge, and about June 1 other ambassadors were to meet on the frontier between the Solomensk trading settlement in the Korela district and the Olonets trading settlement in the Novgorod district, on Lake Ladoga. These ambassadors were to delineate the boundaries and not depart before they had concluded their business amicably.

Tsar Michael Fedorovich renounced all right to the Livonian land and to Korela and to all title, in favor of the Swedish king and his descendants. Trade was to be free and unhindered everywhere between both realms. Swedish merchants were to receive their former depots in Novgorod, Moscow and Pskov, where they would be free to conduct their own religious services in their quarters, but not to build churches of their own faith. Russian merchants were to receive back their depot in Reval, and would be given depots in Stockholm and Vyborg. In those towns they were to conduct religious services in their quarters, but in Reval they would have their church, as they had of old. Old debts by merchants on both sides were to be honored. Ambassadors, emissaries and heralds from Sweden were to be free to travel across the lands of the Muscovite realm to Persia, Turkey, the Crimea and other lands at peace with his majesty the tsar, but traders were not to be allowed to bring their goods with them. Similarly Russian ambassadors, emissaries and heralds were free to travel across Sweden to the Holy Roman empire, Great Britain, the French kingdom, Spain, Denmark, Holland or the Low Countries and any other country at peace with the king, but traders were not allowed to bring their goods with them.

All prisoners of war on both sides were to be set free on the border without any ransom. If any wished to stay behind voluntarily, they were free to do so. Neither side would summon or entice the other's subjects. Fugitives were to be extradited. Lest frontier disputes and incidents upset the peace, they were to be settled on the frontier by the local governors, but if it was too serious a matter, it should be postponed until ambassadors could meet.

On about the first of the forthcoming June, on the exact delineation of the border between Oreshek and Ladoga, on the Lavuia river, the plenipotentiary ambassadors of both realms were to meet, show and have read to each other the confirmatory documents, exchange exact copies with each other, and give the originals back. The Swedish ambassadors were then to go to Moscow, and the Muscovite ambassadors to Stockholm for the final comfirmation.

Should ships or vessels from either country be caught in a storm and driven aground, either in the Baltic Sea or Lake Ladoga, they were to be released without delay with all their cargo that had been salvaged, and the people who live on the shore should help them and guard their possessions. Neither side was to help the Polish king or his son, neither would they plot with or seek to subvert the other in conjunction with other rulers.

On March 5 the high ambassadors sent to Novgorod the tsar's document informing them that peace had been concluded. The tsar wrote: "God has given back into our hands, those of the great legitimate Christian sovereign, our ancient fatherland Great Novgorod which has been ours from time immemorial, but which had been torn away from us, together with you Orthodox Christians. The Swedish king has given it back to us, and merciful God has freed you from such intolerable privations at the hands of foreigners through our labors and royal solicitude for you. Instead of grief, privation and evil, you are receiving now grace, favor and joy, as you now truly see. And you, seeing such ineffable divine mercy and our royal care for you, must pray to God for our health, for our

father and mother and for the whole realm, and you may joyfully
expect our royal favor towards you. And until our patrimony Great
Novgorod is liberated and the Swedes are led out, you must stand
firmly and bravely. You, our pilgrim and metropolitan, and all the
clerical estate must fortify all Orthodox Christians who live in
Novgorod, urging them to rely upon our royal kindness, not to surrender to the Swedes or go over to their side. We wish to reward all
people in everything and give them relief, and the money which we
had to give on your behalf we have collected and sent to the great
ambassadors, and no delay stands in the way of our business at the
session.

"And if any Russians have favored the foreigners and oppressed
Russians or if any gentry or junior boyars have accepted service
tenures or patrimonies in those towns which remain with the
Swedes, or to whom recently the Swedish king or Jacob Pontus (de
la Gardie) has given in those towns, or their own, service tenures or
patrimonies, you must persuade them to rely upon our generosity,
be mindful of the Orthodox faith and us, their natural Christian
sovereign, of the tombs of their parents and their ancestors, and not
attach themselves to the foreign Swedish people, but rely upon our
mercy and not incite their brothers, Orthodox Christians, and burden their souls with such sin or entice anyone or go themselves
from Novgorod to the foreigners, to live in Reval or other towns
which remain with the Swedes, but must abandon all fear of our
disfavor. If you are guilty of any fault, we shall not visit it upon
you; we will cover all faults with our royal compassion. As for
those gentry and junior boyars who had service tenures and patrimonies in the Swedish towns, we shall grant them in their place
service tenures and patrimonies in our towns and, in addition to
that, will favor them with our royal solicitude. You yourselves well
know that whoever committed any transgression did so out of fear
of the Swedes, fearing slaughter, plunder and ruin. You were in
their hands. How were you free not to do as they ordered or serve
them? Nobody need fear our disfavor for any cause. All, from the
greatest to the least, may rely on our royal mercy.

"We have freed Great Novgorod from the heretics in order that
all of you Orthodox Christians may live under our royal favor as
before, and not that our royal disfavor might be laid upon anybody.

Do not be tempted by any allures of the Swedes. They are trying by all means to deceive people, make promises and give bribes to lure people away from our royal favor and bring them to towns under their authority. But henceforth you will not be threatened by their cunning or violence, this you well know. Besides, for apostasy from the true Christian faith and from us, your natural sovereign, from your blood brothers and the tombs of your ancestors, your souls will be lost forever to God, and even though thereafter you come to repentance, there will be no help for you."

LIBERATION OF NOVGOROD

Within two weeks of the conclusion of the treaty Novgorod was liberated, and on March 14 the high ambassadors Mezetsky and Ziuzin entered the city with the miraculous icon of the Virgin taken from the Khutyn monastery. About half a verst from the city Metropolitan Isidore met the icon in a procession with the whole people, with copious tears and great joy.

When they had all entered the Holy Wisdom cathedral the ambassadors delivered the sovereign's gracious word to the metropolitan and all the people. On behalf of the tsar the ambassadors asked after their health, and then delivered a letter in which the sovereign wrote: "Concerning you, our pilgrim Metropolitan Isidore, we have heard from reliable witnesses of your suffering for the common good, and of your healing ministry of the work of God, how you frequently prescribed rigorous fasting for the sake of the Orthodox faith and Christian souls, rooted out many heresies and injustices and set Christian souls towards the light of holy wisdom. Many Christian souls fell away from the Christian faith, compelled by those of the German race to kiss the cross to the king, and others were tempted or compelled to go into their lands. But you, good shepherd, with all the consecrated estate, cast forth your spiritual net, draw them into the imperishable holy wisdom, free many spiritually by your teaching and instruction, and this your solicitude over Christian souls will not be forgotten before God. And you, gentry, crown secretaries, junior boyars, leading merchants and all the people of the Novgorod realm, in consideration of your suffering and grief we wish to reward each according to his deserts. We wish to give you, leading merchants, traders, townsmen, and rural inhabitants tax relief in everything, in accordance with your ruin and poverty. And whatever people were with the Swedes, served them and were obedient to them in all matters, and wantonly transformed their freedom into unfreedom, even to these we wish to extend our royal grace and favor. Nobody should fear anything from us. Since you were in the hands of the Swedes, how could you not do their bidding?"

MERRICK REWARDED

For their service in Novgorod and because the Swedish ambassadors ceded Novgorod the sovereign awarded Mezetsky boyardom, and Ziuzin was promoted from nobleman to lord-in-waiting. There remained one difficult matter, how to satisfy the *mediator*, the Englishman Merrick, for his labors during the conclusion of peace. The boyar Fedor Ivanovich Sheremetev who was given the task of speaking with him, addressed him in the tsar's name. "You, Prince Ivan, according to the instruction of our gracious brother King James, served us, the great sovereign, at the peace conference, favored and promoted our interests and took counsel with our ambassadors, so that our royal name might be honored and exalted; and we will also reward our gracious brother for this his love and friendship, as far as our royal majesty is able. And we praise you for your service and solicitude, and we wish to reward you with our generosity for your service to us, and we will write to our gracious brother about your service and solicitude and be mindful forever of your service and solicitude."

Merrick reiterated his previous request, that English merchants be allowed to travel along the Volga to Persia. Sheremetev replied: "Our Russian traders are impoverished. Presently they are buying goods and cloth in Archangel from the English, taking them from there to Astrakhan and selling them to the Persians, and exchanging them for goods, which is a gain to both themselves and to our treasury. But if the English travel directly to Persia, then they will not sell their goods to the Russians in Archangel and the Persians will not travel with their goods to Astrakhan, but trade with the English in their own country. Also it will be impossible for this reason: the shah is harrassing the sovereign on account of the Iberian land, and in those places through which it is necessary to go to Persia there is war, for the Persians and the Turks are fighting each other. Also it is dangerous along the Volga, because the Great Nogay are wandering about there; this is a matter which should be put off to another time, when our sovereign has settled with the Polish king, the Muscovite realm has recovered from many losses, the shah is at peace with the sovereign and the Turks are at peace with the shah."

Merrick argued that the Russian traders would gain if they could trade in general with the English traders, for the English could give the sovereign's subjects loans against their products, according to the people and industry, to the amount of a thousand, two thousand, six thousand or more without interest. The English would not trade in those goods in which the sovereign's subjects traded with the Persians. It was well known that where more merchants got together there were more goods and therefore more customs dues, and everything would be cheaper. Let people travel from England to Persia and from Persia to England through the sovereign's land.

The boyars said the way was dangerous, but the English merchants were in no hurry. They would wait a year or two and would come when the sovereign ordered, only let the sovereign now give a charter of priveleges. The boyars replied that the English would cease to sell their goods to the Russians, and even if they did sell they would double or triple the prices. The boyars presented all kinds of arguments, but the English could not be put off. The boyars asked about the details of how the English proposed to trade with Persia, and Merrick promised to send it all in a letter.

Then "Prince Ivan Ulianovich" asked permission to explore the Ob river for a route to India and China. The boyars replied that Siberia was far off, more than half a year's journey to the first towns, and that in winter, and even the local inhabitants did not know where the Ob came from and where it went. That region was the coldest of all, there was no more than two months' warm weather, and there was always ice on the Ob so that no boats could travel, and higher up the Ob where it was warmer there were many nomad hordes. Concerning the Chinese realm, it was reputed to be neither large nor rich, and it was impossible to reach it. For the sake of his friendship to King James he would specially send to the governors in Siberia and order them to find out from where the Ob river came and where it went, into what sea, by what kind of vessel was it

possible to travel along it, what hordes lived near the headwaters of
the Ob, what rivers flowed into it, where the Chinese realm was and
how rich, and whether anything could be obtained. But as for now,
since nothing was known for sure, how can we speak of or do anything about it?

Concerning this matter the boyars also asked the conditions under which the English would travel to India. Merrick promised to
reply in writing. The sovereign agreed to the proposal to give Lapps
for the expedition to Novaia Zemlia. Then Merrick asked that pitch
not be exported overseas to any country, even England, because the
export of pitch had also caused the English great marine insurance
losses. He requested permission for the English to mine alabaster
situated one hundred and fifty versts from Kholmogory. He asked
also that they not exile several Englishmen along with other foreigners. The boyars replied that they were not being sent as as result
of disfavor, but because things were very expensive in Moscow; in
Kazan everything was cheaper, and there they would be able to live
more comfortably.

Merrick also petitioned that the English nobleman Aston,[49] who
was suffering from wounds, be sent home, and that his son serve in
his place. The boyars replied that of old nobody was dismissed from
the sovereign's service, and here Prince Artemy Aston had been rewarded according to his worth. Merrick petitioned that at least his
wife be allowed to leave, because they would not have any more
children. The boyars replied that it was unheard of to separate man
and wife.

Finally Merrick presented a petition concerning the Dutch emissary Isaac Abramov (Massa).[50] A brother of Isaac Abramov had
come to the English courtyard to trade in cloth, exchanged sharp
words with the English and during this quarrel uttered an unseemly
word against their sovereign, King James, beckoned towards him
and said: "Your king is just the same as me; he is a man, and I am
a man." He, "Prince Ivan," was greatly grieved that such a base fellow had uttered such unbefitting words about so great a sovereign;
if he had uttered such a word in his own country, in no wise would
he have escaped the gallows. The boyars replied that the tsar's majesty was aware of this, his majesty the tsar was greatly grieved

about this, and was greatly moved with anger that such a base fellow, a mere nobody, had spoken such an unseemly word about so great a sovereign. His majesty the tsar ordered a stern rebuke to be delivered with great grief, and the crown secretary Romanchukov told Isaac Abramov that in the Netherlands he was the very worst of men, and nobody worse than his brother could be found, and it was evident from the fact that he had uttered such an unbefitting word about so great a sovereign that they were base and ignorant men. Isaac excused himself, saying that his brother had acted foolishly out of simplicity, and for this he had rebuked and thrashed his brother.

Merrick was satisfied and shortly thereafter delivered the promised letter saying how the English would travel to Persia. They would travel from Archangel to Yaroslavl overland and then along the Volga. They would build boats near Ustiuzhna Zheleznaia, where there was suitable wood for the purpose, and they had done this before, because Tsar Ivan Vasilievich had placed this forest at their disposal. For the journey along the Volga the English would build covered boats, and a ship for the sea voyage. The seagoing ship would leave Yaroslavl downstream in the spring during floodtime. The skipper would be an Englishman, the carpenters would be Russian hired workers. To defend themselves along the Volga they would bring cannon, firearms, powder, lead and cannonballs. Under Tsar Ivan Vasilievich, when English merchants travelled to Persia past Astrakhan, Astrakhan was being besieged by the Turks and the English, about a hundred of them, joined with the Russians and served alongside them, and his majesty the tsar greatly praised their service.[51]

Merrick pointed out that English merchants never engaged in retail trade and would not take business away from Russian merchants as did the Dutch, who not only sold their goods retail but sent merchandise in small amounts all over the Muscovite realm, thus taking the bread out of his majesty the tsar's subjects' mouths, for which reason during Tsar Fedor's reign they were forbidden to travel any further than Archangel. Concerning transit to China, the way to the East and the far North is well known to Russians, they have been further than the Yenisei; concerning this there was a letter given to

the former tsar, Boris Godunov. He, Merrick, also had a letter on
this matter, but it was not translated. Finally Merrick explained why
pitch could not be exported. If pitch is exported overseas, but hemp
is not also sent there, his majesty the tsar's subjects will gain no
profit from this because sovereigns and authorities should not allow
unfinished or imperfect goods to leave the country and take employment away from their own people. In former years raw wool
was exported to other countries, and because of this many people
were impoverished in England. Having considered the matter more
carefully, his majesty the king forbade the export of raw wool and
thereby the poor people revived since he ordered cloth to be made
in his own country, and now no better cloth is made anywhere in
the world. For this purpose foreign master craftsmen were brought
to England, who made the country and the king's subjects so rich
that there is no king more glorious and richer among his neighbors.
Also recently his majesty the king forbade the export of white cloth
to other countries, since previously foreigners were dyeing and tai-
loring our cloth, from which we became poor, but now this industry
has been returned to the king's subjects.

When the letter had been heard the boyar council was empowered to answer politely that this matter could not be resolved without consulting the tsar, even upon a single article, but as soon as
they had decided they would inform the king. Meanwhile the king
must not be annoyed at his majesty the tsar, for all things henceforth would be governed by their brotherly friendship and love. The
leading merchants[52] and traders were to be asked whether the English merchants should be granted passage to Persia and allowed to
seek along the Ob river routes the way to the Chinese realm, what
duties might the sovereign obtain, and would it be of any profit to
them, the traders? They were also to be queried about iron ore, pitch
and alabaster. The leading merchants replied that they thought the
English merchants were not really concerned about the route to
Persia, but were seeking ways to the Indian realm. They were travelling to India by sea by way of Turkey and Persia, and this route
was very difficult for them, so it would be easier for them to travel
through the sovereign's lands. There would be no profit in it for the
sovereign for, according to the sovereign's charter of privileges, no
duties could be taken from their goods, neither could their goods

be inspected, and the Russians would take exception to this. Here the leading merchants brought up the same objection that the boyars had mentioned to Merrick.

It would be impossible, continued the leading merchants, for Russians to trade alongside the English; the English are strong and rich, and our people cannot compete with them. Concerning the route to China, the leading merchants said that they knew nothing about the Chinese realm, had heard very little about it, did not do any business in Siberia, but they had heard that for long the English had been seeking routes there but had not found them, and likewise they would look for the same route, not find it, and leave. Concerning iron ore, the leading merchants said that if the sovereign allowed the English to seek iron ores in uninhabited places there would be no loss either to the sovereign or any of them; the loss and the labor all would be that of the English. Only if they found it might Russians gain employment from it and, besides, iron would become cheaper because iron did not go from the sovereign's realms overseas, but was imported from overseas. If they found iron which could be poured like bronze, this would be marvellous for the Muscovite realm. The English also built ships, which would bring employment to many poor Russians who would work for them, and Russians would learn the art of shipbuilding.

Concerning the sowing of flax near Vologda, and also canvas, the leading merchants said they thought that the English merchants were snatching at that industry because presently there was no flax coming from Pskov, neither was there any linen coming from Viazma, Smolensk and Belaia. It would harm Russians who trade in linen and flax. As for the argument that they wished to make canvas for their sails, they bring their own canvas with them because Russian canvas is not suitable for sails. Russian canvas is not exported overseas, but flax, cordage and rigging are. There would be losses to those who trade in these, but poor Russians might gain employment with the English when they established a manufactory and started production. But several traders, namely Yudin, Bulgakov and Kotov, said that Russians would suffer no losses, and that flax would be cheaper in the Muscovite realm, and the English merchants would gain very little profit, since they could sow only about five hundred chetverts of flax, neither could they grow any around their shipyards because the ground was unsuitable, and flax would cost them dearly, for if the Russians had seen any business opportunity there, they would have seized it. Concerning pitch they said that if pitch was not allowed to be sent overseas their pitch would be cheaper and the sovereign's subjects would earn less profit. A barrel of pitch fetched a ruble when it was allowed to be exported, but if it was not exported the same barrel would fetch only two grivnas,[53] and even greater losses to the sovereign. But other traders who had served at Archangel as customs chiefs said that, on the contrary, if pitch were not exported there would be even greater revenue for it would be subject to three sets of duties: (1) from the peasants who sold it to the traders, (2) when the merchants sold it to the shipbuilders, and (3) poundage from the vessels. But if pitch was exported overseas these dues would diminish, and there would be no yield from the ships, which would simply carry raw flax and pitch, caulk their ships overseas and shipbuilding would cease for lack of pitch. Poor people would lack employment, and ship's masters would be transferred elsewhere.

On this basis the boyars resolved that without the sovereign's permission nobody should be allowed to export pitch, but in the town of Archangel all foreigners were free to buy pitch. Concerning alabaster, the leading merchants said that the higher hills should not be exploited for the next fifty years, but if they gathered it from the shore where ships might travel more easily, and the English wished to engage in that sort of enterprise, the sovereign's subjects would likewise engage in it.

In accordance with these answers from the boyars, articles of agreement were proposed to Merrick. He agreed to everything, only put off concluding on his own initiative an offensive alliance between the English king and the tsar against the Polish king, although he expressed the firm hope that if the sovereign would correspond concerning this matter with his king, James would help him against Sigismund.

In conclusion Merrick was faced with the problem of disassociating himself from one of the boyars' demands. We have seen how the Muscovite ambassador, Ziuzin, was to have demanded from the English government the return of those Russians who had been sent by Godunov to study.[54] They had not yet been returned to the tsar.

Then the undersecretary Griazev, who had taken the tsar's letter to King James in 1615, reported that the English were hiding these Russians and had converted them to their faith. One of them, Nikofor Alferiev, had been ordained a parson and was living with them in London. Another was a royal secretary in Ireland, and a third was in India as an agent of some merchants. Nikofor was praying to God for the English merchants who went to Russia, and who had brought him out, and he was uttering many blasphemies against the Orthodox faith. The boyars addressed an enquiry to Merrick concerning these four Russian lads, whom he himself had taken from Moscow to England. Merrick replied that they had completed their studies and the English wanted to send them back, but they themselves did not wish to return. The boyars replied: "How can you not send them back, considering they are of our faith. If they do not come back, will they not forsake the faith?" Merrick replied: "There is presently one in England whom they call Nikofor. Another is in Ireland and two are in India. When they are all in England, they will be sent back."

When he took his leave the boyars said to Merrick that the tsar was rewarding him for his service. He replied: "The tsar's kindnesses and rewards are many, but I am happy to serve his majesty the tsar as I ought to do. I was born in my own country, England, but I grew up in Russia. I have not eaten as much bread in my own country as I have in the Muscovite realm. So how thus can I not serve?" Merrick received for his efforts at the peace negotiations with the Swedish ambassadors a golden chain with a portrait of his majesty the tsar, a jewel-encrusted ladle, a Persian robe, pure azure silk with sable and gold thread, images strung with gems and jewels, a black fox hat, a length of velvet, a length of satin, Chinese cloth, five times forty sables and five thousand fox furs.

GUSTAVUS ADOLPHUS ASSESSES STOLBOVO
It is not known whether "Prince Ivan Ulianovich" was satisfied with his business and its outcome, but at least in Moscow and in Stockholm there was great satisfaction over the Stolbovo peace. The loss of several towns was barely felt in comparison to the recovery of Novgorod, and deliverance from the Swedish war coincided with a perilous stage in the war with Poland. But now we were cut off

from the sea! Gustavus Adolphus for his part was very satisfied for
the reasons already mentioned. He spoke thus to the Riksdag in
1617: "God has done a great favor to Sweden in that the Russians,
with whom we have lived for so long in an uncertain state and a
dangerous position, now have had to quit forever that robbers' nest
from which they previously so often had disturbed us. The Russians
are dangerous neighbours. Their frontiers extend to the Northern,
Caspian and Black seas, they have a powerful nobility, a numerous
peasantry, well populated cities, and they can field a large army.
But now this enemy cannot put a single ship on the Baltic Sea without our permission. Large lakes—Ladoga and Peipus—the Narva
region, thirty miles of extensive marshland and strong fortresses
separate us from them. The sea has been taken away from Russia
and God grant that now it will be difficult for the Russians to leap
across these streams."

BORIATINSKY'S MISSION TO SWEDEN

For definitive confirmation of the peace treaty the king appointed as
his plenipotentiary ambassadors to Moscow Gustav Steinbock, Jacob Bat and the secretary Mons Martensson. On the Russian side the
noblemen Prince Fedor Boriatinsky and Osip Pronchishchev and the
crown secretary Kashkin were sent to Stockholm. In September
1617 the Muscovite ambassadors according to the treaty met with
the Swedish ambassadors on the frontier, on the bridge over the
Lavuia river, to show their documents and how they were written. It
happened that they were not written correctly. There arose quarrels
about titles and the business dragged on. They kept sending back to
the sovereign for instruction, whereas the sovereign needed to conclude the matter as quickly as possible. He wrote to Boriatinsky that
the Polish prince Wladyslaw had captured Dorogobuzh and wanted
to advance on Moscow. According to his instructions the ambassadors were ordered to speak to the Swedish ambassadors and, when
they were in Stockholm, they also must address the councillors,
urging the king to help the tsar by sending his army into Livonia,
and the tsar thereafter would recompense him for this. Boriatinsky
was to tell the Swedes that if Wladyslaw conquered Moscow he
would want also to conquer Sweden, that he called Gustavus Adolphus a traitor to him. The Swedish ambassadors replied: "We have

been commanded to speak of this when we are with your sovereign in Moscow; we are not empowered to discuss this with you."

Only on February 15, 1618 did the ambassadors move from the borders, the Swedes to Moscow and the Russians to Stockholm. Boriatinsky and his companions were detained for a long time in Uppsala, and were not brought to Stockholm. They were told that the road was impassable and that the king was burying his cousin.[55] Only on June 2 did they arrive from Uppsala in Stockholm. Here Boriatinsky succeeded in persuading the king to call himself, not sovereign *of* the Izhora land, but sovereign *in* the Izhora land, since not all the Izhora land belonged to the Swedes. Gustavus Adolphus agreed to conclude the treaty to make an alliance against the Polish king, and that neither sovereign would make peace without the consent of the other, but he demanded that the tsar not write to anyone in Livonia and renounce all pretensions to that land so that Swedish merchants might be assigned special quarters in Moscow, Novgorod, Pskov and other places, whence they would request that they be permitted to travel to all Russian towns, trade in Archangel and Kholmogory, engage in fishing in the White Sea, the Lappland shore, the Kola estuary and along Lake Onega; that they be permitted to travel to Lake Onega in their own boats; that they should be free to travel to Persia, Tatary, Crimea and Armenia and back; that ambassadors, heralds and merchants not be confined to their quarters, as was the Muscovite custom, but be allowed to go about simply and freely as among friends, and not as prisoners.

The ambassadors replied that they had no plenipotentiary powers to conclude such an agreement, so the king decided to send his secretary with them to Moscow specifically for that purpose. The ambassadors insisted that the king sign with them a treaty of alliance with Moscow against the Polish king, and send an army for that purpose, but that the other clauses could be discussed in Moscow. The Swedes replied: "We have people in Livonia who are resisting the Poles in the Livonian towns, while we who live here do not fear King Sigismund, as we are living on an island and have water all around us. As long as henceforth the Polish king does not commit any evil against us, why should our king send his troops against the Polish king and unnecessarily place our lives in danger?" The ambassadors replied that the clauses which were the essential basis of the treaty had been written into the Stolbovo agreement and could not be negotiated away, while they had no instructions to conclude any agreement concerning the other clauses. The chancellor replied: "It is true that these clauses were written in, but not exactly in the manner that you describe. It will be necessary to confirm it once again." It was clear that the Swedes either wanted new concessions in exchange for an alliance against Poland, or were waiting to see the outcome of the Polish conflict with Moscow. But it came to an end without their intervention.

III

END OF THE TROUBLES
1616–1619

MILITARY ACTION AGAINST LITHUANIA

After the cessation of talks outside Smolensk, on June 1, 1616 the tsar ordered the commanders to open hostilities against Lithuania. These commanders were Prince Mikhail Konaevich Tinbaev[1] and Nikita Likharev,[2] with a detachment of fifteen hundred men. They probed the environs of Surozh, Velizh, Vitebsk and other places. On the other hand, following reports that the Lithuanians had arrived before Starodub, the commanders Mikhail Dmitriev and Dmitry Skuratov advanced against them with a detachment of about five thousand men. In December news came from Skuratov that they had fought an engagement with the Lithuanians outside Bolkhov, and that the commander Dmitriev had been killed.

To replace the deceased they sent Prince Ivan Andreevich Khovansky who, among other things, was instructed to write personally, and by word urge the Russians in the Lithuanian regiments to be mindful of God and the Orthodox faith, not shed innocent Christian blood and not give their souls over to eternal torment, but forsake the Poles and Lithuanians, make their submission to the great sovereign Michael Fedorovich and come over to his regiments without any fear. The great sovereign would pardon their offenses, generously reward them and hold them in his royal favor without forgetting them. Let them send to Khovansky trusty agents in whom he

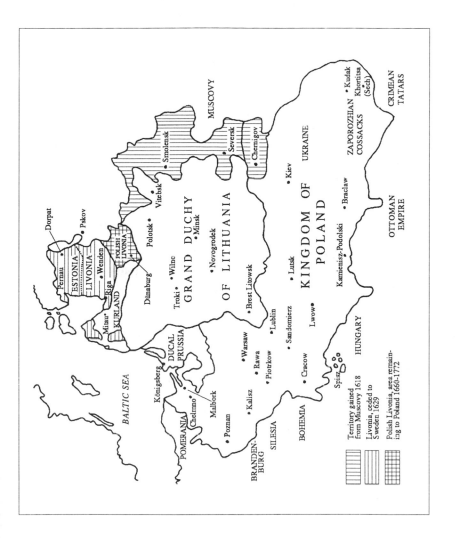

Poland - Lithuania in the Early Seventeenth Century

could trust and bind by oath. The agents were to distribute to the Russians documents from the clergy, in which the hierarchs had written: "We know, lords and brethren, that you serve against your will those who seek our ruin, not considering where you have stood and where you have fallen! Do not deceive yourselves that you are Christians. If the four corners of the earth are crying out against those who conspire with the pope, how can you be Christians when you bow down before the Beast, which Daniel the prophet and John the Evangelist saw speaking blasphemies against God on high?[3] Do not take our word, but learn from the lives of our holy father who came before us. Not only their bodies, but even their fingers have created great miracles. For whom did they commit these great feats, and with whom are they in communion; with the patriarchs and all the ecumenical church, or with the West and the pope? O ye who exalt in your own wisdom! Have regard to your ancestors, where are your parents, where were you born, in what faith were you baptized and nourished, and what memory do you have, of the pious or the impious? When you see standing at Christ's right hand Peter, Alexis, Jonas[4] and Michael of Chernigov[5] and Fedor[6] who suffered much for Christ, and Boris and Gleb[7] who ended their lives in love, when you flee to them will you receive blessing and peace from them, or on account of the embraces and kisses of the sons of Formosus[8] go to eternal perdition? And where will you hide from the defenders of the Russian church? Woe unto you who have abandoned such fathers! Wherefore we pray you, before the time of universal destruction, yours and ours, to desist from such evil intentions and submit to God and His holy intercessors, and you will be saved from the torments of hell. Turn back to the true Christian faith and to the sovereign tsar Michael Fedorovich, and we will forgive you your apostasy, and will persuade the tsar and petition him, pledging our own lives. Once again we promise the tsar's good counsel and generosity. He will reward you with all earthly benefits and receive you as sons and brothers."

MILITARY DIFFICULTIES OUTSIDE SMOLENSK
Prince Khovansky and Skuratov wrote to the sovereign that the Lithuanians, having probed the regions of Karachev and Kromy, had proceeded towards Kursk and they, the commanders, were pursuing

them. The Lithuanians came to Oskol, seized it suddenly and burned it, proceeded to Belgorod and then betook themselves across the frontier. More important were the operations outside Smolensk. Camped outside this town, Mikhail Buturlin and Isaac Semeonovich Pogozhy[9] wrote on October 22 that Gasiewski with his Poles and Lithuanians intended to advance along the Moscow highway, skirt the Smolensk fortresses and encamp at Tverdilishchi on the great Moscow highway.

Acting on this information the sovereign sent Prince Nikita Petrovich Boriatinsky[10] to advance from Rzhev to Dorogobuzh, and from thence to aid the encampments outside Smolensk, deal with the Lithuanians and send to Smolensk grain supplies from Dorogobuzh. In November Prince Boriatinsky announced that he had reached Dorogobuzh with all his forces, but Gasiewski had arrived and taken up position between Dorogobuzh and Smolensk at Tverdilishchi, and had blocked all the roads from Smolensk. Buturlin from outside Smolensk wrote the same, and that no supplies could get through to him from anywhere, and he was under siege by the Lithuanians. Grain supplies and fodder had become scarce, and some soldiers were eating horseflesh. Lithuanians from both sides, from Smolensk and Tverdilishchi, were comming up to the forts every day and causing them great hardship.

SULESHOV AND PROZOROVSKY

So passed the year 1616. On January 6, 1617 the sovereign ordered the émigré Tatar boyar Prince Yury Yansheevich Suleshov and the table attendant Prince Semeon Ivanovich Prozorovsky[11] with six thousand troops to proceed from Moscow to Dorogobuzh to join Boriatinsky. On March 30 Suleshov wrote from Dorogobuzh that he had sent Captains Boiashev and Tarakanov against the Lithuanians. These captains encountered Colonel Wiszel, decisively defeated him and took him prisoner, together with many other Poles; they captured banners, trumpets and kettledrums. In Moscow there was great rejoicing. Gold pieces were sent to Suleshov and Prozorovsky and to all the soldiers who were in the battle.

But in May other news arrived. Suleshov wrote that Gasiewski, joining up with Colonel Stanislaw Czaplinski,[12] had advanced on the forts outside Smolensk and had expelled Buturlin and Pogozhy, who had retreated to Belaia. Czaplinski would have advanced to Dorogobuzh, but he was decisively defeated and lost 240 men. Suleshov and his companions again received gold pieces and were ordered back to Moscow, leaving as many commanders and soldiers in Dorogobuzh, Viazma and Mozhaisk as was necessary, and filling these towns with grain supplies and generally building defenses so that the defenders could hold out securely. Table attendant Prince Peter Ivanovich Pronsky[13] and his companion Ivan Alexandrovich Koltovskoy[14] were sent to Dorogobuzh; but they informed the tsar that they could not enter Dorogobuzh, as the town was encircled by Lithuanians. The sovereign ordered them to take position in Viazma and from there help Dorogobuzh and deal with the Lithuanians. In June the news was worse: the Lithuanians had penetrated the Rzhev district and were preparing to attack Staritsa, Torzhok and Ustiuzhna. In July the commanders wrote from Kashin, Bezhetsky Verkh and Uglich that the Lithuanians already were upon them and were moving into places around Vologda and Beloozero; troops needed to be sent everywhere. Meanwhile news came that Prince Wladyslaw, exalting himself as Russian tsar, was moving directly on Moscow.

WLADYSLAW PREPARES TO ADVANCE ON MOSCOW

As early as June 1616 the Sejm in Warsaw resolved to send Prince Wladyslaw against Moscow, with eight commissioners being appointed to advise him: Bishop Andrzej Lipski of Lutsk;[15] Stanislaw Zurawinski, castellan of Bielsk; Konstanty Plichta, castellan of Sochaczew;[16] Leo Sapieha, chancellor of Lithuania; Peter Opalinski, elder of Srem;[17] Balthsar Strawinski, elder of Mozyr; Jakub Sobieski, son of the governor of Lublin (father of the famous Jan);[18] and Andrzej Mencinski. The commissioners were charged to see that Wladyslaw did not counteract the conclusion of a glorious peace with Moscow, since the war had been undertaken to test the devotion of the Muscovite people to the prince, and that he principally keep in mind the interests of the Commonwealth, not entrusting his cause to the unreliable fortunes of war. Were Wladyslaw so fortunate as to conquer Moscow, let him not be forgetful of his father and his native land. He must also confirm by oath the conditions and sign them with his own hand.

These were the conditions: (1) Unite the Muscovite realm with Poland in an unbreakable union. (2) Establish free trade between them. (3) Return to Poland and Lithuania the territories torn away from them, primarily the principality of Smolensk, and from Severia the towns of Briansk, Starodub, Chernigov, Pochep, Novgorod Seversk, Putivl, Rylsk and Kursk; also Nevel, Sebezh and Velizh. (4) Renounce rights to Livonia and Estonia.

The total strength of the army authorized to advance with Wladyslaw was no more than eleven thousand, despite all the efforts of Leo Sapieha, who contracted even more debts and insisted that a new tax be levied upon Lithuania for the campaign. The majority of the senators wanted to appoint Hetman Stanislaw Zolkiewski as chief commander of the army, since he had earned fame in the Moscow war, had witnessed the Muscovites' oath of allegiance to Wladyslaw, and was greatly respected by them. But Zolkiewski refused, fearing that in the Muscovite realm he would encounter not the respect which had followed him, but rather accusations of perfidy.[19] It was easy for him to find a pretext for his refusal. It was anticipated that Poland would be attacked by the Turks, who were annoyed by cossack raids. As a result of Zolkiewski's refusal the Lithuanian hetman Karol Chodkiewicz was appointed chief commander of the army. He also knew well the road to and from Moscow.

The year 1616 was spent in preparations for war. Various means of attaining success were devised. The king authorized the senators to persuade Prince Vasily Vasilievich Golitsyn to write to the boyars in Moscow about Wladyslaw, but Golitsyn refused. Polish writers say that the Trubetskoy princes, some old man Gotikon and the crown secretary Osipovich appeared before Wladyslaw with an invitation from the boyars. In all probability these were Wladyslaw's old supporters who had remained in Poland, namely Prince Yury Nikitich Trubetskoy[20] and his companions who styled themselves deputies from the Moscow boyars.

Meanwhile the cossacks aroused themselves, scenting war and turmoil. The Don Cossacks sent to Wladyslaw Ataman Boris Yumin and Captain Afanasy Gavrilov to declare that they wished to serve and favor him faithfully. On November 26, 1616 Wladyslaw replied that they should complete what they had begun.

PRIMATE'S SPEECH

In April 1617 the 22-year-old Wladyslaw set out from Warsaw. The archbishop-primate addressed this speech to him: "God gives kingdoms and authority to those who propagate everywhere the Catholic faith, show esteem to those who serve it, and graciously receive their counsel and their directions. God is strong through the intermediacy of your royal highness, and will give the light of truth to those who have sat in darkness and the shadow of death, and lead the deceived upon the path of truth and salvation, even as our nation was led through the intermediacy of our kings Mstislav and Jagailo. Furthermore, in such an important matter upon which all solicitude and care must be focussed, your royal highness must hold yourself in such modesty as is essential in new realms, and attract this cruel people to union and the holy faith not by compulsion and force, not suddenly, but little by little, by the example of yourself and of the priests who will be with you. You will benefit your native land, defend it in all eventualities, unite to it all those districts unjustly torn from it, and will strive to the end that, having received with the help of God the throne there, unite both peoples by means of firm treaties in an indivisible community for the greater advantage and defense of the Christian Commonwealth. We will pray not only to the Lord God to bless your royal highness in this matter, but if there is need of further supplies we will urge the Commonwealth to help you. Only, your highness, endeavor to guide matters to the benefit of the Commonwealth."

Wladyslaw replied: "I go with the intention first of all to have in mind the glory of God and the Holy Catholic faith, in which I have been nourished and strengthened. I will give due thanks to the glorious Commonwealth, which hitherto has nourished me and now is sending me to gain glory, the enlargement of its borders and the conquest of the northern realm."

Wladyslaw set out for Lutsk, which was designated as the rallying point for his army. On the way, at Vladimir-in-Volkynia, he heard mass on Ascension Day, in the Russian Uniate church. There a banner with the Muscovite crest was blessed and handed to one of the Muscovites, a certain Evdokimov (Vitovtov). It is said that this caused ecstasy among the Russian inhabitants of Vladimir.

CAPTURE OF DOROGOBUZH AND VIAZMA

Being compelled to give up part of his army to Zolkiewski, who was preparing to repel the Turks, Wladyslaw returned to Warsaw, from where in August he arrived at Mogilev on the Dnieper, and from thence to Smolensk with Shein and other Muscovites. It is said that in Smolensk the prince and all those surrounding him were very taken up with the conversations between Shein and Nowodworski, the knight of Malta who had taken a significant part in the capture of Smolensk.[21] Nowodworski related how he had taken, Shein how he had defended, Smolensk. The two adversaries became such friends that they swore eternal brotherhood.

At the end of September Wladyslaw left Smolensk to join Chodkiewicz, who was besieging Dorogobuzh. Fear fell upon the Muscovite commanders when they found out that the prince in person was with the army. Ivanis Adodurov, governor of Dorogobuzh,[22] surrendered his town to Wladyslaw as to a Muscovite tsar. The prince triumphantly received his new subjects, kissed the images and crosses which the clergy brought to him, rewarded the musketeers and gave them permission to disperse to their homes. Adodurov and his gentry and junior boyars joined his army.

Having taken Dorogobuzh Wladyslaw, acting on Chodkiewicz's advice, would have set up winter quarters, but news arrived that the governors of Viazma, Prince Peter Pronsky and Prince Mikhail Vasilievich Beloselsky,[23] learning of the surrender of Dorogobuzh, abandoned their town and fled to Moscow. The cossacks were encouraged, seeing that again their time had come, and rushed from Pronsk to plunder the Ukraine. In the small citadel of Viazma sat the governor, Prince Nikita Nikitich Gagarin.[24] He wished to remain, but seeing the townsmen and musketeers fleeing the town, burst into tears and fled with them. At the end of October, Wladyslaw entered Viazma in triumph.

WLADYSLAW'S LETTER TO MOSCOW

Adodurov and Zubov, a native of Smolensk, were sent to Moscow to arouse its inhabitants, and bore this letter to them: "From Tsar and Grand Prince of All Russia Wladyslaw Zhigmontovich to the Muscovite realm, to our boyars, lords-in-waiting, etc." Wladyslaw

wrote that with the extinction of the house of Rurik the people of
the Muscovite realm, considering that it was hard not to have a
sovereign from the royal stem, had kissed the cross to him, Wladyslaw, and had sent ambassadors to his father Sigismund to negotiate
concerning this matter, but the principal ambassador, Metropolitan
Filaret, had disobeyed the instructions given him and had established and promoted his son Michael for the Muscovite throne.
"At that time," continued Wladyslaw, "we ourselves were unable to
come to Moscow because we were not yet of full age; but now we,
the great sovereign, are now of full age to hold the sceptre, and with
the help of God seek our realm of Muscovy which was given to us
by God and confirmed to us by the allegiance of all of you, and
now that we are of full age we can be autocrat of All Russia and by
the grace of God pacify this turbulent realm."

Wladyslaw promised mercy in the event of immediate submission. "And concerning Michael, son of Filaret, if God grants that we
be on our royal throne in Moscow, at that time our royal clemency
will be according to the request of the whole land." Wladyslaw concluded: "We will make haste with sovereign expedition to Moscow,
and we are already on our way. With us will be Patriarch Ignaty[25]
and Archbishop Sergius of Smolensk[26] and the boyar Prince Yury
Nikitich Trubetskoy and his companions."

But this letter had no impact in Moscow. Adodurov and Zubov
were arrested and exiled to distant towns. The pusillanimous governors of Viazma, Pronsky and Beloselsky, were lashed with the knout
and sent to Siberia, their immovable property being confiscated and
given to others. Meanwhile Wladyslaw's movement was halted by
the open mutiny of his army, which had not received any pay for a
long time, and did not wish to endure hunger and cold. They had to
be billeted in quarters in Viazma and the surrounding district.

POZHARSKY IN KALUGA

While Wladyslaw's main force remained there, awaiting pay, the
irregulars under Czaplinski were active. Having devastated everything in their path, they captured Meshchovsk and Kozelsk, but
could not take Kaluga where, in response to the petition of its inhabitants, Prince Dmitry Mikhailovich Pozharsky was dispatched on

October 18; he had at his disposal 5400 troops. Czaplinski took position at Tovarkov, which was situated only one day's march from Kaluga, which received no respite from him. Pozharsky also was not inactive. The struggle went at first with mixed fortunes, but finally Pozharsky was able to force his way into the Polish fortress at Tovarkov and there destroy all their munitions. Another Pozharsky, Prince Dmitry Petrovich,[27] was sent to defend Tver. On the way he was besieged by Lord Sokolowski at Klin. Pozharsky endured, lasted out the siege and convoyed supplies to Tver. Sokolowski arrived before Tver. Pozharsky also held out against him there. After Sokolowski, Colonel Kopyczewski arrived at Tver, stood before the town for two weeks but did nothing against it. Belaia also did not surrender to the Poles.

Wladyslaw's attempt to seize Mozhaisk suddenly did not succeed. The local commanders Fedor Vasilievich Buturlin[28] and Danila Yurievich Leontiev[29] knew of the enemy's movements and were ready to meet him. Learning of this preparedness, and also that the town was strongly fortified and that a strong detachment from Moscow was coming to its aid, Wladyslaw resolved neither to lead his army in an assault, nor to besiege the town in winter, in December, but returned to Viazma, having lost many men, especially Germans, on account of the cold.

When the danger threatening Mozhaisk was known in Moscow, the boyar commanders Prince Boris Mikhailovich Lykov and Grigory Leontievich Valucv[30] were sent there with a detachment of about six thousand men. Volokolamsk was occupied by the table attendants Princes Dmitry Mamstriukovich and Vasily Petrovich Cherkassky[31] with five thousand troops.

UNSUCCESSFUL PEACE NEGOTIATIONS

So passed the year 1617. At the end of the year the lords of the Council reminded the commissioners that it would be better to conclude the war by negotiations and at the end of December the king's secretary, Jan Grydycz, was dispatched to Moscow with a proposal to call a conference from January 20 to April 20, 1618, during which time there would be no hostile action on either side. Prisoners of war were to be exchanged immediately. The boyars answered the emissary that since they saw no credentials from the king or the

Polish Commonwealth they could not enter into relations with the commissioners, that Russian plenipotentiary ambassadors could not enter into negotiations without letters of safe conduct from Wladyslaw, that the time limit until April was too short, that they could not agree to halt hostilities until the Poles had set Metropolitan Filaret and Prince Golitsyn free, and that when the prince delivered safe conducts they, the boyars, would send their ambassadors to the commissioners and would discuss the location of the negotiations and the number of plenipotentiaries.

The first three months of 1618 passed. There was no new onslaught by Wladyslaw but the Poles did not cease to devastate Muscovite districts, neither did the prince quit Viazma and return to Lithuania. With the spring the capital once more was threatened by enemy action. Under these circumstances it was decided in Moscow to compel the Poles themselves to make peace, and at the beginning of April the noble Ivan Gavrilovich Kondyrev[32] and a crown secretary arrived in the Polish encampment and declared that they were prepared to discuss with the commissioners the matter of the conference and the number of plenipotentiaries. They demanded that the Poles quit Muscovite territory, and that if they did so a three-month truce would be concluded. The commissioners replied that their army would not quit Muscovite territory before negotiations had been concluded. These could begin on June 16. Concerning the matter of the location of the negotiations and the size of the ambassadorial suites, this would have to be referred to special commissioners two weeks before the conference.

Spring passed. News came from Warsaw that the Sejm had approved the collection of money for continuation of the war, but not much, and with the condition that the war be concluded without fail within one year. At the beginning of June the Polish army moved out of Viazma and halted at Yurkaevo, on the road between Mozhaisk and Kaluga. There in a council of war Chodkiewicz proposed to carry the war towards Kaluga, in a less devastated countryside, and harass the most famous Muscovite commander, Pozharsky, compelling him to come over to the side of Wladyslaw, which according to the hetman he was prepared to do. Finally, near Kaluga it would be easier to join the army which was crossing the Ukraine with help from Zolkiewski. But the commissioners insisted on a direct advance on Moscow, which would compel its inhabitants to surrender to the prince, as had happened in Shuisky's time. They argued that the diversion to Kaluga would give the Muscovite commanders the opportunity to conquer Viazma and cut the Poles off from Smolensk.

UNSUCCESSFUL ATTACK ON BORISOV, MOZHAISK BESIEGED

This opinion prevailed but rather than advance towards Moscow it was necessary to conquer Mozhaisk, and not leave Prince Lykov in their rear. There was no hope of taking Mozhaisk by storm since they had no siege engines, and therefore they decided to advance on Borisov Gorodishche, take it by force and compel Lykov to come out of Mozhaisk and fight in the open field where the Poles, according to experience, could count on a sure success. The Polish army twice launched an assault on Borisov, and twice were repulsed. At the end of June Lykov wrote to the sovereign that the prince stood before Borisov Gorodishche. Michael ordered Prince Dmitry Mamstriukovich Cherkassky to move over from Volokolamsk to Ruza, whence he could establish communications with Lykov and according to information move to aid him in Mozhaisk. Pozharsky was instructed to move from Kaluga to Borovsk, and from there help Mozhaisk. Kurmash Murza Urusov, with his yurt Tatars and Astrakhan musketeers, was ordered from Moscow to Borovsk. On June 30 Lykov again wrote to Moscow that on the previous day, the 29th, the prince and the hetman had come from outside Borisov to Mozhaisk but the Russians from the fort had come out against them, had repulsed the Lithuanians from Mozhaisk, captured some informers, and the prince had withdrawn to Borisov Gorodishche.

Twenty days passed. Cherkassky arrived at Mozhaisk and on July 21 wrote to the sovereign that on the previous day many Poles and Lithuanians had arrived outside Mozhaisk from Borisov Gorodishche and had deployed at a place near the Luzhetsk monastery along the road from Moscow to Ruza, doubtless with the intention of blocking the road from Moscow to Mozhaisk. Prince Lykov wrote that according to the word of a deserter, the king and the hetman had come with all their forces from outside Borisov to besiege Mozhaisk.

POZHARSKY IN BOROVSK

The sovereign immediately summoned the boyars and resolved to rely upon the commanders Princes Lykov and Cherkassky. If they, according to local conditions, could remain in Mozhaisk, they should pray to God for help and deal with the Lithuanians and correspond with Prince Dmitry Mikhailovich Pozharsky, in order that they might together deal with the Lithuanians as God saw fit. But if they found out that the prince, the hetman and the Lithuanians had come to besiege Mozhaisk, and were expected to operate a tight siege and block the roads, they should not remain under siege but withdraw towards Moscow with all their troops by whatever road was most secure and whenever possible, and must take counsel secretly concerning the evacuation, so that nobody should know. When they decided upon an evacuation route they must send a message directly to Prince Dmitry Mikhailovich Pozharsky, also in secret, so that he might station himself on that route to provide them with fortifications or regiments, and help them. If they decided to evacuate they must leave with commander Fedor Vasilievich Volynsky[33] siege personnel with additional forces, so that they might remain securely under siege in Mozhaisk.

On July 29 Lykov reported that the Lithuanians were advancing upon their forts every day, firing from their cannon and muskets and killing the soldiers, and on the 27th had wounded the commander Prince Dmitry Mamstriukovich Cherkassky. Now the Lithuanians were digging trenches behind the Yakimansk monastery, and beyond the Mozhaia river they had established artillery against their forts, were firing from the trenches on both forts, were causing great hardship. According to Polish accounts, the Russians had more than one thousand men killed.

There was hardship of another kind. Soldiers incited by Bogdan Turgenev, a native of Yaroslavl, Yakov Ostafiev Tukhachevsky, a native of Smolensk,[34] and Dmitry Zhedrinsky, a native of Nizhny Novgorod,[35] came to the commanders with great clamor saying that they had not thought the campaign would cause so much bloodshed.

RETREAT TO MOSCOW

By then the sovereign had decided firmly to order Volynsky to remain in Mozhaisk as the siege commander, while Cherkassky and

Lykov were instructed to withdraw to Moscow with all their troops as best and effectively as they could. Pozharsky, who remained in Borovsk, received a command to move where the commanders specified and help them, and from Borisov rally the besieged with all their supplies, and to act at the same time that Cherkassky and Lykov were withdrawing. When they had withdrawn, Pozharsky was to return to Borovsk. During the first days of August, having chosen a dark and stormy night, in pouring rain, Cherkassky and Lykov silently withdrew from the Mozhaisk forts and on the 6th reached Borovsk, and from there withdrew to Moscow. The Poles immediately occupied Borisov, which had been abandoned and burned by the Russians. There they were joined by Leo Sapieha, who had been to Warsaw in search of money. Instead of money he brought merely a promise and then the army, some of whom had not seen a crust of bread for twelve days, began to mutiny and leave the encampment in droves. With great difficulty the commissioners succeeded in pacifying them, promising to pay them in full on October 28; even so four whole regiments left the encampment, not counting individual desertions already accomplished.

Under such circumstances Chodkiewicz again proposed to deploy between Kaluga and Borovsk, in a less devastated countryside. But the commissioners in no wise would agree. They wanted to conclude the war on time at all costs; of the one-year term less than five months remained and therefore they decided to advance directly on Moscow, directing there a letter in which Wladyslaw wrote that only the counsellors of Michael Romanov believed that he was coming to destroy the Orthodox faith, for that was not his intention.

ASSEMBLY IN MOSCOW

Having notice from Mozhaisk that Wladyslaw was advancing on Moscow, Michael summoned the Assembly on September 9 and declared that he, "praying for God's mercy, promised to defend the Orthodox faith against his enemy Wladyslaw, to remain under siege in Moscow, to fight against the prince, the Poles and Lithuanians insofar as God would help him, whereas they, the metropolitan, boyars and all the people would fight for the Orthodox faith, for him, the sovereign, and for all who endured the siege with him, neither would they be tempted by the prince or any of his deceits."

All the people replied that they vowed unanimously to God to defend the Orthodox faith and their sovereign, endure the siege with him and fight his enemies to the death, not sparing their lives. At the same time dispositions were made as to who was to defend the various sectors of Moscow, and who was to be under their command. Again documents circulated from Moscow around the towns urging that the inhabitants, being mindful of God, the Orthodox faith, their oath of allegiance and their souls, sincerely help the realm in its present need with men and money.

HETMAN SAHAIDACHNY

It was not only Wladyslaw who was approaching Moscow with his small army. From the other side the Little Russian hetman Peter Konashevich Sahaidachny[36] was coming with twenty thousand cossacks, on the way having devastated Putivl, Livny, Elets and Lebedian. The last town was taken because the rural population would not obey the governor. Elets was taken because the governor, Polev, was not accustomed to military matters. Sahaidachny deceived him. He concealed some forces in an ambush, and himself with his remaining forces led an assault. The governor led a sortie against him with all his forces and the concealed force entered the town and occupied it.

But Sahaidachny could not capture Mikhailov. Hearing of Sahaidachny's approach, the tsar ordered Pozharsky to advance from Borovsk against him. Pozharsky moved along the road to Serpukhov, but became gravely ill. The soldiers halted, not wishing to advance with a sick commander against the enemy.

The cossacks took advantage of this opportunity and began to commit brigandage. The sovereign ordered the sick Pozharsky to Moscow and his colleague, Prince Grigory Konstantinovich Volkonsky,[37] to remain at Kolomna and not permit Sahaidachny to cross the Oka. But Volkonsky was in no state to prevent the hetman from crossing and had to shut himself up in Kolomna, where among his regiments there arose differences between the gentry and the cossacks. The latter left Kolomna and halted in the Vladimir district, on the patrimonial estate of Prince Mstislavsky, and from there they laid waste to many places.

ASSAULT ON MOSCOW

On September 17 the prince halted at Zvenigorod and Sahaidachny at the village of Bronnitsy in the Kolomna district. On September 20 the prince halted in the famous Tushino. Sahaidachny appeared near the Donskoy monastery and dispatched his wagon trains to join the prince. The boyars and the army would have come out of Moscow to prevent this junction but, in the words of the chronicler,[38] great fear came upon the Muscovites, and without a struggle they allowed the hetman to join the prince in the encampment near Moscow.

The Muscovites' fear was heightened by a comet, whose head stood above the very city. The tsar and all the people looking upon the star thought that Moscow would be captured by the prince. Meanwhile negotiations proceeded outside Moscow. Wladyslaw demanded submission, calling himself tsar of Muscovy. With tar the boyars smeared out this title of the prince in the documents and dragged out the affair, counting on the arrival of two allies, hunger and cold.

But the Poles did not wish to wait and on the night of October 1st carried out an assault. The besieged were forewarned from the enemy camp and were ready for the defense. Chevalier Nowodworski made a breach in the outer defenses and reached as far as the Arbat gates but there, while affixing a petard to them, was wounded in the hand by a musket shot.

After this the Russians effected a sortie from the gates and came to grips with the enemy, who came under fire from all sides. The Poles held on until dawn but, not receiving any help from their own people, retreated. The lord-in-waiting Nikita Vasilievich Godunov,[39] with 457 men, was in charge of the Arbat gates and the area from the Arbat to the Nikita gates at the time of the assault, while at the gates themselves were Danila Leontiev, Ivan Urusov and the crown secretary Antonov.

An attack against the Tver gates was even less successful because the scaling ladders the Poles brought were too short. The Tver gates and the stretch from the Tver to the Petrov gates, to the Pipe and the Presentation gates, were entrusted to Princes Daniel Mezetsky and Grigory Volkonsky with 562 men, 22 cavalrymen, while the gates themselves were in charge of Vasily Monastyrev, Semeon Danilov and Crown Secretary Golovin.

According to their own accounts the Poles lost thirty killed and one hundred wounded at the Arbat gates. Naturally Hetman Chodkiewicz was blamed for this failure. Why was this assault not kept secret? Why did they believe spies who gave false information about the height of the walls? Why did Nowodworski not receive any help, since the Russians at the Arbat gates would have turned their backs, but they were blocked by the German infantry stationed by the Nikita gates? But according to official Russian sources, there were no Germans by the Nikita gates.

The famous Polish cavalryman Czaplinski died at Vokhna at the hands of a servitor of the Trinity monastery after his failures before that monastery. But at the same time on the Russian side there also perished a famous cavalryman, who had caused much harm to the Lithuanian army. This was Kanay Murza, who was baptized as Prince Mikhail.

NEGOTIATIONS

Negotiations reopened. It was resolved that the plenipotentiaries on the Russian side would be the boyar Fedor Ivanovich Sheremetev, Prince Danila Mezetsky, Lord-in-waiting Artemy Izmailov and the crown secretaries Bolotnikov and Somov. On the Polish side, Prince Adam Nowodworski, the bishop of Kamieniec, Konstantin Plichta, Leo Sapieha and Jakub Sobieski. They were to meet on the Presnia on October 20.

The Russian ambassadors, who were sent on behalf of the boyars and all the Council, received the following instructions: "Only raise your hats at the mention of the king's name if the Lithuanians raise their hats at the mention of the sovereign's name." They were to tell the Lithuanian ambassadors: "We have written that we wish to conclude a fair matter and bring about Christian peace but now you are showing such inconsistency in this matter, for in your speeches you do not name our great sovereign. How therefore can there be a favorable outcome, and why are we ambassadors from both sides meeting? If you do not name our sovereign in your speeches, we shall not name your king." Under those conditions they would speak with them concerning all things, but not mention the king in their speeches. Should by chance the king's name be uttered, it must be in connection with the ruin of the Muscovite realm.

Should the Lithuanian ambassadors demand cities or any reward or compensation for the king or the prince, or any damages, you are to answer: "Such damages were caused by your sovereign and by the Poles and Lithuanians in the Muscovite realm, of which it is impossible to give an estimate, as is evident from the list and from what Fedka Andronov said, that every variety of valuables were sent to the king, and according to the king's letters were distributed to the knights, deputies and Germans, colonels and captains and to the deputies of Sapieha's forces, and also to Sapieha himself according to the agreement with the deputies of his army, and to the Polish and Lithuanian ambassadors. Not to mention the chancellery disbursements, and the expenses for Alexander Gasiewski's household, payments to the colonels and captains according to Alexander's warrants, and also to the Russians, Muscovite cannoneers and musketeers who were with you. The gold, silver and jewelry of all descriptions amount to the value of at least 912,113 rubles and 27 altyns, or in Polish money 340,379 zlotys and 13 groschen."

The plenipotentiaries met and spoke, or rather quarrelled, without dismounting from their horses. Leo Sapieha spoke of Wladyslaw's rights to the Muscovite throne, enumerating the advantages for Moscow of accepting him, the disadvantages if they did not wish to accept him. The Muscovite plenipotentiaries replied: "You did not give us the prince when we all wanted him and long awaited him. At that time much blood was shed, so we chose ourselves another sovereign, kissed the cross to him, and we have crowned him with the royal diadem and cannot depart from him. We wish to conclude a truce between the two realms for twenty years, if you will yield to us Smolensk, Roslavl, Dorogobuzh, Viazma, Kozelsk and Belaia."

The Poles, laughing at these demands, continued to discuss the matter of the prince. The Muscovite plenipotentiaries replied: "Tell us if, apart from the matter of the prince, you want to do any business. If so, we also would like to do business and wish to find with you the means to establish peace on both sides. If you do not cease talking about the prince, we no longer will hold any discussions with you." The Poles retorted: "You will be worse off if you break off negotiations. The sovereign prince is advancing with his army upon the capital, and of what even now is not demolished or ruined, nothing will remain but earth and water." The succeeding conferences, on October 23 and 25, were taken up with disputes over towns which Moscow was to cede to Lithuania, and over the term of the truce. The Poles demanded many towns and designated too short a term for the truce.

WLADYSLAW MOVES TO PEREIASLAVL

Meanwhile cold set in. Wladyslaw struck his camp and moved from Tushino along the Pereiaslavl road. As a consequence, the meeting of plenipotentiaries on October 27 was not on the Presnia but outside the Presentation gates along the Trinity road, and since no agreement was reached the conferences ended because the Polish ambassadors could not remain outside Moscow now that the prince had taken himself off. Under these circumstances Chevalier Nowodworski and his companions sent their own ambassadors into Moscow, namely Krzystof Sapieha, Krasinski and Grydycz, who there concluded a preliminary treaty with the condition that it be confirmed at a conference with the high ambassadors.

The Russians agreed to cede Smolensk, Belaia, Dorogobuzh, Roslavl, Gorodishche Monastyrskoe (Muromsk), Chernigov, Starodub, Popova Gora, Novgorod Seversk, Pochep, Trubchevsk, Serpeisk, Nevel, Sebezh, Krasny and the district of Velizh with all that from time immemorial had pertained to that district. According to Polish accounts, at that time there was great unrest in Moscow. According to our chronicler, about three thousand cossacks, no longer wishing to remain in Moscow and unable to tolerate life without brigandage, mutinied one night, abandoned their fort beyond the Yauza and fled.[40] The tsar sent Princes Dmitry Timofeevich Trubetskoy and Daniel Ivanovich Mezetsky after them to persuade them to come back. The prince persuaded them to turn around, but the cossacks halted at the fort and would not enter the city, fearing punishment. Then the tsar sent other boyars to persuade them, and the cossacks entered the city.

On November 19 Sheremetev and Mezetsky received instructions to meet with the bishop of Kamieniec and his companions and conclude a preliminary truce agreement. Boyar Fedor Ivanovich then was to go to the Trinity monastery, and from there correspond with the Polish commissioners and agree upon the site for a conference.

At the conference he was to demand that the Poles release Prince Ivan Ivanovich Shuisky and Prince Yury Nikitich Trubetskoy, his wife and children, if they themselves wished it, and also to free all Muscovites now with the prince or in Lithuania, if they wished to come to the Muscovite realm. If possible, Sheremetev was to correspond with Prince Shuisky and the others to ask whether it was helpful to mention them in the memoranda of agreement, if they were pleased by the sovereign's solicitude, and whether they wanted the ambassadors to speak concerning them. If so, he should speak of them; if the Russians instructed that he should not speak of them, he should not do so.

The prince, withdrawing from Moscow, moved against the Trinity monastery, but in response to demands for surrender the archimandrite, cellarer and brethren ordered the cannon to be fired at the Polish army. The prince withdrew and halted twelve versts from the monastery in the village of Rogachevo. Hetman Sahaidachny went directly from Moscow to Kaluga and on the way took a fort in Serpukhov, but could not take the citadel. Similarly in Kaluga he succeeded in burning out the fort, but the citadel held out against him. The prince scattered his troops in the regions of Galich, Kostroma, Yaroslavl, Poshekhonie and Beloozero, but in the Beloozero region the governor, Prince Grigory Vasilievich Tiufiakin,[41] caught up with the Poles and defeated them.

DEULINO CONFERENCE AND TRUCE

Meanwhile the plenipotentiaries, Nowodworski, Leo Sapieha and Gasiewski, occupied Svatkovo, ten versts from the Trinity monastery. Arrived at the monastery, Sheremetev sent Solovoy Protasiev to Svatkovo to enquire after the plenipotentiaries' health and invite them to a conference. Sapieha and Gasiewski answered Protasiev angrily, saying that their emissaries, Krzsytof Sapieha and his companions, had been detained a long time by the high ambassadors in Moscow, and had forced them against their will to concede to the Muscovite realm the town of Briansk, which from time immemorial had been the best town in the Severian principality, and had proposed in the draft treaty to give Popova Gora in exchange for Briansk. But they did not know of any such town as Popova Gora, nor had they ever heard of it. Also the boundaries of the Velizh region had not been defined.

Protasiev replied that these three towns had been given in exchange for Briansk: Serpeisk, the Pskov bytown of Krasny, and the town of Popova Gora in the Severian land, and in addition the region of Velizh. Leo Sapieha replied: "We will not discuss this now with you; we will speak with your high ambassadors when we are in conference." Protasiev replied: "If you high ambassadors are going to reopen matters which have been settled, his majesty the tsar's high ambassadors will discuss nothing with you except the agreement which they have concluded and clinched with your emissaries." Gasiewski continued heatedly: "I was myself in Pskov, and know all the Pskov bytowns.[42] There is barely a town at Krasny, it has long been worthless, and is completely abandoned." Then the Lithuanians said that the following day the gentry from both sides should meet and decide upon a conference site, and that at the conference there should be a hundred cavalry and fifty infantrymen on each side. Leo Sapieha added: "When you see your high ambassadors, ask them to send us some fish." Protasiev replied: "No fish has reached our high ambassadors in Moscow from any of the towns whatsoever, on account of your Lithuanians."

The gentry found a conference site in the village of Deulino, which belonged to the Trinity monastery, and was situated along the Uglich road about three versts from the monastery and about five versts from Svatkovo, and the first session took place on November 23. The Lithuanian ambassadors stated that the Muscovite ambassadors had extorted Briansk from their emissaries by force. "You wrote in your notes that we spoke to you concerning the prince, but you stated that this matter was closed. But you should not say that this matter is closed, since this is God's affair. Last Friday at dawn you saw a comet with a tail, and it stood over your Muscovite realm. Because of this star you can see what is happening to you on account of your injustices."

The Muscovite ambassadors replied: "Heavenly signs take many forms, and it is presumptuous for anyone to interpret them. God did not reveal what would happen to which realm on account of it. We think that this sign is for your realm. A heavenly sign is a creation of God. He is its creator, and nobody should draw conclusions from it. And if you should repudiate agreements concluded by your emissaries, whom are we henceforth to believe?"

The Lithuanian ambassadors retorted angrily, and Alexander Gasiewski incited them to every evil. "You extorted many articles which were not in our draft treaty!" the Poles exclaimed. The Muscovite ambassadors replied: "If the letters of credence you gave your emissaries were not in order, whom are we henceforth to believe? Neither, henceforth, can we alter either of these two documents in violation of the agreement and the counsel of our brethren, the great sovereign, the boyars, all his counsellors and all the Great Russian realm."

Gasiewski said: "How can you say you are acting in good faith? You ascribe many Bielsk districts to Rzhev, many Velizh trading settlements have been ascribed to Toropets, and on account of the Bielsk district and the Velizh boundary much blood is still being shed. But now you have come to us with a peremptory demand and insist on having everything your way, and have behaved similarly towards our emissaries. God grant that the Lithuanian ambassadors and emissaries not meet with you in Moscow. We should rather meet in the open field, for there you cannot dictate terms; but it would be disastrous for the Lithuanian ambassadors to carry on negotiations in Moscow. You extort concessions. I myself was in Moscow during the reign of Tsar Vasily and barely escaped alive, and your sovereign extorted by force many articles against my will, which were impossible for me to perform. Previous to that Tsar Boris by force extracted from Chancellor Leo Sapieha a truce for twenty years,[43] and now you have compelled our emissaries by force to do what they were forbidden to do, but we have not concluded a truce with you for that number of years."

The Muscovite ambassadors replied that in Moscow all ambassadors were shown respect, and no concessions were ever extracted by force from such ambassadors. "You say this in order to cover your own injustices, because you never observe the terms of any truce, and you violate your oaths." To this Leo Sapieha replied: "Even though you place a little bird in a golden cage and feed him poppy seed and sugar, but do not give him light and freedom, it will be nothing to him. Likewise a man, when he is not at liberty, also will act not according to his nature. I came as an ambassador to your Tsar Boris, and was detained by him for a long time, and your boyars extorted from me by force more years of truce. Now you are coming to deceive us, but we are still at liberty, and not being detained by you." And they uttered very many angry and unbefitting speeches.

Thereupon the Muscovite ambassadors, seeing that the Lithuanian ambassadors were angry, and fearing a breach with them, took the screed with their notes and compared it with their own, finding in it many articles with added words. For example, to the royal style was added that of Chernigov. To the article providing for the release of Archbishop Sergius of Smolensk was added, "if he so wishes." In the copy held by the Muscovite emissaries it was said of the sovereign "whom now the Russians have as great sovereign of Muscovy," while in the Polish version it was written "who now with them is called Muscovite sovereign." The Lithuanian ambassadors promised to omit the last change, and so on that note they dispersed.

When Sheremetev reported this to the tsar, he was instructed to stand firm, but if they threatened to break off negotiations he was to allow these additions. In accordance with these instructions the Muscovite ambassadors at the second session firmly resisted these additions. The Polish ambassadors answered them angrily, threatening that Hetman Radziwill's regiments, which previously had been engaged in the Swedish war, would now, following the truce with the Swedes, be free to come to the prince's aid. "Evidently you have not had enough of the shedding of Christian blood. You pretend to exchange ambassadors with us, but you keep shifting and deceiving us. But we are not afraid of your deceits, but put our trust in the will of God, our fair dealings with you, and also our knights, in order to deal with you. If we cannot bring matters between us to a favorable conclusion you will bring upon yourselves by your harsh demands a peace such that not one infant will remain in Moscow or any of the other towns. We will not write *whom you now have as your great sovereign.* We accord enough respect even if we write in our copy *who presently among them is called great sovereign.*"

The Muscovite ambassadors argued that in the first session the Poles themselves had promised to leave standing the old formulary concerning the sovereign, *they have*, not *they call.* "Henceforth what can be believed? How can such great and honorable people as yourselves not be ashamed? You give your word, but do not abide by it." The Polish ambassadors replied: "If everyone in the Muscovite realm knew what was good for them, and did obeisance to our sovereign prince, every one of you would be at peace and the shedding of Christian blood would cease. But instead you, being unmindful of your sovereign, have subjected yourselves to some nonentity." Then they uttered unbefitting words about the sovereign.

The Muscovite ambassadors replied: "Then we shall start uttering unbefitting words about your sovereign, and blood will flow again." The Lithuanian ambassadors angrily exclaimed: "We do not expect any truth from you, you do everything underhandedly. We even wrote to you from Warsaw concerning the embassy, and sent Jan Grydycz, so that we might meet with you and discuss matters seriously on the border, but you detained Grydycz for a long time and sent him back empty-handed. Having arrived at Viazma, we again wrote to you, and you replied that we should meet between Viazma and Volokolamsk. We waited for a long time, but you did not come. When we arrived at Mozhaisk we again wrote to you, and you replied that you would meet with us on the Istra river, but there we waited in vain for you. Then you wrote that we should meet on the Khimka, but you refused to meet on the Khimka and sent a message that we should meet outside Moscow, on the Presnia river, and only there did you come and meet with us. You have been trifling with us for nearly two years. Now you have detained us here into the winter, and all the army has come to us complaining that they do not wish to evacuate your country in winter, but are willing to serve the prince all winter without pay."

Leo Sapieha exclaimed: "We vow to you that we will have no further dealings with you. Tomorrow we will set all our troops on you, while we travel to the Sejm in Lithuania." The Muscovite ambassadors replied: "You threaten us with war and, despite the treaty concluded by your own emissaries, wish to shed blood again. But the fortunes of war are in the hands of God, who gives victory to those He helps. Many levies now have been recruited in our towns, and in the spring many troops will come to help us from other lands."

Another complication arose. The Lithuanian ambassadors would not guarantee that the Zaporozhian Cossacks, Lisowski's irregulars and Czaplinski's regiments would obey their orders and immediately quit Muscovite territory at the conclusion of peace. The Muscovite ambassadors replied that they did not wish to hear of this.

The Poles agreed to write that they would take away with them
Lisowski's irregulars and Czaplinski's regiment, but refused to
evacuate the Zaporozhians.

While these disputes were proceeding, Solovoy Protasiev approached the window next to which the Muscovite ambassadors
were sitting and told them what the Lithuanian Madalinski had said
to him: "This night the prince came to the Lithuanian ambassadors
in Svatkovo and said that a missive had come to him from Poland
telling him not to hasten to make peace with the Muscovite ambassadors, and also the prince was to pay the Polish troops for two
quarters of the year." Hearing these tidings, the Muscovite ambassadors made concessions, but the meeting ended without any result.
Gasiewski said: "Even though we make peace and leave your country, your cossacks will find another brigand and our outlaws will
join them, and so without the prince you will have another Dmitry."
The Muscovite ambassadors replied: "You are not yet satiated with
Christian blood. You will not escape God's vengeance."

Sheremetev and his companions were in a difficult situation.
Items of news, each worse than the last, reached them in the Trinity
monastery. There would be no peace; the knights were coming to
the prince and saying that in no way did they want peace with the
Muscovites. The Cherkassians, Sahaidachny and his companions,
had sent to the prince a cossack from Putivl, saying that they would
not leave the Muscovite land. The Don Cossacks were corresponding with the prince, saying that they all wished to serve him. During
the meeting some cossacks approached the ambassadorial suite saying that the Poles, Lithuanians and all the knights were supporting
the prince and hindering him from making peace but they, all the
cossacks, wanted to leave and join the sovereign in Moscow. But
Levka Pivov had visited them saying that in Moscow their cossack
brethren who had come from Lithuania were being executed and imprisoned. For this reason they were not coming over to the sovereign. Some Poles approached the ambassadorial suite saying that
certain Muscovite cossacks had come and asked to be given the
Czaplinski, Lisowski and Cherkassian contingents, saying: "You
Poles are sitting idle. Let us deal with Vladimir, Suzdal and the
other towns." The Poles likewise said openly to the gentry that they
had the son of the Kaluga brigand. He was being taught to read in

Fortress of Marienburg (Malbork)
Place of Imprisonment of Filaret and Other Russian Prisoners
1612–1619

the Caves monastery. Somebody else had been hanged in Moscow, but he had been carried away by the cossacks."[44] The Poles also threatened the gentry: "If the ambassadors do not reach agreement, it will be on your necks that our swords will fall."

The ambassadors had to come to terms at all costs. At the December 1st meeting they agreed to all the changes inserted by the Poles into the Muscovite draft. But again a complication arose. The Poles did not agree to write that the surrender of towns to their side and the release of Metropolitan Filaret should take place simultaneously, namely on February 2, 1619, since Filaret could not travel so soon from Marienburg. The Lithuanian ambassadors had arisen and were leaving the hut, declaring that they were breaking off negotiations, when the Muscovite ambassadors turned them around and persuaded them at last to make an agreement. The Poles said: "For the sake of Christian peace and at the request of you the high ambassadors, seeing your readiness to bargain in good faith, we will concede to you and write into our truce agreement that the release of Metropolitan Filaret Nikitich, Prince Vasily Vasilievich Golitsyn and their companions, the exchange of prisoners and the evacuation and surrender of towns will take place by the same deadline, February 15 according to your reckoning and February 25 according to our Roman calendar."[45]

With this they concluded, and everybody was very content, except for Gasiewski who, during the ratification ceremony wept, saying: "I oppose the taking of this oath. If the boundaries between Velizh, Belaia and Toropets are not delineated I will have to defend my own boundaries perpetually. Already I have defended them on behalf of the king with the shedding of my blood." Having said this, Gasiewski placed the boundary schedule under the cross but the Muscovite ambassadors cast the paper from the platter, saying: "This has nothing to do with our diplomatic task." Gasiewski kissed the cross and wept. The documents were exchanged between the two sides. The Lithuanian ambassadors stood up joyfully and spoke peacefully, quietly, smoothly and sincerely with the tsar's ambassadors.

In the text it was stated: "By the grace of God the high ambassadors (names) of the great sovereign Tsar and Grand Prince Michael

Fedorovich of All Russia, autocrat (title), his majesty the tsar's boyars and all the councillors of his majesty the tsar and all the great realms of the Great Russian tsardom, have spoken with (names), have renounced firmly Prince Wladyslaw and definitely have determined that he shall not be placed upon the Muscovite throne. *But the lords of the Polish Council and their high ambassadors have deferred this matter to the judgement of God.* A truce of fourteen years and six months has been determined between the Great Russian realms of the great sovereign and the great realms of the Polish kingdom and the grand principality of Lithuania. We, the high ambassadors of the great sovereign's boyars and all the Great Russian realm, at the behest of our great sovereign, and in accordance with the counsel of the boyars and all ranks of all of the Great Russian realm, have ceded the towns (names). These towns are to be surrendered with all artillery and ammunition, all townsmen and agricultural peasants of the rural districts, except for leading merchants and traders, who will be free to go to whichever side they please. The clergy, governors, officials and servicemen shall be free to move to Muscovite territory with all their possessions."

In accordance with his previously mentioned instructions Sheremetev sent to Prince Ivan Ivanovich Shuisky and Vasily Yanov, who at that time were in the prince's encampment, asking them whether they wished to come over to the sovereign. He was to tell them that they could rely upon the sovereign's favor, and might come into the Muscovite realm without fear. Shuisky and Yanov replied: "Both you and the boyars know that we are not traitors to the Muscovite realm. We did not desert Moscow for Poland or Lithuania. I, Prince Ivan, and my brothers were handed over, and moreover I know very well that not all of the people of the Muscovite realm handed me over, since many people were not aware of what was happening. By the judgement of God my brothers died, but in place of death the most illustrious king has given me life and has ordered me to serve his son, the great sovereign Tsar and Grand Prince Wladyslaw Zhigmontovich, and I have kissed the cross and sworn to do so. Even were the high ambassadors or the king himself to allow me to go into the Muscovite realm, I would not heed them, for I have kissed the cross, not to the king, but to his son." Vasily

Yanov said: "I was sent to the lord king by all the boyars with the ambassadors Prince Yury Nikitich Trubetskoy and Mikhail Glebovich Saltykov, to ask him to grant his son to reign over the Muscovite realm, and I have kissed the cross to him, the sovereign." Prince Shuisky added: "If my brother boyars, taking pity upon us, have sent to bid us return to the Muscovite realm, let them send to our sovereign Prince Wladyslaw, asking him to release us from our oath of allegiance. If he will release us, we will return to Moscow." It is not known how the matter was resolved on that occasion.

EXCHANGE OF PRISONERS

The exchange of prisoners did not take place within the stipulated time. The matter was protracted until mid-June 1619. The Muscovite plenipotentiaries, the very same who had concluded the Deulino truce, were lodged at Viazma, awaiting the arrival of the Polish plenipotentiaries with Filaret, Shein and other captives. Prince Vasily Vasilievich Golitsyn did not live to see his native land. He died on the way at Grodno and at the king's command was buried at Wilno in the Brethren church[46] of the Holy Spirit on January 27. The archimandrite of the monastery, Leonty Karpovich, preached the eulogy on the text: "The hour will come when even those in the grave will hear the voice of the Son of God," but at the base of the sermon lay the pronouncement of the Greek philosopher that human life is like a comedy. The worthy father was in great difficulty. How was he to praise the deceased, in view of what was known about his relations with the king? The preacher resolved this dilemma by refusing to speak of Golitsyn's life because he did not know anything about it, but called upon his listeners to thank God for such a kind king, who had allowed Golitsyn a burial far grander than any he could have had in Moscow. The orator even called upon the deceased himself to thank the king for having prepared for him such a soft bed for such a long slumber! Later Golitsyn's body was removed to its native soil.

When the Muscovite plenipotentiaries learned that Filaret had left Orsha they sent Andrei Usov to him with the following instruction: if he was able to visit with the metropolitan without any guards or Lithuanians he was to ask him, the sovereign,[47] whether he expected to be exchanged soon, whether there would be any delay, whether the Lithuanians had any evil intentions, or whether he expected

to be harmed during the exchange. The sovereign was to authorize
him to report on all this to the boyars, with instructions as to how
they were to deal with the sovereign. Would it be better to exchange
him ahead of the others, or should all be exchanged at the same
time? How were they to negotiate, and with how many people? The
boyars had about three hundred Lithuanian captives with them. He
should be so gracious as to give them precise instructions and all
tidings. The sovereign tsar had ordered the boyars to report concerning this and learn whether he, the sovereign, had suffered oppression or deprivation. Why were the Lithuanians holding up the
exchange, and what were the Polish lords discussing in the Sejm?
But Usov was unable to have a private visit with Filaret. Meanwhile
a suitable meeting place was found. Along the Dorogobuzh road lay
the hermitage of Pesochna, about two versts off the highway, and
below the hermitage flowed the Polianovka stream, and the distance
from Viazma to the hermitage was seventeen versts.

When the Lithuanian plenipotentiaries arrived at Dorogobuzh,
discussions opened concerning the meetings. Here again Gasiewski
complained. The boyars were not acting according to the treaty. The
Lithuanian captives brought for exchange were few, for in Moscow
many were placed in boyar houses and prisons, and the boyars and
gentry had distributed many others throughout their estates and patrimonies. The boyars were acting unfairly, such as had never been
done in Christendom. Other captives had been given away as gifts
to the Tatars in the Crimea, while others had been transported to
Persia or to the Nogay. Can it really be that Christians give Christians away to pagans? In one prison a hundred and fifty prisoners
were being held, and were being baptized forcibly into the Muscovite faith and compelled to kiss the cross to the sovereign. As for
the king's men, the Germans, Frenchmen, Englishmen, Spaniards
and Dutchmen who had been taken prisoner, the boyars were un-
willing to exchange them, and all this was in violation of the ambassadors' agreement.

Gasiewski was told that all his accusations were ridiculous. The
Lithuanian plenipotentiaries called a meeting for May 27 but the
Muscovites refused on grounds that the number of escorts was not
specified. This annoyed Filaret, who told the gentry sent to him by
the plenipotentiaries: "Why have the boyars postponed the meeting
of Wednesday, May 27? We have had enough of living here, we

have endured hardship and captivity for more than a year or two, yet they merely write letters to us and tell you they are suspicious, as a result of which no letter was sent on to me at Dorogobuzh from them. Are we to write further letters to them? I have written to them three times already. The boyars have long known that I have been brought for exchange. If I were not to be exchanged I would not have been brought out of Lithuania, but would have been returned to Orsha."

While emissaries from the Muscovite plenipotentiaries were travelling to Filaret, heralds from the Lithuanian commissioners were travelling to visit Struys in Viazma. During one of these visits Struys got drunk. After the visitor had sat with him a long time, the guard said that it was time for him to go home. Instead of answering, Struys struck one of the guards on the cheek, another in the chest. The visitor got up and left. The guards told Struys: "The boyars, taking pity on you and wishing to do you a favor, sent the Lithuanian heralds to visit you, but you get drunk and strike us, and so disgrace us, gentry of his majesty the tsar. It would not be honorable for us to engage in fisticuffs with you, but we will detail some musketeers from the guard and order them to humiliate you, since you are unable to act in a dignified manner. Tomorrow hardship will overtake you, since henceforth you will not be able to get drunk and make a fool of yourself." Struys became even more angry and reached for his sword. The Polish herald told the guards: "We know him of old in Lithuania. When he is drunk he himself is unaware of what he does in his anger." After this incident Struys's squires no longer were allowed to go to the market for anything, the musketeers had to do his shopping, and they had orders not to buy anything from the tavern. The guards were forbidden to go to him. If the Lithuanian squires started any quarrel with the musketeers, they were to be beaten with truncheons.

On May 30 the plenipotentiaries met. Gasiewski again asserted that the boyars had enslaved and forcibly baptized many Poles and Lithuanians, forced them to marry and kept them in captivity. Prince Dmitry Pozharsky in particular had sent many of his prisoners around his estates, held them in manacles and confined them in captivity. Those released from prison had been turned loose in bitter frost, naked and barefoot, and all had died. The boyars replied that all these allegations were troublemaking and mischief, and declared on their Christian oath that none of this was true. Then the Lithuanian ambassadors demanded new conditions, including free passage past Briansk to the towns ceded to Poland. Sheremetev and his companions did not agree to this demand, since it was a new one, and so the session ended.

The Muscovite plenipotentiaries immediately sent to inform Filaret that the Lithuanian ambassadors were thinking up new clauses and delaying what he, the great sovereign, had ordered, namely discussion as to whether he should be exchanged for Struys and several of his designated companions, and after that to exchange the remainder. Filaret, having heard out the heralds, burst into tears, saying: "God grant that I may see my son the great sovereign and all the Orthodox Christians in the Muscovite realm!" Concerning the new clauses he said nothing, because many Lithuanians were in the tent with them. Then he asked the herald: "Do the boyars have with them any gift from my son, sables or something? I need to reward those Poles who have looked after my health, so if the boyars have any sables let them send them to me this very day." But Tomila Lugovskoy[48] approached the herald and said: "If the boyars send sables, let them price them at half the standard price, and thus we will know all about it here." The boyars fulfilled this demand, selected seventeen times forty sables,[49] discounted the price, and the same day sent them to Filaret.

In order to get things moving the Lithuanian plenipotentiaries sent to the Muscovites, threatening that if all their demands were not met they would not attend the meeting, would return home taking Filaret, and war would break out again. The Muscovite ambassadors replied: "You have come to us with threats, and seek to extort new clauses from us by force, but we cannot do this in violation of our instructions from the great sovereign, and without the counsel of our brother boyars. We do not fear any of your threats. We have many of our own troops at the ready, and they are nearer than yours."

But such bravery was only in words. The plenipotentiaries could not return to Moscow without Filaret, and therefore they added: "We will discuss among ourselves what additional clauses we may concede, and we will write them down and send them to you. But we can do nothing with regard to road and river communications past Briansk to your towns, or the search and return of people and artillery which were previously in the ceded towns, but are no longer there, since these are new matters."

The Lithuanian emissaries travelling back with this answer called upon God to witness that their plenipotentiaries would not effect the exchange without fulfillment of all the articles, and added: "Your people say about you that there are those among you who do not wish to see the most reverend metropolitan in the Muscovite realm, you are not negotiating in good faith, and actually want Metropolitan Filaret Nikitich to be taken back." The ambassadors replied: "You do not say these things of your own accord but at the instigation of your high ambassadors; if you have conjured up such speeches by yourselves it is not befitting us great boyars to hear them, either from you, or from your ambassadors. It would be befitting for you to speak according to your own understanding, for with us in Moscow there is not one man of rank who does not want to see the great sovereign, the Most Reverend Metropolitan Filaret Nikitich."

Meanwhile Shein informed Sheremetev that they should send him his servant, if he was with him in the encampment, or a servant of his *subordinates* the Saltykovs or Morozovs. The plenipotentiaries ordered a servant of the Morozovs (Boris and Gleb Ivanovich),[50] Pozdney Vnukov, to visit the Lithuanian ambassadors in their encampment. On arrival he was ordered to declare himself to the boyar Mikhail Borisovich Shein. The latter, through the noble Korobyin,[51] told Vnukov that the plenipotentiaries must not hinder the exchange because the Lithuanian ambassadors were hoping for the collapse of the peace treaty and the exchange. Therefore the boyars in the camp should be cautious and on their guard.

The plenipotentiaries took panic, agreed to everything, and the exchange proceeded. On June 1 Metropolitan Filaret approached the Polianovka river in a cart while Shein, Tomila Lugovskoy, all the gentry and other prisoners followed the cart on foot. On the Polianovka two bridges were constructed. Over one Filaret was to travel with all the Muscovites, while over the other Struys and all the Lithuanian prisoners were to cross. Approaching the river Filaret sent the Lithuanian Voronets to tell the plenipotentiaries to send Struys ahead to him without any fear, and the remaining prisoners on both sides would be checked against the lists. But the plenipotentiaries feared deceit and refused Voronets, saying: "There is no way we can release Struys before the great sovereign Filaret Nikitich, neither is there time to check all the prisoners individually against the lists since it is already evening, and if both sides are scrutinized this could go on well into the night. We will trust your list, and whoever on the list does not appear, we will send immediately for him in the encampment."

Filaret sent to the plenipotentiaries a second time, demanding that Struys be sent on ahead, and that they need not fear any evil consequences. They released Struys and with table attendants, crown agents, Moscow gentry, residents and select provincial gentry awaited Filaret on foot by the carriage bridge. As soon as Filaret, Shein, Lugovskoy and all the gentry started to cross the bridge, the boyars ordered the Lithuanian prisoners to cross by their bridge. Having crossed the bridge, the metropolitan alighted from the cart and Sheremetev addressed him with the following speech: "The sovereign Michael Fedorovich has ordered us to do obeisance to *thee*, has ordered us to inquire after *your* health, and concerning himself he has ordered us to say thanks to your prayers and those of his mother he is in good health, and is only grieved that for so long it has not been granted to behold the eyes of your holiness his father."

Then Sheremetev conveyed the homage of the tsar's mother Martha Ivanovna. Filaret inquired after the health of the tsar and the salvation of his mother, and then rewarded and blessed Sheremetev and asked after his health. Sheremetev was followed by Prince Mezetsky, who conveyed the homage of the boyars and all the realm. "The boyars, Prince Fedor Ivanovich Mstislavsky and his companions, lords-in-waiting and all the council of his majesty the tsar and all the Great Russian realm do obeisance to you, great sovereign, and await your sovereign arrival with great joy." Filaret blessed Mezetsky and asked after the health of all the ambassadors. The third plenipotentiary, Izmailov, approached Shein on behalf of the sovereign, inquired after his health, and addressed to him this speech: "Your service, your steadfastness and patience, your suffering on behalf of our Orthodox Christian faith, the holy church of God and us, the great sovereign, and of all the Orthodox Christian community of the Great Russian realms, are well known to us.

Concerning this we, the great sovereign, have been solicitous, and have seen to it that you have been released from such great hardship." The secretary Bolotnikov inquired after the health of Lugovskoy and all the gentry.

FILARET RETURNS TO MOSCOW

Filaret spent the night in the encampment because the exchange had taken place late in the evening. The next day, June 2, he ordered dispatched on his behalf a gift to the Poles, both cavalry and infantry, as a token of respect, food—mutton, poultry, wines, mead and fine loaves—and went on to Viazma. In Mozhaisk he was met by Archbishop Joseph of Riazan, the boyar Prince Dmitry Mikhailovich Pozharsky and the lord-in-waiting Volkonsky. Outside Zvenigorod, in the St. Savva monastery, he was met by the archbishop of Vologda, the boyar Vasily Petrovich Morozov and the lord-in-waiting Pushkin. At the village of Nikolskoe, which is on the Peski river about ten versts from Zvenigorod, he was met by the metropolitan of Krutitsy, the boyar Prince Dmitry Timofeevich Trubetskoy and the lord-in-waiting Buturlin. As he crossed the Khodynka river he was met by the Moscow authorities, all the boyars, gentry and chancellery officials. On June 14, before he had reached the Presnia, the metropolitan was met by the tsar himself, who fell to his knees before his father. Filaret did the very same before his son and tsar, and for a long time both remained in this position, not being able to touch each other or speak on account of their tears of joy. Having greeted his son, Filaret sat on the sled, while the sovereign and all the people went on foot ahead of him, Sheremetev and his companions following Filaret.

After Hermogen the patriarchal throne had remained vacant.[52] Filaret was awaited and Patriarch Theophanes,[53] who had come to Moscow for alms, also was awaiting him. Together with the Russian prelates Theophanes offered the patriarchal throne to Filaret, "for they knew that he was worthy of such rank, especially since he was the tsar's fleshly father, and would be a helper and builder to the tsardom, a defender of orphans and an advocate of the wronged." After the customary refusals Filaret agreed, and was consecrated on June 24.

IV

PATRIARCH FILARET
1619–1633

DUAL POWER

With the return of Filaret Nikitich to Moscow there begins a period of dual power. There were two great sovereigns, Michael Fedorovich, and his father, Most Holy Patriarch Filaret Nikitich, and this was not merely a matter of form. All matters were reported to both, were decided by both, foreign ambassadors presented themselves to both together, duplicate documents were given and two sets of gifts were brought. Concerning the relations of the two great sovereigns with each other, we may gain some insight from the correspondence passing between them when one went on pilgrimage and the other remained in Moscow.

Thus, in 1619, Filaret Nikitich wrote to his son: "Concerning the Crimean matter, O sovereign, what do you, great sovereign, command? To me, the sovereign, it appears that the Crimean ambassadors and heralds should be told that you, great sovereign, value friendship and brotherhood with your brother, their great sovereign tsar, very highly. You should dispatch the ambassador with gifts and inquiries, and dismiss them all soon."

In 1630 Tsar Michael wrote to his father: "It is written, O sovereign, in your royal document that you, great sovereign our father and pilgrim, wish to be in Moscow on the Feast of the Trinity. But it is not convenient for you to be in Moscow on the Feast of the Trinity because it is a great and solemn festival, and for this reason it would be impossible to serve you, O sovereign. The roads are too overgrown for your carriage, and it would be unfortunate if there were no people at hand to serve you. Perhaps it would be better if you, O sovereign, were to hear the liturgy at Pentecost in Taininskoe and also spent the night there, and on the next day, the

Patriarch Filaret
Portrait in State Historical Museum, Moscow

Monday, come to us in Moscow in the morning. But let it be as you, our great sovereign father and pilgrim, wish; whatever you desire will be pleasing to us. We pray Almighty God to grant that you, great sovereign, reach our capital city of Moscow and your sacred throne safe and sound, and that it be granted to us to behold your holy, fair and angelic face, kiss your holiness's head and hand, and bow down and do obeisance."

IMPRESSIONS OF FILARET

Even though Michael's name preceded his father's it is understandable that the experienced and strong Filaret had a very large share in the government during the reign of the inexperienced, young and weak Michael. This inexperience and weakness of the young tsar was taken advantage of by people who did not deserve the right to be close to the throne. Things changed completely when Filaret arrived upon the scene. We can accept the assertion that certain people who were used to having their own way with the young tsar did not wish for Filaret to return, because he would set a limit to their arbitrariness. Others, on the other hand, were pleased that the return of Filaret put an end to the troublesome and harmful rule of the many. Hence we encounter among contemporaries two distinct schools of thought concerning Filaret. According to one version, Filaret not only dispensed the word of God but governed the entire affairs of the land, freed many from violence, and under him there were no men of power except the great sovereigns themselves. Those who served the sovereign during the anarchy but were not rewarded, were sought out by Filaret and rewarded, were held by him in favor and could not be disparaged by anyone. According to the other school of thought, Filaret "was of medium weight and girth, knew the Holy Scriptures in part, in disposition was vindictive and menacing, and so authoritarian that even the tsar himself feared him. He subjected boyars and all the ranks in the tsar's council to perpetual imprisonment and other punishments. Towards the clerical estate he was merciful and not avaricious. He administered all matters pertaining to the tsar and the army."

FATE OF MARIA KHLOPOVA

One of Filaret's chief concerns, naturally, was his son's marriage, with which was bound linkage of the throne to his house and the tranquillity of the realm. As early as 1616 the maiden Maria Ivan-ovna Khlopova[1] was chosen as the tsar's bride and taken into the royal household. According to custom they had changed her name, calling her instead Maria Nastasia, probably in honor of the tsar's famous great-aunt,[2] and had begun to call her tsaritsa, when sud-denly Michael was told that her life was in danger, that she was suffering from an incurable disease, and the unfortunate bride with all her family were exiled to Tobolsk. With Filaret's return Khlo-pova began to move closer and closer to Moscow. In September 1619 she was moved from Tobolsk to Verkhoturie, and in 1620 from Verkhoturie to Nizhny Novgorod. But by then Filaret had no thought of taking up Khlopova's cause; he wanted to marry his son to a foreign princess.

SEARCH FOR DANISH OR SWEDISH BRIDE

In 1621 Prince Alexis Mikhailovich Lvov and the crown secretary Shipov were sent to Denmark, to King Christian,[3] with the follow-ing proposal: "By the mercy of God the great sovereign Tsar Mich-ael Fedorovich is reaching the age of maturity, and the time has come for the sovereign to be married. It is known to his majesty the tsar that his majesty the king has two maiden cousins, and to this end the great sovereign amicably declares to his majesty the king that if he wishes to be in eternal brotherhood, friendship, love and alliance and amity with the great sovereign tsar, then his majesty the king should give the hand of one of his cousins who is suitable in this high matter to the great sovereign." The emissaries were in-structed that if they were told that the king's cousin would convert to the Russian faith for love of her consort, but that it was un-befitting that she be rebaptized, because she was also of the Chris-tian faith and had been baptized according to her own dispensation, they were to reply: "It will be impossible for the king's cousin not to be rebaptized, for we have considerable disagreements with all other faiths. Other faiths instead of baptism by immersion practice only the pouring of water, and do not anoint with myrrh. The king must therefore prepare his cousin for this, and dispatch her with the understanding that she must receive holy baptism."

Should the king or his councillors say "Since she is to be married to the great sovereign, let the great sovereign himself persuade her,

for they would not deprive her of her freedom; or let the ambassadors speak of this with the king's cousin," they were to answer that
it was not befitting that they themselves should speak of this to the
king's cousin because her maidenly modesty was to be prized, and
it was unbefitting to speak at length with her because her highborn
honor must be safeguarded. The ambassadors were to further affairs
by speaking with relatives and those close to the bride using all
means, praising the Orthodox faith and thereby bring the bride to
wish to be of one faith with the sovereign and to accept holy baptism. They must be gracious and friendly to those who were to further this end, and according to measure reward them and hold out
hope of reward from the sovereign.

Should the king should enquire whether his cousin would have
separate towns and income, they were to answer: "If according to
divine scripture the two will be one flesh, what is the point of di-
viding their property? All their sovereign possessions will be held in
common. Whatever the sovereign lady wants will be given to her
unstintingly, and whomsoever she wishes to be rewarded shall with
the advice and permission of her husband be rewarded, and those
Danes who accompany her will suffer no need or restriction. But we
hope that there will not be many people attending her. These should
not be numerous because at the great sovereign's court there are
honorable and venerable boyars, and they have many unmarried
daughters."

Should the king agree to everything, request permission to do
obeisance to his cousins and, approaching them, do obeisance in the
customary manner and kiss hands, and bring the queen and the
maidens on their own behalf forty sables or whatever is appropriate,
then view the maidens attentively from afar, noting their height,
countenance, complexion, color of eyes and hair and natural fea-
tures in general, marking any defects. But view from afar and cour-
teously. If the queen calls them to her side, go and kiss the hand of
the queen and the maidens, but do not take their hand, and having
viewed the maidens, leave, and then learn which is suitable to the
great master, whether she is healthy, of fair aspect, without defects
and of good wit. When a choice was made they were to make an
agreement concerning her with the king, asking how much land and
treasure should be conferred upon the bride. But the matchmaking

concluded without result. Under the pretext of infirmity the king refused to speak with Lvov, who in turn refused to discuss the matter with the king's privy councillors.

Another attempt was made. In January 1623 a proposal was sent to King Gustavus Adolphus of Sweden to obtain for the tsar Catherine, sister of Elector George William of Brandenburg, the king's brother-in-law.[4] But differences of religion constituted an insuperable obstacle to that union, for the tsar adamantly insisted that Catherine be baptized into the Orthodox faith of the Greek dispensation. Gustavus Adolphus replied that her princely grace would not depart for the sake of the tsardom from her Christian faith, would not renounce her spiritual salvation, and therefore he, the king, saw that all efforts in that matter were in vain.

KHLOPOVA'S CAUSE REVIVED

When the search for a foreign marriage partner proved fruitless it was decided to take up again the cause of the erstwhile Russian betrothed, who was living in completely good health in Nizhny Novgorod. They summoned Dr. Valentine Bills and the physician Balthser, who through the agency of the royal carver Mikhail Mikhailovich Saltykov[5] served the tsar's betrothed. Bills and Balthser declared that Khlopova had an eating disorder which would be cured shortly. Then they brought Mikhail Saltykov in for questioning. On what basis had he reported to Tsar Michael that Khlopova's illness was incurable? Saltykov prevaricated and contradicted himself, and it was evident from all of this that he had lied. The sovereigns summoned all their closest advisors, Ivan Nikitich Romanov, Prince Ivan Borisovich Cherkassky and Fedor Ivanovich Sheremetev, and in this family council it was decided to send for Maria's father Ivan and her uncle Gavrila Khlopov, to learn further details of the affair. Ivan Khlopov declared that his daughter was quite healthy until the time she was summoned to the palace. She was overtaken then by a fit of vomiting, which had quickly ceased, and subsequently, during her time of exile, it had not recurred once. They asked her confessor, and he told them the same. Finally Gavrila Khlopov came and explained the matter.

On one occasion the tsar and his close advisers, including some of his new Khlopov relatives, went to view the artifacts in the Armory. Among other things they brought the tsar a Turkish saber, which they all praised. Only Mikhail Saltykov said: "There is a wonder! If only master craftsmen in Moscow could make such sabres." The sovereign turned to Gavrila Khlopov, handed him the sabre and asked him what he thought; did they make such sabres in Moscow? Khlopov replied: "They make sabers like this, but not as good." Then Saltykov snatched the saber from his hand and said that he did not know what he was talking about, or he would not speak thus. Khlopov quarrelled with Mikhail and argued so ably with him that from that time Boris and Mikhail Saltykov disliked him. Therefore, when Maria Khlopova fainted, Saltykov declared that her illness was incurable.

MARRIAGES OF THE TSAR

The sovereigns were not satisfied with this and sent the boyar Fedor Ivanovich Sheremetev and Archimandrite Joseph of the Miracles monastery,[6] together with physicians to Nizhny Novgorod to learn for certain whether Khlopova was really in good health. The unfortunate maiden, to Sheremetev's question as to why she had fainted, replied that the illness came upon her by reason of treachery. Her father Ivan asserted that the Saltykovs had poisoned her, giving her as an aperitif some vodka from the pharmacy. But the most wise statement of all came from Gavrila Khlopov, saying that his niece fainted through immoderate use of sweet dishes. Whatever the case may have been, the Saltykovs' wrongdoing was apparent. They were banished to the countryside, their mother was enclosed in a convent, their service tenures and patrimonies were confiscated into the treasury because "they had hindered the tsar's pleasure and marriage." "You did this treasonably (it said in the decree relating to their exile), being unmindful of your oath of allegiance and the sovereign's great favor towards you. But the sovereign's favor towards you and your mother was greater than you deserved. You were rewarded with honor and proximity to the sovereign, to a greater extent than your brethren, yet you accounted this for nothing, did not concern yourself with the tsar's health but solely with your own enrichment, you filled your own houses and enriched your kinsfolk, stole lands and in all matters wrought iniquity, seeing to it that nobody but you enjoyed the sovereign's favor, yet you showed no benevolence or service towards the sovereign."

The fall of the Saltykovs did not return Khlopova to the palace. The tsar declared that even though she was healthy he would not marry her. It is said that the tsar's mother, to whom the Saltykovs were related, declared that under no circumstances would she agree to that marriage. Khlopova as before remained in Nizhny Novgorod, although it was ordered that her rations be doubled. Having refused Khlopova, the tsar married Princess Maria Vladimirovna Dolgorukova, but the young tsaritsa died within the same year. The next year the tsar married Princess Evdokia Lukianovna Streshneva, the daughter of an insignificant noble. The Khlopova affair showed more than anything what was being done in the palace in Filaret's absence, who had been showered with the tsar's generosity and did not wish to see anyone else close to the tsar.

RELATIONS WITH CRIMEANS AND NOGAY

Concerning the foreign relations with which Filaret Nikitich must be concerned after his return from captivity, it was necessary first of all to send gifts to the Crimean khan, although this was very difficult on account of the exhaustion of the treasury after the Polish war. The Muscovite emissary Amvrosy Ladyzhensky wrote to the sovereign: "I ordered the interpreters to find out from the Tatars, Jews and Muslims who came to the tsar's household and are fed by me whether the khan had spoken with his privy councillors, whether he had read the sovereign's letter, and did the khan or his deputy intend to attack Lithuania? The Tatars, Jews and Muslims told the interpreters that the khan, after reading the letter, said that the Muscovite sovereign had postponed his gifts until the winter, had made peace with the king, but had not written to him concerning this. He is deceiving us since he is delaying the sending of gifts until winter, when it is impossible for us to advance upon Moscow. If he does not give us gifts now in summer, neither will he give us anything in winter or at any time in the future, and having gained such a respite he will oppose us in collusion with the king. The khan had ordered his deputy to send his subordinate to advance on Moscow, and to say that he would attack Lithuania by way of the Muscovite realm.

"And I," continued Ladyzhensky, "hearing that the khan was intending to send his deputy against the Muscovite realm, told the privy councillors that the great sovereign would send his emissary across the blue ice with gifts, and having liberated his father and boyars, would order hostilities with the king to be reopened. The sovereign had postponed the gifts until the autumn because they could not gather them together. Moscow had been under siege, and beyond Moscow there were Poles and Lithuanians in many places, many cities from which the state treasury was usually gathered had been laid waste, there was no communication with me, the emissary, during the entire winter, and many tax-paying townsmen and agriculturalists have joined the musketeers and cossacks, and were demanding pay.

"But the privy councillors replied: 'It would have been possible for the sovereign to have gathered gifts from Moscow alone. The Tatars who were in Moscow say that the people there are even richer than before, and if the khan's deputy comes in person before Moscow the sovereign will give gifts soon enough.' I was completely unable to dissuade the khan from his campaign, or from sending his deputy against your sovereign land. Ibrahim Pasha said to me: 'If the sovereign sends gifts and money during the present summer the khan and his deputy will not attack Moscow, but will attack Lithuania. If the sovereign does not now send gifts, I will not be able to restrain the khan. The khan is mortally offended because the sovereign has made peace with the king and has delayed sending presents until winter, and I can barely restrain him.' Having received this report from his emissary, the sovereign ordered money to be collected from the Crimean fund and treasury revenues from all the chancelleries be given, so that nothing be left, and to dispatch heralds as soon as possible, in two or at the most three days."

Even after this the character of relations with the Crimea did not change. The khan on account of the failure to make presents allowed himself to subject the Muscovite ambassadors to indignity, oppression and torment, and extorted from the ambassadors promissory notes for money with threats that he would order them all sold overseas. But the ambassadors were ordered by Moscow to "speak smoothly and correctly and not hastily, and where it is necessary to maintain a stony silence, cover it with smoothness, so that disputes do not arise."

It was also necessary to smooth over relations with the Nogay, who during the Time of Troubles had dissociated themselves from Moscow, transferred their nomadic pasturelands from the Nogay side to the Crimean and made war on the Muscovite border towns.[7] The governor, Prince Alexis Mikhailovich Lvov, and Crown Secretary Ivan Griaziev,[8] who had been sent to Astrakhan as early as 1616, were successful in their mission, brought the Nogay murzas and all the people in the encampment under the tsar's hand in direct servitude and led them from the Crimean to the Nogay side, took as hostages in Astrakhan the murzas, their brothers, children and leading men of the encampments. From the more distant nomadic lands they summoned Alba-Murza, his brothers and cousins, and with them up to fifteen thousand people from the encampments from near Khiva and Bukhara to Astrakhan. They bound them by agreements and ordered them to occupy nomadic pasturelands with the Astrakhan murzas and yurt Tatars. Finally Lvov and Griaziev managed to obtain from the Nogay about fifteen thousand Russian captives.

SWEDISH AFFAIRS

With Sweden there were at first long disputes over the delineation of frontiers. Between the Muscovite realm and the districts ceded to Sweden there was a strong bond, namely unity of faith, and the Muscovite government sought to support it. In 1619 Isidore's successor, Metropolitan Makary of Novgorod,[9] in accordance with the tsar's decree distributed throughout these districts documents of which the model was written in Moscow. In the documents it was stated: "Since you were formerly of our ecclesiastical flock and servants of the Christian faith, I have no wish to cast you off, but desire all the more to unite you to us. Even though you are now under the authority of another ruler, all the same you must not separate yourselves from your spiritual heritage. Therefore I remind you how previously you were sheep of our flock and sons of the church, so now you should stand firm, in nothing abandoning our blessing. Be manly and strong, do not let anything cause you stumble, do not in any way diminish your previous traditions, hold to the holy apostolic faith transmitted to us by our fathers, and by the order of our great sovereign you may travel freely to and from Great Novgorod in matters of the spirit."

The Swedes regarded with suspicion the correspondence between the Novgorod metropolitan and the Russian clergy in the districts ceded to them, and demanded that the metropolitan correspond with the Swedish governors concerning spiritual matters, and not directly with Russian priests. The governor of Novgorod reported concerning this to the sovereign, who replied: "In accordance with our decree we have ordered Metropolitan Makary of Novgorod to write and act concerning priests according to the command and documents of the most holy sovereign Filaret Nikitich. But if according to this decree there should be occasion to write to the Swedish marshal, it will be the task of you, our boyars, to write to the marshal in consultation with the metropolitan. But the metropolitan shall not correspond with the marshal because he is an ecclesiastic and of exalted rank, for whom it is improper to correspond with foreigners."

The Swedes feared most of all lest the Novgorod metropolitan break off altogether spiritual relations with the Orthodox population of the ceded regions, who then would be compelled to flee in hordes into Russian territory. This is why the Swedish government anxiously besought the Muscovite authorities that the Novgorod metropolitan send priests and consecrate churches in Korela and the other ceded regions. Nevertheless the Russian clergy got on badly with the Lutherans, and monks and priests fled to Novgorod. The Swedish authorities, in accordance with the treaty, demanded their extradition. On this occasion the tsar wrote to the governor of Novgorod: "You will not surrender without our decree any monks or parish clergy who live on our side, or any who flee from the Swedish side and appear on ours. If the Swedish authorities write to you to demand them, you are to answer that hitherto on our side they have not been sought out, but when they are sought out we will inform them. Also, you should write to them that they should not inflict hardship or persecution on our people on account of their faith. If they are oppressed and persecuted on account of their faith they will be compelled against their will to flee." In addition the tsar ordered the governor not to detain fugitives in borderland places, but to send them into more central regions or to Moscow.

Of interest also is the tsar's letter to the Novgorod governor concerning fugitives who were not of the clergy. "You are to correspond with the Swedish governors and carry out an exchange of

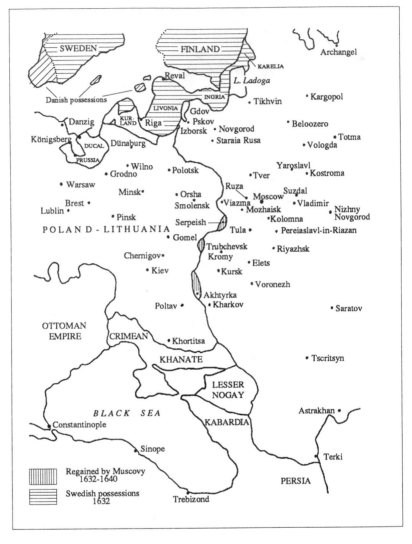

Muscovy and Its Western Neighbors
1613–1645

fugitives, taking into consideration the reason for their exile or surrender, since from our side many fugitives have been surrendered to
the Swedish side, while from their side to ours there have been very
few. Many have not been surrendered but have been kept against
their will, in violation of the peace treaty. Those people whom you
have identified in your investigation on our side, but whose names
are not in the Swedish lists, you are to settle under our protection in
court villages in regions somewhat removed from the frontiers. You
are to give them subsidies and exemption from taxation as you see
fit, according to the nature of the person and the agricultural land.
They are not to live near the frontier, in order that knowledge of
them will not reach the Swedish towns, and nobody will write to us
concerning them. Settle them on our lands in freedom and accustom
them to our favor with kindness, subsidies and tax exemption, so
that they will be eager to settle on our agricultural land. If they are
settled against their will, they will flee back and talk in the Swedish
towns among their fellows. A quarrel will arise and it will be impossible to conceal fugitives."

It was necessary also to act in a similar manner towards those
Russians coming from the towns ceded to Sweden to Novgorod for
the purpose of trade. On this matter the Novgorod governor received the following letter from the tsar: "You wrote that Russians
are coming to Great Novgorod from the Swedish side to trade, and
have petitioned to be allowed to enter the Stone City to the cathedral church of the Holy Wisdom to pray at the tombs of the Novgorod miracle-workers, and that you have no instructions concerning
this. You must order investigations of these people, whether they
have wavered in their faith and were being tempted to the Lutheran
faith. If they are firm in their Orthodox faith, you may allow them
to approach the churches located in the suburbs but not allow them
into the Stone City to visit the cathedral church. If you learn concerning these men that they have wavered in their Orthodox faith,
you are not to allow them into the suburban churches either, and
above all take care that our Orthodox faith is not mocked." It was
permitted for Russians to travel to both sides to visit relatives: "But
take care that Russians do not come to Novgorod for purposes of
espionage."

With regard to the Swedes who had come to Novgorod to learn the Russian language, the governor ordered: "Receive them and order ecclesiastical subdeacons in the suburbs to teach them to read Russian, but unbaptized foreigners are not to be allowed into churches; the subdeacons are to be given strict instructions to this effect. If any of these foreigners wish to be baptized into our Orthodox faith, they are to be baptized; but once baptized they are not to be allowed to return to their own land, and they are to be told before baptism that they will not be given permission to leave our side. They are to be sent to us in Moscow or they may remain in Novgorod. Each may go to whomsoever he pleases, but those who receive these baptized foreigners into their service must give surety for them in writing. Those foreigners who are now studying in Novgorod and wish to go home are to be allowed to leave with their previous documents. Foreigners are to be received to learn our language only if they are sent by their fathers, brothers and uncles, and not such men as will run away frivolously."

Neither side wished to provide a pretext for a breach of relations. Moscow wished to be at peace and recoup whatever forces it could, and this not for war with Sweden. Gustavus Adolphus was occupied in the west. He sincerely desired peace in Moscow, and wished for an alliance with the tsar against Poland. The Zaporozhian Cossacks were in uproar, of which Gustavus Adolphus wished to take advantage. He sent his high ambassadors Bremen and Horn to Moscow with a request that the tsar send his decree to the Zaporozhian Cossacks to detach them from the Polish crown. The boyars replied that this was impossible inasmuch as the Cherkassians of the Zaporozhie were subjects of the Polish king, and between the Muscovite realm and Poland a truce had been concluded.

In 1626 Swedish ambassadors visited Moscow. One was Georg Bengart, while the other, to the amazement of the Russian court, was called Alexander-Liubim Dementievich Rubets, or Rubtsov,[10] and on the way he entered a Russian church. The tsar sent to ask the bailiff what language the ambassador spoke, did he eat fish on fast days, by what authority did the bailiff allow him into a church, how did he stand and pray in the church, and how was he dressed? Rubtsov replied that he was a Russian, had suffered for the Orthodox faith at the hands of King Sigismund and had been imprisoned at Marienburg for eleven years and had been freed by King Gustavus Adolphus. Despite this, in the village of Cherkizovo the bailiff did not allow Rubtsov into the church, but when he arrived at Moscow the bailiffs said to them on behalf of Crown Secretary Gramotin: "It is known that you were once a subject of the Muscovite realm and of the Christian Greek faith, and after that you were a prisoner of the Lithuanian king in Marienburg. Did you hold fast to our Orthodox faith while in Marienburg? Did you not turn to the Roman or other faith, and how do you now hold to the Orthodox faith?" After a satisfactory answer they allowed the ambassador to enter a church. Then he petitioned that he be allowed to see the image of the Immaculate Virgin, be allowed to hear mass in the cathedral church, be granted an audience with Most Holy Patriarch Filaret and receive his blessing. In his petition he stated that he had been imprisoned in Marienburg for the Christian faith, and had not had a spiritual father for a long time; therefore the patriarch might instruct that he be given the reserved sacrament wherever the opportunity arose, whether on the road or at the time of death, so that he could take communion, for Most Holy Patriarch had known him in Marienburg. He was admitted to the Dormition cathedral, where he visited with the patriarch.

Rubtsov strictly speaking did not come as an ambassador to the Moscow court but with the aim of setting out through Muscovite territory to Belorussia and Zaporozhie. In his letter the king informed the tsar of his successes in Prussia against Sigismund of Poland, and added: "If your majesty the tsar wishes to take vengeance for the great injustice committed by the Poles against your land and subjects, your majesty the tsar could never choose a more opportune time, because the Tatars have invaded the Polish land on one side, and we have invaded it from the other. We think that a certain great sovereign might invade Lithuania on a third front. We declare this to your majesty the tsar amicably for the sake of the friendship which exists between our two rulers." The boyars answered: "The great sovereign rejoices that King Gustavus Adolphus has taken towns from his enemy, and he will always be glad to hear that your sovereign has defeated his enemy the Polish king utterly, and has conquered his lands. The king is sending Alexander Rubtsov to Belorussia and Zaporozhie. It will be impossible to allow

Alexander transit, because a truce has been made between the Russian realm and Poland. The great sovereign takes in good part the sound advice to avenge himself upon King Sigismund, and he will consider it, but now, during the years of the truce, it is impossible inasmuch as this would be violation of a solemn oath and a sin upon his soul. But if the king commits the slightest injustice before the expiry of the period of grace, the great sovereign stands ready to attack the Polish king, and will correspond henceforth with King Gustavus Adolphus concerning this matter." With this the ambassadors returned home. Patriarch Filaret sent letters to the archbishop of Tver and metropolitan of Novgorod, in order that in their eparchies they permit Rubtsov to enter the churches, because he had suffered in Marienburg for the Orthodox faith, had been sentenced to death and that he, the patriarch, had witnessed his sufferings.

Involved in the great struggle for Protestantism against the house of Habsburg, Gustavus Adolphus at the beginning of the year 1629 sent to Moscow his ambassadors Monier and Bengardt with a declaration that "in the past year God had aided him against the Polish king, and it was possible for him to lead his army unhindered through the whole of Poland were he not impeded by the Holy Roman emperor and the papist conspiracy, for they had come nigh with a great force and were besieging the strong commercial city of Stralsund, which stood upon the Baltic Sea.[11] His majesty the king, to protect himself and his great realms, and also his many neighbors and coreligionists, had come with a great army to help and relieve that city, and in this he succeeded. It is truly well known to your majesty the tsar that the Holy Roman emperor and the papalists had subjected to themselves the majority of Protestant princes in Germany and had taken the best harbors in Denmark, Mecklenburg and Pomerania. There they now very busily are preparing to gather the next year a great and mighty armada in the Baltic Sea, and with it not only hinder trade but also subjugate neighboring realms such as Sweden, Prussia and Denmark to themselves and to papal servitude. His majesty the king is mindful of the fact that your majesty the tsar earlier bethought himself how great a danger hung over his head and that of his realm. As soon as the Holy Roman emperor and the papalist conspirators get hold of the Swedish land they will seek the ruin of the Russian people and the eradiction of the ancient Greek faith. Thus you must give thought to this as soon as possible. Evidently you do not intend to open war before the expiry of the years of truce with the Polish king; but the poor and oppressed people in Denmark and Germany need help! His majesty the king wishes to act with all his forces. Such a large army needs supplies, but grain has not grown in Sweden on account of the heavy rains. Thus the king is requesting permission to buy in your lands and convey to his army fifty thousand measures of rye and other provisions. And if your majesty the tsar wishes to promote peace by money or grain, Almighty God will reward your tsardom more highly than other lands. The pope, the Holy Roman emperor and all the house of Austria are seeking means to become rulers of the entire universe, and now they are very close to achieving this aim. And when we see our neighbor's house on fire, we must help him put it out, in order to preserve our own property. It is now time for your majesty the tsar to take thought how to help your neighbors and protect yourself."

The boyars replied: "The great sovereign has reflected with us at great length on this, and wishes to wreak revenge upon the Polish king for his injustices, to assist your sovereign and other Christian realms of the Protestant faith by every means, to prevent the evil intentions of the Holy Roman emperor and the papalists from reaching us, and to help all of you. Let the king only write how much provision he needs, and the great sovereign will order it purchased free of tolls in any year when there is a favorable harvest. The sovereign has ordered his subjects to trade with your sovereign's subjects freely, without tolls on any goods".

When negotiations concerning matters of state were concluded the ambassadors presented complaints from Swedish merchants. In the Novgorod customs house they did not receive proper accounts, but merely were told: "Put down your money, we will count it out." When the Swedes drew up their own accounts it appeared that they were being greatly overcharged. The Swedes could not walk about the streets because people shouted at them, calling them sprat eaters and chicken thieves and various other insulting words. From Narva, Izhora, Oreshek and other borderland places drivers could not travel to the Russian towns because heavy tolls are exacted from them. Swedes are not being allowed to learn Russian in the Russian towns. Musketeers, standing by the gates, do not allow Russian merchants to visit the Swedish merchants in their hostel.

Early in 1630 the same Monier came a second time to Moscow with news that Gustavus Adolphus had concluded a truce with the Polish king in order more conveniently to concentrate all his forces against the Holy Roman emperor, and with a request to buy free of duty grain, groats, pitch and saltpetre. The tsar sent word that he was not angry at the king for his truce with Poland, for it had been concluded out of necessity; he repeated that from his side he would not await the expiry of the truce and would move to take vengeance upon the Polish king for his injustices, only he would ask Gustavus Adolphus to keep this matter secret. Concerning the king's request, normally it would not be advisable to sell so much grain at short notice because that year the grain harvest was short, but out of friendship and love he would permit the purchase of 75,000 quarters of rye and four thousand quarters of millet duty free. The Swedish sovereign thanks to this great friendship has been in amity and good counsel with his majesty the tsar. It was permitted further to buy two hundred barrels of groats, and also saltpetre where they could find it.

The following year, 1631, permission was granted to purchase for the king fifty thousand quarters of grain. That year there first appeared at the court of Moscow the Swedish agent Johann Meller. Explaining the role of the agent, the king wrote to the tsar that Meller would supervise all relations more easily and with fewer hindrances, and that similar officials resided with other great kings and sovereigns. Meller was to report to the boyars concerning various rumors concerning the intentions of Poland and of the Catholic powers in general against the Muscovite realm. Among other things, the agent reported that in Smolensk it was being said that as soon as the Poles opened hostilities nearly all the boyars' slaves would flee to the Polish side, as they would be glad of freedom. The agent also related the words of his sovereign: "If his majesty the tsar could look into my heart he could guess how much I wish him well." He declared that in the event of war between the tsar and Poland the king would give him two of his own regiments with good commanders. At the same time the Swedes, striking fear into the Muscovite court at the dangerous machinations of King Sigismund and Emperor Ferdinand,[12] assuring them that Gustavus Adolphus and his army were the bulwark of the Russian realm, their vanguard regiment fighting in Germany for the Russian realm, persuaded the tsar to allow passage for two Swedish emissaries to the Zaporozhians to incite them to rebellion against Poland. The emissaries received these instructions: to declare to the cossacks the Swedish king's goodwill towards them, a favorable disposition based upon the struggle against their common enemies and the persecution which people of the Greek faith had suffered from the Jesuits along with the Protestants. The king personally wished to reward them, having heard of their military exploits. Reckoning them to be friends of faith and freedom, the king by this token considered them to be enemies of the pope, the very antichrist, and the king of Spain, who wished to deprive all peoples of freedom. The emissaries were to declare to the cossacks that King Gustavus Adolphus would reward them much more handsomely than the Polish king, demanding nothing but devotion to himself, and therefore they should send plenipotentiaries into Livonia for definitive negotiations. Finally the emissaries were to hint at two services which Gustavus Adolphus expected from the cossacks, namely to assist him at the election of a Polish king, and to send their army into Austrian territory.

In August 1631 in accordance with the instructions of the great sovereigns an inhabitant of Putivl, Grigory Gladky, was summoned to the Chancellery for Foreign Affairs and asked whether he could conduct from Putivl to the Zaporozhian Host two foreigners sent from Sweden to the Zaporozhians, and where they should be led, whether to Kiev or some other Cherkassian town. Gladky replied that the Zaporozhian Cossacks were living in various towns but when they were called to service they rallied wherever they were summoned, but mostly they gathered in Maslov Stav, about a hundred and fifty versts from Kiev, but this settlement of Maslov Stav was deserted. If the sovereigns wanted him to travel with these foreigners to the Cherkassians, he was ready to go. If he was asked on the way who they were and where they were going, he would reply that they were going to the Zaporozhian hetman, but for what reason he did not know; he had merely been hired to drive a cart with provisions. He would then conduct the foreigners to the trading settlement of Wisniowieck, where Zaporozhian Cossacks were living, and when the foreigners said they were travelling to the hetman the cossacks would conduct them to Hetman Timokha Arendarenko,[13] who was living in Konev, or would bring them as far as Kiev. But the sovereigns sent word to Gladky that he should be so good as to take the foreigners to Kiev, to Bishop Isaac of Lutsk,[14] and to Porfiry and Andrei Boretsky, brothers of Metropolitan Job,[15] who would find a way to the Zaporozhian Host, but they were not to deal with Hetman Timokha or the cossacks serving the king.

Gladky set off with the foreigners and in October returned to Moscow with the news that since neither Bishop Isaac nor the Boretskys had been in Kiev to meet them the foreigners had hired some monastic servitors to take them by way of the Dnieper to the new hetman, Ivan Petrizhitsky-Kulaga, whom the cossacks had selected to replace the former hetman, Arendarenko. A week later Andrei Boretsky had arrived. Gladky had given him the sovereigns' letter and questioned him about the previous letters. Boretsky took the sovereigns' letter and wished personally to take it to the Zaporozhians, and concerning the previous letter said that Bishop Isaac of Lutsk, on the occasion of the burial of Metropolitan Job Boretsky, had given both documents, those of the sovereigns and of Patriarch Cyril of Constantinople,[16] to Peter Mogila, archimandrite of the Caves monastery,[17] but so far Peter had not forwarded them to the Zaporozhian Cossacks. When he, Boretsky, had reminded him, Peter had replied: "These letters are enough to get you impaled," and after that Boretsky dared not raise the matter again. Soon news arrived in Moscow that Hetman Kulaga had placed the Swedish emissaries under arrest and had informed Hetman Koniecpolski of this.

RELATIONS WITH ENGLAND

In entering into close relations with Sweden it was necessary to reckon with England, which considered it had a right to the gratitude of the Muscovite government for even having made close relations with Sweden possible. The complicated situation of the Muscovite government had not ended with the Stolbovo peace because at the time of its conclusion a menacing cloud was gathering over Moscow from the direction of Poland. In July 1617 the noble Stepan Volynsky and Crown Secretary Mark Pozdeev[18] were sent to England to express thanks for the assistance in peace with Sweden, and requesting help against Poland. The ambassadors were to ask

King James to communicate to the Danish and Swedish kings and the rulers of the Netherlands the request that they ally with Moscow against Poland inasmuch as it would be impossible for King James himself to send his army against Poland due to the great distance. There were certainly reasons for the Danish and Swedish kings or the rulers of the Netherlands to oppose the Polish king. He was seeking to deprive the Swedish king of his realm.[19] The Danish king was related to the elector of Brandenburg[20] and Prince Wilhelm of Courland, and the Polish king wished to annex the whole of Prussia and expel Wilhelm from Courland.[21] He was corresponding with the pope about the rulers of the Netherlands, wished every misfortune upon them, desired to interfere with their faith and the faith of the English, and spoke all varieties of unbefitting words about their sovereign.

The ambassadors were to insist that the English king immediately assist the great sovereign with money, demanding two hundred or one hundred thousand, or at the very least eighty or seventy thousand rubles, but not to accept less than forty thousand. Were the ambassadors asked to give a solemn oath that the tsar would repay the king, they were not to agree to this pledge, pleading the absence of instructions to this effect, and petition the king to send his own ambassadors to Moscow. They must point out that Tsar Fedor had sent a large sum of money to the Holy Roman emperor, although there had been no written agreement between them. As a last resort they could give a note and ask for cash in the form of reichsthalers and gold pieces, to pay the soldiers sooner. Finally the ambassadors were instructed to insist that the young men sent during Godunov's reign for instruction be sought out by all means and returned.[22] After being handed over they must be held very correctly and subjected to no oppression and hardship lest they flee, and be reassured about everything.

As a result of this embassy, in 1619 the English ambassador Dudley Digges[23] arrived in Archangel with money, but he evidently learned of the siege of Moscow by the Poles, and returned to Kholmogory, handing the matter over to the noble Finch and the commercial agent Fabian Smith, who set out for Moscow. The tsar at first did not receive them as ambassadors because they were not mentioned in the king's letters of conduct, but later he received them. An interim payment of twenty thousand was taken from them, with a promise to pay it back.

When the war with Poland was concluded Merrick arrived in Moscow in July 1620 and was received by the tsar and patriarch. The patriarch sat alongside the tsar to his right, his velvet seat was moved together with the tsar's seat, but the image over the patriarch was a special one with a torture chamber; to the right of the patriarch near the window stood a cross on a golden orb. The metropolitans, archbishops and bishops sat to the right of the patriarch, while the boyars, lords-in-waiting and upper gentry as before sat to the left of the sovereign in golden robes and black hats. On the right hand, in the place of the lord-in-waiting, not far removed from the clergy, sat the lord-in-waiting Nikita Vasilievich Godunov and the treasurer Trakhaniotov,[24] because Godunov had met and announced the ambassador, while Trakhaniotov had announced the gifts. Godunov, when announcing the ambassador, had addressed both sovereigns, but kissed the ambassador's hand only on behalf of the tsar. The ambassador directed his speech to both the tsar and the patriarch. The patriarch listened to the speech, stood, bowed in the customary manner and asked after the king's health, and the tsar arose at the same time at his father's prompting and the ambassador presented two documents, one for the tsar and the other for the patriarch. Merrick spoke to the tsar and patriarch separately (calling the tsar his imperial majesty), saying that the king was pleased at the conclusion of peace with Poland and the freedom of Filaret. Then he gave duplicate presents to the tsar and the patriarch. The tsar was given a crystal salt cellar, inlaid with gold, precious stones and jewels, a unicorn inlaid with gold, a silver lion and ostrich embellished with gold, five gilded silver goblets, two silver flagons inlaid with gold, a wash basin and an ewer of gold inlaid with silver, a stone vessel with a golden lid and saucer, various silken materials and cloth, two Indian parrots and a wild Indian antelope; for the patriarch crystal dishes inlaid with gilded silver, four goblets with gilded lids, an ewer and a wash basin of silver inlaid with gold, velvet, a globe and armchairs upholstered in cherry-colored velvet, embroidered with gold thread.

During discussions with the boyars Merrick declared that Dudley Digges had brought a hundred thousand rubles to help the tsar, yet

Finch and Smith had not handed over the money. He had given only a small portion of it, forty thousand reichsthalers or twenty thousand rubles. The king, when he sent the money, requested no promissory note, ordering the ambassador to speak only of a confirmatory letter with the tsar's seal. Then Merrick complained that English merchants had suffered great losses, namely 144,000 rubles, on account of the Time of Troubles from plunder, and because the impoverished people were not buying their goods and, finally, because the Russian coinage had depreciated. Previously the ruble had been equal to fourteen English shillings, but now the ruble was worth no more than ten shillings. Apart from this they had suffered losses from embezzlement of merchants' money by factors and servants, who also had betrothed themselves or married Russian natives, or who had entered the tsar's service, and purposely had become Russian subjects in order to defraud the English merchants and avoid rendering account to them.

Consequently Merrick was requesting that no factor or servant be permitted to marry or enter service in Russia without the permission of a leading English merchant. They must first travel to England to settle accounts with their employer and only then be allowed to enter the tsar's service. Finally Merrick once again requested passage along the Volga to Persia. Again the sovereign summoned the leading Muscovite merchants, told them of Merrick's request and added that in exchange for passage to Persia the English would give appropriate aid to the treasury. "The sovereign tsar and the most holy patriarch have commanded that you, the leading merchants, be informed of this, and that it also be declared to you that you all know very well that on account of our sins the Muscovite realm is suffering all manner of scarcity because of war, and the state treasury is depleted. Apart from customs and tavern duties, none of the sovereign's money is being collected, for tax exemption has been given to the towns. We formerly collected for the treasury fifths, and tallage from you, the leading merchants and traders, but we have ceased this on account of your financial difficulties. Yet servicemen, cossacks and musketeers have arrived in the towns, and we must pay them every year. The tsar's expenses and petitions from servicemen, gentry and boyars have increased, but we have nothing with which to pay them. If for our sins some enemy attacks

us the treasury is not prepared, neither can we gather it from anywhere. Yet if we grant the English merchants passage to Persia, will
this not cause hindrance and impoverishment for the Muscovite
leading merchants and traders?"

"We do obeisance for the great sovereign's favor," the leading
merchants responded. "In answer to the question whether we should
grant passage for the English merchants to Persia, let the great sovereigns do as they please. We, the leading merchants and traders,
will speak according to our best understanding, only let the sovereign show mercy and not lay his disfavor upon us for speaking
plainly." The boyar Prince Ivan Borisovich Cherkassky and the
crown secretary Gramotin told them to speak frankly without fear,
and they questioned each of the leading merchants individually in
detail. The leading merchant Ivan Yuriev said that if the English
were allowed passage along the Volga to Persia the sovereign and
the Russian merchants would suffer losses, because many traders
from Moscow and the lower towns were travelling to Persia. They
came from Moscow, Yaroslavl, Kostroma, Nizhny Novgorod, Kazan
and Astrakhan. From each barge arriving at Astrakhan a toll of four
altyns per ruble was exacted.[25] Should the English begin to travel to
Persia, these barges will cease to come to Astrakhan. If the English
are charged duty there will be great profit to the sovereign's treasury, but business will be taken away from our traders, because they
cannot compete with the English. If only because the sovereign
would derive great help from it, the English could pay a heavier
duty. Let God and the sovereign decide that. But they personally
could stand to contribute to the tsar's treasury for a while, even
though this might entail a loss.

The leading merchant Grigory Tverdikov[26] said: "The sovereign
may do as he pleases, but as the leading merchants see it, the tsar is
considering this out of necessity. Let the tsar order the English to
trade only with their own overseas goods, and not deal with the
Persians in Russian goods. Russian goods go there, such as sables,
bone, fish teeth, bales of linen, and Russian leather. They also bring
into Russia reichsthalers from the German realms, which bring great
profit to the sovereign and also to them, the merchants, the exchange on reichsthalers being very profitable. But if the reichsthalers go to Persia the sovereign's treasury will suffer loss and

depletion. Reichsthalers and old Muscovite coinage will be paid for Persian goods, and silver will be scarce in the Muscovite realm, causing hindrance and scarcity to our traders."

"When the ruin of the Muscovite realm occurred," Grigory Nikitnikov said, "and it was thought that it would be conquered by the Polish king, the Dutch immediately sent one hundred thousand rubles to the Lithuanian king that he might grant them exclusively passage to Persia. Even should the English now give generously into the sovereign's treasury the tsar may do as he pleases, but it would be fruitless to grant passage to Persia without receiving anything in exchange. It would be more profitable for the sovereign to negotiate simultaneously with the English and the Dutch, who will bid against each other. It would be unthinkable to charge them only a small duty, since as a result the Muscovite traders would lose their business to them. The sovereign should not think of this since the whole land would present a petition that we exact heavy tolls for the Persian trading route and thereby enrich ourselves, and the sovereign obtain greater revenue."

Rodion Kotov[27] stated that "Our brethren are afraid that as soon as we grant the English passage to Persia their commerce will become established, but it is difficult to guess how this trade will affect us. Should they engage in both the wholesale and retail trade, it will be each for himself. At present in the town of Archangel there is unequal trade. At first humble people arrive with insignificant wares and trade in them, and then they come with larger merchandise and also trade in them. The lesser merchants do not remain so, and each trades according to his measure, as happens there. If some Persians trade with the English in Persia while others visit Astrakhan, can we exclude only the English from the Persian market? There are many eager traders in Persia who are after Russian goods."

The remaining merchants were against allowing passage unless the English gave more money into the treasury. They also said that the merchants from Yaroslavl and Nizhny Novgorod must be asked, for they did the most business with Persia.

As a result of these answers the boyars asked Merrick what goods the English merchants would be taking to Persia. What would they buy there, and where would they sell these goods within the

Muscovite realm, or would they export them beyond the sea? What profit would there be in this for the sovereign's treasury, what duties would they pay, or how much money would they give into the treasury? Merrick replied that they would take to Persia cloth, reichsthalers, tin ore and other English goods, and in Persia then would buy raw silk, dye, rhubarb, muslin, calico, precious goods and taffeta. But these goods, which they would bring into the Muscovite realm and then export, would not be expensive."

"This may be so," said the boyars, "but what profit is there for the sovereign's treasury, since the trade will be in Persia?" Merrick replied: "If his majesty the tsar orders the building of a hostel and marketplace for traders of other countries there will be a great increase in the customs dues." The boyars asked: "What duties would the English pay?" "I have had no instructions concerning this," Merrick replied. "But if you boyars think that your treasury and people will suffer losses as a result of our trade with Persia, I will cease to speak about it, for my king does not wish the sovereign and his people to suffer any losses."

In this manner the subject of customs dues demolished the whole matter at one blow, inasmuch as the English were hoping to take their goods to Persia duty free. They spoke of other matters. The boyars answered Merrick's complaint that the new coinage was minted lighter in weight: "After Tsar Fedor Ivanovich there was in the Muscovite realm much unrest, much devastation and laying waste of lands, the tsar's treasury was exhausted and the number of servicemen multiplied and they could not be paid. Christian sovereigns of neighboring countries gave no aid. Thus against our will the coinage began to be minted lighter so that the sovereign would have money for reconstruction and to pay his servicemen. This is also nothing new; this has happened in many countries in wartime. Not only did gold and silver coins become more expensive and lighter than before, in many countries trade also was conducted with copper or leather coinage, and now copper coinage is in use almost everywhere. But as soon as any country returns to normal, so also does the currency. The English merchants have begun to sell their goods more dearly than before. Under previous sovereigns they sold gold-washed silver for three rubles an ingot, and pure silver for two and three quarters, yet now they charge five rubles or more for an ingot and the silver they bring in their vessels is not the purest, but is mixed with copper, and the cloth they bring is also worse than before. Less is supplied, it is shorter in length and when it is soaked it shrinks, but the price is higher by half. The English merchants are not the only ones arriving in the Muscovite realm, but also traders from other lands, yet they do not demand any exchange for their money."

"I swear upon my life and honor," Merrick answered, "that the silver is not worse than before. Concerning the cloth, the king has given strict information that cloth is to be made well, and manufactured according to previous standards. The king does not wish to live by deceit." With regard to receiving English factors and servants into their service, the boyars replied: "We do not take foreigners into the tsar's service against their will, nobody is forced to marry, and nobody is forced to stay against his will. But if anyone petitions the tsar to be taken into his service, the great sovereign does not insult him, shows kindness to all foreigners and does not drive them from the tsar's favor. Thus during the reign of Boris Fedorovich young junior boyars' sons were sent to England for learning, and were detained there against their will, and Nikofor Alferiev abandoned our Orthodox faith and, who knows by what temptation, became a parson. The king must immediately send them back, lest brotherly friendship and love be broken." Merrick replied that one had died, and two others were in India. When they returned, they would be sent on; but Nikofor had declared that he did not wish to return to Moscow and the king would not allow him to be sent against his will. "Besides, we cannot talk about that," added Merrick, "since I do not have any instructions on the matter."

Merrick requested that a special guardian for the English merchants be appointed from among the boyars. To this they replied that the Chancellery for Foreign Affairs alone was, and in the future, would be responsible for the English merchants, and the conciliar secretaries of the foreign chancellery would report to the tsar. Merrick requested the tsar to return the twenty thousand rubles sent to him by the king to aid him against the Polish king. The request was based upon the fact that the king was short of money, and must help his son-in-law, Frederick, count palatine and king of Bohemia.[28] The money was handed over. Concerning the waste lands previously demanded by Merrick, he himself dropped the request. "His majesty the king has decided that it is unbefitting to cultivate land in a strange country."

FIRST FRENCH AMBASSADOR TO MOSCOW

As soon as the business with the English was concluded the French arrived with the very same demands. As early as 1615 the tsar had dispatched to France his ambassadors Ivan Kondyrev and the crown secretary Neverov with the announcement of his accession to the throne and with a request for aid against the Poles and Swedes. "We have sent to you," it said in the sovereigns' letter, "to inform you of our accession and to declare to you the wrongs of King Sigismund and of past and present Swedish kings. And you, our beloved brother, great sovereign King Louis, should assist us, the great sovereign whenever you can."

Naturally Louis XIII offered no assistance. But in the autumn of 1629 there arrived for the first time in Moscow a French ambassador, Louis Deshayes de Cormenin.[29] According to the tsar's command the governor of Novgorod sent his bailiff Okunev with a horse to meet him. The bailiff wanted to ride to the ambassador's right hand, but he would not travel on the left or move from the meeting place. The bailiff told him that the sovereign had been visited by Turkish, Persian, German and other ambassadors, and all had travelled on the left. The Frenchman replied that Turkey, Persia and Crimea were not Christian countries, whereas the king was a Christian, and therefore he must not travel on the left, and he had instructions about this from the king. The bailiff asked him why he had not made this plain before setting foot on the sovereign's territory. The ambassador replied that he did not know the Russian custom, and therefore he had not written. He wished to return to Yuriev in Livonia, got off the horse which the governor had sent him, left the transport on which he as travelling and mounted a cart, saying that he had been insulted and would die as a result. He was told that no one was allowed to depart the sovereign's land without the sovereign's permission. "If I am not allowed to leave," he replied, "I shall stay where I am and buy food and drink with my own money; but I will not ride on the left." And he stayed there until nightfall.

Finally the Frenchman saw a way out: let him be accompanied by two bailiffs. One would ride on his left side, the other on his right, while he would ride in the middle. Okunev, after consulting the archbishop of Pskov, agreed, and himself rode on the right-hand side of the ambassador while on the left rode a junior boyar disguised as a bailiff. Okunev reported that the French, while travelling along the road, subjected the sovereign's bailiffs to violence and insults, but the ambassador did not call them off, and they did not heed the bailiffs.

Arrived in Moscow, the ambassador petitioned that the sovereign order them to be given French and Rhenish wine. The sovereign had sent them gifts and drink, but they were not accustomed to this kind of beverage. They also requested to be supplied with vinegar. Wine and vinegar were given. Then he demanded that when presented to the sovereign he wear a sabre, since Kondyrev had worn a sabre in the presence of his king. Also that when pronouncing his majesty the tsar's title he be allowed to keep his hat on. He also demanded carriages. All these demands were refused.

In reply the boyars first of all pointed out that in the king's letter the tsar's title was not written out in full. The ambassador replied: "In my sovereign's realm it has been the custom from the beginning that in letters to all great sovereigns their names and titles are not written; also the names and titles of our own sovereign are not written, and we cannot introduce any novelties." The boyars said: "Why was a document dispatched with Kondyrev, in which the tsar's name and style was written in full?" The ambassador replied that the king had ordered this done at Kondyrev's request. "And if the sovereign's title is to be written as it is spoken, there are many places which we cannot remember written in the title." The boyars said that until now such a formula had not been used by any sovereigns. The ambassador replied: "If it is pleasing that his sovereign should write the sovereign's full title every time the tsar's name is mentioned, he would bow his head at the mention of the name of God and the king."

When the dispute over titles ended the ambassador declared his articles. (1) The king wished to be in firm friendship and love with the tsar. The king would not object to whatever was pleasing to the tsar in his own realm, whether goods or armed forces. (2) Trade between subjects of both countries was to be free of both customs and duties. (3) French merchants in the Muscovite realm were not to be deprived of their freedom or kept in confinement. They could maintain priests and teachers of their own faith. They were to have a headman and he was to regulate them in all matters. (4) In the West there was the house of Austria which included a special prince (the king of Spain), a friend of the Holy Roman emperor and of the imperial family, and they were allied to the Polish king, and gave him considerable aid. This Austrian prince was the enemy of the French king, and the Polish king was the tsar's enemy. These princes derived profit from the fact that they sent trading expeditions into the eastern land and thereby helped the Polish king. Thus if the tsar were to be in friendship and love with the French king, and would order the French to be given free trading privileges in the Muscovite realm, its sovereign would do harm to the house of Austria and deprive them of their eastern trade. Their power would be diminished and they would cease to aid the Polish king. (5) His majesty the tsar should allow the French to travel to Persia through his realm. The tsar and his subjects would derive great profit from this. The English, Dutch and Brabançons bought goods in France, sold them at great price in the Muscovite realm, and only brought very ordinary goods, whereas the French would import goods of the very best quality and sell them at the proper price. Whereas, his majesty the tsar is the head and leader of the eastern lands and of the Greek faith, and King Louis is the leader of the western land,[30] if the tsar and the king are in friendship, love and unity, the forces of the tsar's enemies will diminish. The Holy Roman emperor and the king of Lithuania were united, so the tsar and the French king should be friends and be in alliance against their enemies. The French king was the friend of the Turkish sultan. Knowing the latter to be our friend, and that his majesty the tsar is the leader of Orthodox Christendom of the Greek faith, the king had instructed his ambassadors in Constantinople to assist in all matters those Russians and Greeks who came to them in Constantinople. Such great sovereigns as the king of France and his majesty the tsar are everywhere renowned. There are no other such great and mighty sovereigns, and all their subjects obeyed them in everything, unlike the English and the Brabançons, who all did just as they pleased. They bought up cheap goods in Spanish territory and sold them at high prices in Russia. The French, on the other hand, would sell everything cheaply.

The boyars answered, refusing exemption from duties and transit to Persia, saying that French merchants could buy Persian goods from Russian merchants, except for forbidden goods such as white salt and saltpetre. They also refused to let the French have teachers of their own faith, on grounds that other foreigners in Moscow did not have them, even though the ambassador asserted that there were twelve Greek churches in Paris, and that the French were accustomed to going to their confessors four times a year, and could not be without their spiritual fathers. Thus Cormenin went away without obtaining anything.

DUTCH EMBASSY

On the heels of the Frenchmen, Dutch ambassadors arrived in August 1630. These were Albert Conrad Burgh and Johann Veltdril. They petitioned the great sovereigns Michael and Filaret to show favor to Dutch traders, and declared in the name of the States-General and Prince Frederick Henry of Orange,[31] that they had commenced hostilities against the king of Spain and his advisers, the pope of Rome and the Holy Roman emperor, who sought to introduce the accused papalist faith everywhere, and eradicate the Orthodox Christian faith. They were also hostile to his majesty the tsar. Thus the States and Prince Frederick Henry had ordered them to declare to his majesty the tsar that they wished to be in friendship and alliance with him, and wished to increase their trade within the Muscovite realm. When they were in friendship with his majesty the tsar and their trade increased, there would be great harm done to the papalists. The Dutch carry on trade in Lithuania, in Dantzig they buy charcoal, potash, linen and hemp at high prices and pay the Polish king heavy duties, and there is great gain for the Lithuanian traders, but it is known to the States and Prince Frederick Henry that these goods enter Lithuania from the Muscovite realm. His majesty the tsar must therefore decree that Muscovites should not export goods—potash, linen and hemp—to Lithuania, but instead send them to the town of Archangel, and the Dutch would buy these goods from them; there would be great profit to the tsar's treasury, and the Polish king would suffer a further loss of one hundred thousand reichsthalers, and his subjects be without trade and in scarcity. When his majesty the tsar agreed to this, the States and Prince Frederick Henry would strictly forbid their subjects to send their ships to load in Dantzig, but instead proceed to Archangel.

Besides this, the States and Prince Frederick Henry bade them declare that his majesty the tsar had shown favor to foreigners, had bidden them buy grain, but all this grain was now in Holland. Foreigners sold it to the Dutch in Archangel and took a great profit for themselves at double the price. The tsar must allow the Dutch to come to Archangel and to Moscow for free commerce with Russian traders, and take from them moderate duties, such as are taken from other foreigners. Their high mightiness the States also commanded them to request his majesty the tsar and his holiness permit the export of grain and saltpetre to the Netherlands, as much as possible, in exchange for which the States would seek the tsar's subjects to import from the Netherlands all manner of goods, money and munitions, and afford all manner of aid to his majesty the tsar.

The ambassadors were told that it was impossible to allow so many nameless Dutch traders to do business in Moscow and other towns because the sovereign's subjects would suffer great oppression and loss from this. Therefore they, the ambassadors, must inscribe the names and number of the Dutch who wished to trade in Moscow and the other towns, since the English do not have many people there. The sovereign and his holiness the patriarch instructed the Dutch to keep in Moscow an agent as the English did. Concerning the sale of potash, linen and hemp exclusively to the Dutch, it was stated that when the Dutch had an agent in Moscow who could negotiate with the Muscovite traders, and the Dutch might buy these goods in Moscow and specified towns.

"We have heard by rumor and we know for certain that the Muscovite realm has extensive lands," the ambassador said, "and has much soil on which to grow grain, but which is uncultivated. If your majesty the tsar and your father his holiness the patriarch will allow Dutch traders to come in great numbers, some of them who are skilled in agriculture may, if they wish, petition the great sovereign to be allowed to cultivate these abandoned lands. The Dutch would cultivate such lands according to their own method and produce many articles, as is their custom. From this the tsar's treasury will derive great profit in the form of duties, and the Muscovite traders stand to gain much. From Sweden, from the West and East Indies and Holstein came emissaries who ask the States to allow Dutch traders and various people to come and cultivate abandoned lands. This the States did not permit, but they have ordered us to request of your majesty the tsar that various Dutch people be permitted to enter the Muscovite realm for trade and agriculture."

In the Council it was decided to refuse permission to cultivate, and to allow no one to enter except those traders specifically listed. The proposal to sell grain and saltpetre exclusively to Dutch merchants was declined also. The sovereigns ordered that only 23,000 quarters of rye of the grain consigned to Astrakhan be sold to the Dutch ambassadors. The amabassadors requested permission for the Dutch along the Dvina river and in the town of Archangel to fell trees and buy from Russians large oak or pine timbers and build ships from them in Archangel, and to export other timber home beyond the sea. This was granted on condition that the Dutch hire Russians to fell trees, and that they buy only from Russians.

Finally the ambassadors asked that the Dutchman Ernest Phillips and his company be allowed exclusively to trade with Persia for thirty years by way of the Muscovite realm, and in return the company would pay annually fifteen thousand rubles into the tsar's treasury. The answer was that this was impossible. The English king had been refused because of the petition of the traders of the Muscovite realm. The boyar asked the ambassadors: "Have you instructions on anything besides trade?" Replied the ambassadors, "We have no instructions about anything besides trade, but trade is a weighty matter. In all realms sovereigns derive great profit from friendship, but their subjects derive profit from trade." To this the boyars replied that "Friendship and love between sovereigns derives not through trade alone."

DANISH AMBASSADOR

Following the Dutch there appeared the Danes with the very same proposal. In June 1631 the plenipotentiary Danish ambassador Malteiul Gizingarski arrived in Moscow to conclude peace terms and with representations (1) That between both states there should be free trade. (2) In 1630 the Danes had been permitted to purchase three thousand shiploads of grain. The grain had been purchased, but not in full. Could the remainder be purchased duty free, and henceforth no duty charged on grain? (3) That the Dutchman David Nikolaev be permitted to act as agent for the Danish merchants, and be given a charter granting him the status of leading merchant.[32] (4) That Danish merchants be permitted free passage to Persia. (5) That he, the ambassador, be permitted to inspect the tomb of Prince Johan.[33]

The ambassador was told that the boyars had no permission to grant passage to the shah's lands. Concerning the agent, there would be a ruling after peace had been concluded. Grain purchases would be permitted over three years to a maximum of 75,000 quarters of rye, 25,000 a year. Let it be so. The request for duty-free trade was refused. Concerning the question of concluding peace, the tsar would send his ambassadors to the Danish king. The boyars appended a complaint of their own to their reply. In 1623 six Danish ships had sailed to the sovereign's land, to the Kola anchorage, and had massacred the tsar's subjects, and furthermore the Danes said this was done at the command of their king to recover the belongings of the foreigner Klim Yuriev, who had come to the Kola fort in 1620. This foreigner Klim Yuriev, while at the Kola fort, had committed brigandage, spoke unbefitting words about the sovereign and his land, picked many quarrels and intended without the tsar's permission to travel to Pustozersk. Because of this he had been taken temporarily to Archangel, an inventory had been taken of his possessions, and he had been allowed to depart overseas and his goods returned to him.

The ambassadors petitioned that in the future they be allowed to buy more grain than previously, that the duties levied on grain be returned and not charged in future. In answer they were told that it was impossible to predict how good the grain harvest would be, or how high the prices. Instructions were given not to charge duty on the unpurchased grain to be exported in 1632. Finally, the ambassador returned to the principal matter. "I was sent," he said, "to conclude peace, and do not understand why this matter has been referred to other ambassadors who are being dispatched to Denmark." The boyars replied that he had been sent alone, without colleagues, and therefore the tsars could not kiss the cross before him alone at the conclusion of peace, since things were not done in this way. The ambassador replied that everywhere his king sent only a single ambassador, and he was acccredited according to the king's documents. But in Moscow it was feared that conclusion of peace with Denmark might harm friendly relations with Sweden, and therefore the boyars answered the ambassadors: "We cannot conclude any agreement with you because you have received no instructions about the tsar's friend King Gustavus Adolphus. Does King Christian wish the same friendly relations with King Gustavus Adolphus as with our sovereign?" The boyars proposed to draw up memoranda of agreement and kiss the cross to the ambassador, that neither side would commit provocations, harm or injustice against the other, pending signature of a permanent peace. The ambassador agreed, but when the time came to draft the document a quarrel arose. Under no circumstances would the ambassador agree to place in his copy the king's name after the tsar's, and so he was dismissed without a document and without a reply "on account of his obstinacy." At his farewell audience he was not permitted to say anything in his defense. He was allowed an audience with the tsar, but there was no bench for him. Thanks to his obstinacy the tsar and patriarch did not permit him to sit down, and he did not have a table.

EMBASSY TO DENMARK

Following this obstinate man, in December 1631 Muscovite ambassadors, the nobles Vasily Korobyin, Ivan Baklanovsky[34] and Crown Secretary Griaziev, set off for Denmark, with instructions to insist that the tsar's name be written before the king's. Should they say that the Swedish king in his documents wrote his name before the tsar's, they were to reply: "The Swedish king is his majesty the tsar's friend, he has shown our great sovereign much friendship, love and justice. Our great sovereign is moved with respect to the Swedish king by his imperial friendship and love on account of his many favors, and furthermore peace was concluded with the Swedish king at a time when the Muscovite realm was in ruin and the Swedish king in all things seeks the honor and exaltation of his majesty the tsar."

A grim reception awaited the ambassadors. In Copenhagen they were lodged with a merchant, the house was poor and cramped, and they could not get any rest. There was nowhere to store their supplies or shelter their retinue. Many sentries were posted outside the ambassador's lodging, soldiers with weapons kept a strict guard over them. The sovereign's men were not allowed out of the house, and nobody was allowed into the house to visit the ambassadors. The ambassadors asked the interpreters what this meant. They replied that these hardships were inflicted by reason of the complaints of Ambassador Malteiul and especially the interpreter Klim Blom, who allegedly on their arrival and departure had been greatly insulted, had been confined, had suffered shortage in everything and had been dismissed empty-handed. After receiving them the king did not invite the ambassadors to dinner, but instead sent food to their lodging. Furthermore the king's secretary declared that they, the Danes, would first drink a toast to the king, and afterwards to the tsar and then to the patriarch, following the Muscovite custom of drinking to their own sovereign first. The ambassadors did not agree, and did not drink to the king's health. The Danes drank alone and afterwards the ambassadors did not propose a toast to the tsar.

They began to discuss a definitive peace treaty. The king did not agree that his name be placed after that of the tsar, the ambassadors were dismissed merely with letters expressing amicable sentiments, and thus they achieved nothing.

HUNGARIAN EMBASSY

In 1630 there arrived in Moscow ambassadors from Bethlen Gabor, who called himself king of Hungary.[35] These were two Frenchmen, one Charles Talleyrand, marquis d'Assedeville, the other Jacques Roussel. The latter slandered his companion before the Muscovite government, accusing him of evil intentions, and the unfortunate d'Assedeville was placed in custody at Kostroma. The duke of Soissons, who took an interest in the fate of d'Assedeville, asked the English king, Charles I, to plead with the Russian tsar for his release. The king agreed and together with Frederick Henry of Nassau sent documents concerning this matter to the tsar and patriarch in 1632. The Frenchman Gaston de Charon brought the documents, and he received the following written reply for the English king: "Bethlen Gabor, king of Hungary, sent his ambassadors to us. He wrote of friendship and love in his letters, saying that he had delegated to us his ambassadors, Charles Talleyrand, whom your majesty describes as now being a marquis, and Jacques Roussel. When these ambassadors were with us news came that King Bethlen Gabor had died, and his ambassador Charles wished to depart our realm to the Spanish king, wishing to embroil the Turkish sultan, Murad[36] with the Spanish king. But since we are in friendship and cordiality with the Turkish sultan, we ordered this Charles to stay in our Muscovite realm temporarily, lest he embroil the sultan with the Spanish king. So now, until we have corresponded with Sultan Mur-ad and thoroughly investigated this matter, we cannot release him." In 1635 King Louis XIII himself sent to Moscow a letter in which he asked the tsar to release Talleyrand. The request was granted.

RELATIONS WITH PERSIA

We have seen that Tsar Michael initiated very amicable relations with Shah Abbas of Persia, who even sent money to help him. In 1618 Prince Mikhail Petrovich Boriatinsky,[37] the nobleman Chicherin[38] and Crown Secretary Tiukhin were sent from Moscow to Persia with thanks for the aid sent, and also with a request for even more money to pay soldiers in the event of war with Poland. These ambassadors received a dry reception. The shah ordered the junior member, Crown Secretary Tiukhin, to be brought to him, and he had to listen to a stern lecture against the usual treatment accorded in Moscow to foreign ambassadors, a treatment against which European governments already had strongly protested. Abbas told Tiukhin heatedly: "I order you to tell this word for word to your sovereign, and see to it that you do not conceal a single one of my words, so that there may not be confusion or quarrels between us. I will fulfill your sovereign's request and desire, and send him money from my treasury, but I am annoyed at your sovereign for this reason. When my ambassadors were with him they were penned in their quarters like cattle in Moscow and in the towns of Kazan and Astrakhan. Not a single person was allowed out of the house, they were not allowed to buy anything, and musketeers were placed at the gates. I shall also order such a guard to be placed upon you, and shut you up so tightly that not even a bird will be allowed to fly in.

Not only will you not see a bird, but not even a bird's feather. In another matter your sovereign shows me lack of love. Your governors in Astrakhan, Kazan and other towns cause our traders to suffer losses. They take tolls from them two or three times as much as before, and not only from my traders, but even from my own personal goods, and forbid goods to be purchased on my behalf. One petty matter concerns a hawk which one of my traders purchased for me in Astrakhan. The governors took the hawk away from him, and imprisoned the Tatar from whom he had bought it for trading in forbidden goods! You have brought me from your sovereign some birds as a present, but I shall only take a feather from each, and set them all free. Let them fly where they will. And if in my lands any official causes your traders to suffer loss, I will immediately order his belly ripped open."

After that the ambassadors were not dismissed for a long time. Prince Boriatinsky died in Persia, but Chicherin and Tiukhin returned in 1620 together with the shah's ambassador Bulat Bek. In the letter given the latter the shah wrote: "We desire that between us great sovereigns there should be friendship, love and unity as before. And if you are concerned about something which happens in our realm, you must declare it to us, and cheerfully we will do your bidding. You write to us of friendship, love and unity, and we wish for nothing but friendship and love." The ambassador declared to the boyars concerning the shah's wish that the tsar order towns to be established in the Kumyk lands,[39] so that between the shah and the tsar there shall be no other neighbors, and both shall be formidable to their enemies. The ambassador also complained about wrongs committed against Persian merchants by governors, customs officials and interpreters.

The conciliar secretary in turn complained about the poor welcome accorded the Muscovite ambassadors Prince Boriatinsky and his companions. He further complained that the shah's soldiers were laying waste the lands of Iberia[40] and Georgia, despite the fact that these lands were Orthodox and under the authority of the Muscovite sovereign.[41] With this Bulat Bek set off.

Meanwhile the wretched crown secretary Tiukhin paid dearly for having gone to the shah on his own and for having listened to his lecture. When Chicherin and Tiukhin from Astrakhan informed the tsar how their business had fared in Persia, the sovereign spoke with the boyars, saying that Tiukhin, by visiting the shah alone without his companions was acting in violation of previous customs to an extent unheard of, and therefore must be suspected of wrongdoing. As a consequence of this suspicion the sovereign ordered a trustworthy nobleman sent to meet the ambassadors. He was to intercept them on the road from Kazan and Nizhny Novgorod, take Tiukhin's possessions and letters from him, make an inventory and reseal them, and send Tiukhin himself to Moscow. Despite the fact that Chicherin and the interpreter vouched for Tiukhin, proving that he had visited the shah against his will, the boyars found various other sins and passed the following sentence: "For this and all the other things, because Mikhail Tiukhin was alone with the shah, and went up to his bailiff Hussein Bek in the forecourt and called him his brother, took with him Polish and Lithuanian prisoners of war from the Moscow jail, and in Persia received into his service a Little Russian cossack who had apostasized to the Muslim faith, he is to be interrogated rigorously, for it is known that he did this for the sake of wrongdoing and treason, or at someone's instructions." The unfortunate was given seventy strokes, was twice reprimanded and was burned with hot pincers on his back, but he did not confess to wrongdoing or treason. Concerning the Lithuanian prisoners of war he said that they had been given to him according to the regulations on presentation of the petition. He had received the Cherkassian lad into his service in Persia to act as an interpreter. The bailiff had called him brother (*kardash*), and he had reciprocated without any evil intention. Despite this the boyars sentenced Crown Secretary Tiukhin to be sent for his wrongdoing and treason to Siberia, and to be imprisoned in one of the lesser Siberian towns.

The Muscovite ambassadors dispatched to Persia in 1621, Korobyin[42] and Kuvshinov, got quite a different reception from that accorded to Boriatinsky and his companions. Abbas showered them with favors, raising his hands and eyes to heaven, and said: "My realm, my people and my treasury are all not mine, but belong to God and the sovereign Tsar Michael Fedorovich. God and the great sovereign may do as they please with it all." In 1624 the shah's ambassadors Rusan Bek and Bulat Bek brought Patriarch Filaret a valuable present, Christ's seamless garment, stolen from Georgia.

But neither the Persians in Moscow nor the Russian ambassadors in Persia fared well. The tsar complained to the shah about Rusan Bek, saying that he had done many unbefitting things and had behaved disrespectfully to the tsar's majesty, and Rusan paid for this with his head. Muscovite ambassadors Prince Grigory Tiufiakin, Grigory Feofilatiev and Crown Secretary Panov[43] arrived in Persia together with Rusan. The shah complained about them to the tsar, because when they arrived in Persia he, Abbas, was outside Baghdad and had asked the ambassadors to send some gefalcons there. This they did not do and then proposed to send him two or three live birds, but instead sent him birds' tails and feathers. Master glaziers accompanied them from the tsar to the shah but these craftsmen were not sent to him when the shah demanded them. They did not present themselves to the shah on grounds that they could not appear together with other ambassadors. When the shah summoned them to the square to view equestrian exercises, they did not obey, and did not appear. Finally they did not come to the shah wearing the clothes he had presented to them.

In all these matters the ambassadors had acted according to the letter of their instructions, and the boyars declared to the shah's ambassador that Tiufiakin and his companions were not to blame. Despite this, the tsar believed the shah when he said they had angered him, and ordered severe punishment to be inflicted upon them. In fact disfavor was placed upon the ambassadors because, when at the shah's table and the tsar's health had been drunk, they did not drain their cups. For this they deserved to be executed, and sentence was pronounced, but the tsar, at the intercession of Tsarevich Alexis and in response to the plea of his father, Patriarch Filaret Nikitich, ordered that they merely be imprisoned and their service tenures and patrimonies confiscated. Apart from these charges, another offense was discovered. In the town of Ardebil Prince Tiufiakin had ordered the theft of a Tatar youth, whom he sold in the Kumyk land, and also in the Kumyk land he ordered a maiden stolen and secretly abducted her, placing her on his vessel.

V

RELATIONS WITH POLAND
1619–1634

FLAWS OF THE DEULINO TRUCE

Even after the Deulino peace no relations existed with Austria. Early in 1632 Emperor Ferdinand II's ambassador approached the border but was not received because his suite was composed of Poles, with whom a breach was already impending. The Chronograph[1] which, as we have seen, is not very favorably disposed towards Filaret Nikitich, reproached him for allegedly being to blame for a second Polish war because he wished revenge upon the Poles for the privations he had suffered at their hands. We have no way of defining Filaret's feelings with regard to Poland, but we must point out that whatever these feelings may have been, war was inevitable.

The Deulino truce was agreed to in Moscow because means were lacking to wage war successfully. The desire was for respite, no matter how slight, to recoup forces and release the sovereign's father from captivity. But it was impossible to remain for long in the position Tsar Michael was placed by the Deulino truce. Wladyslaw had not renounced his rights to the Muscovite throne, nor would the Polish government grant Michael his proper title; and this against a background of incessant clashes, which disrupted relations between the two realms. The Russians could not enter into proper relations, because they demanded that the Polish authorities in their documents name Michael Fedorovich as great sovereign, and they refused. But the refusal alone was not a significant matter measured against the fact that several of them dared write unbefitting expressions, insulting him and casting aspersions on his election! Was, in addition to this, Filaret's vengefulness needed to reopen hostilities at the first available opportunity?

ANNOYANCE AT POLISH GOVERNORS

As early as September 1619 the tsar's governors of Viazma had written to the king's governors of Dorogobuzh complaining that they did not term Michael as tsar. "We, according to our instructions and to justice," they responded, "ascribe the title of tsar to the great sovereign Wladyslaw Zhigmontovich of All Russia, and henceforth we will ascribe it to him since God has given it to him, and has confirmed it in your souls, the souls of the Muscovite nation, of all ranks. Are you acting justly in that you are calling Michael Fedorovich Romanov sovereign of Moscow, insulting your own legitimate sovereign? We will not dispute with you or begin a quarrel since the Lord God will carry out His will. The high ambassadors spoke at length about this great matter when they established the present peace, but they did not agree and were not reconciled on this matter, nor did they abandon the title and rights of the prince to the Muscovite realm, and even though they agreed to leave the matter to the judgment of God it was Almighty God himself who began and concluded this matter concerning which it was inscribed in the truce documents. Therefore we await God's judgment."

In 1619 the boyars sent the emissary Kireevsky[2] to the lords of the Polish Council with a document, in which they wrote: "You, lords of the Council, should beware, and refrain from reopening and put out of your minds this matter which is past, closed and abandoned, and on account of which much Christian blood has been shed. God did not grant the realm to your king's son, so you must not describe Prince Wladyslaw as sovereign of a realm which is not his. As for what you write in your missive concerning Prince Ivan Ivanovich Shuisky and Yury Trubetskoy,[3] alleging that they stand firmly in justice, serve the prince and receive kindness and favors from him, it is known to us that you are detaining Prince Ivan and others and not permitting them to return to the Muscovite realm, and you have done this in violation of the ambassadors' agreement. As for the prince's kindness and favors to Prince Ivan and Prince Yury, we also know that Prince Ivan goes on foot and serves at his own expense, and at times is assigned to guard duty or service with the haiduks. Prince Yury is slightly better off, he is a little more highly esteemed, only he frequently treads in fear of your Polish squires."

PRINCE IVAN SHUISKY RETURNS TO MOSCOW

The Polish lords replied that in accordance with their petition the king had ordered Prince Shuisky to be allowed to leave for Moscow. But with regard to the principal matter, discontent was growing in Moscow. The boyars dispatched to the conference at Polianovka[4] were given the instruction: "In the towns ceded to the Lithuanian side traitors to the Muscovite realm were made governors: Larka Korsakov in Dorogobuzh, Yushka Potemkin in Serpeisk, Ivashka Meshcherinov in Nevel. They write missives to the sovereign's governors concerning various matters but it is unbefitting for the governors of his majesty the tsar to correspond with traitors. When the boyars are in conference with the Polish lords they must tell them that in the ceded towns there are traitors to the Muscovite realm appointed as governors, who are discourteous to all the Muscovite realm. If they are placed in the border towns, quarrels and disturbances will be inevitable."

QUARRELS BETWEEN RUSSIAN AND POLISH GOVERNORS

This representation was not acted upon and in August 1620 Meshcherinov forwarded a document to the governor of Velikie Luki in which the name of Michael Fedorovich was written without the sovereign title. The governor reported this to Moscow and received thence a document, which was to be sent to Meshcherinov on behalf of the Velikie Luki town official. In the document it was stated: "You write unbefittingly in your missive, you write about the great sovereign without the sovereign title, which is not only boorish on your part, but also improper in taking away from the great sovereigns the honor accorded to them by God. His majesty the tsar's governor is amazed at your colleague, in that he writes unbefittingly, not safeguarding the state of peace. As for you, fiendish cur, we cannot expect anything else since you have forgotten God, the Orthodox faith and your native land. What good can be expected of you? On account of your brigandage you will suffer not only the judgement of God in the next life, but also condign punishment in this world. It will not be long before you, perjurer and apostate, base haiduk and rustic boor, will be slain in a tavern or some other place thanks to your evildoing."

Not only did governors, alluding to the terms of the peace, refuse to call Michael Fedorovich tsar, they even demanded that Russian governors not call him tsar, and hurled insults at him and cast aspersions on the legitimacy of his election. The Lithuanian governor of Serpeisk wrote to Khitrovo, Muscovite governor of Mosalsk: "You write to us documents not according to the peace treaty; you exalt your Michael as tsar as if you did not know, you yourself and this Michael, that all the Muscovite realm has kissed the cross to our prince. Peace has been concluded between realms, and not with Michael. Kireevsky journeyed to Lithuania not on behalf of Michael, but on behalf of the lords of the Muscovite council!"

Governor Miron Veliaminov of Kaluga[5] answered that missive thus: "From your letter it is obvious that you are not of noble birth, but the bastard of an unlettered knave. According to your unlettered, utterly base and simpleminded nature you expect us to revile our great sovereign like fiendish curs. It is unbefitting for you dogs to open your mouths to utter blasphemies against the Lord's anointed."

This document elicited an even sharper reply: "You describe Michael Romanov, a subject of the sovereign Tsar Wladyslaw Zhigmontovich of All Russia, whom the brigands and cossacks, in conjunction with Kuzma Minin, placed upon the Muscovite throne without consulting you, the boyars and nobles. He is not now sitting upon his own throne, but one which of old has belonged to sovereigns and sons of sovereigns, not of monks."

"You presently call your ruler king of Sweden,"[6] Veliaminov replied. "You dishonor the king and his children with quarrelsome and unlearned speeches. Of old you have done with your sovereigns as you pleased. They bear you no malice because you thrust them upon the throne and then cast them down, as you did King Henry,[7] and then you poisoned King Stephen,[8] who wished to rule over you as befits sovereigns. Also previously the great sovereign Patriarch Filaret Nikitich in secular life was a great senator and privy councillor. God denied the great realm to your Wladyslaw on account of the injustices committed by his father and by him, on account of your blatant lies and greed. Henceforth Wladyslaw will never see the Muscovite throne. He may wander through strange lands and perhaps disappear, or his stepmother[9] may dispatch him to the next world, or his maternal uncle, which would be nothing new for you."

The Serpeisk governor was not slow to reply in kind, the insults flew faster and quicker and the matter finally came to blows.

THE POLES THREATEN THE SOVEREIGN

The boyars sent the Polish lords a copy of the Serpeisk governor's document, declaring that they would not tolerate such things, and demanded punishment for such insults. The lords replied that they had not violated the peace in any way and informed them that pretenders were at hand, although the king did not look favorably upon them. "You yourselves know that from your Muscovite nation there are several who call themselves sovereigns' sons, who again are distributing documents and summoning free people to them, corresponding with the Zaporozhian and Don Cossacks, and following the example of Dmitry desire to advance on the Muscovite borderlands in arms. On account of this there has been much unrest in your borderlands, but the king has given strict instructions that none of his people dare join them."

Concerning Tsar Michael, the Polish lords replied that he was inscribed in the truce agreement as Michael Fedorovich, and not as sovereign, for Wladyslaw had not renounced his rights. Concerning the Serpeisk governor's documents, the Polish lords replied: "We have read through and seen that copy, which is how soldiers and servicemen, who do not know the proper written formula in which to write to foreign realms, write in plain words."

In October 1620 emissaries Alexander Sliezen and Nicholas Anforowicz came to Moscow on behalf of the lords of the Council with the same words: "Wladyslaw has not renounced his rights to the Muscovite throne, and has not released any of you, including Michael Fedorovich whom you now call your sovereign, from your oath of allegiance." Again the Polish lords wrote describing rebel conspiracies to threaten the boyars, wishing to demonstrate that it was in the king's power to restrain or loose a pretender upon the Muscovite realm. "At the time," wrote the Polish lords, "when the commissioners at Orsha were paying off the army, they led him apart from the army and proposed a new design. They began to spread among the army documents in the name of Tsarevich Ivan Dmitrevich of Moscow,[10] in writing and with the Muscovite seal. In these documents it was written that he was alive and was asking

Sigismund III of Poland
Contemporary Engraving

that the soldiers, remembering his father's generosity towards them, should come to the Muscovite land and help him gain his patrimony, the Muscovite realm, and he promises them a fair reward. Many in the army believed this, and wanted to enter his service, but the commissioners persuaded them with many words that this was a hoax, and threatened them in the king's name not to have anything to do with this criminal undertaking. All the father's sons heeded them, and dispersed to their homes, but several cossacks and squires went to the Zaporozhian Cossacks urging that together they lead this Ivan into the Muscovite land. The king immediately sent missives to all the borderland places, and to the Zaporozhians sent a menacing command that they all disperse from the borders."

TURKS URGE WAR ON POLAND

Polish affairs were in this state when in August 1621 a Turkish emissary, a Greek named Thomas Cantacuzene, arrived in Moscow. If we are to credit the report of the French ambassador in Constantinople, De Césy,[11] the Byzantine patriarch Cyril, the Dutch emissary and several Turkish magnates were instrumental in arranging this embassy. Sultan Osman[12] wrote that he was attacking the Lithuanian king. In order that the tsar might take advantage of this opportunity to avenge himself upon the Poles and strengthen his friendship with the sultan, he must also attack the king with all his forces. Grand Vizier Husayn was sending a personal message to his beloved friend, the Muscovite king, that the time had come to gird up bravely for war, and that the tsar must not let slip this opportunity. Patriarch Cyril of Constantinople wrote in a similar vein to Filaret Nikitich. Cantacuzene declared in the name of the sultan: "Rumor has come to us that your son sent a subsidy to the Polish king, and himself wants to go. He should not have done this, but should ally himself with us against the Polish king. And when the sultan conquers the Polish land and captures towns, he will give the Russian towns, Smolensk and others, to your son as a free gift. It is well known to the great sovereign your son and to you, great pastor—continued Cantacuzene—that in the German lands, in the domains of the Holy Roman emperor, there is great strife with the Lutherans, and many lands have fallen away from him. In Hungary and Transylvania, Sultan Osman has placed Bethlen Gabor, in Wallachia the son of the governor Mikhna and in the Moldavian land my father-in-law. He has ordered them to oppose the emperor and prevent him from aiding the Polish king. The emperor is now left to his own resources and cannot defend himself. Sultan Osman expressly sent me here as a man of the Greek faith, in order that you might believe all I say and will rely upon my sovereign in all things. He truly resisted the Polish king for ten years and even went on campaign, and sent me from his journey there. Also Patriarch Cyril of Constantinople ordered me to urge your holiness strongly that his son ally with the sultan and not send help to the Polish king. I pledge my soul to the sovereigns that Sultan Osman wishes to be in firm fraternal friendship with your son and wants to ally against the Polish king."

"The boyars have concluded a truce with the lords of the Polish Council," Filaret Nikitich replied, "and several towns have been ceded to Lithuania. My son ordered this truce to be concluded solely for my sake. There is now neither correspondence nor amity between my son and the Polish king or his son. It is impossible to forget their injustices and the ruin of the Muscovite realm, since we have only to look upon it. Should the Polish king violate the peace in the slightest way, my son will send the army against him for the sake of the sultan's love, and the troops are ordered to be at the ready. My son has not given, nor will ever give, any help to the Polish king against the sultan. In order that the sultan may trust my word in this, let the Most Holy Patriarch Cyril assure him that our word will never change." With that Cantacuzene was dismissed.

THE ASSEMBLY OF 1621

On October 12, 1621 there was an Assembly before the great sovereigns in the great golden Palace of Facets. At the Assembly there were three metropolitans, those of Novgorod, Rostov and Krutitsy, archbishops, bishops, archimandrites, abbots, synodal elders, archpriests and all of the Holy Synod. The boyars were present—Prince Fedor Ivanovich Mstislavsky and his companions, the lords-in-waiting, councillors, table attendants, crown agents, Moscow nobility, crown secretaries, residents of the capital, provincial gentry, selected chancellery officials, captains, hundredmen and junior boyars of all the towns, leading merchants, tradesmen, Don atamans and cossacks and men of all ranks of the Muscovite realm.

The great sovereigns spoke of the injustices and perfidy of the inveterate enemy of the Muscovite realm, King Sigismund, his son Wladyslaw and the Poles and Lithuanians. "King Sigismund has violated the terms of the peace. From many of the Lithuanian border towns officials write not according to the ambassadors' agreement, they call Prince Wladyslaw tsar of All Russia, and many incursions are made from the Lithuanian side. In the regions of Putivl, Briansk, Velikie Luki and Toropets, Lithuanians have begun to invade the sovereign's land. They establish forts and trading settlements, appropriate villages, hamlets, forests and waters, they extract saltpetre at seventy places in the Putivl region, they catch fish and kill all manner of wild animals, they attack borderland gentry and junior boyars, kill them, chase them from their estates and do not release all their prisoners, but keep them in captivity and humiliation. From Serpeisk the Lithuanian officials in their missives do not write in a seemly manner, with many insults such as would not befit even those curs, or even their king.

"Because of the evil intention of the Lithuanian king, in the past year the lords of the Council delegated to the sovereign's boyars their emissaries and in their documents they wrote in an improper manner deliberately aimed at a breach of the peace. The sovereign's name was written without the sovereign title, and they separated the sovereign from the genealogy of the tsars. They forbade Tsar Ivan Vasilievich to be described as his grandfather, or Tsar Fedor Ivanovich as his uncle.[13] And if King Sigismund and the lords of his Council do not set these wrongs to right, the great sovereign, begging favor from God and according to his father's blessing, on behalf of the holy churches of God, the Orthodox Christian faith, his own honor and of all the people of the Muscovite realm, will oppose the Lithuanian king and his son, regain his honor and avenge the wrongs committed against all the people of the Muscovite realm.

"And now Turkish Sultan Osman has sent to both great sovereigns his ambassadors, to the end that they should unite against their common enemy the Lithuanian king, and the Crimean tsar also would attack Lithuania. King Gustavus Adolphus has sent word more than once, seeking an alliance against the Polish king. And they, the great sovereigns, still being solicitous of Christendom and not wishing to see bloodshed, have ordered the boyars to send a document from themselves to the lords of the Council concerning all these matters. If the lords of the Council return the herald to the boyars empty-handed, if they write the sovereign's name without the sovereign title, or write unbefitting words, if they describe the prince as tsar and do not set harmful matters right, the great sovereigns no longer will endure such injustices and will correspond with the rulers of Turkey, the Crimea and Sweden, and will send their army against Lithuania. But if the Polish king now keeps silent, and the lords of the Council in their decline lessen their pride and injustice, when they are subjected to war and oppression from the Turks, Tatars and Swedes, then later, when they obtain the slightest relief from their enemies, all the more will they plot against the Muscovite realm.

"There is also another danger. If the great sovereigns do not now ally with the Turkish sultan, the Crimean tsar and the Swedish king against the Polish king, they could invoke great hostility from the Turks, Tatars and Swedes."

The Assembly petitioned the sovereigns, for the sake of the holy churches of God, their sovereign honor and their realm, strongly to oppose their enemy. And they, the Holy Synod, would pray to God for victory and peace while the boyars, lords-in-waiting, etc., and all the servicemen would be glad to fight on behalf of their sovereigns and their realm, not sparing their lives. The gentry and junior boyars petitioned the sovereigns to reward them too, and order them to be mustered in the towns. Everyone who was capable must serve, and not one man must be among the defaulters. The leading merchants and traders petitioned that they would be glad to contribute money to aid the sovereign's treasury, as much as they were able, according to their means.

PREPARATIONS FOR WAR

As a consequence of all this the boyars, gentry and crown secretaries were sent throughout the towns the muster gentry, junior boyars and foreigners, as many as were fit for service. On the third day after the Assembly the herald Borniakov was dispatched from the boyars to the Polish lords with this missive: "If henceforth you do not write the name of our great sovereign according to his royal dignity, and abuse him, and if your border governors do not write the sovereign's name according to his royal dignity, and not as in the present diplomatic documents which your ambassadors have taken from the Muscovite ambassadors, and if your ambassadors do not address our ruler as great sovereign and describe the prince in every place as prince and not tsar, and if the prince is not described according to the ambassadors' agreement, then we his majesty the tsar's boyars, declare to you for the last time that we, the boyars and all the people of the Muscovite realm, no longer will tolerate this and, beseeching God's favor, will defend our sovereign's honor and avenge the wrongs you have committed against us."

On February 2, 1622 Borniakov returned from Lithuania and brought the boyars a missive from the Polish lords. In the document the king's name was written not according to the customary style, but with additional titles and claims. Concerning the prince it was written that the boyars and all the land had elected him tsar and had kissed the cross to him, "your present sovereign, Michael Fedorovich, who was a table attendant, in league with other table attendants, his colleagues, swore allegiance and subjection to the prince," and of this the prince could not be deprived. If need be, the boyars could petition the prince and ask him themselves. Tsar Michael Fedorovich was inscribed in the document with the bare name, not with the sovereign title. Scurrilous words were written concerning Tsar Ivan Vasilievich, saying that he was born of Princess Glinskaia, whose father had betrayed the Polish king, and now Glinsky princes were serving the king.[14] Concerning the borderland officials who wrote unbefittingly of the sovereign, the Polish lords gave no satisfaction, nor did they mention the matter in their document. They also made no amends in the matter of border incursions and other damages, saying only that if the boyars wanted to discuss sovereign titles, the prince's proper style and the conclusion of a proper peace, they must send high ambassadors for this purpose to the border between Viazma and Dorogobuzh.

On receiving this document on March 14 the sovereign ordered his documents on the injustices of the Lithuanian king and the lords of his Council to be distributed to the towns. In these missives, it was declared that even after Borniakov's arrival the governors of Briansk had spread copies of letters from the governors of Pochep in which the sovereign also was named in an improper fashion, in abbreviated form, and the prince was called tsar of All Russia. Therefore the sovereign commanded all boyars, governors, gentry and junior boyars of all towns and all servicemen to be ready for immediate service, and await the tsar's documents.

But the documents announcing the opening of the campaign did not arrive. Sultan Osman's preparations against Poland ended in failure. Osman returned to Constantinople and was killed by the janissaries. Poland gained respite from that quarter. A truce was concluded with the Swedes, who were victorious in Livonia. Without allies the Muscovite government could not resolve to open hostilities with Poland.

CRIMEAN RAIDS

How feeble were Muscovy's resources is evident from the fact that Crimean brigands in small bands ranged with impunity in May and June 1622 over the districts of Epifan, Donkov, Odoevsk, Belev, and Dedilov, while the commanders passively sat in the towns. The sovereign sent Ivan Veliaminov to tell the commanders: "Even without instructions you ought to be at the ready with all your men because you are field commanders, and as soon as news comes of the Tatars you must hasten to meet them and not let them make war. Also because of simplemindedness and stupidity, having come close to the Tatar encampments, you took no reprisals upon them, you did not attack them in their encampments or send patrols after them, you did not follow their trails, you did not wait for stragglers to catch up and did not know how to safeguard them. A few Tatars appeared before Dedilov. They were about three versts from the town quarter, but Prince Gagarin dared not come out from Dedilov against them. He sent a few hundred men, and came himself when the Tatars had retreated. This Tatar warfare is the result of the commander's negligence and apathy. Perhaps also, in exchange for bribes, he dismissed the soldiers to their homes, and so had no forces to combat the Tatars. They must not act in this way in the future."

Under these circumstances, instead of an army, Prince Vasily Akhamushkovich Cherkassky was sent to the Lithuanian frontier as ambassador to a peace conference. The Polish lords sent Prince Samuel Sanguszko. They met only once. Sanguszko did not speak of significant matters, such as the title and brigands who were spreading missives with insults against the sovereign, calling him a halfwit, saying that he had no instruction on these matters, but spoke solely of border disputes. They parted without achieving anything.

FOREIGN MERCENARIES AND TACTICS

Nevertheless there was no warfare for nine years after that. Yet preparations were being made. The instability of the Russian army was apparent, and it was decided to hire foreign mercenaries. More significantly, a decisive step was undertaken which previous rulers had not made. Russian soldiers were ordered to learn foreign tactics. In January 1631 the senior colonel and knight Alexander Ulianovich Leslie[15] was sent to Sweden to hire five thousand infantrymen. Two ambassadors were sent to Sweden, the table attendant Plemiannikov and the undersecretary Aristov, to purchase ten thousand muskets and ammunition, and five thousand swords. If the colonel hired less than five thousand men in Sweden, he was to travel to Denmark, England and Holland to hire the remainder. Plemiannikov was to do the same if he could not purchase all the necessary arms in Sweden. Leslie was also to recruit German master craftsmen acquainted with the latest methods of cannon manufacture, like the Dutch master craftsman Koet was doing in Moscow. He was also to obtain a blacksmith, a machinist, a wheelwright and also master craftsmen who knew how to cast iron cannonballs. In February, Colonel van Damme was sent to recruit a *regiment* of good and skilled soldiers. There were altogether 66,690 foreign soldiers in the Muscovite realm in 1631. In June 1631 the sovereign, having taken counsel with his father the holy patriarch and having spoken with his boyars, ordered the boyars and commanders Prince Dmitry Mamstriukovich Cherkassky and Prince Boris Mikhailovich Lykov to be sent to Dorogobuzh and Smolensk. When these commanders received their appointments, they more than ever began to look to the foreign colonels, Alexander Leslie and his companions, the commanders of their regiments, and the foreign soldiers. They observed them and brought them into service.

PRECEDENCE DISPUTE BETWEEN CHERKASSKY AND LYKOV

Nearly a year went by. In April 1632 King Sigismund died. An interregnum in Poland set in, an elective Sejm, disorders. It was necessary to seize the opportunity but that very April Prince Dmitry Mamstriukovich Cherkassky petitioned the great sovereigns, bringing an action against Prince Boris Mikhailovich Lykov. "Prince Boris Mikhailovich does not wish to serve alongside Prince Dmitry. He says that Prince Dmitry orders his men about, and that the practice is hard for him, because Lykov is senior to Prince Dmitry, and has served the sovereign for forty years, and that for thirteen years he has commanded his own forces, and has not been under anyone else's command or anyone else's colleague."

The sovereigns ordered Prince Andrei Vasilievich Khilkov and the crown secretary Dashkov to make inquiry of the boyar Prince Cherkassky, whom Lykov had told that he would not serve alongside or allow his men to be ordered about by him. Cherkassky replied: "You sovereigns yourselves well know that Prince Boris Lykov in the past year and now also has petitioned that Prince Dmitry not be his colleague because thereby he would be disparaged; but he, Prince Dmitry, was ready for the sovereign's service. So they, the sovereigns, should be gracious to him and allow him to present his defense against Prince Lykov."

The great sovereigns ordered that Prince Lykov be told the following: "He was appointed the past year and was ordered to serve alongside Prince Dmitry Mamstriukovich Cherkassky. Yet he, Prince Boris, a year ago from now as he was going into the cathedral church said to holy Patriarch Filaret, right in the cathedral, such words as any man who remembers God and his oath of allegiance would not utter, and was given a year to prepare for service. When the time for that service arrived, in order to justify his idle arrogance and obstinacy he brought an action against Prince Cherkassky, saying that he could not serve alongside him because Prince Dmitry Mamstriukovich was of harsh disposition and it would be unprofitable for them to be together in the sovereign's service. By his haughty and frivolous posture he had refused to do his duty, had dishonored Prince Dmitry Mamstriukovich Cherkassky and had caused great unrest among the sovereign's servicemen. Therefore the great sovereigns ordered that Prince Dmitry Mamstriukovich Cherkassky receive compensation for his dishonor from Prince Boris Lykov, in the amount of double his salary, twelve hundred rubles."

They thought for two months about with whom to replace Cherkassky and Lykov. Finally in August they appointed the boyar Mikhail Borisovich Shein and the lord-in-waiting Artemy Izmailov. They were accompanied by 32,082 troops and 158 pieces of artillery. Other commanders advanced from Rzhev Volodimirov, Kaluga and Sevsk.

INSTRUCTIONS TO COMMANDERS

The commanders were given instructions to avenge the wrongs committed by the Polish and Lithuanian king, and to recover the towns yielded at sword point to Poland and Lithuania and return as before into the Muscovite realm. The commanders at first were to advance light detachments of nimble forces and seize Dorogobuzh suddenly. If unsuccessful, they were to advance to that town with all their regiments, and employ all means possible, but not remain outside Dorogobuzh for long. They were to send secret missives to the townsmen, who were Russians, urging them to remember their Orthodox faith and their oath of allegiance to the sovereign, serve the sovereign, deal with the Lithuanians and surrender the town. If they did not succeed in capturing the town quickly, Shein and Izmailov were to leave lesser commanders outside it and proceed to Smolensk to deal with that town the same way as they had Dorogobuzh. The campaign was undertaken with the aim of returning Smolensk, Dorogobuzh and their districts to the Muscovite realm. Therefore the commanders were ordered that, once arrived before Smolensk, they immediately distribute missives around the districts of Smolensk and Dorogobuzh to the elders, sworn officials and all the people, calling upon them to rally for the liberation of Smolensk and its region and its reunification with the Muscovite realm. Let all the people of the district come to them in their encampment with supplies and sell them at the going price. The soldiers were warned more than once not to take from anyone without paying, not to plunder or assault anyone, not to lay waste the districts or drive away all the people by reason of their violence. In order to investigate those accused by petition, the rural inhabitants were to elect special judges to form half the tribunal. These judges were enjoined strictly to investigate these petitions faithfully, the soldiers were not to hinder them in any way, and the commanders personally must oversee the activity of these judges.

GATHERING SUPPLIES FOR THE ARMY

Since the soldiers had been given a large salary the colonels of the Russian and foreign soldiers, and the cavalry and infantry colonels, were assessed a direct monthly subsistence deduction. Since there was no hope of dealing with the Lithuanians without a large additional army, the sovereigns took counsel with men of all ranks that they give money to pay the troops, that a fifth be levied from all traders, and from the boyars, lords-in-waiting, crown agents, table attendants, gentry, crown secretaries and all officials to take whatever was offered. The metropolitan of Krutitsy and several other prelates and abbots declared in the assembly how much they would give from their domestic and cellar funds. The remaining clergy and population declared that they would give money, and receipts would be issued to anyone who gave.

The collection of money in Moscow was entrusted to Prince Dmitry Mikhailovich Pozharsky, Archimandrite Levky of the Simonov monastery,[16] Moisey Glebov[17] and two crown secretaries. In the provinces, archimandrites, abbots and senior gentry collected the money, while leading merchants and traders were to elect from among themselves upright men who, having sworn an oath, were to declare how much was to be given by whom from his possessions and trading profits. All money collected in this manner was to be sent to Moscow, to Prince Pozharsky, who would inscribe these contributions accurately in the register, according to category. Apart from this, supplies of grain and meat were gathered directly from the countryside—biscuits, groats, oats, malt, butter and bacon. Prince Ivan Boriatinksy and Ivan Ogarev were entrusted with the collection of these supplies and their distribution. Men of all ranks provided transport of these supplies to the forces outside Smolensk.

SUCCESSFUL BEGINNING TO THE WAR

The war opened successfully. On October 12 Serpeisk surrendered to Captain Prince Gagarin; on October 18 Dorogobuzh surrendered to Captain Sukhotin and Colonel Leslie. The sovereigns ordered Shein to advance from Dorogobuzh to Smolensk and, so that the customary obstacles would not stand in the way of successful operations, ordered that commanders, captains and gentry must serve without any precedence, and that the muster rolls for this war would have no bearing.[18] Belaia surrendered to Prince Prozorovsky; Roslavl, Nevel, Sebezh, Krasny, Pochep, Trubchevsk, Novgorod Seversk, Starodub, Ovsey, Druia, Surozh, Baturin, Romen, Ivangorodishche, Mena, Mirgorodok, Borzna, Propoisk, Yasenichi and Nosenichi all surrendered. The suburbs of Polotsk were taken and burned with the help of the Orthodox Russian citizens. The suburbs of Velizh, Uswiat, Ozerishche, Luzha, Mstislavl and Krichev were all captured. Shein and Izmailov laid siege to Smolensk. Its governor Stanislaw Wojewodski held out for eight months and was preparing to surrender because of shortage of supplies when help came.

KING WLADYSLAW AIDS SMOLENSK

Matters had changed for the better in Poland during these eight months. The late King Sigismund's son Wladyslaw had been elected king and his first task was to come to the aid of Smolensk. Twenty-three thousand troops were assembled, the cossacks were permitted to invade and lay waste Muscovite possessions, thus encouraging the Crimeans to do the same. The Lithuanian chancellor, Radziwill[19] commented in his notes: "I do not argue whether in the theological sense it is good to incite pagan peoples against Christians, but in the political sense it is very good." In fact the Crimeans devastated the Muscovite borderlands. Many soldiers, hearing that the Tatars were attacking their service tenures and patrimonies, dispersed from outside Smolensk.

On August 25, 1633 King Wladyslaw arrived outside that city and halted on the Borova stream, seven versts away. First of all Wladyslaw wanted to drive the Russians from Intercession hill where Colonel Mattison, who was in Russian service, was entrenched, and next to him in a blockhouse Princes Prozorovsky and Beloselsky. On August 28 the crown hetman moved against this

Wladyslaw IV
Reigned 1632–1648
Portrait Bust by Georg Pfründt
Moscow, Pushkin Museum

blockhouse by way of the Zapresk side along the lower road, but
was beaten back with heavy losses. At the same time the king penetrated by way of Intercession hill into Smolensk, from which the
besieged effected a sortie and captured Mattison's trenches, but they
were driven from them by the formations sent by Prozorovsky and
Beloselsky.

On September 11 there was a fresh attack on Mattison and on
Prozorovsky's blockhouse. The fighting went on for two days and
two nights until the commanders, consulting with each other and
with the colonels, decided that the sovereign's troops lacked the
strength to withstand the Poles and Lithuanians as well as hold the
blockhouse on the Intercession hill. They withdrew Mattison to their
blockhouse, while several of the foreigners deserted to the Poles.

Having news of this, the tsar wrote to Shein: "We submit this entire matter to the judgment of God and His just mercies. Many such
things occur in military affairs, the arrival of hostile forces does
happen, but then God's mercy still exists. You have performed the
task entrusted to you by us, the tsar, and have maintained order.
And if it is impossible for our lord-in-waiting Prince Prozorovsky to
hold out in his encampment, and if the infantry cannot hold the
earthen blockhouses, then you, our boyar Mikhail Borisovich, must
order Prince Semeon Borisovich (Prozorovsky) with all his troops
to join you in the encampment in one place." Shein replied to this
with a report that Prozorovsky had crossed to an encampment on
the other side of the Dnieper, and several cannon and supplies had
been abandoned in the trenches. The Russians, when they left, had
intended to set fire to them, but the rain extinguished the flames.
When the Russians had gone, the king in person had inspected the
abandoned trenches. In the words of the Poles, the huge earthworks,
equal in height to the fortifications of Smolensk, had been dug with
immense labor. If they had to be taken by storm, much blood would
have been shed.

"You have done well by concentrating our troops in one place,"
wrote the tsar to Shein and Prozorovsky. "We have ordered our
boyars and commanders, Prince Dmitry Mamstriukovich Cherkassky and Prince Dmitry Mikhailovich Pozharsky with many troops, to
set out from Moscow against our enemy. The table attendant Fedor

Buturlin is proceeding from the Severian land to you outside Smolensk, while the table attendant Prince Vasily Akhamashukov Cherkassky and Prince Efim Myshetsky already have been dispatched to you. Troops are on their way from Novgorod, Pskov, Toropets and Velikie Luki. You should tell all the troops to be hopeful, they can expect help soon, so they should resist the enemy strongly and bravely."

Meanwhile the Poles in Shein's rear captured and burned Dorogobuzh, where war supplies had been cached. Shein reported that on October 6 the king with all his forces had crossed the Dnieper from Intercession hill to the Bogdanov pathway upstream and had established an encampment in the rear of their blockhouse across the Moscow road about a verst from the blockhouse, and had deployed infantrymen and towers opposite the large blockhouse on the hill. On October 9 Shein led his men out against the enemy. The Polish cavalry put to flight part of the Russian infantry, but was compelled to flee from the other part, and the onset of night put an end to the action. According to Polish accounts, the Russians lost two thousand killed, the Poles had many wounded, a few killed, but there was great loss of horses. Shein wrote that the enemy were in control of all the roads, and there was no way of getting through to him. At the end of October the Russians began to suffer food shortages, especially fodder for their horses. Gunfire continued between the two blockhouses. The Poles fired from Skervonkovoia hill on the Russian encampment, whereas the Russians were firing from lower ground and could not inflict any great harm on the enemy, but when they began to fire cannister shot the shrapnel flew up to the king's blockhouse.

Shein called a council of war and solicited opinions as to whether it was possible to strike at the king's blockhouse, and from what side. Colonel Leslie, the most senior of the foreigners, urged striking at the enemy. Colonel Sanderson, an Englishman, gave the opposite opinion. Leslie began to argue, calling Sanderson a traitor, and Shein was barely able to separate them. It was decided to follow Leslie's advice. But on December 2 the Russians, who were suffering from cold, went out into the forest for wood. The Poles attacked, and five hundred were left on the field. When news of this misfortune reached the blockhouse, Leslie persuaded Shein to go out and reckon for himself how many Russians had fallen. Sanderson accompanied Shein and Leslie. Leslie suddenly turned on him and pointed to the corpses, saying: "This is your doing. You told the king that our men were going into the forest." "You lie!" exclaimed the Englishman. Then Leslie, without saying a word, pulled out his pistol and shot Sanderson dead right in front of Shein.

Because of hunger and cold in the Russian encampment there was great mortality. Hearing of this the king, during the last days of December, wrote to Shein and the foreign officers urging them to throw themselves on his mercy, instead of perishing in vain by the sword and through sickness. Shein for a long time refused to let the foreign officers see the king's letter, arguing that foreigners had no right to participate in any negotiations, because they were hired servitors, and he also referred to the policy of the Poles, who permitted foreigners in their service to have no dealings with the enemy. The Poles delivering the letters replied that with them it was another matter, because foreigners were fully subordinate to the hetman, which was not the case with the Russians. Leslie, when he killed Sanderson, did not submit to Shein's judgment and remained unpunished. After long disputes the Russians yielded. Colonel Rozverman took the paper on behalf of the foreigners, while Sukhotin received it on behalf of Shein. Having read the paper, Shein sent it back without reply on the basis that it contained unbefitting words, and that should the Poles refuse it, the emissaries must throw it on the ground and leave.

WLADYSLAW'S TRIUMPH

But in mid-January 1634 Shein, under cover of negotiations concerning exchange of prisoners, began to display his readiness to enter into a peace agreement with the king, compelled particularly, it is said, by the foreign mercenaries, who were not as accustomed to hunger and cold as the Russians were. The mercenaries told Shein that the only course was to petition the king for mercy through the Lithuanian hetman and other senators, and surrender entirely on the king's terms. These terms were that Shein first must surrender all Polish defectors and free all prisoners of war. Foreigners would be given their freedom on condition that either they returned to their country or entered the king's service. Russians were also free to enter the king's service, those who wished to do so. The foreigners were to swear that they would never again fight against the king or the kingdom of Poland, or in any other way harm it. Russians were to swear that until the expiry of four months they would not occupy any cities or strongholds, would not unite with any Muscovite forces and would undertake no activity hostile to the king. They were to surrender without concealment all banners, all artillery and all weapons left behind by soldiers who had been killed. The soldiers who remained alive might leave with the weapons they carried, traders could leave with their swords, or with spears if they did not have swords, and all provisions must be left within the encampment.

Shein agreed. On February 19 the Russians marched out of the blockhouse with banners reversed, with extinguished fuses, quietly, without drumbeat or music. Drawing level with the place where the king sat on horseback, surrounded by senators and soldiers, the Russians had to lay their banners down on the ground, the standard bearers were to step back three paces and wait until the hetman, in the name of the king, ordered them to take up their banners. Then, raising their banners, rolling their kettle drums and beating their drums, the Muscovite army immediately set off along the Moscow road, taking with them twelve regimental cannon by special permission of the king. Shein himself, and all the commanders and leading officers, dismounted and bowed low to Wladyslaw, after which at the hetman's order they remounted and continued on their journey.

MOSCOW DURING THE SMOLENSK DISASTER

Meanwhile what was happening in Moscow? Princes Cherkassky and Pozharsky were held up in Mozhaisk, evidently because not all the forces had assembled. There was also no money. Patriarch Filaret died on October 1, 1633. His place was taken by Archbishop Joseph of Pskov[20] "at the behest of Tsar Michael Fedorovich and with the blessing of Patriarch Filaret, because he had been a junior boyar attached to the court. He was a virtuous man in his nature and his life, but he lacked boldness before the tsar," says the chronograph.[21]

Michael summoned an Assembly on January 28, 1634 and declared that the Polish king, seeing the valiant stand of Boyar Shein, all the commanders and troops, and observing the hardship outside Smolensk and victory over his men, had bribed the Crimean tsar, who had sent his son with many troops, and they had conquered and burned many borderland towns. The gentry and junior boyars of the border towns, seeing the Tatar invasion and hearing that many of their service tenures and patrimonies had been taken, departed Smolensk leaving only a few men before the town. The Lithuanian king, hearing that the sovereign's men were dispersing, had come before Smolensk. The sovereign's men had slain many Lithuanians, had captured many informers, banners and kettledrums, and the informers under interrogation said that King Wladyslaw and the Lithuanians had marched to repel the boyar Mikhail Borisovich Shein, retain Smolensk for Lithuania as before, and invade the Muscovite realm in order that, in accordance with the designs of the accursed Roman pope, he might pervert the Orthodox into his own heretical faith and utterly ruin the Muscovite realm. The king had inflicted great harm upon the sovereign's men, and closed the roads to them. Now the sovereign was sending against the Lithuanians Prince Dmitry Mamstriukovich Cherkassky and his companions. But it was impossible for these troops, and those who had stood without respite outside Smolensk, to serve without pay. But the cash in the sovereign's treasury, which in past years was gathered through the sovereign's skilled management, and not by special levies from the land, for the most part had been distributed to the troops. Whatever money still remained must be disbursed immediately to pay the troops and provide them subsistence. In the past year, in accordance with the resolution of the Assembly, a fifth tax was collected. But many of the leading merchants and traders cheated on their payment of fifths, not reckoning their commerce and their profits. In past years the Muscovite realm was in ruin, there was no money and no treasury, but when a fifth tax was assessed, much more money was collected than now, even though people were worse off. Thereafter the Muscovite realm enjoyed peace and tranquillity for a long of time, and people's fortunes were much increased. Therefore they must now give money.

The men of all ranks replied that they would provide money according to their means, as much as they were able. The sovereign ordered Prince Boris Mikhailovich Lykov, the lord-in-waiting Korobyin and Archimandrite Feodosy of the Miracles monastery[22] to collect this special levy and the fifth tax.

THE COMMANDERS EXECUTED

On February 1 the nobleman Satin reached Moscow with news from Shein that on account of the Lithuanians the sovereign's men were suffering great hardship and severe shortage of food supplies and salt. The commander wrote that the Polish colonels were talking of a truce, had agreed that each army retire behinds its own lines, and that high ambassadors must sit and discuss peace. The sovereign ordered Shein to agree to a truce if the king and all his troops would withdraw to Poland, and if the Poles allowed the sovereign's auxiliary troops, who were to bring up artillery and the treasury, to join Shein. Meantime the sovereign ordered the lord-in-waiting Prince Grigory Volkonsky to Mozhaisk to confer with the commanders, Princes Cherkassky and Pozharsky, how most expeditiously to aid the sovereign's troops outside Smolensk. Could they advance to Viazma and Dorogobuzh? The boyars replied that they could, and the sovereign ordered them to prepare to advance; but on March 3 Cherkassky informed the sovereign that Shein had made a truce with the king and was on his way back to Moscow. On the next day, March 4, Moisey Glebov was instructed to meet Shein and ask him the terms of the truce with the king? How many artillery pieces and how much ammunition had he surrendered to the king? How many troops were coming with him, how many sick had he left at Smolensk, and how many had entered the king's service?

Shein could guess that in Moscow he would receive an ungracious welcome. Glebov did not bring any greetings for him, although he told the troops that their service, zeal, hardship and fortitude against the Poles and Lithuanians as they fought, without sparing their lives, was known to the sovereign and all the Muscovite realm. Shein sent the articles of the agreement and a list of the soldiers lost or who remained with the king. There were very few in the last category, eight men, six of them Don Cossacks. Altogether 8056 men accompanied Shein from Smolensk, though of that number many had to be carried sick, and had died on the way, while others had been left in Dorogobuzh, Viazma and Mozhaisk. Many foreigners had changed sides, gone over to the king or died on the way, but exactly how many was not known, since the commanders for several days had been asking the foreign colonels for lists of their men, but they had not given them. Two thousand and four sick were left at Smolensk.

When Shein arrived in Moscow he was sentenced as a traitor and was put to death. Before the execution the crown secretary read out the following accusation: "You, Mikhail Shein, did not leave Moscow on the sovereign's service as the sovereign entrusted you to do when he personally took leave of you. You recalled your previous services to him with great haughtiness, alleging that your previous great service to the sovereign was higher than that of any your brother boyars, alleging that while you were serving many of your brother boyars were sitting by their firesides and could not be found. You reviled all your brethren before the sovereign with great reproachfulness, and said that in service and in nobility of ancestry there were was none equal to you. The sovereign, taking pity upon you and sparing you on account of your service to the crown and the land, not wishing to vex you while on your way, kept silence before you in all these matters. The boyars who were at that time in the sovereign's presence, even though they heard such rude and abusive words, which no other person ought to have heard from you, also refrained from answering you, in order not to upset the sovereign."

Following this Shein and Izmailov were accused of dilatoriness in that they had lost the initiative, confused the troops and, waiting for rainy weather, had set off on a long march, not heeding the orders of the sovereign and the patriarch, and by their dilatoriness had given the Poles the opportunity to fortify themselves in Smolensk. They did not write to the sovereign concerning the unfavorable state of affairs, and if they did write, they did so briefly and untruthfully. While waiting for sapping operations to be completed they did not approach the city at the right time, but in broad daylight. When they were advancing Shein ordered the artillery to fire on the sovereign's troops, as a result of which many were killed. He did not heed the Russian troops or the foreigners; he did not execute the sovereign's business or allow anyone else to perform it. Shein and Izmailov took the best villages and hamlets and divided them up between them, confiscating from them many revenues and giving none to the troops. Also included in the accusation was the strict observation of the tsar's order that the soldiers take nothing without paying or in general harm the inhabitants of the Dorogobuzh and Smolensk countryside. "You ordered beaten mercilessly with the knout servicemen who went into the Dorogobuzh or Smolensk countryside in search of fodder for their horses, thus preserving the Smolensk and Dorogobuzh countryside and all their supplies for the king." In this matter it should be remarked that servicemen were allowed into the Smolensk and Dorogobuzh countryside when there was no scarcity in the encampment, but when scarcity set in they could not leave of the camp.

The indictment continued: "You, in defiance of the tsar's command, treasonably and on your own initiative kissed the cross to the king, abandoned much artillery and supplies, merely persuading him to leave twelve cannon on the sovereign's side, and even these cannon you, Shein, by your treason, gave up to the king altogether. You also surrendered thirty-six men who had transferred their allegiance from the king to the sovereign, who constantly visited the king's encampments to gather information and travelled to Moscow on the sovereign's business, and the king ordered all these men executed. And when you passed through the Polish regiments you laid down your reversed standards before the king and bowed to the ground before the king, which caused great dishonor to the sovereign's name."

Finally, there is a curious accusation. "When you were a prisoner in Lithuania you kissed the cross to Sigismund, the former Lithuanian king, and his son Prince Wladyslaw, promising to do all they asked. And when you came to the sovereign in Moscow, fifteen years ago, you did not declare that previously you had kissed the cross to the king, but kept this cross-kissing secret. And now, when you were before Smolensk, by your treason to the sovereign and all the Muscovite realm, you fulfilled your oath to the Lithuanian king, satisfied him in everything, wished him well and betrayed the sovereign."

The deputy commander Izmailov was beheaded also. The most guilty of all, if we are to believe the death warrant, was Izmailov's son Vasily. "You, Vasily, when you were before Smolensk, committed brigandage, committed the greatest treason of all to the sovereign, by fraternizing with the Lithuanians Zakhar Zarutsky and Madalinski and those traitors to the sovereign Yushka Potemkin, Ivashka Meshcherinov and others. You invited them to your quarters in the encampment, feasted with them, honored them and gave them gifts, while you and your brother Semeon received gifts from them, entertained them overnight; they were with you and spent the night with you, and came to you with their own food and drink and accompanied you to your camp, and you discussed with them everything of use to the Lithuanian king. And you, Vasily, when you were outside Smolensk, and from Smolensk arrived in Mozhaisk, praised the Lithuanian king, saying: 'How can our puny Muscovite forces fight against such a great sovereign monarch? Ivan was a great tsar, yet he did not draw his sword against the Lithuanian king, nor did he fight against him.'[23] Also you, Vasily, when you heard of the death of the great sovereign Patriarch Filaret Nikitich, said many villainous and unbefitting words, such as it is not seemly to write."

Princes Semeon Prozorovsky and Mikhail Beloselsky were sentenced to exile in Siberia, their wives and children were dispersed among the towns and their possessions confiscated by the sovereign. These commanders were spared the death penalty because, as it was stated in the sentence, all the soldiers bore witness to Prozorovsky's zeal and Beloselsky's sickness! Ivan Shein, the son of the chief commander, guilty only by association with his father, was spared the death penalty at the request of the tsaritsa and the tsar's sons and daughters, but was sent with his mother and wife to the Lower Towns.[24] Artemy Izmailov's other son, Semeon, was beaten with the knout and sent to prison in Siberia because before Smolensk he committed brigandage, fraternized with Lithuanians, said many unbefitting words and gave presents to the Lithuanians. Gavrila Bakin suffered the same punishment because when he was in Mozhaisk he praised the Lithuanian king and the Lithuanians in front of the Russians, calling the latter rustics. Liubim Ananiev was beaten with the knout and sent to prison in Siberia because he had lived all the time in Shein's household, was in his house as a spy, and listened to what they said about him, and provoked quarrels between the commander and many prominent men. Timofey Izmailov, Artemy's brother, was employed in the sovereign's business in Moscow as an official in the Chancellery of the Exchequer. According to the sovereign's decree, Timofey was dismissed from the treasury office, and on account of his brother Artemy's treason he and his wife and children were banished to Kazan.

Shein's fate is easily explained. The military history of the Muscovite realm long since had revealed the shortcomings of the Russian army in its struggles with the Swedes and Poles, its lack of military skill. The authorities understood this very well and tried to remedy the deficiency. Foreigners were summoned, Russians began to learn foreign methods. But these first steps forward naturally could not lead immediately to appreciable results. Having collected together an army and money and hired foreigners, they sent to Smolensk the commander who was famed for the defense of the town. But defending a town and besieging it are two different matters. Shein did not succeed in compelling Smolensk to surrender by reason of hunger, and soon was besieged himself by King Wladyslaw. There his position was quite different from what it had been when he was inside Smolensk. It was not simply that his little fort was not as strong or as comfortably placed as Smolensk, which was so well protected from Skowronski's murderous batteries. Rather it was the fact that earlier Shein was surrounded by soldiers and citizens ready to fight to the death for their sacred interests, whereas in the blockhouse the foreigners impertinently broke discipline, objected to his authority over them and the hunger and cold, and demanded agreement with the enemy. The Russians were asking, how with their rustic methods they could fight against the Lithuanian king and his troops? From Moscow there had been the single promise that commanders would come to their aid from all sides, but in three months this promise had remained unfulfilled. No treason on Shein's part is evident. Why then did they try in Moscow to convict Shein of treason? The reason is clear: Shein by his mockery of them in the sovereign's presence had mortally offended many powerful people. On that occasion, as the sentence naively records, they were silent because they needed him, and Filaret probably would not have betrayed his fellow-sufferer to the people who sat idle at home. But now Shein's failure had eclipsed his former services. Filaret was no longer living, and powerful men hastened to avenge their dishonor.

CHRONOGRAPH'S VERDICT ON SHEIN

The Chronograph,[25] which refers slightingly to Filaret Nikitich, thus explains the reasons for Shein's failure. "The tsar, following the advice, or more precisely, the orders of the patriarch, summoned from Denmark and other German lands to help him colonels, famous and brave men, and with them a multitude of soldiers, opened his royal treasure and unsparingly rewarded the foreigners, and gave the foreigners free Russians to learn military art. The tsar did not desire to campaign himself against the Poles, as he was a kindly and mild man who did not wish to shed blood. Had he placed his hope in the omnipotent God and gone himself, then I think he would have succeeded in the venture. They sent Shein. He took cities like birds' nests, because the Poles did not expect the Russians to advance. But God punished Shein because when he was released from captivity he had sworn an oath to the king not to fight against Lithuania, and this was known to the tsar and to the patriarch. When Boyar Mikhail approached Smolensk he placed his fortresses close to the very city, filled gabions with earth in front of the cannon, constructed all kinds of battering rams, took counsel with the commanders and colonels and a considerable part of the fortifications were destroyed by the cannon. The foreign colonels were conducting sapping operations and blowing up the walls. In a word, everything was going according to plan. But then the tsar and the patriarch fell into *consternation* and distrust on account of the oath Shein had sworn to the king. The Moscow boyars, stung with envy, began to slander him, and informed Shein while serving with the regiments that in Moscow there were many denunciations against him. In the regiments there arose great murmuring against him on account of his haughtiness and lack of zeal and, because of his haughtiness, relations with the commanders and the foreign colonels worsened. He dishonored them, vexed the soldiers, gave them no leave to go around the villages in search of fodder for their horses, began to write discourteously to Moscow, while from Moscow letters came containing only criticism and disfavor. He became even more annoyed on account of this. And if Artemy Izmailov and his son Vasily had not restrained his anger he would have perished on account of his grief and pride. King Wladyslaw arrived before Smolensk with not a very large force, but acted efficiently. He sent to Mikhail Shein, reminding him of his oath. Shein again grew downcast, again became angry at his troops and conducted no operations for a long time. The Russians in the forts became sick through constriction and shortage of food, and there was a great plague, while no help came from Moscow and no supplies were sent."

VALIANT DEFENSE OF BELAIA

Having allowed Shein to depart Smolensk, the king advanced on Belaia, hoping to take that town easily, but things turned out differently. The Polish army arrived at Belaia half dead from hunger and cold. The king established himself in the Mikhailovsk monastery two miles from the town and sent to the governor to demand his surrender, citing the example of Shein. The governor replied that Shein's example instilled in him bravery, not fear. The king ordered the town to be surrounded by trenches and mines to be dug. But the mines only brought grief to the Poles. The forward troop commanders were so covered with earth that they could barely be dug out. Gunfire caused no hardship to the besieged. Emboldened by their success at Smolensk, the Poles threw off all caution. The Russians took advantage of this and effected a sortie against Weiger's regiment and captured eight standards almost before the Poles were able to take up their arms. How burdensome the siege of Belaia was for the Poles is seen in Chancellor Radziwill's advice that the town no longer be called Belaia (White) but Krasnaia (Red), on account of the great bloodshed. Hunger reached such extremes that the king himself had half a chicken for dinner, saving the other half for supper, while for the rest a piece of bread with cold water was a delicacy. Because of this scarcity, sickness and mortality set in among the army. On the other hand there was news that the Turkish army was approaching the Polish borders. Under these circumstances the king needed to conclude peace with Moscow as quickly as possible, a perpetual peace which would secure Sigismund's gains for

Lithuania. The Polish lords first sent peace proposals to the boyars. Understandably these proposals were received eagerly, and in March 1634 Fedor Ivanovich Sheremetev and Prince Alexis Mikhailovich Lykov were designated as high ambassadors to meet with the Polish commissioners, Bishop Jakub Zadzik of Chelmno[26] and his companions. The meeting was to take place on the Polianovka river, in the same place where previously there was an exchange of prisoners. The king stayed not far off, in concealment.

POLISH-RUSSIAN NEGOTIATIONS

The talks began as before, with the same altercations and rehashing of old business. The Poles insisted that King Wladyslaw had a right to the Muscovite throne, and that the Russians had broken the Deulino truce by sending Shein against Smolensk before the expiry of the truce. Among other things, the Poles said: "We know for certain that the war began at the instigation of Patriarch Filaret Nikitich. He began it and blessed all of you." The Muscovite ambassadors declared that if Wladyslaw would not renounce the Muscovite title they would not discuss the matter further. They said: "Both we and all the people of the great Russian realms have a principal and primary duty to safeguard the sovereign's honor, and we are all ready to die to the last man for our sovereign." Then the Poles, agreeing with the demands of the Muscovite ambassadors, proposed eternal peace on the basis of the peace terms concluded by King Casimir with Grand Prince Vasily the Dark.[27] King Wladyslaw was to be compensated for his renunciation of the Muscovite throne and the title of tsar with an annual pension of one hundred thousand rubles and compensation for losses sustained in the recent war. The Muscovite ambassadors answered that these words were unbefitting. "We henceforth refuse to discuss such matters with you. It is unprecedented to ask of us questions such as never before were or in the future never will be put. On this we, all the people of the Muscovite realm, insist and stake our lives." The Poles protested that Michael Fedorovich had given Gustavus Adolphus towns and money for some unknown reason, but Wladyslaw would be compensated for his renunciation of the Muscovite realm.

After protracted disputes, the Poles said: "When we have brought negotiations concerning eternal peace to a successful conclusion, we will petition the king to absolve you of your oath of allegiance and cede his title to your sovereign. But you must declare what you will give our sovereign in exchange." "Do not represent it as a concession or a gift," the Muscovite ambassadors replied, "that the king wishes to divest himself of the Muscovite title. Your sovereign cannot give it to ours because our great sovereign reigns over the Muscovite realm through the gift and will of Almighty God, by reason of his ancient royal honor inherited from his great sovereign ancestors. But our oath, that of the Muscovite people, has been washed away in blood by your sovereign king and his injustices, so now we are cleansed of it." Finally they spoke of the current situation. The Poles declared that without cession to the king's side of all the towns yielded according to the Deulino truce, but which had been seized by the Muscovites when the truce was broken, they would not discuss anything. At each meeting the Muscovite ambassadors conceded one or two towns, but the Poles constantly demanded all of them. An order came from Moscow. In exchange for Dorogobuzh, Novgorodok, Serpeisk and Trubchevsk and for renunciation of the title the king was to be given ten thousand cash, which could be increased to seventy thousand, or at the utmost a hundred thousand. At that time Bishop Zadzik sent word to Sheremetev that the king had dispatched his regiment to Mozhaisk. He had persuaded the king to send Krzystof Radziwill's regiment[28] when a junior boyar arrived from Moscow to the king with news that Shein and Izmailov had been executed, which fueled great popular agitation, and there had been great conflagrations in Moscow and nearly all the city was burned. In Mozhaisk the soldiers also set fires and dispersed. The king wished to deal with Mozhaisk and advance on Moscow but he, the bishop, had halted the Lithuanian troops, and the king stood on the Viazma river twenty versts from Semlevo.

At the next session the Polish commissioners demanded all the towns ceded at Deulino, and also several more, in return for the release of the tsar and people from the oath to Wladyslaw. The Muscovite ambassadors replied that the tsar must pay nothing for such a release since Tsar Michael had not kissed the cross, because at the time he was not fully grown. For surrendering the title the commissioners demanded not cities, but money. The Muscovite ambassadors refused. Then the Poles got up noisily and wanted to break off negotiations. The Muscovite ambassadors began to offer money according to their instructions. The Poles remained. They began discussions among themselves, several left the tent where the talks were going on towards Polianovka stream and there began to discuss matters further with their colleagues. The gentry relayed to the sovereign's ambassadors that the Polish commissioners were going to the king, who was resting in the woods on the bank of the Polianovka river. After turning over the matter between themselves the Poles rejected the proposals of the Muscovite ambassadors, who in turn refused to cede any towns. The Poles grew angry, once again rose from their seats, and the sovereign's ambassadors also stood up and wished to leave the tent. The ambassadors talked standing for more than three hours, sometimes speaking very loudly, at other times they feigned ease, as though they were coming to a good understanding. After raising their voices, they parted company. They reproached one another and rehearsed all former quarrels and injustices. The Poles at last walked out of the tent, announcing that they wished to break off the talks.

Then the Muscovite ambassadors conceded Dorogobuzh to them, but they did not agree. They ceded Novgorod Seversk, but they did not agree. The commissioners left the tent, only leaving Zadzik and Radziwill, governor of Wilno, who continued the talks. Of all the towns ceded according to the Deulino truce they would only yield Serpeisk, but demanded Trubchevsk and a hundred thousand rubles cash. Then they lowered the price, coming down to twenty thousand. The Russians agreed to this, on condition that the king be given the money secretly, that no mention must be made in writing, only Bishop Zadzik and Radziwill would know of it, they would not tell their colleagues, and when the treaty was completed by kissing the cross the bishop alone would take the money and issue a receipt. The Polish delegation agreed to call Michael Fedorovich tsar because the Polish government had recognized that title before, when they had called Wladyslaw tsar. But while they did not dispute the title of tsar, they did quarrel about the title "of All Russia." "Your sovereign describes himself as ruler of "All Russia," they told the boyars, "but Russia is in both the Muscovite and Polish realms. Thus in the Polish memorandum of agreement your great sovereign should be described as tsar *of his Russia* so that the title not contain any pretentions to Polish Russia, and in the Muscovite

memorandum of agreement and henceforth in the tsar's documents
to the Polish king must be written *of All Russia* as before." The
Muscovite ambassadors refused. "It is improper to do so. You have
Little Russia, which belongs to Poland and Lithuania and does not
affect his majesty the tsar's intitulation *of All Russia*. To change it
for your sake from *of All Russia* to *of his Russia* is out of the
question." Having settled the dispute over the title, the ambassadors
clasped hands on a *perpetual agreement*. It was May 17.

ETERNAL PEACE

When the terms of the perpetual agreement had to be drafted the
Polish side renewed the attempts made by Leo Sapieha in Godunov's reign, and proposed additional articles. (1) To be in eternal
friendship, as people of a single Christian faith, one language and
Slavic nation. The Muscovite ambassadors added here the condition
that the great sovereign must have his name written with full intitulation. (2) To have common enemies. To which the Muscovite
ambassadors added that the king's enemies must be specified, and
the terms of the treaty would be written accordingly. (3) Not to ally
with other nations to each other's detriment, but to have common
relations with them after taking counsel with each other. If a treaty
had been concluded to the detriment of the new ally, it must be
broken. (4) In case of an enemy attack they must defend each other.
Answer: our sovereign has common borders with only two neighboring states, Sweden and Crimea, and we are in treaty relations
with both of them, so we cannot afford any help against them. (5)
Subjects of both sovereigns shall be free to travel to the other sovereign for service at court, in the army or in the provinces, and shall
be free to return. Answer: Russians cannot marry Poles and Poles
cannot marry Russians on account of the difference in their religious faiths. It is improper to sell patrimonial estates to someone
outside the country, something which never has been done. (7)
Subjects of both realms shall be free to send their children either for
service or for learning. Answer: Concerning this the great sovereigns will correspond with each other. (8) That Poles serving the
Muscovite sovereign be allowed to establish churches of their own
faith on their estates, that there may be Catholic churches in Moscow and other towns. Answer: there never have been churches of

other faiths within the Muscovite realm, neither would there be any in the future. (9) The king and the great Muscovite sovereign shall strive together to have artillery, ships and men on the Livonian Sea and upon the Great Sea, to extend their frontiers. Answer: the sovereign's warships have never been on the Livonian or Great Sea, neither did he intend to have them anywhere or for any reason. But if this is necessary for the king, let him correspond about the matter with our sovereign. (10) As a token of our special union there shall be two crowns: one in Poland which the Muscovite ambassador shall place upon the king's head at the time of his coronation, and another in Moscow which the Polish ambassador likewise shall place upon the Muscovite sovereign's head. (11) On the occasion of the king's death the lords of the Council shall deliberate on the election with the sovereign and all ranks of Muscovites. (12) If the tsar is elected king, he will live for two years in Poland and Lithuania, and one year in Moscow. To all these latter articles, there was a single answer: let the sovereigns correspond with each other.

On the tsar's draft document it was written: "People who flee from one side to the other shall not be extradited because if we extradite fugitives there will arise great disputes, and harming of souls, and it will be impossible to fulfill this clause in any way. The Muscovite and Polish realms are great and extensive, and fugitives will go to live in distant and border towns in secret, making it impossible not only to find them but even their place of residence." As a consequence the plenipotentiaries were persuaded to strike the article concerning fugitives from the memorandum of agreement, but resolved that brigands who had fled across the border to escape punishment for their crimes shall be found and extradited. The Polish commissioners demanded that the patriarch, on behalf of the true tsar, of future tsars and the whole land kiss the cross on the perpetual agreement, and that in addition two men from each of the border towns kiss the cross. The Muscovite ambassadors replied: "The great sovereign the most holy patriarch administers the church of God, and does not concern himself with the tsar's business, or with any political or secular matters. Also the men from the border towns shall not kiss the cross because the perpetual agreement will be confirmed when we, the ambassadors, kiss the cross on it, and furthermore the sovereigns will confirm it, and furthermore the

townsmen may do nothing without the sovereign's authorization."
The Polish ambassadors insisted that the patriarch, the spiritual authorities, boyars and representatives of all ranks kiss the cross on
behalf of themselves and their children, and should involve all the
earth besides. They said that with them, in Poland, everyone would
kiss the cross. "Your archbishops and bishops must kiss the cross,"
responded the Muscovite ambassadors, "because they are members
of the Senate, but our patriarch and clergy do not kiss the cross on
any matters. In the Muscovite realm never have the boyars or any
other persons kissed the cross alongside the sovereign, neither can
they do so now. The conclusion of the peace shall be firm in the
sovereigns' souls, and we the high ambassadors give confirmation
on behalf of the boyars and all the people."

The Polish delegation protested that the senators and boyars must
kiss the cross in the event of the death of the king or the tsar. To
this the Muscovite ambassadors replied that "It is unheard of that
the boyars shall kiss the cross alongside our sovereign. We are all
slaves of our great sovereign and are entirely subject to his royal
will, and we cannot give any such undertaking without his authorization." The Poles continued to insist that the patriarch kiss the
cross, but the Muscovite ambassadors replied that "The patriarch
cannot be here because according to the law of our Greek faith it is
forbidden for patriarchs to assist at the kissing of the cross. They
hold a spiritual rank, they are the foremost servants of Christ,
higher than all bishops or archbishops, and they cannot take part in
the swearing of any human oath." The Muscovite ambassadors also
argued that the boyars and men from the borderlands should not
kiss the cross.

It was agreed that the tsar and king send to bordering Christian
and Muslim rulers to announce their perpetual agreement. They
agreed as to how many men should constitute their respective ambassadorial suites. Ambassadors on both sides were to arrive with a
hundred retainers, emissaries with thirty and heralds with six. Ambassadors and emissaries shall not be detained for more than two
months. The Polish commissioners demanded that both sovereigns
be permitted to hire troops, the king in the Muscovite realm and the
tsar in Poland. The Muscovite ambassadors laid aside that article
until they could inform the sovereign, because this was a new matter. The Poles demanded that payment to the Zaporozhian Cossacks

be made by the sovereign annually since they had a document to that effect and, furthermore, such payments had been made in the past. "The payment made to the Zaporozhian Cossacks, for what service it was given, and the nature of the document they have, we do not recall," responded the Muscovites. "We think that it possibly relates to the time when the Zaporozhian Cossacks served our sovereign, and if now they serve the sovereign again they will be paid according to their service."

While the talks were going on the ambassadors received a document from Moscow telling them to demand from the Polish ambassadors the artillery taken from Shein at Smolensk. They were to ask this as a mark of the king's favor. "To this end you shall stand and speak unhurriedly, since by now the Poles cannot break off negotiations. It is known for certain to the sovereign that the Turkish sultan has advanced on Poland, in Poland and Lithuania there is great fear of the Turks, and that the king has returned to Lithuania. Had the sovereign known about this in good time, he would not have instructed the ambassadors to yield so many towns. The chief ambassadors, the boyars and lords-in-waiting, shall speak forcefully, and the others shall be calm and cloak themselves in composure and conversation, that the treaty shall not be broken and they shall not be without glory." They fulfilled their instructions. The Muscovite negotiators spoke to the commissioners about the return of the cannon, spoke of the twelve artillery pieces the king allowed Shein but which through treason he had not conveyed to his sovereign. The commissioners replied that they would report concerning this to the king, to which the Lithuanian hetman, Radziwill, added: "You spoke to us of the twelve cannon which Shein did not return, allegedly because of treason to his sovereign. You must not speak these words or write them in your letter because our sovereign took all this artillery by his own armed might and not through any treason. The twelve cannon which he gave back to Shein he gave me in affection and not because he was forced to do so, and these cannon are now in my possession, not the king's, and it is not befitting to give them back, because Shein made a gift of them to me."

The Polish delegates demanded that their merchants be allowed to trade in Moscow and in the towns of the Moscow region, but the Muscovite ambassadors agreed only that they be allowed to trade in the border towns. As for trade in Moscow and the other towns, this

matter was postponed until the Polish ambassadors could meet with
the tsar in Moscow. It was agreed to release prisoners of war on
both sides without restriction, although the Poles did not accept the
demand of the Muscovite ambassadors not to release those who had
accepted the Orthodox faith or who had married in Russia. In the
draft treaty sent from Moscow the condition was written that the
Orthodox faith remain inviolate in the towns to be ceded to Poland.
The Polish commissioners spoke of this with great vehemence:
"How can you suspect us of such bigotry? Each man guards his
own, and does not seek to build another's house. We do not forbid
any man to hold fast to his own faith. We will promise this under
oath, but it would be invidious to write this in the memorandum of
agreement, inasmuch as the king would be embarrassed to appear to
be a destroyer of faiths." And they noisily refused. Whereas the
Muscovite draft treaty opened with accusations that the Poles had
broken the truce, etc., the commissioners declared that they could
not let such a document pass. "An eternal peace has been concluded," they said, "yet accusations appear at the very beginning of
the document! We do not wish to reproach you, and we do not reproach you." They quarrelled about this for two hours and finally
decided to omit the offending words.

All this ended on June 4. Taking their leave, the Polish delegates
said: "Such a great and glorious matter has been done as no previous sovereigns ever were able to achieve. On this very spot where
such a great and glorious matter has been achieved, where the tsars
have stood, let us for the sake of eternal memory erect two large
mounds and raise on them two stone columns, one on the Muscovite
and the other on the king's side, and let us inscribe on them the
sovereigns' names, the year and month and also in what manner and
by which ambassadors such a great deed has been achieved."
Sheremetev and his companions did not agree to this proposal, re-
plying that "Such customs there have never been in the Muscovite
realm, and there is no way we can do this. All this was achieved by
the will of God and at the command of the great sovereigns and will
be written down in the diplomatic books." Sheremetev informed
Moscow of this and received the following reply: "The sovereign's
ambassadors have done well to refuse the Lithuanian ambassadors'
request, since they were asking something unprecedented, and

henceforth you are to refuse the Lithuanian ambassadors' requests when they propose to dig mounds and erect columns, inasmuch as this is unbefitting and to no good purpose, for this good deed was achieved according to the will of God, and not for the sake of senseless pillars and mounds."

LYKOV'S MISSION TO POLAND

At the beginning of 1635, for the ratification of the eternal peace by the king's oath the high ambassadors, boyar Prince Alexis Mikhailovich Lykov-Yaroslavsky and his companions, were dispatched to Poland. These were their instructions. "Insist firmly and without fail that the king place his lips upon the cross, and not upon the dish." An even more interesting second article states: "When the king orders the cross to be placed upon the document, the ambassadors shall be certain that this cross of the king's does not have a crucifixion,[29] and if the king insists on following Lutheran fashion by kissing the Gospels, find out what the king's faith really is." If they insist, continued the instruction, that Polish merchants come freely to Moscow and other towns, they were to reply: "This is impermissible since if many Polish and Lithuanian merchants begin to come to Moscow and other towns they will bring with them teachers of the Roman faith and convert people to their faith. But our true Orthodox Christian faith of the Greek dispensation until now has stood firm and unshakeable, and henceforth shall continue to stand, shielded and protected by God for all time, and we will not accept any other faith. Other foreigners will come to Moscow, merchants of the Lutheran and Calvinist faiths, and there will be conflict with the Romans on account of that faith. Thus merchants of the Roman faith will quarrel with the Lutherans and Calvinists, for quarrels between them over matters of faith are inevitable. But, while being firm, agree that Polish merchants may come to Moscow."

The lords demanded from the ambassadors yet another new article, that there be a common currency between the two realms. "It is impossible to establish a uniform price," the ambassadors answered. "With you in Poland and Lithuania the prices in zlotys and efimki are unequal. The zloty with you is worth one ruble, twenty-one altyns and four dengas in Russian money, yet in Moscow a

zloty can be purchased for thirty altyns.[30] An efimok can be purchased among you for thirty altyns, yet in Moscow for no more than
sixteen altyns. It is also impossible because in Poland and Lithuania trading is done in zlotys and efimki, and copper groschen and
schillings are used for small purchases, whereas in the Muscovite
realm we use Russian copecks and Moscow dengas. Although they
are fractional, they are coined out of pure silver."

THE MISSING TREATY

After all negotiations were complete a severe complication arose for
the Muscovite ambassadors. As early as the Polianovka meeting
between Sheremetev and Zadzik it was agreed that the Poles surrender the original agreement by Zolkiewski concerning the election
of Wladyslaw and all other papers relating to the Time of Troubles.
Now the lords of the Council informed Lvov that they were looking
for the treaty but could not find it anywhere. "Until the hetman's
treaty and all the other papers are surrendered to us," said the ambassadors, "we will conduct no business, neither will we be present
when the king kisses the cross. An amazing business! Did you not a
long time ago kiss the cross, and did not your high ambassadors and
senators swear and kiss the cross that the hetman's treaty and all the
papers would be given to his majesty the tsar's ambassadors in
Warsaw, and now they say that they cannot find the treaty."
Krzystof Gasiewski and Albert Gizycki visited the ambassadors and
said: "We told the king and the lords of the Council that you would
do no business without the hetman's treaty. On account of this the
king became concerned and the lords of the Council all grew sor-
rowful, and the king ordered the treaty to be sought in every nook
and cranny." Then Jakub Zadzik, Crown Chancellor Albrycht Radziwill and the chancellor of Lithuania, Alexander Gasiewski, visited
the ambassadors and said that the treaty could not be found in the
king's treasury. When Hetman Zolkiewski brought that treaty to
Smolensk to give to King Sigismund it was not known whether or
not the king took it from him; all that is known is that the king did
not gain the Muscovite realm for his son. They thought that the
treaty was either with Zolkiewski, or with Leo Sapieha or with the
notary Sokolinski, who all had died, and now the king was search-
ing for the treaty at Zolkwa, Zolkiewski's estate, and also from

Sapieha's son and Sokolinski. If they could not find the treaty the king would pledge by kissing the cross that henceforth neither he nor any future king would make any claim to the throne by reason of the hetman's treaty, and never for all time would call it to mind, and this would apply to the lords of the Council and the whole Polish Commonwealth. Pledges concerning that treaty would be written as you, the high ambassadors, yourselves order.

"You wish to give a written guarantee concerning the hetman's treaty," said the ambassadors, "but you have made a written assurance about it and kissed the cross, and then lied. And you, lords of the Council, how is it that you have committed such injustices as are unheard of in Christian realms? Did you not kiss the cross, knowing of that treaty that it was in the king's treasury? And now you are saying that you cannot find it!" The lords replied: "We ourselves are very embarrassed that we could not find the treaty, only this occurred without guile, not by deceit. God sees this, may God destroy us body and soul if we are concealing the treaty. Write to your great sovereign for a decree, and our sovereign will send his herald to his majesty the tsar. He will write that he, the king, will kiss the cross on this, and will set his hand and seal to it, and they, the senators, will set their signatures to it on behalf of the whole land, saying they could not find the treaty." The ambassadors continued to swear, and finally resolved to write concerning the matter to the sovereign.

The tsar sent an answer that he was agreeable to the understanding concerning the hetman's treaty, but only on condition that the king must write concerning this matter to all realms.

RATIFICATION CEREMONY

April 23 was designated as the day when the king would ratify the treaty. The church was magnificently decorated. By the high altar burned six candles in gold candlesticks. The crucifix and statues on the altar were made of the same metal. The music thundered from four choirs. Discussions began as to whether the Muscovite ambassadors were to enter the church in front of the king or behind him, or lead him by the hand as was the custom. They declared that to lead the king by the hand was unbefitting, and it was an even greater sin to lead anyone to an oath-taking, much more so a king.

They agreed to go before the marshal. When the procession got under way the ambassadors demanded that the king in the presence of all sign the promised pledge with his own hand. The king complied with all their wishes, and they were greatly pleased, saying: "Now we see that you are dealing sincerely with us, and there will be eternal peace." They requested that the king and tsar always call each other brother. Agreement to this also ensued.

The king entered the church with a numerous suite. Apart from his courtiers, he had with him two archbishops and sixteen lay senators. Having prayed before the high altar, the king sat in an armchair. The archbishop opened his sermon. Since according to custom he frequently introduced Latin texts and sentences, one of the ambassadors told the Lithuanian chancellor, Radziwill, that the preacher must be forbidden to use Latin words which they could not understand. Radziwill smiled at the simplicity of this notion, as he himself relates. At the end of the sermon the archbishop gave the king a cross and the oath. The king loudly read the oath and, adding the condition concerning the hetman's treaty, kissed the cross. But the ambassadors demanded that there be a special oath regarding the hetman's treaty, and that the king kiss the cross a second time, which would greatly pacify the ambassadors. After the king, six senators took the oath. At the end of the ratification ceremony the king, having taken the documents, gave them to Prince Lvov and said: "I hope that with the help of God we will have a firm and permanent friendship with your sovereign, my brother. Give into his hands this token of our brotherhood and bow to him in my name in a friendly manner." The ambassadors bowed low. The archbishop began to intone the Te Deum, and all the while salutes were fired from cannon. This ceremony, unprecedented to this time, was observed from the choir by the papal nuncio and the Florentine ambassadors.

The ambassadors dined with the king and were his guests at an entertainment, "and the entertainment was how the Assyrian tsar Holofernes came to Jerusalem, and how Judith saved Jerusalem."[31]

SHUISKY'S REMAINS RETURNED TO MOSCOW
But after the entertainment the ambassadors were obliged to perform a mournful commission. Michael had ordered them to request

from the king the corpses of the Shuiskies—Tsar Vasily, his brother Dmitry and the latter's wife. In the instruction it was stated: "If the Poles demand money for Tsar Vasily's corpse, you may give up to ten thousand or even more, according to measure, but you are to say 'This is utterly unheard of, to sell dead bodies. We will give no money for Dmitry Shuisky or his wife, since they were not royal personages.'" When the ambassadors raised the matter with the lords of the Council, they replied that they would report to the king, and added: "It is not befitting to give up the body. We have attained everlasting glory in that a Muscovite tsar and his brother lie with us in Poland; they were buried with honor, and a fine stone chapel was built over them." To this the ambassadors replied that "Tsar Vasily's body is already lifeless, there is not profit in it whatsoever, and we will give you mementoes of what happened with us," and they presented Crown Chancellor Jakub Zadzik with ten times forty sables, and gave smaller presents to various other people. Then the lords of the Council said: "We will report concerning this to his majesty the king and advise him to surrender the body."

Soon the ambassadors were informed that the king had agreed. Zadzik and Alexander Gasiewski told them: "His majesty the king has instructed us to inform you that he has commanded that the bodies of Tsar Vasily and his brother are to be surrendered out of love to his brother your sovereign. If Sigismund were still king, he would not have yielded for anything. Even if you had showered his chambers with gold, he would not have released a single bone." The crown secretaries of the embassy travelled to the capital together with the king's chamberlains and guards. The coffins were in the ground. When the crown secretaries ordered the ground broken they saw beneath them a stone chamber, and in this chamber three coffins, one on the right hand and two to the left. The last two were placed one on top of the other. The solitary coffin on the right hand was Tsar Vasily's; on the left, the upper one was Prince Dmitry's, the one underneath that of his wife. The bodies were exhumed with respect. The ambassadors, with all the table attendants, gentry and all their suite, met them on the road from the village of Jezdowo to the suburbs of Warsaw with great honor. The ambassadors ordered new coffins to be made, and the old coffins be sealed and placed within the new ones. The king sent a golden Turkish globe and bosses forged of gold, and silver nails with which he ordered Tsar Vasily's coffin to be sealed. For Prince Dmitry's coffin he sent some green velvet, and for the princess's coffin some green Chinese silk. The king also released the bodies with great respect, but to the senators and the king's privy councillors sables to the value of 3674 rubles had to be given to obtain this release.

On the morning of June 10 the lament began to sound and the people swarmed out to Dorogomilovo to meet Tsar Vasily's body. From the Dorogomilovo trading settlement to the St. Nicholas church on the Arbat the body was carried on the heads of junior boyars from the provinces, and behind the body walked Bishop Raphael of Kolomna,[32] archimandrites, abbots and archpriests who had been designated to meet the body at Viazma. Behind the body walked the ambassadors, Prince Lvov and his companions. At the church of St. Nicholas Yavlenny, Metropolitan Paul of Krutitsy[33] and Archimandrite Joseph of the New Savior monastery met the body, and with them were all the priests and deacons of the Wooden City with candles and tapers. There the body was met by the boyars Prince Suleshov and Boris Mikhailovich Saltykov, and the lord-in-waiting Mikhail Mikhailovich Saltykov in mourning garb. Servicemen, leading merchants, and ordinary merchants, having there met with the boyars, were also all in mourning. From the church of St. Nicholas the body was carried through the Arbat gates by way of the Exaltation of the Cross street to the Stone Bridge which led the way across the Neglinnaia river into the Kremlin. It was borne on the shoulders of the Muscovite gentry. Patriarch Joseph with all the Holy Synod met the body by the St. Nicholas of Zaraisk church, a wooden chapel which stood by the Stone Bridge, in mourning vestments and, commencing the proceedings according to the clerical estate, followed the body, which was carried into the Kremlin through the Deposition of the Robe gates. When they drew level with Tsar Boris's palace all the bells rang out and the body was carried into the Archangel cathedral through the front doors facing the Treasury Court. The sovereign met the procession by the Dormition cathedral, not going up to the bier. Behind the sovereign were the boyars, councillors and privy councillors, all in mourning. In the Archangel cathedral they sang the great requiem, and the interment was on the next day, June 11.

APPENDIX

KOSTOMAROV ON IVAN SUSANIN

From the distortions of Polish historical literature we move to the distortions of the Russian. The reasons for these distortions are set forth very ably in Professor Kostomarov's recently published article "Ivan Susanin." "In important events," says the author, "it is sometimes necessary to differentiate two sides, the objective and the subjective. The first consists of actuality, that aspect in which the event occurred during its own time. The second is that aspect in which the event impressed itself upon the memory of posterity. Both the one and the other have the significance of historical truth; sometimes the latter is more important than the former. So also historical personages take on the image of a completely different life than they had with contemporaries. Their deeds acquire a much greater significance, their qualities are idealized. They are attributed motives which they possibly did not have at all, or had to a far lesser degree. Later generations select the type of concepts and tendencies which are familiar to them."

These completely true sentiments serve as an introduction to a piece of historical research in which the author attempts to prove that the famous deed of Susanin is doubtful. What is the nature of his evidence? "Until the nineteenth century," says the author, "nobody thought of seeing in Susanin the savior of the tsar's person, or of considering his deed an act of historical importance standing above the common level." But in the same article he cites the charter given by Tsar Michael in 1619 to Susanin's son-in-law in Kostroma, in which it is stated: "When we, the great sovereign, were in Kostroma, the Poles and Lithuanians came into the region, and Bogdashka's father-in-law Ivan Susanin misled them, and they tortured him with great and immeasurable torments, trying to get him to say where we, the great sovereign, were at that time. But Ivan, though he knew all about us, and where we were at the time, suffered immense torments from the Poles and Lithuanians, but did not tell them where we were at that time, so the Poles and Lithuanians tortured him to death."

The charter was confirmed in 1633 and 1641, in 1691 in the name of Ivan V and Peter, and in 1767 on behalf of Catherine II. In the document it states explicitly that the enemy asked where Michael was and tortured him, since naturally they needed the information. Susanin knew, but did not tell. Evidently neither in the seventeenth nor in the eighteenth century did anyone think of trifling with Susanin, or to ask the question whether he really saved the tsar. Did he really need to suffer torture and death? The enemy were very few in number; what danger could they have posed to Michael? They did not concern themselves with such minor details; they simply looked at the fact of the matter. Danger threatened, and Susanin saved the tsar from it. Consequently we have before us several important personages—Michael, Peter, Catherine—who even prior to the nineteenth century thought they saw in Susanin the savior of the tsar's person, and so considered his feat to be out of the ordinary.

But perhaps only these people so regarded Susanin's deed? The author of the article says that we are accustomed from the schoolroom to imagine Susanin as the hero-savior of the tsar and the fatherland. But can he indicate a time when this custom began? He points to Shchekatov's geographical dictionary (1804), where Susanin's feat is first recounted in details which are lacking in Michael's charter. The author of the article finds a contradiction between Shchekatov's account and the charter, namely that in the charter it is stated that the tsar was living at Kostroma, whereas Shchekatov states that he was in the village of Domnino. We should not be surprised at such discrepancies. It is well known how traditions transmitted orally are embellished and distorted until they are written down and printed. But the fact of the matter is that the embellished and distorted tradition attests to the importance of the event transmitted.

The author of the article states: "Somebody (either Shchekatov himself or the person from whom he was borrowing) imagined that Tsar Michael Fedorovich was at that time in the village of Domnino." But if we move that imaginer back from the year 1804, where will the author of the article order us to halt? The author finds new distortions, notable details in the accounts of Glinka and Prince Kozlovsky, and without evidence attributes these details to the imaginations of these writers. But the author himself introduces Prince Kozlovsky's footnote concerning the Nazarov chronicle, which was in the possession of Svinyin, and includes new details not included by Prince Kozlovsky in his account.

Therefore everything tends to indicate to us that there are several traditions concerning the event, with various details, and this directly attests to us the genuineness and importance of this event, however it happened. In the time of Nestor, when some brethren were still alive who remembered the conversion of Russia, several contradictory accounts were current as to the precise place where Vladimir received baptism. Is it possible on this basis to reject the event itself and deny its significance? Finally is there really an unreconciled contradiction between Tsar Michael's charter and the accounts of Shchekatov and others? In the charter it is stated that Michael was at Kostroma, but in the narratives that he was in the village of Domnino. But do we not even now use the names of towns to denote those of districts? "Where did he go?" we ask. "To his estate in Riazan" is the answer, when the traveller never stays in the town of Riazan, but rather in the Riazan countryside.

Further on Kostomarov proceeds to cast suspicion on the very existence of the event as it is depicted in Michael's charter, pointing out that "concerning this event there is not a word by contemporary narrators, either Russian or foreign." We will not speak of foreign writers since the author does not burden us by indicating in which foreign accounts he would expect to find mention of Susanin. As far as the Russian chronicles are concerned, the author asserts that they were fairly generous with their tales!

Let us challenge the author to prove this novelty. The Muscovite chronicler (who he was, we do not know) lightly touches on the most important events in the life of the country and the capital. Is there anything remarkable in that he did not know about a local event, an event occurring in Kostroma, a deed performed in the backwoods by an obscure individual? It could be argued that the event involved the most eminent person in the realm, the newly elected tsar! But let us ask whether we really know much about this personage from the chronicles? When, following Michael's election, it was necessary to dispatch to him a solemn delegation, it was not known where the newly elected tsar was! What had happened to Michael up to March 13, 1613 neither Moscow nor her chronicles knew, and even Kostomarov attributes Susanin's feat to the time before March 13. News of Susanin's feat might have been brought to Moscow with the arrival there of the new tsar and his mother, which did not take place very rapidly; then the news had to be disseminated from the court. How long would it have taken to reach the person who left us his record of contemporary events? And how many circumstances there were to have prevented news from reaching him or, having reached him, to have prevented it from being introduced into the record! It is well known how the impression of events is weakened when knowledge of them comes long after they occur. Kostomarov points out that the Nikon chronicle was definitively compiled during the reign of Alexis Mikhailovich, when Susanin's descendants already had their charters. But was the chronicle really compiled in the same manner that historical works are now compiled, according to archival sources? The available chronicles were transcribed; that is how a definitive compilation was made!

Leaving aside the chronicles, Kostomarov turns to contemporary acts, and also finds that where one would certainly expect to find mention of Susanin's feat "if those who then spoke and acted knew something of that nature." By these words the author wishes to show that not only is the chronicler an obscure individual, but even people in ruling circles knew nothing about Susanin. Among such acts which ought to have contained mention of Susanin, Kostomarov includes those which contain the reproaches of the Muscovite against the Polish government for all that had been done by it and its subjects in Russia during the Time of Troubles. Among these reproaches, in Kostomarov's opinion, there must have been reproaches against the dishonorable attempt on the life of the tsar, who was saved by Susanin. But one page later the author himself destroys his case by explaining that the term "Poles and Lithuanians" in the document must mean rebel cossacks, and not a detachment of the Polish army proper. How, he asks, could the Muscovite government reproach the Poles for a crime of which they were not guilty?

It is also interesting that Kostomarov demands of the metro- pol-
itan who delivered the speech at Michael's coronation skillful descriptions of current events, among which he ought to have mentioned Susanin. Since he did not mention him, he concludes that the
metropolitan knew nothing about him. Yet the metropolitan mentioned neither Minin, Pozharsky nor Trubetskoy. Finally, most
interesting of all, Kostomarov demands that Michael's mother, refusing the throne on behalf of her son before the delegation from
the Assembly, should have mentioned Susanin. The basic argument
for the refusal was that the youthful Michael could not maintain
himself upon the throne, since grown men had been unable to maintain themselves there, for the Russian people were pusillanimous
and did not support their tsars, but replaced them. Kostomarov demands that this basic argument be destroyed by introducing into
evidence events proving the opposite, by which delegates from the
Assembly, arguing against Martha, could use best of all to prove
their basic opinion, that the new tsar had nothing to fear, that the
Russian people had done penance, had come to themselves, were
united, and instead of pusillanimity were showing resolve to sacrifice their lives for the tsar.

"The charter to Bogdashka Sobinin," concludes the author, "was
issued almost eight years after the time of Susanin's death. Can we
assume that the newly-elected tsar could neglect for so long such an
important service rendered him? Of course, he knew nothing about
it. Thereby we may all the more readily assert that Michael Fedorovich, when he acceded to the throne, immediately rewarded all
those who in the years of adversity had befriended his family. Thus
in March 1614 the peasants of Tarutino received a charter of tax
exemption for having shown kindness to Martha Ivanovna when she
was sent into exile during the reign of Boris. This service was of
course significant, but Susanin's service, had it been known about at
the time, was a hundred times more worthy of recognition. Why
was this heroic deed for so long forgotten, when it had the greatest
right of all to the tsar's attention?" Here the author neglects the
most important circumstance, which fully resolves all bewilderment.
Who was there to be rewarded? If Susanin had been tortured but left
alive he would have been rewarded more promptly and handsomely
than the inhabitants of Tarutino. But he was no longer among the

living, he had no wife or sons, but only one daughter, a cast-off piece of flotsam according to the conceptions of that time (and of the present day). Yet she was rewarded after all!

Further on Kostomarov, while agreeing with the explanation that inexact terminology is used in the charter—Poles and Lithuanians instead of rebel cossacks—says: "Perhaps among the number of brigands who fell upon Susanin there were Lithuanians, but in no way was there any organized detachment with the political aim of seizing and killing Michael. Perhaps it was a small cluster of petty brigands into which some Lithuanian stragglers had wandered. But such a cluster could not at that time have posed any danger to Michael Fedorovich, who was staying in a fortified monastery, and was surrounded by junior boyars. Under interrogation by such brigands Susanin could have dared say where the tsar was, and the brigands would have remained in the position of the fox looking up at the grapes. But let us suppose that Susanin, motivated by blind loyalty to his boyar, did not wish to say anything whatsoever to these brigands. Who saw how or why he was tortured? If there were others present the brigands would have tortured them also, and either would have tortured them to death as they did Susanin, or would have found out from them where the tsar was. If the brigands really did seize him alone, then only God could ascertain why he was tortured. In short, there is some kind of inconsistency and lack of clarity, something improbable. Susanin's martyrdom was something all too common in those days. At that time cossacks were roving about the countryside burning and torturing peasants. It is likely that the brigands who fell upon Susanin were precisely that kind of petty bandits, and the incident subsequently so largely glorified was one of many similar incidents in that year. Some time later Susanin's son-in-law took advantage of it, obtaining for himself the charter of tax exemption. We can see the way he chose. He appealed to the tender heart of the nun (Martha Ivanovna), and she asked her son. The son did not refuse his mother's plea. In that century everyone sought to avoid taxation insofar as he was able!"

To answer this it must be said, first of all, that it is in vain that Kostomarov, by diminishing the significance of the rebel detachment, seeks to minimize the danger threatening Michael, and thus lessen or deny the importance of Susanin's feat. Does Kostomarov really know the size of the forces defending the Hypatian monastery while Michael was living there prior to his acceptance of the tsardom? We will even suppose that these forces were large; but even with Pozharsky in Yaroslavl there were many troops, yet the cossacks got together a conspiracy to kill him, and it was only by chance that their design did not succeed. Consequently the danger to the tsar had nothing to do with the size of the brigand detachment, but in the aims its leaders set themselves. They would better be able to achieve their purposes by secret assassination rather than a frontal attack upon Kostroma or a siege of the Hypatian monastery. Concerning the question as to who saw Susanin tortured, there can be any number of satisfactory answers. The usual methods of bands similar to that which fell upon Susanin are well known. They would find out who knew what the brigands needed to know, and then they would torture the one who knew, while the others who pointed him out would either stand around or lie down half dead through fear. In putting forward an alleged inconsistency, something unclear and improbable in the event, Kostomarov wishes at all cost to debunk Susanin; but the matter cannot end with this debunking. In place of the hero Susanin it is necessary to create a rogue, a deceiver, his son-in-law Sobinin, who fabricated the story that his father-in-law was tortured to death for the sake of the tsar, and wheedled a tax exemption charter for himself. We do not know whether we can allow ourselves to believe such things, having no clear evidence from the sources, on the basis of only a few considerations which will not hold up even at the first glance! Sobinin, according to Kostomarov's words, appealed to the nun's tender heart; but the author forgets that by this time the monk had come, who was not exactly noted for his tender heart. This was Filaret Nikitich, who had taken the government into his firm hands. It is true that in this century everyone who could avoided taxation; but Kostomarov would have us believe that at that very time a tax exemption charter was granted to a man who appeared with some unsubstantiated yarn about how his father-in-law had been tortured to death on behalf of the tsar.

But most curious of all is the conclusion of Kostomarov's research. "By a sheer coincidence that which our bookmen in the nineteenth century thought up about Susanin (evidently the 1619 charter belongs to the nineteenth century!) appeared in almost the same vein at the opposite end of the Russian world, in the Ukraine. When in 1648 Hetman Bogdan Khmelnitsky was in pursuit of the Polish army a certain South Russian peasant Mikita Galagan volunteered to act as a guide to the Polish army, deliberately led them into a swamp and impenetrable forest, and gave the cossacks the opportunity to destroy their enemies. This heroic feat of self-sacrifice differs from Susanin's in that it really happened."

How can we say it really happened? Everyone thought that Susanin's feat also really happened, but suspicions arose all the same. Nobody believes in these words, especially when it is known what a murky source are the Little Russian chronicles, in which even the date of Bogdan Khmelnitsky's death is incorrectly given. Here he will find a similar tale about Galagan (when, in the words of the *History of the Battle of Prezel*, Galagan was sent by Khmelnitsky) where it says only that the Poles moved into an unfavorable position because of the unreliability or hostility of their guide. How delighted Kostomarov would be if in some chronicle or chronograph some reference could be found to Ivan Susanin, namely that the enemy were unable to discover Michael's whereabouts because of the unreliability or hostility of their guide! Thus Kostomarov in relation to the one event casts suspicion upon a primary source, a document, on the basis that there is no such information in sources of lesser reliability, while at the same time proclaiming that a heroic act was truly achieved, of which only a murky source knows, and about which nothing is known in any primary source.

We have seen that Kostomarov has used in vain methods of petty historical criticism to undermine the information about Susanin's historical act. Encountering such a phenomenon, the historian immerses himself in the state of the national spirit, and if he sees the heightening of moral forces of the nation, as there was during the Time of Troubles, if he sees the heroic deeds of Minin, Pozharsky, Rzhevsky, Filosofov and Lugovskoy, he will not fail to recognize as being worthy of belief the heroic deed of Susanin, will not submit the martyr to fresh torture by asking whether he really was tortured, or why he was tortured! The historian should act in the same way with regard to Galagan's feat. He should not quibble over whether there is any mention of such a deed in this or that chronicle, or look

at different sides, at north and south. He knows that during the ep-
och of Khmelnitsky in the south there was that same heightening of
moral forces in the Russian people, evidenced by the enemy themselves, who write that among the Russians they could not find a
single spy, and that even if you burned a Russian prisoner alive he
would not betray any information about his fellows. Knowing this,
the historian does not cast doubt upon the credibility of Galagan's
brave deed, and even will say that there were many Galagans whose
names were not inscribed in any chronicle. Under the influence of
the great events of the seventeenth century, which laid the ground
for the greatness and unity of the Russian people, the historian will
not remain a Great or Little Russian historian, and in place of a
single Russian life will not highlight in his account the strife between the Drevliane and Poliane, the Radimichi and Viatichi.

NOTES

Additional information on personalities and topics found in the text and notes is available in Joseph L. Wieczynski, ed., *The Modern Encyclopedia of Russian and Soviet History* (MERSH); Harry B. Weber, ed., *The Modern Encyclopedia of Russian and Soviet Literatures (Including Non-Russian and Emigre Literatures)* (MERSL); David R. Jones, ed., *The Military-Naval Encyclopedia of Russia and the Soviet Union* (MNERSU); Paul D. Steeves, *The Modern Encyclopedia of Religions in Russia and the Soviet Union* (MERRSU), all published by Academic International Press.

CHAPTER I

1. The Assembly of the Land (*zemskii sobor*) was a gathering in which representatives of various strata of society met to discuss matters of importance. Some historians have seen the Assembly as an abortive step towards a permanent "states-representative monarchy," but this view is generally discounted. See entry by Richard Hellie in MERSH, Vol. 45, pp. 226-234.

2. Feodorit (1551-1617) was a close relative of the Sheremetev family, who was persuaded by Patriarch Job to enter the monastic life. Formerly he had owned a service tenure in Riazan province, which places his entry into religious life not earlier than 1589. The name of Brother Feodorit appears among those of the commissioners empowered to investigate the death of Tsarevich Dmitry in 1591, though perhaps this is not the same Feodorit. From 1604 he was archimandrite of the Savior monastery in Riazan. The archiepiscopal throne became vacant on the elevation of the Greek incumbent Ignaty to the patriarchate under False Dmitry I. Feodorit was consecrated by Hermogen, at that time metropolitan of Kazan. During the reign of the pretender the archiepiscopal palace which had been confiscated from his predecessors was restored to him. He seems to have let things pass under False Dmitry, at whose coronation and marriage he assisted (according to foreign observers, although he is not mentioned in official documents). He also assisted at the coronation of Vasily Shuisky, and greeted the remains of Tsarevich Dmitry a few days later. The new Dormition cathedral, begun in 1598 by Mitrofan, the first archbishop of Riazan, was completed by Feodorit. In 1609 the incorrupt remains of St. Vasily, a former bishop of Riazan, were exhibited in the new cathedral, before being given their final resting place in the Nativity cathedral. Feodorit ordered two copies of the

miraculous icon of Our Lady of Riazan to be made; one he placed in the church of the village of Fedotievo, from whence the original had come in 1489, and the other he placed in the Nativity cathedral. His services to Russia during the patriarchate of Hermogen were so great that he is mentioned among the foremost saviors of the country in 1612. Aided by his friends the Volkonsky princes, especially Prince Mikhail, he prevented Pereiaslavl-in-Riazan from going over to the enemy. He bitterly mourned the deposition and forcible tonsure of Vasily Shuisky by Zakhar Liapunov, and later the designs of King Sigismund against the Orthodox faith. In conjunction with the authorities of the Riazan land, namely Pozharsky, Prokopy Liapunov and Archpriest Dmitry, he called upon the people to come to the defense of the Orthodox faith. Hermogen was starved to death by the Poles, Liapunov murdered by the cossacks, and Pozharsky was wounded, so for a time Feodorit was regarded as the foremost leader of the national resistance. In February 1613 Feodorit was authorized by the Assembly of the Land to proclaim the election of Michael as tsar. He was also dispatched to Kostroma to urge Michael to accept, taking with him the miraculous icon of the Dormition painted for the sainted Metropolitan Peter of Moscow. He subsequently played a prominent part in the Assembly of the Land, on many of whose documents his name appeared. He died at Pereislavl on September 10, 1617 in his 66th year, and in the twelfth year of his episcopacy.

3. The New Savior (Novospassky) monastery was originally dedicated to the Transfiguration, and was built on the site of the present Danilov monastery at the end of the thirteenth century. The community moved within the Kremlin in 1330 at the behest of Ivan Kalita, and for a time was the foremost monastery in the Kremlin. Until the founding of the Ascension convent it served as the burial place for female members of the ruling house. In 1462 the community was relocated once again, to the Taganka, where it was rededicated as the New Savior monastery. From the end of the fifteenth century it was the burial place for prominent boyar families related to the ruling house. Late in the sixteenth century it was fortified with towers and defensive walls, and the defenses were subsequently reinforced.

4. The Simonov monastery was founded in 1370 as a forepost defending Moscow on the left bank of the Moscow river on the southeastern approaches. In 1404 the building of the stone conventual church was completed. In the mid-sixteenth century it was newly constructed with defensive walls and towers, several churches and household offices. It was converted into a plague hospital during the 1771 epidemic, but recommissioned as a monastery in 1796.

5. Avraamy Palitsyn, in secular life Averky Ivanovich, entered the monastic life involuntarily in 1588, allegedly being implicated in the plot against Boris Godunov by the Shuisky family. Initially confined to the

Solovetsk monastery in the far north, he later was transferred to the Trinity monastery, of which he became the cellarer in 1608. The cellarer was the business manager of the monastery and, prior to the takeover by the state in the eighteenth century of the monasteries' landed properties, also managed the monastic estates and their peasant population. Apart from writing his famous history, Avraamy took part in the embassy to Sigismund III outside the walls of Smolensk in the fall of 1610, and played a leading part in the liberation of Moscow from the Poles in 1612 and the election of Michael Romanov in 1613. In 1618 he was one of the defenders of the monastery against the forces of Prince Wladyslaw. In 1619 he was banished once again to the Solovetsk monastery, where he died in 1626. See entry in MERSH, Vol. 26, pp. 195-197.

6. Fedor Ivanovich Sheremetev (1576-1650) was orphaned at an early age. His father was killed in the Livonian war in 1577, and his mother died in 1583. During his minority his estate was administered by his sister Elena Ivanovna, widow of Tsarevich Ivan Ivanovich. His earliest recorded service was in 1591, when the Tatars were threatening Moscow. In 1592 he was at the christening feast of Tsarevna Feodosia, and in 1597 was at the reception of the imperial ambassador in the Palace of Facets. He was briefly governor of Chernigov in 1598, but was back in Moscow in time to witness the confirmatory charter concerning the election of Boris Godunov. Sheremetev seems to have shared in the fate of the Romanov clan in 1600, since he was in semi-honorific exile as governor of Tobolsk from 1601 to 1603, and then there is a gap in his service record until 1605, when he was sent with a large army to the relief of Kromy. From his petition to Prince Wladyslaw in 1610 it is also apparent that Boris confiscated some of his estates in the Riazan region. With the advance of False Dmitry I, Sheremetev found himself at Orel, where he greeted the pretender with bread and salt, crosses, icons and pealing of bells. When Dmitry restored to favor those who had been in bad odor during the reign of Boris, Sheremetev was not forgotten, and was appointed to the boyar council, which Dmitry renamed the Senate. He also was put in charge of a levy of eighteen thousand men from the regions of Novgorod and Pskov, intended for Dmitry's proposed Crimean campaign. Probably the troops which infiltrated the capital on the night of Dmitry's murder were commanded by Sheremetev. When Astrakhan under its governor Prince I.D. Khvorostinin declared for False Dmitry II, Sheremetev was ordered to recover the city. Despite the help of the Nogay khan, Ishterek, he was unable to do so, and set up his camp on the island of Balchik, about three versts upriver in the Volga delta. Many merchants from Astrakhan and the Caspian littoral sought refuge at Balchik. Although he was never able to recapture Astrakhan, he did pacify many of the towns of the lower Volga, and also recruited levies from the various native peoples, including Cheremiss, Mordvin and Chuvash. He then sent aid to the governors of Nizhny Novgorod, A.A. Repnin and A.S. Aliabiev, enabling them

to repel the rebels, not only from the city itself, but also from Balakhna, Vorsma and the village of Pavlovo. On the way Sheremetev defeated rebel detachments at Cheboksary and Sviyazhsk, and remained at Nizhny Novgorod until the dry season. Murom swore allegiance to Tsar Vasily even before Sheremetev arrived there, but Kasimov surrendered only after a prolonged resistance. Vladimir surrendered also without a struggle, and there Sheremetev made his headquarters. Despite Tsar Vasily's urging that Sheremetev proceed immediately to the relief of the Trinity monastery, he felt unable to advance further while leaving Suzdal untaken in his rear. An attempt to capture Suzdal was defeated by the pretender's governors Pleshcheev and Prosovetsky, reinforced by a detachment led by Lisowski from the forces besieging the Trinity monastery. Retreating to Vladimir, Sheremetev corresponded with various other towns loyal to Moscow, principally Yaroslavl. Informed of Skopin's movements, he eventually managed to link up with the Russo-Swedish expeditionary force at Alexandrovskaia Sloboda on November 11, 1609. Thereafter Skopin assumed command of the combined forces and Sheremetev faded into the background. After the deposition of Vasily Shuisky, Sheremetev loyally supported the candidacy of Prince Wladyslaw. He was one of the boyars virtually held prisoner in the Kremlin from February 1611 to October 1612, but after a brief absence from Moscow played a leading part in the Assembly of the Land in 1613, and was one of the deputation sent to bring the newly-elected Tsar Michael to the capital. From then on until his retirement in 1646 he played a leading part in the government. Before the return of Filaret, and after his death, he was virtually the head of the chancellery network and the factual leader of the boyar council, although in the earlier years he was theoretically outranked by the easy-going Prince F.I. Mstislavsky. He also accumulated fabulous wealth, as his will and the enormous endowments made to leading monasteries attest. He finally took monastic vows under the name Feodosy at the St. Cyril monastery near Beloozero, and died there February 17, 1650.

7. Prince Vladimir Ivanovich Bakhterianov-Rostovsky (?-1617) is first mentioned in 1580 as governor of Staraia Rusa, together with Ivan Kriuk-Kolychev, with whom he got involved in a precedence dispute. In 1582 he was one of the governors of Novgorod, and in 1586 commanded the main regiment at Briansk. He returned to Novgorod in 1596, with Luke Osipovich Shcherbatov as his colleague. In 1596 he was sent to Tiumen with grain supplies and money. He was governor of Terka in 1599, fought with the Turks in the Caucasus and was captured in a skirmish, then ransomed the following year. He is not attested again until the Time of Troubles, when apparently he sided with False Dmitry II. After the fall of the Tushino camp he proceeded to Moscow, where he was promoted boyar by Vasily Shuisky. He was also the first to bring news to Moscow of the death of the pretender and the collapse of his army. In 1611 his name appears on two

acts: (1) a letter to Shein in Smolensk, and (2) a letter to King Sigismund requesting the speedy dispatch of the tsar-elect, Prince Wladyslaw. In 1613, as seen here, he was included in the delegation sent by the Assembly of the Land to Michael at Kostroma. Later he was appointed governor of Nizhny Novgorod, where he remained until his death. He corresponded with the governor of Yaroslavl in 1615 concerning the activities of Lisowski. His only son Peter fought in the ranks of the First Militia Force, and died in 1618 without heirs.

8. Fedor Vasilievich Golovin, lord-in-waiting, died 1625.

9. The Holy Synod (*Osviashchenyi sobor*) was an assembly of the bishops, heads of monasteries and other prominent clergy of the Russian Orthodox church, and is not to be confused with the lay board of the same name set up by Peter the Great to administer church affairs.

10. Fedor Nikitich Romanov (1553-1633) was arrested in 1600 along with his brothers Ivan, Vasily and Alexander, and was forcibly tonsured under the religious name of Filaret. During the reign of False Dmitry I he was appointed metropolitan of Rostov but during the rule of Vasily Shuisky was passed over for the patriarchate in favor of Metropolitan Hermogen of Kazan. Returning to his see of Rostov, he was captured by the forces of False Dmitry II, brought to Tushino and forced to accept the patriarchal title. Escaping to Moscow after the fall of the Tushino camp, during the interregnum he was dispatched with the high embassy to King Sigismund III at his encampment outside Smolensk. Failing to reach agreement over the candidacy of the king's son, Wladyslaw, the members of the high embassy were interned in Poland. Filaret languished in the fortress of Marienburg until he was exchanged for Colonel Struys in 1619. Returning to Moscow, he assumed the patriarchal throne and was the factual ruler for his feeble-minded son until his death in 1633.

11. Pereiaslavl-in-Riazan, as opposed to Pereiaslavl-Zalessky (see Note 37, below).

12. The Hypatius monastery was founded in 1330 on the site of a miraculous appearance of the Blessed Virgin Mary. Its founding is associated with the name of Chet Murza, allegedly the ancestor of the Godunov family, who took the baptismal name of Zakhary.

13. Grishka Otrepiev was the runaway monk allegedly assuming the identity of Tsarevich Dmitry (presumed dead since 1591) who in 1603 appeared in Poland and successfully asserted his claim to the Muscovite rulership. He ruled from June 1605 to May 1606. His detractors frequently refer to him as the brigand or the renegade monk (*rasstriga*).

14. Ivan Martynovich Zarutsky (?-1614) first took part in the Bolotnikov rebellion, and then joined forces with False Dmitry II, on whose behalf he commanded a band of Don Cossacks, and was named boyar by the pretender. After the collapse of the Tushino camp he first went to King

Sigismund at Smolensk, but then returned to Dmitry in Kaluga. After the murder of the pretender he joined the First Militia Force, and after the murder of Liapunov assumed leadership. In 1612 he attempted to organize the assassination of Pozharsky; when this failed he fled to Astrakhan. With the approach of Tsar Michael's troops and a popular uprising within the city, Zarutsky fled to the Ural steppes but was handed over to the Muscovite authorities by his own cossacks, and was impaled by the Serpukhov gates of Moscow. See entry in MERSH, Vol. 45, pp. 176-182.

15. The Ivan Susanin story periodically is called into question. The Appendix contains Soloviev's rebuttal of Kostomarov's challenge, and more recently an attempt to debunk the Susanin legend by Yu. Chernichenko, "Uravnenie s izvestnym" (Comparison with What is Known), *Zvezda* 1974, No. 4, was roundly refuted by V.I. Buganov, "Vopreky fakty" (In Face of the Facts), *Voprosy istorii*, 1975, No. 2.

16. Prince Dmitry Mikhailovich Pozharsky (1578-1642) had been the military commander of the Second Militia Force, which in 1612 finally had liberated Moscow from Polish occupation. Although he was the undoubted hero of the liberation movement, he appears to have suffered a comparative eclipse during the reign of Michael. This might have been because he is known to have favored the candidacy of the Swedish prince, Karl Philipp, or because men of greater prominence absent from the scene during the time of crisis now had returned to resume their proper places. During the reign of Michael, Pozharsky seems to have been called to action when the skill and prestige of such a military leader was needed, but at other times was relegated to relative obscurity. See entry by Daniel B. Rowland, MERSH, Vol. 29, pp. 151-156.

17. Prince Ivan Fedorovich Troekurov, boyar, died 1621.

18. Ivan Petrovich Sheremetev (1586-1647) is first mentioned as a table attendant in 1606 at the court of False Dmitry I. In 1611 he swore allegiance to Prince Wladyslaw, but then appeared in the encampment of the Militia Force, though perhaps he was implicated in the murder of Prokopy Liapunov on July 25. He and his brother Vasily then made themselves scarce for a while, but in September reappeared in Trubetskoy's army outside Moscow. He urged the cossacks to kill Pozharsky and prevent the Second Militia Force from reaching Moscow. In the late autumn of 1611 he was sent by the boyar council to be governor of Kostroma. In March 1612, when Kuzma Minin advanced from Kineshma to Kostroma, he was met on the Ples river by some of the inhabitants, who warned him that Sheremetev did not wish him to enter the town. Pozharsky ordered the Militia Force to halt in the outskirts. The inhabitants of Kostroma were divided, although eventually those who supported Pozharsky gained the upper hand and would have killed Sheremetev, had not Pozharsky intervened personally to save him. Pozharsky then appointed Sheremetev governor of Yaroslavl and

in this capacity Sheremetev greeted the newly elected Tsar Michael and his mother on March 21, 1613 as they passed through the town on their way to Moscow. Sheremetev accompanied them as far as the Trinity monastery, and on April 23 was sent ahead to announce to Moscow the tsar's impending arrival. At the Trinity monastery Michael declared that he would proceed no further because of the disordered state of the land. It was Sheremetev whom the Muscovite commanders sent to the tsar to urge him to continue his journey. Between 1613 and 1618 he played an important part in court ceremonial functions, and in September 1614 he was sent briefly to Mtsensk to command the vanguard regiment to counter a threatened Tatar invasion. He does not appear to have been in service between 1618 and 1622, but in June of the latter year he was sent to Riazan, again to command forces on the Tatar frontier. From 1625 he was at court functions, assisted at the birth and christening of the tsar's children Irina, Pelagia and Alexis, and accompanied the tsar on pilgrimages. He disappears from court records between 1630 and 1633. In 1634 he was appointed boyar with a salary entitlement of four hundred rubles, and named governor of Kazan, where he stayed until 1636. On March 8, 1638 he escorted the remains of Prince Johan (died 1602) to the city gates of Moscow on their way back to Denmark at the request of King Christian IV. Between April and September 1638 he was at Krapivna guarding the frontier against the Crimeans and Nogay. In 1639 he was appointed head of the Chancellery for Military Recruitment. In April 1640 he was entrusted to conduct negotiations with the Polish envoys, and was given the title lord lieutenant of Rostov. Between 1640 and 1647 he was in charge of the Vladimir Judicial Chancellery. In 1642 he was in a precedence dispute with Prince Andrei Vasilievich Khilkov, head of the Moscow Judicial Chancellery, which he considered inferior to the Vladimir post. He won, and Khilkov was imprisoned. On January 28, 1644 Sheremetev met with Prince Waldemar. At the end of 1644 he negotiated with the Turkish ambassador, and in January 1645 with the Polish ambassador Stempkowski. Then he got into a precedence dispute with Prince Nikita Ivanovich Odoevsky, and as a result spent a time in prison. On September 28, 1645 he held the sceptre at the coronation of Tsar Alexis. He continued to head the Vladimir Judicial Chancellery until his death on July 8, 1647. Prior to his death he took the monastic tonsure under the name of Jonas (Iona).

19. Prince Fedor Ivanovich Mstislavsky (?-1622) was the son of a prominent political and military figure during the reign of Ivan IV. Ivan Fedorovich was one of the more prominent advisers of the tsar during the 1550s and then, together with Prince I.D. Belsky, was joint head of the lands of the realm (zemshchina). He also was named to the council of regency on the death of Ivan the Terrible, but in 1585 fell from power and entered a monastery. Fedor Ivanovich is first mentioned in court service in

1575, and became a boyar in 1576. With his father's banishment to a monastery in 1586 he became the ranking boyar in the duma. In 1598 he was put forward by some as a candidate for the throne, but he refused to be considered. He was loyal to Boris Godunov and on one occasion even was offered the hand of the tsar's daughter Xenia, since apparently he had been a widower since 1586. When he declined, the tsar refused him permission to marry at all. This prohibition was lifted by False Dmitry I in 1606, but there is no evidence that he took advantage of this dispensation. His military record was not very distinguished, although when reputedly he was wounded fifteen times at Novgorod Seversk in December 1604 he was given a hero's welcome in Moscow by Boris. On the other hand, he was defeated soundly by Bolotnikov on the Serpukhov highway in October 1606, and was forced to lift the siege of Kaluga when the relieving column under the bogus Tsarevich Peter arrived. Both in 1606 and 1610 he refused to be considered as a candidate for the throne, but he was one of the "seven boyars" who formed the interim government after the deposition of Vasily Shuisky in July 1610. After the liberation of Moscow by Minin and Pozharsky he temporarily went into seclusion at Yaroslavl, but was present at the final session of the Assembly which elected Michael Romanov. It is estimated that in 1613 he was the wealthiest lay landowner in Muscovy; since his two sons predeceased him, the line became extinct with his death on February 12, 1622. See entry by Emily V. Leonard, MERSH, Vol. 23, p. 160.

20. The Palace of Facets was constructed between 1487 and 1491 by the Italian architects Marco Ruffo and Pietro Antonio Solario. The name is taken from the eastern facade of the building. The interior contains an audience chamber five hundred square meters in area, with a series of vaults supported by a central column. This chamber was used for ceremonial receptions, meetings of the boyar council and sessions of the Assembly of the Land.

21. The Ascension convent was founded in the fourteenth century by Evdokia, wife of Grand Prince Dmitry Donskoy, within the Kremlin behind the Savior tower. It superseded the Transfiguration monastery as the burial place of female members of the ruling house. The convent, along with the adjoining Miracles monastery, was demolished during the 1930s to make room for the School of Red Commanders.

22. Maria Nagaia was Ivan IV's last wife and mother of Tsarevich Dmitry, who after the death of her son and the ensuing tumult in Uglich was forced to take the veil under the name Martha. Michael's mother, Xenia Romanova, also took the religious name of Martha, which makes matters a little confusing! Martha Nagaia recognized False Dmitry I as her long-lost son, but changed her tune after he was murdered. Since this last change of mind suited Vasily Shuisky's purposes very well, she was allowed to remain in the special apartments assigned to her as dowager tsaritsa in the Ascension convent.

23. Prince Ivan Mikhailovich Vorotynsky (?-1627) is first mentioned as being imprisoned during the reign of Ivan IV, then released on the death of his father in 1577. Under Ivan IV he served as governor of Murom, and in 1582 was sent to Kazan to pacify the rebellious Cheremiss. In 1585 he incurred the hostility of the regent Boris Godunov by his partisanship of the Shuisky interest and was exiled to "distant places," only to return in 1592 when he was promoted boyar and appointed chief commander at Kazan. He returned to Moscow in 1598 and apparently remained loyal to Boris until the latter's death. He was one of the first to swear allegiance to False Dmitry I, and was one of the delegation sent to greet the pretender at Tula. Within a year he was in opposition to him and was party to his overthrow. During Shuisky's reign he was loyal to the tsar, and fought against False Dmitry II and other opponents. He was also a close confidant of Patriarch Hermogen, and as such suffered persecution from the interim boyar regime in Moscow. He was placed under arrest and forced to sign a document calling for the surrender of Smolensk. According to some accounts, he was considered briefly as a candidate for the throne but when Michael was elected Vorotynsky was among the deputation sent to Kostroma. He subsequently served as governor of Kazan, led the embassy to Smolensk and later, when Michael was absent on pilgrimage, was left in charge of the capital. In his last years he retired from service, and on his deathbed was tonsured under the name Jonas.

24. Vasily Petrovich Morozov, lord-in-waiting since 1600 or 1601, boyar 1608, died 1631.

25. Prince Danilo Ivanovich Mezetsky (?-1639) had been a favorite of Boris Godunov. In 1608, under Shuisky, he was appointed lord-in-waiting. He was one of the signatories to the armistice concluded with Hetman Zolkiewski at Tsarevo-Zaimishche in June 1610. He was later one of the plenipotentiaries at the Deulino peace talks, receiving boyardom in 1618. He headed the Chancellery of Artillery 1626-1628 then retired to a monastery, taking the monastic name David.

26. Prince Dmitry Timofeevich Trubetskoy (?-1625) is first mentioned as being among the defenders of Novgorod Seversk against the forces of False Dmitry I in 1604. In 1608 he deserted the cause of Tsar Vasily Shuisky and was appointed table attendant and later boyar at the Tushino court of False Dmitry II. There he was joined by his cousin Prince Yury Nikitich Trubetskoy, who had been exiled by Shuisky for alleged treason during the Bolotnikov rebellion. On the other hand, Prince Dmitry's uncle, Prince Andrei Vasilievich Trubetskoy, remained in Moscow, and after the overthrow of Shuisky became one of the "seven boyars" in charge of Moscow during the ensuing interregnum. At the same time Prince Dmitry obtained command of a band of cossacks, and was among the besiegers of the city with the First Militia Force. After the murder of Liapunov he remained with

his cossacks in the vicinity of Moscow while the Second Militia Force was forming under Minin and Pozharsky. Unlike his colleague Zarutsky, he made his peace with the Second Militia Force and with them participated in the liberation of Moscow. It appears that he was considered for the vacant Moscow throne, but was bought off with lavish grants in the Vaga region of lands which formerly belonged to the Godunov and Shuisky families, and which more latterly King Sigismund III had granted to Mikhail Glebovich Saltykov. Under the new reign he took part in the liberation of Novgorod from the Swedes, but later became involved in an embarrasing precedence dispute with V.P. Morozov, in which his compromising relations with the Poles were dragged up. He was among the delegation sent to greet Metropolitan Filaret on his return in 1619. Some time later he was appointed governor of Tobolsk, where he died in 1625. See entry by Daniel B. Rowland, MERSH, Vol. 39, pp. 241-244.

27. The Dormition cathedral (Uspensky sobor), built by the Italian architect Aristotle Fioravanti between 1475 and 1491, was the main cathedral of the Kremlin, where such ceremonies as coronations and royal weddings were conducted.

28. Prince Ivan Borisovich Cherkassky (?-1642), son of Prince Boris Kanbulatovich, first is mentioned in 1598 at the election of Boris Godunov. In 1600-1601 he was implicated in the sorcery charges brought against the Romanov family. His property was confiscated and he was exiled to Siberia. While he was on his way there, the bailliff received orders to halt at Malmyzh and await the tsar's pleasure. Cherkassky and his uncle Ivan Nikitich Romanov, then were ordered to serve at Nizhny Novgorod. On September 17, 1602 the sentence of banishment was lifted, and Cherkassky returned to the capital in November. Nothing further is known of his service under Boris or False Dmitry I. Tsar Vasily appointed Cherkassky to the court office previously occupied by the pretender's favorite, Prince Ivan Andreevich Khvorostinin, but was dismissed shortly afterwards. With the attack of False Dmitry II on Moscow in the fall of 1608, Cherkassky was placed in charge of one of the regiments stationed on the Khodynka. He seems to have seen little further action until 1611, when he fought under the command of Prince Ivan Semeonovich Kurakin on behalf of Prince Wladyslaw in the Vladimir region. Kurakin was defeated, and Cherkassky taken prisoner. His fortunes changed for the better when his kinsman Michael was elected tsar. Cherkassky was promoted boyar on July 11, 1613, two days before the coronation. The return of Filaret in 1619 improved his lot still further. His first active service under the Romanov regime came in September 1618, when he was sent to Yaroslavl to raise troops for the defense of Moscow. During this campaign he inflicted heavy losses on renegade cossacks operating in the environs of Yaropolch. On his return to Moscow early in 1619 he was invited to the sovereign's table, and after the

banquet awarded a sable robe and a silver goblet. In the autumn of 1624 and the spring of 1627 he was in charge of the Chancellery of Musketeers. During his long career he also served as Treasurer, and as head of the Chancellery for Service Foreigners and the Chancellery of the Apothecary. It is known that he was married, but he died without surviving issue, so his immense fortune was divided between the Sheremetev family and his Cherkassky relatives, Princes Dmitry Mamstriukovich and Yakov Kudenet-ovich.

29. Ivan Nikitich Romanov (?-1640) is first mentioned in 1591, when he was summoned to Serpukhov to participate in the campaign against the Tatars. He returned with land grants, gifts and expressions of the tsar's goodwill. In 1597 he was present at the reception of the imperial ambassador Abraham Donau, and in 1599 was ceremonial cupbearer for Tsar Boris at the reception of Prince Gustav of Sweden. When the Romanov family fell into disgrace in 1601 Ivan Nikitich was sent to Pelym, where he was joined for a while by his brother Vasily, who died on February 15, 1602. The following month the terms of his exile were alleviated, and he was escorted to Ufa, and later was employed in some administrative capacity at Nizhny Novgorod. He was permitted briefly to return to Moscow, but spent the rest of Boris's reign under house arrest at his estate near Klin. In 1605 he was bidden to attend the coronation of False Dmitry I, and thereafter was promoted boyar and named to Dmitry's Polish-style Senate. During the reign of Shuisky he was ordered, together with a number of other boyars and commanders, to Kozelsk. He was also one of the groomsmen at the tsar's marriage on January 17, 1608. He served as second in command at different times to Prince I.I. Shuisky and Prince M.V. Skopin-Shuisky. In 1610 Ivan Nikitich was responsible for persuading Patriarch Hermogen to withdraw his initial objection to the candidacy of Prince Wladyslaw, and his signature is prominent upon the letter of the boyars to the inhabitants of Kostroma and Yaroslavl urging them to discountenance the First Militia Force commanded by Trubetskoy and Zarutsky. Yet when the Second Militia Force liberated Moscow he also signed the confirmatory charter proclaiming the election of his nephew Michael. He was also part of the family regency council, consisting of himself, Prince Ivan Borisovich Cherkassky and the boyar Fedor Ivanovich Sheremetev. The senior boyar, Prince Fedor Ivanovich Mstislavsky, also made Ivan Nikitich his executor shortly before his death without heirs in 1622, and Ivan Nikitich on his behalf distributed his fabulous wealth among various religious foundations. As related here, he was involved in a number of precedence disputes in which it was generally ruled that, although the plaintiff came from a more illustrious family, Ivan Nikitich, as uncle of the tsar, must take precedence. In order to avoid more such unseemly incidents Ivan Nikitich seems to have made himself scarce at court. In any case he was fabulously rich, although it is not known

whether the estates confiscated by Boris in 1601 were restored to him. For ceremonial receptions of ambassadors he provided large contingents of armed and mounted men from his estates; for example, in 1626 forty of the 177 members of the guard of honor were provided by Ivan Nikitich at his own expense. During the Russian-Polish war of 1632-1634 he contributed large amount of provisions for the troops besieging Smolensk, also at his own cost. Ivan Nikitich died July 18, 1640. His widow Uliana Fedorovna attended the first marriage of Tsar Alexis on January 16, 1648 and died October 23, 1649. Ivan Nikitich had eight children, but only two, Nikita and Martha, survived him. Martha married Prince Alexis Ivanovich Vorotynsky. Nikita was a lifelong bachelor, and with his death in 1654 his estates escheated to the crown.

30. Ephraim, second metropolitan of Kazan, was consecrated December 26, 1606. After the death of Patriarch Hermogen the suffragan metropolitanate of Krutitsy was also vacant with the death of its incumbent Pafnuty. Metropolitan Isidore of Novgorod was in the power of the Swedes, which led the Second Militia Force to look to Ephraim as the spiritual leader of the Russian church. He took the initiative in convoking a synod of Russian bishops meeting in conjunction with the Assembly of the Land. He consecrated Jonas, archbishop of Sarai and the Don, as metropolitan of Krutitsy, but continued to act as head of the church until his death in December 1613, on the seventh anniversary of his consecration.

31. In Russia and other Orthodox countries it is customary, in addition to birthdays, to celebrate the feast of the saint after whom a person is named.

32. St. Michael Malein was a tenth-century abbot of the Kimenos hermitage on Mount Athos.

33. Kuzma Minin (?-1616) was described as a *miasnik* but to judge from the extent of his personal fortune he must have been quite a successful retailer, rather than merely a simple butcher. On September 1, 1611 he was elected territorial elder (zemskii starosta) of Nizhny Novgorod, and thereafter took charge of the national movement to raise forces and collect money for the liberation of Moscow. Together with Prince Dmitry Pozharsky he led the Second Militia Force and was a prominent member of the Council of the Whole Land created at Yaroslavl to discharge functions normally exercised by the central government. In 1613 he was promoted to the rank of conciliar noble, and many state documents of the early years of Michael's reign bear his signature.

34. The Stroganov family was descended from peasants in the northern maritime region. Fedor Lukich Stroganov became firmly established in the region of Solvychegodsk. There his son Anika (1497-1570) acquired a saltworks in 1515, and from there expanded the industrial properties of the family considerably. In 1558 Ivan IV gave Anika and his descendants

extensive territories along the Kama and Chusovaia rivers; in 1566 the Stroganov lands were taken into Ivan IV's crown estates at their own request. The Stroganovs mentioned here were Anika's grandsons, who had taken part in Yermak's original expedition to Siberia, and for their pains were given additional landholdings. During the Time of Troubles they gave considerable material assistance to the Muscovite government and also, as seen here, responded to similar appeals from the government of Michael. In 1610 they were given the title "distinguished people;" under the Romanov regime also their services were not forgotten. See entry by V.I. Buganov, MERSH, Vol. 37, pp. 224-226.

35. The Greater Nogay Horde had accepted Russian suzerainty since the reign of Ivan IV, and Boris Godunov had confirmed this tributary status by conferring princely rank upon the murza Ishterek. Evidently Ishterek was now taking advantage of the turmoil in Muscovy to make a bid for independence. The leaders of the Lesser Nogay Horde, which had not sworn allegiance to Moscow, were tributary to the Crimean khanate.

36. Shulgin had been town secretary, but assumed command of the Kazan levies after the murder of the governor, Bogdan Belsky, which Shulgin probably incited. Ivan Birkin had been sent by the Second Militia Force to raise recruits in Kazan, but Shulgin recalled the Kazan levies. Some obeyed, but others remained with Birkin and entered the service of the Yaroslavl militia. There ensued a further schism in the ranks of the Kazan levies when Ivan Birkin and the Tatar captain Lukian Miasnoy quarrelled over seniority, and Birkin left in high dudgeon. As can be seen from this passage, Shulgin's attitude towards the new government continued to be ambiguous. See Volume 15, pp. 256-257.

37. Pereiaslavl "beyond the forest", to distinguish it from Pereiaslavl-in-Riazan, or the Pereiaslavl in the Ukraine, now known as Pereiaslavl-Khmelnitsky.

38. The Cherkassians were a Caucasian tribe who members frequently served as auxiliaries in the Russian and Polish armies. Soloviev, however, tends to apply the term to cossacks in Polish service. On the Cherkassians, see Volume 14, Chapter I, Note 20.

39. Prince Ivan Nikitich Odoevsky "the Younger" (?-1629), youngest son of Prince Nikita Romanovich Odoevsky, is first mentioned in 1586 in the suite of Tsar Fedor Ivanovich. In 1590 he took part in campaign against the Swedes, and in 1591 played a part in the repulse of the Crimean Tatars from Moscow. In 1598 he participated in the Assembly of the Land which elected Boris Godunov, and went on the Serpukhov campaign of the same year. He does not appear to have been on active service again until 1611, when he was governor of Vologda, and he was there in 1612 when the city was captured, burned and then abandoned by roving cossacks. Odoevsky barely managed to escape to the encampment of the Second Militia Force.

There he quickly attained a prominent position, and his signature appears on most of the documents of the provisional government. He was present at the electoral assembly in 1613 and later that year was ordered to proceed against Zarutsky, who was reputed to be at Epifan. After the campaign against Zarutsky described here, he was promoted boyar in December 1613 and thereafter seems to have specialized in relations with the cossacks, supervising their pay arrangements, sending commanders to deal with renegade bands, and establishing trading links with Persian and Armenian merchants. In 1615 he was once again in Astrakhan, but thereafter information concerning him is lacking until 1618, when he was in Moscow taking part in the assembly concerned with the defense of the city against the advancing Poles. Later that year he was appointed to the Vladimir Judicial Chancellery. In 1620 was appointed governor of Kazan, where he remained until 1624, when he was recalled to Moscow to reassume his duties at the Vladimir Judicial Chancellery. There he remained until his death in 1629. His remains were interred in the Trinity monastery.

40. *Chronicle of Many Rebellions*, pp. 275-276. As his main chronicle source Soloviev in these chapters uses the *Chronicle of Many Rebellions* (Letopis o mnogikh matezhakh), which was compiled around 1658 at the court of Patriarch Nikon. It was basically a continuation of the *New Chronicler* (Novyi letopisets), the official court chronicle compiled around 1630, but incorporates other documentary sources, especially in the latter part, which is especially preoccupied with the religious reforms carried out by its patron. It was edited and printed by N.I. Novikov in 1771, with a second edition in 1788. Citations in this volume are from the second edition.

41. Marina was of course a Catholic, not a Lutheran.

42. Prince Ivan Dmitrevich Khvorostinin (?-1614) was appointed table attendant some time before 1598, and then served in a subordinate capacity in command of cossacks in various Tatar campaigns. He also was assigned to escort duty for foreign emissaries between 1598 and 1602. Later in 1602 he was appointed governor of Borisov, but was recalled to Moscow in the following year. He was appointed to the boyar council at the Easter festivities of 1604, and on March 3, 1605 was among the delegation attending the English ambassador. Under False Dmitry I he was named to the tsar's inner council. In 1607 he was appointed by Shuisky to be governor of Astrakhan. There, apparently crediting rumors of Dmitry's survival, he roused the city against Shuisky and resisted all attempts of the expeditionary force under F.I. Sheremetev to recapture the city for Moscow. Ivan Zarutsky, when he broke with the Second Militia Force, eventually made Astrakhan his base. He was at first made welcome but, on becoming aware of the real nature of Zarutsky's regime and the probable permanence of Romanov rule, Khvorostinin began to send secret messages to Shah Abbas and the commanders of the Terek Cossacks, discouraging them from any further support for

Zarutsky. The rebel leader seized Khvorostinin and executed him on September 16, 1614, along with five hundred of the more prominent citizens of Astrakhan.

43. After the fall of the Tushino encampment, False Dmitry II set up his headquarters at Kaluga; hence he is frequently referred to as the Kaluga brigand.

44. Prokopy Petrovich Liapunov (?-1611) came from an important landowning family in the Riazan region, and was one of five brothers, of whom Zakhar is the most important after Prokopy himself. The Riazan gentry as a whole were hostile to the regency and rule of Boris Godunov, and supported False Dmitry I. There is no indication what, if any, reward the Liapunovs received for this support, but they were very active in opposition to his successor, Tsar Vasily Shuisky. Prokopy and another prominent Riazan landowner, Grigory Sunbulov, led a contingent of insurgent Riazan gentry to join the Bolotnikov rebellion but when the main force of Bolotnikov's army composed of rebellious peasants and runaway serfs arrived before Moscow conflict arose as to the goals of the rebellion, and so Prokopy brought at least some of the Riazan contingent over to the side of Vasily Shuisky on November 15, 1606. He received conciliar boyar rank from the tsar, and also the post of governor of Riazan, which apparently he held for the remainder of his life. Prokopy and his brother Zakhar played a prominent part in the defeat of the rebel forces on the Vosma river, June 5-7, 1607, and was also present at the siege of Tula. He was wounded in 1608 while attempting to clear his native province of supporters of False Dmitry II, and was forced for a while to retire from active service. Despite the fact that they were praised for their loyalty to the tsar and were held in high honor, the Liapunov brothers tried to get the popular hero, the tsar's kinsman Skopin, to seize the throne. Although Skopin refused to have anything to do with the plot, he soon afterwards died, according to the Liapunovs and many others poisoned by his jealous kinsmen. When the tsar's untalented and unpopular brothers Dmitry and Ivan suffered disastrous defeat at Klushino the Liapunov brothers played a leading part in the deposition of Vasily Shuisky. Although Zakhar was induced to take part in the high embassy to promote the candidacy of Prince Wladyslaw, Prokopy tended to support the second pretender. After the death of False Dmitry II at the hands of his Tatar bodyguards, Prokopy was responsive to the appeals of Patriarch Hermogen to unite all Russians in defense of the land and the Orthodox faith. The part Prokopy played in the First Militia Force is well known, and is described in detail in Volume 15. As a result of cossack intrigues and Polish disinformation, he was murdered July 22, 1611. See entry by John Wiita, MERSH, Vol. 19, pp. 238-241.

45. See Chapter II, Note 44; also Note 18, above.

46. Marcin Kazanowski (1566-1636) took part in the Wallachian campaign of 1600. In 1610 he fought in Russia under the command of Hetman Zolkiewski, under whon he also fought the Turks in 1617. In 1618 he took part in Wladyslaw's Moscow campaign, but became embroiled in a quarrel with Hetman Chodkiewicz. He was captured by the Turks at the battle of Cecora in 1620, but soon escaped to fight the Swedes under the command of Stanislaw Koniecpolski. He became castellan of Halycz in 1622, a crown colonel in 1628, governor of Podolia and Polish crown hetman in 1633.

47. Jan-Piotr Sapieha (1569-1611), prefect of Uswiat, a military leader in the battle of Kirchholm against the Swedes in 1605, and on the royalist side in the Zebrzydowski rebellion in 1607. With the connivance of King Sigismund III he joined the forces of False Dmitry II at the head of a band of seventeen thousand men, and commanded the force besieging the Trinity monastery on behalf of the Tushino government. Rather than obey the call to rally to the king's forces in 1609, he continued to operate independently, but later co-operated with Hetman Zolkiewski and the king. He died during the Kremlin siege in 1611, leaving behind a diary which is a valuable primary source for the Time of Troubles.

48. A reference to the night of May 17, 1606 when False Dmitry I was deposed and murdered, and Marina herself was in great peril.

49. Abbas I "the Great," born 1577, ruled 1588-1629, came to the throne after the reign of his weak and semi-blind father. He was faced with the twofold task of reasserting authority against the *kizilbash*, the Turkmen tribesmen who had been responsible for bringing the Safavid dynasty to power, and of expelling Ottoman and Uzbek troops from Persian soil. To this end in 1590 he signed a truce with the Ottoman empire and set about the creation of a standing army and administration, both staffed largely by *ghulams* (Georgian, Armenian or Circassian converts to Islam). In 1598 he resumed the offensive against Persia's external foes, first defeating the Uzbeks and regaining control of the province of Khorosan; then from 1602 he won a series of victories against the Turks. His reign is also notable for the transfer of the capital to Isfahan, which developed into a brilliant commercial and artistic center. Carpet weaving and tiles became major export industries, as Persian rugs and ceramics began to appear in the homes of European burghers. The dark side of his reign was his morbid fear of conspiracy, which led him to order the execution or mutilation of many members of his own family, including three of his sons. Abbas therefore died without an heir capable of succeeding him.

50. Peter, Alexis and Jonas were metropolitans of Moscow and were the first of the "Moscow miracle-workers". Peter (1308-1326) was the first metropolitan to reside in Moscow. Alexis (1354-1378) officially transferred the seat of the metropolitanate to Moscow, and was regent during the minority of Dmitry Donskoy. Jonas (1448-1461) was nominated by Grand

Prince Vasily II to replace Isidore, who had supported the resolutions on church union at the Council of Florence-Ferrara. Jonas, moreover, was confirmed by a synod of Russian bishops without reference to Constantinople. As a token of this independence, the same synod canonized Peter and Alexis.

51. A region of present-day Georgia, where the Cherkassky clan originated.

52. A verst (anglicized form, Russian *versta*) is an old Russian linear measure equivalent to about one kilometer or two-thirds of a statute mile. For a table of weights and measures, see the beginning of this volume.

53. *Chronicle of Many Rebellions*, p. 286.

54. Fedor (Fedka) Andronov was a merchant who attached himself to the court of False Dmitry II, then joined the armies of Sigismund III at Smolensk. The king appointed him to the boyar council in Moscow, where he served as treasurer. He became the foremost collaborationist, and was seized on the orders of Pozharsky before he could escape Moscow. He was impaled outside Moscow in October 1612. See entry in MERSH, Vol. 1, pp. 225-226, and also Vol. 15, pp. 191-199, of this series.

55. *Chronicle of Many Rebellions*, p. 288.

56. Gerasim (?-1615) was formerly archimandrite of the Archangel monastery of Yuriev-Polsky from 1596 to 1605. Between 1605 and 1612 he was superior of the Spaso-Evfimiev monastery at Suzdal, where he was consecrated archbishop in 1612, occupying that see until his death. In 1612 he was consecrated also as *locum tenens* of the Kazan metropolitanate, since Metropolitan Ephraim was effectively in charge of the patriarchal see. In 1613 he was a leading signatory of the Confirmatory Charter, and evidently a man of considerable authority. On his death in 1615 he was succeeded at Suzdal by Arsenius of Elasson.

57. Prince Boris Mikhailovich Lykov-Obolensky (?-1646) took part in various diplomatic receptions between 1593 and 1597. He was a signatory to Boris Godunov's confirmatory charter in 1598, and accompanied him on the Serpukhov campaign in the summer of that year. He was in the reception party for both of Tsarevna Xenia's suitors, Prince Gustav of Sweden and Prince Johann of Denmark. Late in 1602 he was appointed governor of Belgorod, where he remained for the rest of Boris's reign. Absence from court for several years was the result of the unsatisfactory outcome of several precedence disputes and apparent dissatisfaction with Tsar Boris. He became one of the closest followers of False Dmitry I, who sent him to the borderland towns to administer the oath of allegiance. He was appointed boyar April 13, 1606 and later married Anastasia Nikitichna Romanova, sister to Metropolitan Filaret. Under Vasily Shuisky he took a leading part in the struggle against the Bolotnikov rebels. In 1608 he was sent to the

relief of Briansk, and then operated against False Dmitry II from his head-quarters at Orel. Although he did not desert to Tushino, he was suspected of sympathies in that direction, especially since an expeditionary force un-der his command failed to engage Lisowski by reason of yet another prece-dence dispute. After Shuisky's deposition, he was one of the "seven boyar" commission which acted as an interim government pending the arrival of the newly-elected Wladyslaw. He presented a petition to Wladyslaw, from whom he received two small villages in the Riazan region; the only trouble was that King Sigismund simultaneously had granted the same villages to Ivan Mikhailovich Saltykov. Lykov was also one of the signatories on let-ters to Shein demanding the immediate capitulation of Smolensk, and on another letter asking the ambassadors to urge the immediate dispatch of Prince Wladyslaw to Moscow. Like the other boyars held captive in the Kremlin, Lykov was absent during the initial deliberations of the 1613 As-sembly, but was one of the signatories on Michael's confirmatory charter. After the coronation he brought a precedence dispute against the tsar's uncle Ivan Nikitich Romanov, but eventually consented to take his place at the tsar's table below the Romanovs. In May 1614, when Moscow was threatened with a Tatar attack, Lykov was put in charge of the defenses along the Yauza river. In September of the same year he was given the task of pacifying the southern borderlands, and defeated Zarutsky's marauding cossacks near Balakhna. He also operated against renegade cossacks and foreign mercenaries around Vologda and Beloozero in 1615. He rounded up three thousand cossacks and brought them to Moscow, where they swore allegiance to Tsar Michael. In September 1617 he was sent to Nizhny Nov-gorod to recruit forces in anticipation of Prince Wladyslaw's advance on Moscow, and in June 1618 he took part in the relief of Mozhaisk. In 1619 he was head of the Chancellery for Criminal Affairs, and was sent to Nizh-ny Novgorod to muster service cavalrymen. Between 1620 and 1622 he was senior governor of Kazan. In 1623 he headed the Chancellery for Investiga-tions. He attended both marriages of Tsar Michael, in 1624 and 1626, and in the latter year also superintended the refortification of Mozhaisk. He was head of the Chancellery for Monasteries 1628-1629, and from 1629 to 1635 headed the Chancellery of Posts. In 1632 he became involved in a prece-dence dispute with Prince D.M. Cherkassky. He lost, and was forced to pay damages in the amount of twelve hundred rubles, and both litigants were removed from command of the Smolensk expediton. In view of what hap-pened to Shein and Izmailov, this was perhaps a blessing in disguise! In 1634 he was in charge of the extraordinary tax levies to defray the expense of the Smolensk war, and from 1635 to 1642 he headed the Chancellery for Kazan and Siberia. When in January 1639 two of Michael's sons, Ivan and Vasily, died, Lykov kept vigil over the bodies day and night. In 1640 he was one of the commission of seven boyars left in charge of state affairs while Tsar Michael was absent on pilgrimage. Lykov died June 2, 1646 and was buried in a stone chapel adjoining the St. Paphnutius monastery of Borovsk.

58. Tikhvin is first mentioned in 1383 as the St. John the Baptist parish in the Obonezh "fifth" of the Novgorod lands. Between 1560 and 1764 it was a proprietory settlement of the Mother of God monastery of Tikhvin. It became a regional center late in the eighteenth century. In 1941 it was the scene of a bitter contest between German and Soviet troops for control of the southern shore of Lake Ladoga. Soviet success considerably shortened the supply line to the beleaguered city of Leningrad.

59. Stepan Vasilievich Chemesov (?-1639) is first attested in 1612 as deputy governor of Volokolamsk. He was sent to Tikhvin in December 1614 but his campaign against the Swedes, as related here, foundered upon cossack indiscipline. In 1616 he was appointed deputy governor of Putivl, from where in 1617 he was ordered to join Governor Protopopov of Briansk to stem the Lithuanian advance. In 1624 he was serving at court, in 1624-1625 was governor of Mtsensk, and in December 1626 escorted the Swedish ambassador Rubtsov from the frontier to Novgorod and Pskov. Between 1627 and 1629 he was again in attendance at court, and from 1630 to 1633 was governor of Saratov. In July 1633 he was assisting the boyar S.V. Golovin in supervising the construction of defense works against the Crimeans between the Moscow river and the Tver gates. In 1635 he was charged with the defense of Moscow between the Tver and Presentation streets. He is last mentioned as being at the tsar's table in 1639.

60. The Donskoy monastery was founded in 1591 on the site where the Muscovite forces made their stand that year against the Crimean invaders. The smaller cathedral, built 1591-1593, is still an active church. Other buildings, including the larger cathedral, were added in the late seventeenth and early eighteenth centuries. Among those buried in the cemetery are Peter Chaadaev and the historian Vasily Osipovich Kliuchevsky. Since 1935 the monastery has been an architectural museum.

61. Alexander Jozef Lisowski (1575-1616) was a colonel of the Polish army and the organizer of irregular military bands known long after his death as *lisowczyki*. He joined the forces of False Dmitry II at Starodub in 1607 and the rest of his life was spent campaigning in Russia, either in the service of the pretender or of King Sigismund III. See entry in MERSH, Vol. 20, pp. 60-62.

62. Artemy Vasilievich Izmailov (?-1634) is first mentioned in 1593, serving at Livny, where he took part in negotiations with the Crimean ambassadors. Between 1597 and 1604 he was deputy commander in various regiments guarding against Tatar attacks. On the occasion of False Dmitry I's marriage to Marina he was appointed conciliar noble and court falconer.

Later he served Tsar Vasily loyally against the Poles. In 1607 he commanded operations successfully near Kozelsk, for which service he was promoted
lord-in-waiting. Subsequently he was appointed to the court rank of majordomo, and in 1609 was sent to receive the Tatar contingents coming to aid
Tsar Vasily. In 1611 he raised levies in Vladimir to aid the First Militia
Force, and was constantly engaged in the liberation struggle. He was a signatory to Michael's Confirmatory Charter, and was prominent in court ceremonies. He was one of the negotiators at the conferences leading to the
Truce of Deulino in 1618. During the tsar's absences he was usually third
or fourth in the commission of boyars left in charge of the capital. He became involved in several precedence disputes, one of which earned him a
term of imprisonment. He also served as governor of Valuiki and Astrakhan. In 1632 he was second in command of the Muscovite forces during
the Smolensk war. Along with his superior Shein he was executed for his
failure in 1634. His son Vasily was also executed, his brother Semeon exiled to Siberia, while Artemy's brother was exiled to Kazan.

63. A kinsman of Prince Dmitry Pozharsky, who had led the advance
guard of the Second Militia Force during its advance on Moscow in 1612.
See Chapter III, Note 27.

64. Prince Yury Yansheevich Suleshov (1584-1643) was the son of a
prominent emigrant from the Crimean Horde. He held the rank of table attendant under Boris Godunov, by whom he was sent early in 1605 to Novgorod Seversk to reward Prince Yury Nikitich Trubetskoy with gold. He
remained as table attendant, apparently third in that rank, under Tsar Vasily
Shuisky. In 1610 he married Martha Mikhailovna Saltykova, a cousin of
Michael's mother. He took part in both Militia Forces and in January 1611
his name appears on the charter granting the Vaga lands to Prince Dmitry
Timofeevich Trubetskoy. He played a prominent role in Michael's coronation in July 1613. He was involved in a number of precedence disputes and
won all of them, but not all the losers remained in inferior position to him
throughout Michael's reign. In 1614 he was on active service against Zarutsky, along with Prince Ivan Nikitich Odoevsky "the Younger." In 1615-
1616 he was sent to Kazan to deal with the Cheremiss rebellion, but got no
further than collecting levies in Nizhny Novgorod. Early in 1617 there occurred his most important military feat, when he beat off the Poles who
were trying to capture Dorogobuzh. His last military campaign was in 1618,
when he was one of the commission of boyars entrusted with the defense of
the capital. During the siege of Moscow he was joined by his brother Mahmet Shah Murza, who received the baptismal name Vasily. In 1619 both
brothers were awarded estates in the Murom and Nizhny Novgorod regions.
In 1621 he served in the Chancellery of Investigations, conducting a review
of service tenures in the Riazan and Meshchera regions. He was appointed
governor of Tobolsk in 1623, apparently an honorific exile, since he had

alienated too many people during his tenure at the Chancellery of Investigations. Nevertheless Filaret showed considerable favor to his brother Vasily Yansheevich, and he himself was given considerable freedom of action by Prince Dmitry Mamstriukovich Cherkassky, who as head of the Chancellery for Kazan was his immediate superior. In many ways, Suleshov's governorship was a turning point in the history of Western Siberia. He handed over to his successor Prince D.M. Trubetskoy on May 29, 1625 and was rewarded richly for his services, taking his place in the boyar council once again. In 1626 he was present at the tsar's marriage to Evdokia Stresh-neva, and became one of the longest serving judges in the Chancellery of Investigations, from 1626 also heading the Office of Chancellery Affairs. Between 1628 and 1630, in addition, he served on the Chancellery for Criminal Affairs. In 1630 he was appointed governor of Novgorod, and his brother also disappears for seven months from the records, giving rise to speculation that this was yet another honorific exile. He was recalled in 1632 and served once again on the Chancellery for Criminal Affairs for three and a half years. He also led the donkey at the consecration of Patriarch Joseph in 1634, and in 1635 was one of the boyars receiving the remains of the former tsar, Vasily Shuisky, at the Arbat gate. After retiring from the Chancellery for Criminal Affairs, Suleshov was inactive for eighteen months. In early 1638 he again was appointed governor of Novgorod after which, in 1640, he retired from active service but remained in attendance at court and on the tsar's pilgrimages. He died February 7, 1643, his funeral being conducted by Patriarch Joseph. He was buried in the Simonov monastery.

65. Prince Alexis Mikhailovich Lvov (?-1654) is first mentioned in 1607, when he recaptured Arzamas for Tsar Vasily. In 1610 he was one of the three governors of Nizhny Novgorod. In 1612 he was at Yaroslavl with Pozharsky, and was one of the signatories on Michael's Confirmatory Charter, with the rank of table attendant. He was one of the delegation sent to the Trinity monastery to persuade Tsar Michael to complete his journey to Moscow, and later took part in the coronation ceremony. In 1614 Lvov and Perfily Sekerin were ordered to campaign against the Lithuanians, and were joined on the campaign by Kazan princes, Tatar murzas, Chuvash and Cheremiss contingents. In 1615 Lvov was governor at Rylsk, together with Grigory Andreevich Aliabiev. In 1616 he was sent with Suleshov to Nizhny Novgorod to gather troops against the rebellious Tatars and lowland Cheremiss. From 1618 to 1620 Lvov was governor of Astrakhan, together with Prince Andrei Andreevich Khovansky. He was one of the ambassadors sent to Denmark to negotiate the possible marriage of Prince Waldemar to one of the tsar's daughters. In 1621 he was appointed to the Chancellery for Military Appointments, and in 1625 he received the Persian ambassador. In 1627 he petitioned the tsar, complaining that he had been in Astrakhan when the rewards were handed out to the defenders of Moscow; his petition

was granted, and he was promoted to the rank of lord-in-waiting. From then until 1647 he sat on the board of the Chancellery of the Royal Household. In 1628 he was at the reception of the Persian ambassador and in 1630-1631 met with the Swedish ambassador Anton Monier. In 1632 he was one of the commissioners in charge of collecting supplies for the Smolensk campaign and the recruitment of military levies from the estates of those landowners who did not serve in person. He subsequently served as one of the Muscovite emissaries at the peace talks in 1634, with the title of Lord Lieutenant of Suzdal. For his part in the successful negotiations Lvov was promoted to boyar and given additional estates. In January 1635 he was sent to Poland to receive confirmation of the peace treaty from Wladyslaw IV, and also to secure the release of the remains of the Shuisky princes. In 1638 he was sent to Tula with the delegation greeting the Crimean khan. In 1639 he kept an all-night vigil over the bodies of the tsar's sons Ivan and Vasily, who died in January and April respectively. In February 1644 he once again was sent as a plenipotentiary to Poland to obtain clarification of the tsar's title and rectification of the borders, and also with secret instructions to find out about a new pretender, alleged to be a bogus son of the late Tsar Vasily. Lvov was further rewarded for his services, being greeted on his homeward journey in the tsar's name at Mozhaisk, and later given trading immunities in Yaroslavl. He continued to serve at court under Tsar Alexis, and died childless. His first wife was Yevlampia Mikhailovna Nagaia, who died in 1632. The name of his second wife is unknown.

66. Denis Grigorievich Aladyin, a Moscow noble, was sent, as related here, to King Sigismund with a demand that he release the interned Muscovite ambassadors. He later served, in 1615, as governor of Oskol. In 1616 he took part in the defense of Moscow, and in 1618 he was governor of Rostov. In 1626 he was appointed governor of Sanchursk, although it is apparent that some time prior to this he had served in a similar capacity at Cheboksary.

67. Nicholas Struys was a Dutch mercenary officer in Polish service who played a prominent part in the final phases of the Time of Troubles. After the capitulation of the Polish garrison in the Kremlin he was kept captive in Muscovy until the exchange of prisoners which took place in June 1619 (see Chapter III). Thereafter he returned to Holland.

68. Mikhail Glebovich Saltykov had been employed on a number of diplomatic missions on behalf of Boris Godunov and False Dmitry I. He later threw in his lot with the second pretender, and later with the Poles, playing a prominent part in the collaborationist regime in Moscow in 1610-1611. Thereafter he left Russia for permanent exile in Poland, where he died in 1621. See entry in MERSH, Vol. 33, pp. 45-49.

69. Wladyslaw IV, born 1595, king of Poland, grand prince of Lithuania and titular king of Sweden 1632-1648, titular tsar of Muscovy 1610-1634, was the son of Sigismund III and his first wife, Archduchess Anna of

Austria. At the age of fourteen he was proposed by the Russian supporters of False Dmitry II as the next ruler. To this end they negotiated with Hetman Zolkiewski the treaty of February 4, 1610. Zolkiewski defeated an army loyal to Tsar Vasily Shuisky at Klushino on June 24, and the tsar was deposed less than a month later. The interim boyar administration, fearful of the proximity of Dmitry's forces, compelled the inhabitants of Moscow to take the oath of allegiance to Wladyslaw on August 27, and dispatched the high embassy under Filaret and Golitsyn to negotiate with King Sigismund at his encampment outside Smolensk. The Muscovites were alienated quickly by obvious Polish bad faith, and the death of False Dmitry II on December 11 removed the immediate threat which had induced the boyar administration to endorse the Polish candidature. The continued resistance of Smolensk held up the advance of the royal army until June 2, 1612, by which time the Polish garrison in Moscow was closely besieged, surrendering in October. Wladyslaw's supporters attempted an advance on Moscow, but were turned back at Volokolamsk. In February 1613 Michael was elected, but the war continued. In 1617-1618 Wladyslaw launched another attempt to make good his claim, but lacked the means to conduct a proper siege. The Truce of Deulino, curiously enough, ran out about the time that Sigismund III died, on April 30, 1632, while Wladyslaw did not ensure his election until November. During the interregnum, their confidence boosted by the Swedish alliance, the Muscovites attempted to regain Smolensk. Russian plans went awry and instead of Smolensk they gained only minor territorial concessions, but the Truce of Polianovka was a diplomatic success in that Wladyslaw renounced his title to the Muscovite tsardom in exchange for a secret payment, which some sources put at twenty thousand rubles, others at two hundred thousand. Ironically, when the Russians demanded the return of the original "hetman's treaty" of 1610, the royal archives were in such a chaotic state that the document could not be found. Wladyslaw was popular at his accession, but was quick to squander this fund of goodwill. He was anxious for religious peace, and sanctioned the re-establishment in Poland-Lithuania of the Orthodox hierarchy, which had taken place illegally in 1620, but was unable to resist clerical pressures for the suppression of the schools and printing houses of the Orthodox Brethren (See Chapter III, Note 46). In foreign affairs his continued claim to the Swedish throne prevented him from being drawn into the antiimperial camp during the Thirty Years' War by the offer of Austrian Silesia. Instead, by his marriage to the Austrian archduchess Cecilia Renata, he committed himself to the Habsburg cause and a renewed war with Sweden. In the first round of the conflict he drove the Swedish garrisons out of the Prussian ports, and in 1636 concluded the advantageous Truce of Stumsdorf (Sztumska Wies), but the Austrian marriage was construed by the Swedes as a breach of the truce. In 1637 Bohuslaw XIV, the last native duke of

Pomerania, died, and most of his territory was seized by Sweden, while Wladyslaw was forced to abandon his attempts to build a fleet to challenge Swedish hegemony on the Baltic. The duke of Prussia did homage to the Polish crown for the last time in 1641. Wladyslaw's second marriage, to Princess Marie Louise Gonzaga, led to promotion of a new anti-Turkish crusade, in which the king attempted to enlist the aid of the cossacks. The Sejm frustrated his designs and the cossacks, furious at being left in the lurch, rose up under their hetman, Bogdan Khmelnitsky, in a revolt that led ultimately to the Muscovite annexation of the Ukraine and the loss of all that Poland had gained from Muscovy as a result of the Time of Troubles. Wladyslaw died May 20, 1648, having heard of Khmelnitsky's victory over the royal army at Zheltye Vody. He was succeeded by his brother Jan Kazimierz, who renounced the Polish claim to the Swedish throne under the terms of the Treaty of Oliwa (1660), abdicated the Polish throne in 1668 and died in French exile in 1672. See entry on Wladyslaw IV in MERSH, Vol. 44, pp. 15-18.

70. Ivan Tarasievich Gramotin (?-1638) first appears at the court of False Dmitry I, but was also party to the coup which overthrew him. Instead of being granted high office by Shuisky, he was appointed town secretary to Pskov, where he distinguished himself by his rapacity, which played no small part in provoking the subsequent disorders in that city. He fled from Pskov to Tushino after the revolt of September 1608. In 1609 he and Mikhail Glebovich Saltykov were sent to the Trinity monastery, where Gramotin made a speech to the defenders, falsely asserting that the war was over, and that Shuisky had made his submission to Tsar Dmitry. After the fall of the Tushino encampment Gramotin was one of the deputation which proceeded to King Sigismund III, urging him to become the protector of Muscovy. He became the king's trusted advisor on Muscovite affairs, and after the deposition and forcible tonsure of Shuisky was appointed keeper of the seal and conciliar secretary, and from January 1611 was assistant to the Chancellor for Foreign Affairs. He served with the High Embassy led by Filaret and Golitsyn, but when this failed and Moscow was relieved by Minin and Pozharsky, he travelled with King Sigismund back to Warsaw. While in exile he contrived to ingratiate himself with Filaret, and on his return to Moscow in 1618 was reappointed conciliar secretary. He enjoyed a distinguished career under Tsar Michael, although from 1626 to 1632 he was exiled to Alatyr, evidently having incurred the patriarch's disfavor. Restored to favor in 1634, he received the privilege of attaching the -vich (of) suffix to his patronymic. See entry in MERSH, Vol. 13, pp. 92-94.

71. Vasily Osipovich Yanov (dates of birth and death unknown, fl. 1605-1618) during the reign of Boris Godunov was a secretary in the employment of Prince Vasily Kordanukovich Cherkassky, who at that time was governor of Smolensk. Yanov took part in the investigation of the alleged treason of the city's inhabitants in 1605. During the reign of Vasily

Shuisky he apparently enjoyed the particular confidence of the tsar. In 1609 he was appointed conciliar secretary, but after Shuisky's deposition became an ardent supporter of Prince Wladyslaw. For this reason Prokopy Liapunov particularly singled out Yanov's house and possessions for destruction. In order to bring the prince's candidature to a speedy conclusion, the boyars dispatched Yanov along with Princes Mikhail Glebovich Saltykov and Yury Nikitich Trubetskoy to the king's encampment outside Smolensk. Unlike Saltykov and Andronov, who were guided by selfish motives, Yanov seriously was convinced that the Polish candidature was in Muscovy's best interests, and remained loyal to Wladyslaw to the extent that, when in 1618 he was offered a safe return to Moscow, he declined.

72. Wilno (Polish), Vilnius (Lithuanian) or Vilna (Russian) was the historic capital of Lithuania, and is presently capital of the Lithuanian republic.

73. Matthias (1557-1619), Holy Roman emperor from 1612. As archduke he served as stadholder in the Netherlands from 1578 to 1581, and from 1593 was governor of Upper and Lower Austria. With the increasing mental instability of his brother, Emperor Rudolph II, Matthias came into increasing conflict with him. Aided by his able advisor Melchior Klesl, in 1608 he seized the rulership of Upper and Lower Austria, Hungary and Moravia. The naming of his first cousin, the fanatically Catholic Archduke Ferdinand of Styria, as his successor in Bohemia and Hungary sparked off the Bohemian revolt of 1618-1620 and the rebellion of Bethlen Gabor in 1619. Both these events were subsumed by the general conflict of the Thirty Years' War.

74. Prince Andrei Andreevich Khovansky (?-1629) later served as governor of Astrakhan (1615-1620) and Tobolsk (1626-1628). To prevent foreign navigators from using the water route from Archangel to Mangazeia, he sent forces to the Kara straits and had a fort constructed there. He also repelled the intrusions of Kalmyk warriors into the regions of Tara and Tobolsk. Later Michael ordered him to settle peasants in Siberia to cultivate crown land and find new sources of crown revenue in the Siberian towns. After serving his tour of duty at Tobolsk Khovansky was appointed governor of Nizhny Novgorod, but died soon after taking up his duties.

75. Prince Semeon Nikitich Gagarin (?-1632) served for twenty-two years as governor of various towns (Tsarev-gorod 1610-1611, Toropets 1611-1613, Belev 1613-1614, Nevel 1614-1615, Kazan 1616-1619, Viazma 1619-1620, Verkhoturie 1627-1629, Novgorod 1631-1632). At Nevel he withstood a siege by the Lithuanians and was richly rewarded by the tsar. In the interval between his postings to Viazma and Verkhoturie (1620-1627) Gagarin served as escort to the Turkish ambassador when he was received by Patriarch Filaret in 1621-1622, and served the Persian ambassador in a similar capacity in 1625. As far as his military commands were

concerned, he was appointed to the vanguard regiment at Dedilov in 1622, in anticipation of a Tatar attack, but entered a precedence dispute with Prince Vasily Petrovich Shcherbatov, who was in charge of the main regiment at Tula. Gagarin, allegedly disgruntled at the tsar's refusal of his petition, failed to attack the Tatars at the village of Dolgoe. He was in attendance at the tsar's table in 1625-1626, but his appointment to a governorship in Siberia during the following year shows that he had not entirely lived down that particular blot on his escutcheon.

76. Prince Ivan Andreevich Khvorostinin (?-1625) began his career at the court of False Dmitry I, apparently as the pretender's homosexual favorite. During the reign of Vasily Shuisky he was exiled to the monastery of St. Joseph of Volokolamsk, from which he returned to Moscow in 1610 or 1611. During the reign of Michael he was given a series of arduous military assignments but, being under constant suspicion of heresy, was banished for a second period of monastic confinement on charges of heresy, drunkeness and "lack of firmness towards treasonable activity." He was released in 1624 but shortly afterwards voluntarily became a monk, and died at the Trinity monastery the following year. See entry in MERSH, Vol. 16, pp. 204-206.

77. Probably Boris Ivanovich Nashchokin, who was governor of Tobolsk 1608-1609, Nizhny Novgorod 1614-1619, Voronezh 1620, Astrakhan 1632-1635 and Nizhny Novgorod again in 1642. There is no record of Nashchokin ever having been governor of Mozhaisk, but there is a gap in the records for that town between July 1611, when Timofey Mikulin was governor, and March 1614, when Smirnoy Elizariev Otrepiev was in command.

78. Prince Dmitry Mamstriukovich Cherkassky (?-1651) could claim kinship, through the marriage of his aunt, Maria Temriukovna, to Ivan IV, to the ruling house. Temriuk was a ruler of Kabardia, and is reputed to have been fabulously wealthy. His second son, Mikhail, accompanied his sister to Moscow, and served in the crown estates (oprichnina) corps until he fell into disgrace and was executed in 1571. Temriuk's eldest son Mamstriuk remained in Kabardia, where he inherited much of his father's wealth, and appears to have been on good terms with Moscow. By 1601, however, Mamstriuk had been murdered, and his son Dmitry fled to Russia, where he was taken into Muscovite service. After Shuisky's defeat on the Khodynka river (July 25, 1608) Cherkassky deserted to Tushino, where he was awarded the title of boyar; he and Trubetskoy were the last two Tushino boyars to remain with False Dmitry II at Kaluga. After the murder of the pretender he swore allegiance to Wladyslaw along with the other inhabitants of Kaluga, and on January 24, 1611 arrived at Sapieha's encampment. Forsaking the Poles, he joined the First Militia Force and was dispatched against Hetman Chodkiewicz in 1612. He established his base at the Antonov monastery,

whence he cleared Uglich of roving cossack bands. For these deeds he was given a hero's welcome in Yaroslavl. He remained with the Second Militia Force, and was with it for the liberation of Moscow. His name appears on the charter granting the Vaga lands to Trubetskoy, and he took part in the early deliberations of the 1613 Assembly. After the initial rejection of Trubetskoy and Michael Romanov, the cossacks went into a circle and proposed Cherkassky as a compromise candidate. Cherkassky, though a foreigner, was in Muscovite service, and had exalted connections in Muscovy. His most recent feats had raised his stock in the Second Militia Force and he was indeed to have an illustrious career under Michael, becoming a table attendant in 1613 and receiving in 1618 a boyar rank more legitimate than his Tushino title. He served as head of the Chancellery for Kazan from 1624 to 1636, and died in 1651.

79. Mikhail Matveevich Buturlin (?-1648) held the court rank of table attendant in 1608, but went over to Tushino to serve False Dmitry II. He helped the pretender to flee to Kaluga in 1610, and on his own initiative executed the loyalist governor Ivan Ivanovich Godunov. He was also responsible for the murder of the Tatar khan, Uraz Mohammed, which in turn led to the revenge killing of the pretender by his Tatar bodyguards. When Marina declared her infant son tsar, Buturlin and Prince Yury Nikitich Trubetskoy took them both into their custody, declaring that they would swear allegiance to whomsoever was able to conquer Moscow. Buturlin was present at the liberation of Moscow, but was absent on campaign at the time of the coronation, being occupied with Zarutsky in the environs of Pereiaslavl-in-Riazan. Later in 1613 he and Cherkassky were ordered to relieve Kaluga, but the Poles retreated to Viazma and Dorogobuzh. The Muscovite commanders went on to capture these towns, and Belaia as well. Buturlin then proceeded to the siege of Smolensk, but was wounded and ordered to return to Moscow. In 1616 he was ordered once again to the Smolensk front, and in 1618 was one of the defenders of Moscow. After that he is frequently mentioned in accounts of court ceremonies. He was governor of Tula in 1620, and in 1622 was appointed governor of Pereiaslavl-in-Riazan. Subsequently he served mostly at court until 1640, when again he was appointed governor of Tula. He was promoted lord-in-waiting in 1646, and the next year began a third tour of duty at Tula, where he died.

80. Prince Ivan Andreevich Khovansky (?-1621) fought in 1607 on behalf of Tsar Vasily against the forces of False Dmitry II and the Poles, and then with the First Militia Force. In 1611 he was defeated by Lisowski near Zaraisk. Later he captured Rzhev and Staritsa from the invading Swedes and laid siege to Belaia. During the absence of Prince Dmitry Pozharsky on pilgrimage, in conjunction with Kuzma Minin he led the Second Militia force from Yaroslavl to Rostov. In 1615 he was sent to command the Muscovite forces besieging Smolensk. Subsequently he commanded the forces

opposing the Lithuanians in the province of Severia, but when he allowed the enemy to break through near Belgorod, he was recalled to Moscow. In 1616 he was appointed head of the Vladimir Judicial Chancellery, and was governor of Novgorod from 1617 to 1619.

81. Miron Andreevich Veliaminov (?-1641) was governor of Vladimir on behalf of both pretenders. He became a Moscow noble in 1627 and lord-in-waiting in 1640.

82. There were several persons of that name on active service at the time. Unfortunately Soloviev does not give any patronymic in the text, while his Soviet editors have omitted this particular Pushkin completely from their index.

83. Stepan Ivanovich Istlenev (?-1647) was promoted to the rank of Moscow noble in 1627. In 1631 he headed the Chancellery for Stonework, and in 1641 the Chancellery for Slavery. Soloviev renders his surname as Islenev, but elsewhere it is rendered as I have amended it.

84. In the list of governors of Bolkhov: "Table Attendant Stepan 'the Younger', son of Volynsky served through 1614 to October 1615." See A. Barsukov, *Spiski gorodovykh voevod* (Lists of Town Governors), St. Petersburg, 1902, p. 17. Perhaps he is identical with the Stepan Ivanovich Volynsky (?-1629) who served as emissary to England in 1617.

85. Prince Ivan Semeonovich Kurakin (?-1632) is first mentioned in 1606 as governor of Smolensk. He later became prominent in the circle of boyars plotting to overthrow Dmitry and put Shuisky upon the throne. He fought successfully in 1607-1608 against False Dmitry II, against whom he defended Briansk, but things rapidly deteriorated after he handed his command over to the tsar's brother, Prince D.I. Shuisky. In the spring of 1608 Kurakin inflicted a decisive defeat on Lisowski, relieving the siege of Kolomna. In 1609-1610 he fought alongside Skopin to clear the Moscow region of outlaw detachments. The ineffectiveness of Tsar Vasily led Kurakin, Mstislavsky and others to look for a foreign prince. Kurakin initially favored Wladyslaw, but later became a supporter of King Sigismund, and was among the boyars remaining in the Kremlin until the bitter end in October 1612. After the election of Michael he seems to have been employed on various military actions against the Poles, but in 1615 was sent into honorific exile as governor of Tobolsk, where he remained until 1620.

86. *Chronicle of Many Rebellions*, p. 302.

87. The Suma fort (ostrog) was founded on the southern shore of the White Sea between 1584 and 1586, and became a dependancy of the Solovetsk monastery.

88. Prince Vasily Vasilievich Golitsyn was, along with Metropolitan Filaret, the leader of the high ambassadors interned in Poland. Golitsyn, therefore, although his pedigree was outstanding, was out of the running at the 1613 Assembly. As will be seen in Chapter III, after the Truce of

Deulino he was on his way to be repatriated when he died at Grodno, and on the orders of King Sigismund was buried in the Brethren church of the Holy Spirit at Wilno on January 27, 1619. His body later was returned to Muscovy. See entry in MERSH, Vol. 48, pp. 166-167.

89. Afanasy Petrovich Zheliabuzhsky (?-1641) was sent in 1611 to Hetman Sapieha on behalf of Fedor Kirillovich Pleshcheev with messages from the gentry, cossacks and townsmen. In 1614, as related here, he was sent on behalf of Tsar Michael to Sigismund III and Metropolitan Filaret, and on his way visitied the captive Shein on the estates of Chancellor Leo Sapieha. He brought with him a document from the Polish magnates proposing a meeting of plenipotentiaries on the border between Smolensk and Viazma. Later Zheliabuzhsky was sent with a letter from Tsar Michael to Ataman Osip Petrov and all the Don Host, with a promise of five thousand rubles' cash payment and the prospect of further employment.

90. Mikhail Borisovich Shein (?-1634) is first mentioned in 1598 when he attested the confirmatory charter of Boris Godunov's election. In January 1605 he saved the life of the Muscovite commander Prince F.I. Mstislavsky, and was awarded the rank of lord-in-waiting. After taking part in the struggle against Bolotnikov, in 1607 he was appointed boyar and in April 1608 was appointed governor of Smolensk. He was still there when the fortress was besieged by the Poles in September 1609, and was taken prisoner after its capture on June 3, 1611. Ironically, as will be seen later in this volume, he was appointed to command the force to retake Smolensk in 1632, but was executed in 1634 for his failure. See entry by Daniel B. Rowland in MERSH, Vol. 34, pp. 196-198; also entries by G. Edward Orchard, MERSH, Vol. 32, pp. 136-138 and Vol. 36, pp. 46-53.

91. Prince Ivan Ivanovich Shuisky (?-1638) began his career in the household of Tsar Fedor Ivanovich. Although the date of his birth is unknown, he was probably much younger than his brothers Vasily and Dmitry, since he outlived them both by twenty-six years. He was named boyar in 1596, but there is no record that he saw active service during the reign of Boris. After his brother's accession he was sent to the relief of Kaluga, which was being besieged by Bolotnikov, but without success. He was similarly unsuccessful in his mission to interdict the progress of Jan-Piotr Sapieha towards the siege of the Trinity monastery, being defeated at Rakhmantsevo. After this poor record he does not seem to have been called to active duty again, but he became jealous of his successful kinsman Skopin, whom he slandered to the tsar. The chief blame for the poisoning of the popular hero fell on his brother Dmitry, but the hatred Ivan felt for Skopin was well known, and so he shared the fate of his two brothers in being handed over to the Poles. Vasily and Dmitry died in Polish captivity in 1612. Ivan was allowed rather more freedom but had to fend for himself in dire poverty, at times being placed under guard by a troop of hussars. When the Truce of Deulino was concluded he refused to return to Muscovy until

Wladyslaw released him of his oath of allegiance. He finally appeared at Michael's court in 1630, thereafter taking part in diplomatic receptions as well as presiding over the Moscow Judicial Chancellery and, after 1634, heading the Chancellery for Investigations. He died without heirs, and with him the Muscovite branch of the Shuisky family became extinct.

92. Leo Sapieha (1577-1633) was the younger brother of the military commander Jan-Piotr Sapieha. Leo was appointed king's secretary in 1580, royal notary 1581-1585, chancellor of the grand principality of Lithuania 1589-1623, governor of Wilno 1623-1633 and grand hetman of Lithuania 1625-1633. He had served as ambassador to Moscow in 1600. See Volume 14, pp. 18-25.

93. Marienburg (Malbork) was founded in 1274 by the Teutonic Knights on the bank of the Nogat river, and from 1309 was the residence of the grand master. Under the terms of the Treaty of Torun in 1466 it was ceded to Poland. The city was an important strategic point in the Polish-Swedish wars of 1626-1629 and 1655-1660.

94. Mikolaj Olesnicki (1558-1629). Soloviev in this volume renders his name as "Oleshinsky," which is strange, since he got it right in a previous volume (14 of this series). Olesnicki began his career at the court of Stefan Bathory. He was sent to the Netherlands during the Dutch revolt. Later he supported Chancellor Jan Zamoyski's backing of Sigismund Vasa's candidacy for the Polish throne, and was sent to Lithuania to rally supporters there. As a reward for this service he received extensive estates in Belorussia. In 1590 he was a deputy to the Sejm for Sandomir, and became one of the gentry delegates to the War Council. In 1598 he was appointed Castellan of Malagoszcz. Some time after that he converted to Catholicism. In March 1606 he accompanied Marina to Moscow, where he brought up the matter of church union with Dmitry. He was kept prisoner after the overthrow of the pretender, but later was released by Shuisky. He did not regain the frontier, but joined the forces of False Dmitry II, who awarded him estates around Belaia, near Smolensk. He later returned to Poland with Alexander Gasiewski, with whom he presented a joint report on Muscovite affairs to the Sejm. At the Sejm of 1609 he and Leo Sapieha were the most ardent advocates of armed intervention in Muscovy. In 1613 he was awarded the castellanate of Radom, in addition to that of Malagoszcz. In the same year he was appointed commissioner to supervise payment of soldiers taking part in the Moscow campaign. In 1613 and 1614 he put down a gentry confederation opposed to further imposts to finance the Moscow campaign.

95. Krzystof Mikolaj Dorohostajski (1562-1615) was educated at Strasbourg and Freiburg, and served in the Dutch-Spanish wars. He later took part in Stefan Bathory's campaigns against Russia, in the Swedish campaigns of 1600-1601, and was present at the siege of Smolensk in 1611-1612. Although a loyal supporter of King Sigismund, as a Calvinist he was a leading advocate of religious toleration.

96. The *sejm* was the Polish parliament, which developed in the fifteenth century and took final shape in 1493. The constitution *Nihil novi* ("nothing new") of 1505 stated that the king could not introduce any innovations without the consent of the Sejm. The Sejm was composed of three estates: king, senate and deputies, elected by the gentry and to a limited degree by some towns. It had legislative powers, voted taxes, controlled state expenditure and decided on war and peace. Ordinarily it was convoked every two years, but every third Sejm was held in Lithuania, normally at Grodno. A special session after the coronation of each king was held at Cracow. Decisions of the Sejm generally had to be unanimous.

97. Prince Alexis Yurievich Sitsky (?-1644) became a boyar in 1615, and served in the Chancellery for Kazan.

98. Jan Karol Chodkiewicz (1560-1621) studied at the Jesuit college of Wilno and then, between 1586 and 1589, at the Jesuit academy of Ingolstadt, Bavaria, where he read philosphy and law. He was appointed to his first military command in 1595 when, under the command of Zolkiewski, he helped put down the cossack revolt led by Nalivaiko. In 1599 he was appointed elder of Zmud, in 1600 deputy hetman of Lithuania, and in 1603 administrator of the occupied territories in Livonia. He took part together with Zamoyski and Zolkiewski in the Wallachian campaign of 1600 and the Livonian war of 1601. He was first commandant of Kokenhausen, conquered Dorpat in 1603, Weissenstein in 1604 and Riga in 1605. His Livonian campaign was crowned with a brilliant victory over the Swedes at the battle of Kirchholm in 1605. In the Zebrzydowski rebellion he won a signal victory over the insurgents at Guzow (July 5-6, 1607). Returning to the Swedish front in 1609, he captured Pernau and defeated the Swedish fleet at Salis. Appointed against his better judgement to command the relieving force sent against Moscow in 1611, he was greatly hindered by mutiny amongst his troops, whose pay was in arrears. He was also a personal enemy of Leo Sapieha and the Potocki brothers. He fought unsuccessfully against the Muscovite militia force from October 10, 1611 to September 7, 1612. He returned to Smolensk, where he succeeded Jakub Potocki as commandant of the royal garrison. In 1617-1618 he took part in Prince Wladyslaw's expedition to Moscow, capturing Dorogobuzh and Viazma, but failed in his attempt to capture Mozhaisk. He also took part in the Turkish campaign of 1620-1621 and after Zolkiewski fell in the battle of Cecora assumed command of the royal forces, but died before the end of the campaign.

99. Alexander Gasiewski (?-1636), ambassador to the reigning False Dmitry, was for a while imprisoned in Moscow by Tsar Vasily Shuisky. He later returned to Muscovy in command of a contingent of royal troops. After the departure of Hetman Zolkiewski from Moscow he was Polish commander in the Kremlin until its capitulation in October 1612. He later

played a prominent part in the negotiations leading to the Truce of Deulino in 1618, and was appointed palatine of Smolensk.

100. "Tolochanov" is perhaps a misreading of "Molchanov." The latter would fit here, as he is known to have been a boon companion of False Dmitry I, while to the best of my knowledge no Tolochanov is mentioned elsewhere. For further details regarding Molchanov, see Volume 15, Chapter I, Note 22.

101. Tushino was formerly a village near Moscow, now well within the Moscow city limits. It is first mentioned as having belonged to the boyar Ivan Rodionovich Kvashin in the fourteenth century. Originally called Korobovskoe, it was renamed after the sobriquet of Kvashin's youngest son, Vasily Tusha. In 1570 it was given by the widow of Prince P.I. Teliatevsky to the Trinity monastery, in whose possession it remained until the 1760s. When it became the headquarters of False Dmitry II in 1608 it was fortified by earthen ramparts and wooden palisades. Within it were built a villa for the pretender, a residence for the so-called Patriarch Filaret, quarters for Polish and Russian troops, and offices for the Tushino chancelleries. When it was abandoned in March 1610 Tushino was burned to the ground. Archeological excavations carried out between 1898 and 1901 uncovered sabers, musket barrels, spearheads, axes, blacksmiths' implements and other artifacts, which are preserved in the State Historical Museum, Moscow.

102. Prince Alexander Petrovich Zasekin (?-1611) occupied a number of important military commands in the 1580s and 1590s, and was involved in a number of precedence disputes. He was commander the Great Regiment in the Muscovite stand against the Tatars on the Pakhra river just outside Moscow in 1591. In 1600 he received the Persian ambassador and was sent with the return embassy, returning to Moscow in 1603. In 1605, in accordance with the request of False Dmitry I, he escorted Simeon Bekbulatovich to Moscow, and later that year was appointed governor of Toropets. In 1609 he was commander of the troops in Pskov for False Dmitry II, and sent to the Polish governor of Dorpat requesting auxiliaries for the upcoming campaign against Great Novgorod. In 1610 he was a supporter of Wladyslaw's candidacy, but later he aligned himself with the cossack commander Zarutsky. In 1611 he was one of the members of the boyar council who voiced their sympathy with Patriarch Hermogen's call for national resistance, as a result perishing at the hands of the Poles occupying the Kremlin.

103. Prince Fedor Andreevich Meshchersky was a boyar who had supported consistently both pretenders.

104. Prince Yury Dmitrievich Khvorostinin in mentioned in the sources as lord-in-waiting in 1610.

105. Ivan Mikhailovich Saltykov (?-1611) was the son of Mikhail Glebovich. He originally served the collaborationist regime alongside his father,

but then forsook the Poles and recaptured Ladoga from the Swedes. Despite this he was arrested by the citizens of Novgorod and cruelly put to death on false charges of treason.

106. Stanislaw Zolkiewski (1547-1620) was appointed field hetman of the crown in 1588, and in 1594-1595 took a leading part in suppressing the Nalivaiko rebellion in the Ukraine. In 1608 he was named governor of Kiev. He played a leading part in the Polish intervention during the Time of Troubles, and after Shuisky's deposition was instrumental in coming to an agreement with the interim boyar administration to admit a Polish garrison and to elect Prince Wladyslaw as tsar. When it became apparent that King Sigismund was attempting to advance his own claims to the Muscovite throne, Zolkiewski no longer wished to take part in the enterprise and abandoned the royal camp. He nevertheless retained the confidence of the king, who appointed him high crown hetman in 1613 and chancellor in 1617. He was killed while fighting the Turks at the battle of Cecora in 1620.

107. Fedor Kirillovich Pleshcheev (?-1633) was sent to Pskov in 1607 by the Tushino authorities to administer the oath of allegiance to False Dmitry II. The local inhabitants asked the Muscovite governor, Sheremetev, and the town secretary Gramotin to protect them against Pleshcheev, but instead they plundered the inhabitants and people of the surrounding countryside. When rumors spread that the Swedes were approaching the people arose on September 1, 1608 in favor of Dmitry, and accepted Pleshcheev as governor. Soon thereafter he was transferred to Suzdal, where he remained for two years, conducting a lively correspondence with Jan-Piotr Sapieha. He accompanied Lisowski to many surrounding towns, such as Shuia, Kineshma, Lukh and Vladimir, which had gone over to Dmitry. When it was proposed that Pleshcheev return to active service, the inhabitants of Suzdal petitioned that he should remain, rather than have Andrei Prosovetsky and Nekhoroshy Babkin as governors. Pleshcheev remained, with Prosovetsky as his deputy. After the fall of the Tushino encampment Pleshcheev declared for Wladyslaw and came to Zolkiewski, offering his submission, provided that he and other Tushino followers retain the same rank as they had enjoyed under the pretender. When the boyars refused to agree to this condition Pleshcheev returned to the pretender and was appointed governor of Serpukhov. In 1611 he joined the First Militia Force under Prokopy Liapunov and thenceforth supported the national liberation movement. In 1613 he was sent by Tsar Michael at the head of a detachment to relieve the Swedish siege of Tikhvin, but at Ustiuzhna learned that the inhabitants had repelled the Swedes. In 1616 he was given command of a sector of the Moscow defenses, from the Neglinnaia river to the Frolov gates, alongside Prince F.I. Lykov. He was governor of Belgorod in 1618-1619, and in 1623 was sent to Kashira to fortify it against the Nogay Tatars. He was deputy

governor of Tobolsk in 1623-1625. Between 1625 and 1628 he is mentioned five times as a table guest of the tsar, and was one of the groomsmen at Tsar Michael's second marriage. He served in the 1632 campaign at Sevsk, and was governor of Novgorod Seversk at the time of his death on December 28, 1633.

108. The Merchants' Hundred (gostinnaia sotnia) was one of the privileged corporations of merchants created in the late sixteenth century and lasting until the early part of the eighteenth century. Members were excused from government taxes, were excluded from the jurisdiction of local authorities and enjoyed other privileges although, unlike the leading merchants (gosti), they did not have the right to travel abroad. In return for these privileges they were obliged to provide financial services to the government and make good any shortfall in goods required by the crown. See entry by A.N. Kopylov, MERSH, Vol. 13, p. 77.

109. Krzystof Radziwill (1585-1640), field hetman of Lithuania in 1615, castellan and governor of Wilno in 1633, crown hetman of Lithuania, 1635. He fought in the Livonian campaign in 1622, recapturing Mitau from the Swedes.

110. The text of the treaty between Zolkiewski and the Moscow boyars, together with pertinent documents, is reprinted in the *Sbornik Imperatorskogo Russkogo Istoricheskogo Obshchestva*, Vol. 142, Moscow, 1913, No. 9.

111. Vasily II (1415-1462), grand prince of Moscow from 1425, entered into a treaty of friendship and alliance with Grand Prince Casimir IV of Lithuania in 1449. This treaty for a time secured Muscovy's western frontier.

CHAPTER II

1. Soloviev only gives the surname, but Stepan Mikhailovich Ushakov is recorded elsewhere as having been deputy governor of Kostroma in 1615-1616. He had earlier served as ambassador to Austria.

2. In fact Michael was only sixteen years of age and notoriously dimwitted.

3. Ivan Fomin (fl. 1609-1659) was a translator in the Chancellery for Foreign Affairs and fluent in several languages. He was first employed by Tsar Vasily Shuisky in the translation of foreign military manuals. As related here, he was sent to Emperor Matthias in 1614 to sort out the mess left by his predecessor Ushakov. He remained in Vienna for about eighteen months, until relieved by Lukian Miasnoy. There is no trace of him again until 1640, when he was sent as ambassador to Denmark to complain about the failure of the duke of Holstein to fulfill his obligations with regard to

the Persian trade, and also to sound out the possibilities for the marriage of Prince Waldemar to one of the tsar's daughters. Fomin returned to Russia with portraits of the king and prince, which he had obtained with great difficulty. In the 1650s it is known that Fomin served in the Chancellery for Foreign Affairs, and was busy making various translations from the English. He accompanied the 1654 and 1657 embassies to the Ukrainian leader Bogdan Khmelnitsky and the Grand Notary Ivan Vygovsky. He last appears in the archives of the Privy Chancellery, where he is mentioned as having been on a mission to the duke of Florence, but the purpose of this mission is not specified.

4. Rudolph II (1552-1612), Holy Roman emperor from 1576, son of Maximilian II and Maria of Spain. His reign was marked by an erosion of imperial power. In 1606 he was compelled to make considerable concessions to the Hungarian aristocracy, and by the Letter of Majesty of 1609 was forced to grant the Protestants of Bohemia religious freedom. Also by reason of mental infirmity he was obliged to yield the rulership of Upper and Lower Austria, Hungary and Moravia to his brother Archduke Matthias.

5. *Tu, felix Austria, nube.* Soloviev is alluding to the old adage, *Bella gerant alia, tu felix Austria nube; nam quae Mars aliis, dat tibi regna Venus* (Let others wage war; you, happy Austria, marry. For those kingdoms which Mars gives to others, Venus passes on to you).

6. Lukian Miasnoy was a Tatar captain from Kazan who accompanied the levies from Ivan Birkin, destined for the Second Militia Force at Yaroslavl. Apparently Birkin and Miasnoy quarrelled on the way over seniority, and the dispute flared up again at Yaroslavl. The supporters of Birkin left, but Miasnoy remained "with twenty princes and murzas, thirty gentry and a hundred musketeers." See Volume 15, p. 265, and p. 338, Note 68. See also above, Chapter I, Note 36.

7. Melchior Klesl (1552-1630), the son of a Protestant banker, converted to Catholicism with the remainder of his family at the age of sixteen. He studied philosophy at Vienna, receiving his doctorate, and later was appointed provost of St. Stephen's cathedral and chancellor of the university. In 1582 he became councillor to the bishop of Passau, and in 1588 administrator of the bishopric of Wiener-Neustadt. In 1590 he became the foremost proponent of the counter-reformation, being appointed chairman of the Reformation Commission, charged with the reconversion of the towns of Upper and Lower Austria, other than Vienna. In 1598 he was consecrated bishop of Vienna and the following year became chancellor to Archduke Matthias, who during the following decade became increasingly the factual ruler of the Habsburg empire. In 1611 Klesl became head of Matthias's privy council and, when Matthias became emperor in 1612, was in charge of virtually all imperial affairs of state. The emperor obtained for him, from

the pope, nomination to the College of Cardinals in 1615. At the outbreak of hostilities in Bohemia Klesl at first counselled against concessions to the Protestants, but later changed his mind. Consequently in 1618 he was arrested by the younger archdukes, Ferdinand of Styria and Maximilian of Tyrol and was imprisoned in the Georgenburg monastery near Schwaz. At the intercession of the pope, he was released from captivity in 1622, and was allowed to live in exile at Rome. In 1627 he received permission to return to Vienna, where he spent the last three years of his life.

8. Sables generally were presented as gifts to foreign dignitaries in multiples of forty.

9. Solovoy Ivanovich Protasiev, a musketeer captain, is among the signatories of Michael's confirmatory charter in 1613. In the summer of the same year he was sent with Crown Secretary Mikhail Danilov to the Turkish sultan with proposals of friendship and alliance. He returned to Moscow in 1614. In 1615 he was ordered to travel to Turkey, again with Danilov and Ivan Grigorievich Ododurov. In 1617 he was assigned to escort John Merrick, and at the beginning of 1618 was one of the escorts of the Persian ambassadors.

10. Ahmed I, Ottoman sultan, born 1519, ruled 1602-1617. His authority was weakened by numerous wars and rebellions, and the disadvantageous peace with Austria in 1606 was a blow to Ottoman prestige. In order to recoup his finances he was compelled to make extensive commercial concessions to the French, Venetians and Dutch.

11. Semeon Samsonov, Moscow crown secretary. In 1611 he was serving at Novgorod, where he is said to have incited the murder of Ivan Mikhailovich Saltykov. The next year he took part in the Nizhny Novgorod militia force, and accompanied Lopata to Yaroslavl. He was also among the first units of the Second Militia Force to reach Moscow. In 1615 he was sent on a mission to Constantinople, where he was detained with the embassy for thirty months. In 1621 he served in the Chancellery of the Royal Household, 1625 the Chancellery of Crown Revenues, and in 1625 was assigned to Astrakhan.

12. Azov was at this time an important stronghold; in modern times its importance has been eclipsed by Rostov-on-Don. It is one of the most ancient settlements of the Black Sea littoral, and in the tenth and eleventh centuries belonged to the Russian principality of Tmutorokan. In 1067 it was seized by the Polovtsians, who named it Azak. It was in turn subject to the Golden Horde and in 1471 was conquered by the Turks, who made it a major fortified center. Between 1637 and 1642 Azov was occupied by Don Cossacks, but was abandoned when the cossacks failed to obtain Muscovite backing (see Volume 17 of this series). It was conquered by Peter the Great in 1696, but was retroceded to Turkey in 1711. Azov definitively became part of the Russian empire under the terms of the Treaty of Kuchuk Kainardji in 1774.

13. *"s Mertvogo Dontsa."* The meaning of this expression is unclear.

14. The Mius is a small river which flows into the northeastern arm of the Sea of Azov, slightly to the west of the fortress.

15. Yurts were Tatar encampments and the lands pertaining to them. Since the cossacks were semi-nomadic, the term is also applied here to their habitations.

16. The Zaporozhian Host Cossack army (voisko zaporozhskoe) was the official title of the Ukrainian cossack army, not to be confused with the Zaporozhian Sech, or camp, which is a geographical location. The Sech was a cossack stronghold situated on islands in the Dnieper river below the present-day town of Zaporozhie. The cossacks of the Sech clung to their independence and democratic traditions; as a significant factor in Moscow's fight against the Poles and Turks they were treated circumspectly by the Muscovite government. Under the Truce of Andrusovo (1667) the Sech came under Muscovite protectorship, but was abolished by Catherine II in 1775.

17. In other words, the cossacks who were causing the trouble were technically Muscovite rather than Polish subjects.

18. Alexis Ivanovich Ziuzin (?-1618) first appears as a signatory to Boris Godunov's confirmatory charter in 1598. Between 1603 and 1605 he was serving as a military commander on the steppe. There he received letters from Boris's widow and Patriarch Job that the tsar was dead, and a letter from False Dmitry I informing him of his accession. Later he received instructions ordering him to exhume the body of Vasily Nikitich Romanov, who had died in exile, and bring it back to Moscow. He was governor of Ustiug in 1610 and 1611, Kargopol in 1612. On June 22, 1612 Ziuzin sent to the Russian and Swedish commanders in Novgorod, forbidding them to send tax collectors into Kargopol, and in December he was obliged to defend the town against marauding Poles. In the spring of 1613 he was at the Trinity monastery with Tsar Michael, who sent him with letters to the Assembly demanding the eradication of brigandage. As related here, he was sent as ambassador to England on July 7, 1613, returning to Moscow in October 1614. Also, as will be seen later, Ziuzin was a prominent member of the Russian delegation in peace negotiations with the Swedes, and it was he who entered the liberated city of Novgorod bearing the miraculous icon of Our Lady of Khutyn. On his return to Moscow, Ziuzin was promoted to council rank as lord-in-waiting. In 1617 he attended the Persian ambassador, and in 1618 received the Polish and Swedish ambassadors. He is also mentioned as being among the besieged during Wladyslaw's expedition.

19. John Merrick (1559-1638) was the son of a founding member of the Muscovy Company and began his apprenticeship while accompanying his father on a visit to Russia in the years 1573-1575. He became the Company's agent at Yaroslavl in 1584, and chief agent in Russia in 1594. In

1596 he was admitted to full membership of the Company. He also served as a diplomatic conduit for messages between the governments of Tsar Fedor and Boris Godunov and that of Elizabeth I. Merrick resigned his post in 1600 but resumed it in 1603, and proved indispensible to the embassy of Sir Thomas Smith in 1604-1605. He remained in Russia throughout the Time of Troubles, preserving the interests of the Company through bewildering changes of regime, returning only for brief periods of home leave. In 1612 he acted as intermediary for a proposal to establish an English protectorate over part of northern Russia, but when he returned to Russia Tsar Michael had been elected and Merrick confined himself to conveying the conventional courtesies from King James I. Michael requested English mediation in peace negotiations with Sweden, for which James appointed Merrick, conferring a knighthood upon him before his departure. On this occasion Merrick stayed three years in Russia (1614-1617). His attempts to gain further concessions for English merchants achieved only limited success, whereas from the Russian side proposals for a military alliance against Poland were totally unsuccessful, although a small monetary loan was advanced and delivered in 1618. Merrick's last visit to Russia occurred in 1620-1621, when he obtained repayment of the 1618 loan and a new charter for the Muscovy Company. In 1627 he became governor of the Company, as well as the English government's chief adviser on Russian affairs. See Geraldine M. Phipps, *Sir John Merrick. Merchant-Diplomat in Seventeenth-Century Russia* (Newtonville, Mass.), 1980; also her entry in MERSH, Vol. 21, pp. 237-239.

20.   James I instructed his ambassadors to Denmark and Sweden, Robert Ans-truther and James Spens, to mediate between the two countries to bring an end to the War of Kalmar. Peace was concluded by the Treaty of Knäred, January 21, 1613. See Michael Roberts, *Gustavus Adolphus*, pp. 69-71.

21.   James (1566-1625), king of Scotland from 1567, king of England from 1625, was actually the son of Mary Stuart and Henry, earl of Darnley, although some suspicions were cast on his paternity by Bishop Andrewes: "Verily may he be called another Solomon, since he is the son of David," an allusion to the queen's notorious affair with David Rizzio. Unfortunately there is no satisfactory explanation for the expression "son of Andrew" which Merrick allegedly uses here, unless it is an allusion to St. Andrew as patron saint of James's native Scotland.

22.   Isidore, metropolitan of Novgorod (?-1619), first took vows in the Solovetsk monastery, of which he became abbot in 1597. In 1604 he was elected metropolitan of Novgorod. In 1605, on the death of Tsar Boris, he was one of the commisioners sent, along with Peter Basmanov, to administer the oath of allegiance in favor of the new tsar, Fedor Borisovich, to the army encamped outside Kromy. He had barely returned to Moscow after

fulfilling this commision when he heard news of Basmanov's treason. On June 1, 1606 he presided over the coronation of Tsar Vasily Shuisky. In 1608 when Skopin was in Novgorod negotiating the Swedish alliance Isidore and the citizens of Novgorod, seeing that Shuisky's enemies were becoming more numerous, wrote to the tsar offering him safe refuge in Novgorod. When the Swedes forced their way into the city in 1611 Isidore conducted religious services by the walls, encouraging from afar the courageous resistance of Archpriest Amos. Yet after the city had been captured Isidore and the governor, Prince I.N. Odoevsky the Elder, concluded an agreement with De la Gardie, recognizing Prince Karl Philipp as suzerain of Novgorod, and undertaking to bring the rest of Muscovy into alignment with this agreement. After the election of Michael Romanov the Swedes still held on to Novgorod, which was evacuated after the Peace of Stolbovo in 1617. Tsar Michael sent a letter to the metropolitan and all the people of Novgorod promising full amnesty for their temporary lapse from allegiance, since they had not been in any position to resist Swedish might. After the liberation of Novgorod Isidore asked for permission to resign his office and retire to the Solovetsk monastery, but by the time this permission arrived he had died. He is buried in the Holy Wisdom cathedral in Novgorod.

23. Prince Ivan Nikitich Odoevsky "the Elder" (?-1616) is first mentioned in 1578 attending the table of Tsar Ivan IV. In 1590 he accompanied Tsar Fedor on campaign against the Swedes. Later that year he was sent on a tour of inspection of the Oka frontier. In 1591 he took part in the defense of Moscow against the Crimean Tatars, and distinguished himself in that campaign. He was at the Assembly which elected Boris Godunov in 1598, and later the same year took part in the Serpukhov campaign. In 1601 he was sent on another inspection tour of the southern defenses. After that there is no mention of him in the service records until he took part in the marriage ceremony of False Dmitry I to Marina in May 1606, on which occasion he was promoted boyar. In 1608 he was similarly present at the marriage of Tsar Vasily Shuisky to Princess Maria Buinosova. The following year he repelled the forces of False Dmitry II from the sector of the Moscow defenses adjoining the Arbat gates. In 1610 he received from Shuisky his fateful appointment as governor of Novgorod. Shortly afterwards Shuisky was deposed and the interim boyar government sent Ivan Mikhailovich Saltykov to administer to the citizens of Novgorod the oath of allegiance to Prince Wladyslaw. Both Odoevsky and Metropolitan Isidore treated Saltykov with suspicion, declaring that they would not swear allegiance to anyone until they had official instructions from Moscow, neither would they let any of Saltykov's followers into the city. Meanwhile the First Militia Force was sending its own emissaries around the towns, in the case of Novgorod Vasily Ivanovich Buturlin (see below, Note 36). Buturlin on his own initiative opened negotiations with the Swedes. As early as March 1611 De la Gardie approached the city without any serious

opposition, and persuaded the inhabitants that he would abide by the Treaty of Vyborg, concluded on behalf of Tsar Vasily in 1609. Buturlin relayed Liapunov's offer to promote the candidacy of a Swedish prince, and ignored Odoevsky's advice to fortify the city against the Swedes. Troops were allowed across the Volkhov to buy in the markets, while De la Gardie was permitted to set up his headquarters in the Kolmov monastery. This considerably softened the defenses of Novgorod, which on July 16 was occupied completely by the Swedes. Odoevsky and Isidore, besieged in the citadel with no means of resistance, were forced to negotiate. The city was forced to accept the protectorate of the Swedish king, and the citizens were made to promise to bring the dependent territories into subjection. Apart from that, the inhabitants were to hold no independent communication with Moscow. De la Gardie for his part agreed not to devastate the Novgorod lands, to respect religious customs, and not to annex to the crown of Sweden territories other than those already ceded by the Treaty of Vyborg. Odoevsky felt troubled by this agreement, even though the king had rewarded him richly with estates in September 1611.

In December of the same year Odoevsky and Isidore were compelled to send plenipotentiaries to Stockholm to offer the Russian throne to one of the Swedish princes. They wanted to preserve the unity of the country, even if it meant accepting a ruler from Sweden. To this end, in mid-1612, they sent emissaries to Prince D.M. Pozharsky at Yaroslavl. Pozharsky accepted, on condition that the prince convert to Orthodoxy. Later Odoevsky sent another mission to the Second Militia Force, but this time the emissaries were told that such a decisive matter could be decided only by a full Assembly of the Land. With the election of Michael, Odoevsky was placed in a delicate position. Karl IX had died, and the new king, Gustavus Adolphus, declared that he was sending his brother, Karl Philipp, to Vyborg, where he was to be met by plenipotentiaries from Novgorod to confirm his election to the tsardom. Odoevsky was instructed to send a delegation led by Archimandrite Cyprian of the Khutyn monastery to swear allegiance to the prince, who would then proceed to Novgorod. The Swedish commanders accompanying the prince now declared that Karl Philipp had not come to rule over Novgorod alone, but over the entire Muscovite tsardom. This the plenipotentiaries could not promise, and so the prince departed for Stockholm. Meanwhile in Novgorod De la Gardie had handed over his command to Evert Horn, who began to make harsher demands, giving the citizens the choice between rule by Karl Philipp or direct annexation to the Swedish crown. They opted for the prince, but then Horn announced that Karl Philipp had renounced the Novgorod throne. The citizens of Novgorod then revolted, expressing their wish to be reunited with Moscow, and Prince Nikofor Meshchersky openly voiced his defiance to Horn. Odoevsky also sympathized, and appealed to Moscow for help. He devised a ruse whereby he told Horn that he would swear allegiance to the prince, but first he wished to send to Moscow to remind the boyars of their previous oath of allegiance. The delegation, led by Archimandrite Cyprian, told the boyars that the inhabitants of Novgorod had acted under duress, and appealed to Michael to intervene before Novgorod was utterly ruined by the Swedes. As related here, there was simultaneous official and clandestine correspondence between Novgorod and Moscow, while open hostilities flared up once again between Muscovy and Sweden. Unfortunately Odoevsky did not live to see the fruits of his efforts, since he died in 1616.

24. Jacob Pontus de la Gardie (1583-1652) was the son of Pontus de la Gardie, a French nobleman who entered the service of the Swedish king, commanded Swedish armies against Russia, and was drowned at Narva in 1585. Jacob thus was orphaned at an early age and was brought up at the Swedish court. He served his military apprenticeship in the Livonian war, was captured at Wolmar in 1601 and spent four years in Polish captivity. After a spell in Western Europe in the service of Prince Maurice of Orange, he later re-entered Swedish service in both diplomatic and military capacities, leading a force of Swedish and foreign auxiliaries at the request of Tsar Vasily Shuisky to relieve the beleaguered city of Moscow in 1609-1610. The expedition, conducted in conjunction with the forces of M.V. Skopin-Shuisky, was a success, but Skopin died, and the Swedes' paymaster, Shuisky, was deposed, leaving the Swedish expeditionary force to fend for itself. Some of the foreign mercenaries under De la Gardie's command entered the service of the Polish victors of the battle of Klushino; others chose to go home, while the main force moved off into northern Russia to await reinforcements. With the complicity of the Russian military governor, these forces occupied Novgorod in the summer of 1611. De la Gardie was very active in the negotiations with the Militia Forces, first that of Prokopy Liapunov and then that of Minin and Pozharsky, with a view to placing the Swedish prince Karl Philipp on the Russian throne, and it is just possible that had the prince been less dilatory in making his journey to the Russian frontier his candidature might have succeeded. After the election of Michael Romanov the Swedes, frustrated in their attempts to place one of their princes upon the Russian throne, continued their occupation of Novgorod and the Baltic littoral, though they were less successful in seizing strongholds in the north such as Kola, the Suma fortress and the Solovetsk monastery. Further south, the Swedes gained control of Koporie, Yama, Ivangorod, Oreshek, Gdov, Porkhov, Staraia Rusa, Ladoga and Tikhvin, and in 1615 an attempt, commanded by King Gustavus Adolphus in person, was made to take Pskov by siege. During this time the troops were commanded by De la Gardie, who was also military governor of Novgorod. After the failure of the Swedes to take Pskov peace negotiations began in earnest, culminating in the Peace of Stolbovo, which was signed in February 1617. Sweden returned Novgorod to Muscovy, but retained the

provinces of Karelia and Ingria. De la Gardie was awarded the title of count in 1615, and played a major part in the Swedish participation in the Thirty Years' War. He also married Ebba Brahe, the king's former mistress. In 1619 he was appointed governor of Reval, and in 1622 governor of Swedish-held Livonia. After the death of Gustavus Adolphus in 1632 he was appointed to the Council of Regency during the early part of the reign of Queen Christina. His son Magnus (1622-1686) was ambassador to Paris, the lavishly rewarded favorite of the young queen, and one of the organizers of the Swedish invasion of Poland in 1655. Jacob also wrote memoirs of the Muscovite campaigns, *Thet svenska i Ryssland Tijo ahrs krijgs-historie*, Stockholm, 1671. See entry in MERSH, Vol. 48, pp. 5-6.

25. Karl IX (1550-1611) was the youngest son of King Gustav Vasa, and in 1560 was invested as duke of Sudermania. When his cousin, King Sigismund III of Poland (reigned 1587-1632), also became king of Sweden in 1592, Karl led the movement against the new ruler's attempts to reintroduce Catholicism. At the Riksdag held at Söderköping he was appointed regent, and in 1598 thwarted Sigismund's armed attempt to regain effective rule. In the following year Sigismund was declared deposed. Karl continued as regent until officially proclaimed king in 1604. Neither Sigismund nor his son Wladyslaw IV (reigned 1632-1648) ever renounced their rights to the Swedish throne, though the claim was renounced in 1660 by Wladyslaw's younger brother Jan Kazimierz (reigned 1648-1688, died 1672). Sigismund fought three unsuccessful wars (1600-1611, 1617-1620 and 1621-1629) to regain his Swedish crown.

26. Gustavus Adolphus (1594-1632) succeeded his father Karl IX as king of Sweden in 1611. His early years were marked by compromise with the Swedish aristocracy, whose leader Axel Oxenstierna eventually became his closest collaborator. One of the problems Gustavus Adolphus inherited was the Swedish intervention in Russia, as well as the War of Kalmar with Denmark. He managed to extricate himself from both but became heavily involved in the Thirty Years' War, in which he led what generally is regarded as the prototype of the modern standing army. In 1632 he concluded an offensive alliance with Russia against Poland, but the alliance became ineffectual when the king was slain on November 16, 1632 at the battle of Lützen. See Michael Roberts, *Gustavus Adolphus. A History of Sweden 1611-1632*, 2 vols., London, 1953.

27. Karl Philipp (1601-1621) was the candidate for the Russian throne favored by both Prokopy Liapunov and later by Prince Dmitry Pozharsky, but the candidacy foundered upon the failure of the prince to present himself in Russia on time. It is also believed that his mother, the regent Queen Christina, was less than enthusiastic about the venture. Karl Philipp later accompanied his brother on campaign against Poland in Livonia during the early stages of the Thirty Years' War. He participated in the capture of

Riga in September 1621, but died of camp fever at Narva in November of the same year. See G. Edward Orchard, "The Election of Michael Romanov," *Slavonic and East European Review*, Vol. 67, No. 3 (1989), pp. 378-402.

28. Cyprian, (?-1635) archimandrite of the monastery of the Transfiguration of Our Savior on the Khutyn, later metropolitan of Novgorod. He became archimandrite in 1611, when the Swedes occupied the Khutyn monastery. Cyprian was sent by Metropolitan Isidore to Odoevsky in Sweden to urge the speedy dispatch of Prince Karl Philipp. He was detained there under harsh conditions until the election of Michael Romanov. He arrived in Moscow in 1614 to explain the circumstances of his mission, and urged the tsar's government to come to the aid of Novgorod. In 1620 he was consecrated missionary archbishop for Siberia, and tried to bring the native peoples into submission. The governors, however, not only failed to help, but even ignored him. He baptized many pagans, and founded monasteries and convents in Turinsk and Tara. He also started new settlements and the compilation of the first Siberian chronicles. In 1624 he returned to Moscow, and was appointed metropolitan of Krutitsy. In 1625 he composed verses in honor of the presentation of Christ's seamless robe to Moscow by the Persian shah Abbas. He then served as metropolitan of Novgorod from 1627 until his death in 1635.

29. The Khutyn monastery was founded in the late twelfth century by Varlaam of Khutyn (?-1193) about ten versts upstream along the Volkhov from Novgorod. It was originally dedicated to the Transfiguration of Our Savior but later was dedicated also to its sainted founder, who was a member of one of the ancient Novgorod boyar families. It played a prominent part in the political life of independent Novgorod, and in the mid-fifteenth century came under the tutelage of the rulers of Moscow. The main conventual church was built in 1515, the refectory in 1552, the chapel of St. Gregory of Armenia was first built in circular form in 1445, reconstructed in octagonal form in 1535. The dormitories and household offices were reconstructed in the seventeenth century. The monastery was damaged severely during the second world war, but is now in the process of restoration.

30. Evert Horn was De la Gardie's second-in-command during the entire Russian venture, from the initial intervention in 1609 until he was killed in a skirmish outside Pskov in September 1615.

31. Soloviev frequently refers to the Swedish prince simply as "Philipp." I have taken the liberty of correcting the author and using the prince's full name.

32. The city of Novgorod since ancient times had been divided administratively into five wards *kontsy*, (or "ends"), each of which was also responsible for the administration of·one of the "fifths" (piatiny) of Novgorod's vast colonial territories.

33. Prince Nikofor Fedorovich Meshchersky later served as governor of Verkhoturie from 1643 to 1646, and died in 1652 while serving as governor of Surgut.

34. Prince Ivan Fedorovich Khovansky, boyar, died 1625.

35. Neither is mentioned in the official lists as governor of Tikhvin. Pleshcheev was governor of Tikhvin in 1614.

36. Vasily Ivanovich Buturlin (dates of birth and death unknown, fl. 1606-1651) is first mentioned in the capacity of court cupbearer, pouring wine at the wedding feast of False Dmitry I. In 1608 he repulsed the first sudden attack of the second pretender's chief commander Roman Rozynski, and then conducted several successful operations against Lisowski and his Tushinites. In July 1609 he was appointed governor of Vladimir. In 1610 he fought at Klushino and was taken prisoner by the Poles. He was released when the Poles captured Moscow and the boyars swore allegiance to Prince Wladyslaw. He nevertheless secretly encouraged Prokopy Liapunov, urging him to advance on Moscow, and when the First Militia Force had infiltrated the capital he continued to communicate with the liberation movement. He was discovered and fled to Liapunov's encampment, whence he was dispatched to Novgorod to request De la Gardie's aid against the Poles, and to offer the Russian throne to one of the sons of King Karl IX of Sweden. De la Gardie countered by demanding the cession of the northern towns, and negotiations dragged on. Some allege that it was Buturlin who gave De la Gardie the idea of seizing Novgorod, but most Russian sources attribute this misfortune to a misunderstanding between Buturlin and the Novgorod governor Prince Odoevsky. Buturlin left the city, plundering the market stalls in the town quarter, arguing that if he did not do so, the Swedes would. He withdrew with his forces to Bronnitsy, where he once again established contact with the Militia Force. He was sent by Avraamy Palitsyn to Vladimir and the "lower towns" with documents calling for the collection of funds and the recruitment of armed men for the militia. He took part in Michael's coronation and then went to Yaroslavl to recruit forces, with which he was to proceed to Torzhok to join up with Trubetskoy. While fulfilling this task Buturlin was taken prisoner by the Swedes who were besieging Gdov. Russian sources cease to mention him, but the Swedes say that he became a Swedish subject, retained his noble status and adapted his name to read "Wasilius Butterlin", distinguishing himself in the Swedish army during the Thirty Years' War. In 1638 he was made a regimental quartermaster, a colonel in 1649, and received a coat of arms in 1651. He married a Swedish noblewoman, Anna Knudsen, but died childless.

37. Count Axel Oxenstierna (1583-1654) was educated at Rostock and other German universities. Subsequently he was appointed to the exchequer and became a leading member of the Council of State. On the death of Karl

IX he extorted a charter from Gustavus Adolphus guaranteeing the nation against excessive royal power. The king appointed Oxenstierna as his chancellor in January 1612. This initiated a long period of collaboration between king and chancellor, who drew up a parliamentary law (riksdagsordning) in 1617 and a constitution for the upper house (riddarhusordning) in 1627, placing the government of Sweden on a firm footing. After the death of Gustavus Adolphus at the battle of Lützen in 1632, the burden of rulership fell largely upon Oxenstierna's shoulders. He was the leading figure in the Council of Regency, and admitted the young Queen Christina to council meetings when she attained the age of fourteen. Despite this, he came into frequent conflict with his young and gifted erstwhile pupil after she came of age in 1644, although he attempted in vain to dissuade her from abdicating in June 1654. Oxenstierna died twelve weeks later.

38. See Chapter I, Note 24, above.

39. Fedor Leontievich Buturlin, lord-in-waiting 1618, died 1640.

40. Anthonis Goeteeris, *Journael der Legatie ghedaen inde Jaren 1615 ende 1616* (Journal of the Embassy Dispatched in the Years 1615 and 1616), The Hague, 1619. Goeteeris was apparently treasurer (*Pennighmeester ende Dispensier*) of the embassy, as well as its rapporteur.

41. The town of Korela, founded in 1295, was repeatedly a bone of contention between Sweden and Russia. It had been in Swedish hands from 1581 to 1595 but had been won back in Boris Godunov's Swedish war, and ceded to Russia under the terms of the Treaty of Teusen. It was captured by the Swedes in 1611, but was retaken by Peter the Great in 1710. When the Swedes took it over, it was renamed Kexholm, and this name was retained until 1948, when it was renamed Priozersk.

42. The battle of Klushino (June 24, 1610) was a resounding defeat for the forces of Tsar Vasily Shuisky, under the command of his effete brother, Prince Dmitry Ivanovich. After the battle many of the foreign mercenaries under Swedish command deserted, some of them going over to the Polish side.

43. Prince M.V. Skopin-Shuisky (1586-1610), a kinsman of Tsar Vasily Shuisky, was sent to Novgorod in 1609 to recruit Swedish auxiliaries for the relief of Moscow. He was successful in his mission, and entered Moscow in triumph in the spring of 1610. He was poisoned to death a few weeks later, probably at the instigation of the wife of Prince D.I. Shuisky, who was heir apparent to the throne, and jealous of Skopin's popularity. Skopin's death was followed quickly by the defeat of the Muscovite forces at the battle of Klushino and the deposition of Shuisky.

44. This is untrue. It was Zakhar Liapunov and his companions who deposed Shuisky and had him tonsured forcibly. Neither Zolkiewski nor his other Polish captors recognized the validity of the former tsar's involuntary monastic vows and neither, for that matter, did Metropolitan Filaret.

45. Yuriev (Russian), Dorpat (German) or Tartu (Estonian) was inhabited as early as the fifth century A.D., but is first mentioned in the year 1030 under the name Yuriev as a foundation of Yaroslav the Wise. In 1229 it was captured by the Teutonic Knights, who renamed it Dorpat, and made it the seat of a Catholic bishopric. From the thirteenth to the sixteenth century, Dorpat was an important member of the Hanseatic League. It was conquered by Russia in 1558, in the initial campaign of the Livonian War, but was ceded to Poland in 1582. From 1625 to 1704 Dorpat was in Swedish hands. A German university was founded in 1632 but was closed in 1710, being reopened in 1802. In 1918 part of the university was evacuated to become the core of the university at Voronezh.

46. A reference to the 1595 Peace of Teusen (Täysinä) by which Sweden retroceded Korela and renounced its claims to the Kola peninsula. In return Russia recognized Sweden's title to Estonia and Narva.

47. Some groups of Lithuanians, led by Captains Chmieliewski and Pagaliewski, angry at arrears in pay, deserted to the Second Militia Force at Yaroslavl. Chmieliewski was also responsible for alerting Trubetskoy to Zarutsky's treacherous designs in May 1612, and played a prominent part in the repulse of Chodkiewicz from Moscow. The Lithuanian auxiliaries, as seen here, subsequently saw action against the Swedes around Novgorod.

48. The Holy Wisdom cathedral (Sofiiskii sobor) is the most ancient historical monument in Novgorod. It was built on the orders of Prince Vladimir Yaroslavich between 1054 and 1050 to replace the wooden cathedral which had been destroyed by fire. A second storey was added in the twelfth century, and between 1108 and 1144 the cathedral was adorned by frescoes, fragments of which still remain. The western facade boasts the Korsun gates, fashioned at Magdeburg in the mid-twelfth century. From the twelfth century it became the cathedral church of the archbishops and later metropolitans, and also for a time housed the city treasury.

49. Sir Arthur Aston had been a mercenary in Russian service, but was accused of plotting with the Poles. As a result of Merrick's intercession he was given leave to depart from Russia, but immediately left for Poland and later appeared in England recruiting mercenaries for service in Poland. At the insistence of the Russian ambassador, Pogozhy, he was confined for a while to Marshalsea prison, but was released a few days after the ambassador's departure.

50. Isaac Abrahamszoon Massa (1587-1643) was for many years Merrick's rival, and his career runs curiously parallel. Arriving in Moscow at the age of thirteen in 1600, he stayed there for eight years, and on his return wrote a fascinating *Short History of the Muscovite Wars*, tr. and ed. G. Edward Orchard, Toronto, 1982. He was employed on a number of subsequent commercial and diplomatic missions, and was well known at the Russian court. See entry in MERSH, Vol. 21, pp. 133-136.

51. A reference to the adventures of Thomas Bannister and George Duckett in 1569. See *Early Voyages and Travels in Russia and Persia*, ed. E.D. Morgan and C.H. Coote, London: Hakluyt Society, 1886.

52. Leading merchants (gosti) were the highest stratum of the Russian mercantile community. They numbered about thirty in the seventeenth century. Although the rank was not hereditary, it was not unknown for a son to inherit his father's rank. In return for very considerable privileges the *gosti* also had to perform, on the average of one year in five, quite onerous financial services for the tsar. See entry by Samuel H. Baron, MERSH, Vol. 13, pp. 74-77.

53. About 20 copecks. One value given for a grivna is twenty Moscow dengas, the denga being equivalent to half a copeck.

54. See Volume 14, p. 48.

55. Soloviev's text reads "brother," but in Russian the term is used much more loosely than in English, and could be used to describe a cousin. Gustavus Adolphus's only brother Karl Philipp did not die until 1622, but his cousin Johan, duke of Ostergötland (born 1589), younger brother of King Sigismund III, died in 1618. Johan was next in line for the Swedish throne after Sigismund's deposition, and his uncle Karl waited until Johan had come of age and renounced his rights before himself assuming the kingship in 1604.

CHAPTER III

1. Mikhail Konaevich Tinbaev (dates of birth and death unknown) was probably the son of Kanay Murza. Shortly after the halt of the peace talks near Smolensk he was ordered to accompany Likharev into enemy territory and harry the Lithuanian borderlands. Proceeding by way of Volok and Pogoreloe Gorodishche, they captured informants on the Belaia river and caused great havoc behind the Polish lines.

2. Nikita Paramonovich Likharev (dates of birth and death unknown) was later, in 1626, governor of Briansk.

3. The Beast is used as an allegorical term in the biblical books of Daniel and Revelation. In Daniel 7 four different beasts symbolize four pagan kingdoms. In Revelation a beast from the sea symbolizes the Roman empire (13:1); a beast from the earth symbolizes the provinces of Asia (13:11), and a beast from the Abyss portrays the Antichrist (11:7 and 17:8).

4. The Moscow miracle-workers. See Chapter I, Note 50.

5. Michael of Chernigov (1179-1246) was executed at Saray on the orders of Batu Khan, allegedly for refusing to bow down before the golden idol of the Mongol ruler. He and his boyar Fedor, who was executed along with him, became known as the Chernigov miracle-workers. See entry by

Martin Dimnik, MERSH, Vol. 22, pp. 52-54, and also his monograph *Mikhail Prince of Chernigov and Grand Prince of Kiev* (1224-1246), Toronto, 1981.

6. Possibly a reference to the boyar martyred along with Prince Michael of Chernigov (see previous note), or else Prince Fedor Ivanovich of Starodub, executed at the Horde on the orders of Khan Uzbek on June 23, 1330, and also revered as a martyr of the Russian church.

7. When the first Christian prince of Russia, Vladimir, died in 1015, his eldest son Sviatopolk "the Damned" tried to consolidate his position by getting rid of his two half-brothers, Boris and Gleb. Within a short time of one another they were murdered, each refusing to allow his followers to defend or avenge them. They thus exemplified unwillingness to resist injustice by force or to raise their hands in fratricidal strife. They were the first Russian saints to be canonized, and their feast day is celebrated July 24.

8. Formosus, pope (891-896), whose posthumous trial is one of the most bizarre incidents in church history. In 864 he was made cardinal bishop of Porto by Pope Nicholas I, who sent him to promote the conversion of Bulgaria. He was later placed in charge of missions to the Frankish kingdom, but then incurred the enmity of Pope John VIII, fled Rome and was excommunicated. Subsequently he was absolved by Pope Marinus I, who restored him to his see of Porto. Eventually he was elected pope, but tried to evict the Lombard rulers of Spoleto, Guy and Lambert, by inviting the Frankish king Arnulf to invade Rome. In 896 Arnulf was crowned emperor by Formosus, but suffered a paralytic stroke while preparing to attack Spoleto. Formosus died shortly thereafter. His Spoletan enemies exhumed his body, propped it up in a chair, and subjected it to a trial, in which a deacon answered for the defendant. His election was declared invalid, his consecration fingers were cut off, and his body was thrown into the Tiber. These actions divided Rome politically and the successor of Formosus, Stephen VI, was imprisoned and murdered. Pope Theodosius II reinstated the ordinations performed by Formosus, and his body was solemnly reinterred. Pope John IX annulled the proceedings of the "Cadaver Synod" and quashed all the enactments of Stephen VI.

9. Isaac Semeonovich Pogozhy (?-1631), also rendered as Pogozhin or Pogozhev, is first mentioned at the marriage of Tsar Vasily Shuisky in January 1608. In 1611 he took part in the First Militia Force under the command of Trubetskoy, until the cossacks swore allegiance to the Pskov pretender. Pogozhy then joined the Second Militia Force at Yaroslavl. In June 1613 he and Fedor Semeonovich Pleshcheev were sent to the defense of Tikhvin, though not before Pogozhy had brought a precedence suit against his colleague. In 1614 Pogozhy repelled the Swedes before Bronnitsy. He accompanied Tsar Michael on pilgimage to the Trinity monastery

in September 1614, and attended the English ambassador in January 1615. He subsequently fulfilled other diplomatic tasks. In December 1615 he was sent to the theater of operations around Smolensk along with Mikhail Matveevich Buturlin. In October they were able to inflict heavy losses on Gasiewski's encampment, but then quarrelled with each other. They then informed the tsar that Gasiewski was intending to skirt Smolensk and advance on Moscow along the main highway, joining forces with Prince Wladyslaw. The tsar ordered Prince N.P. Boriatinsky from Rzhev to Dorogobuzh to reinforce Buturlin and Pogozhy, but he failed to do so. Gasiewski skirted Smolensk and dug in at Tverdilishchi, cutting off the supply route to the Muscovite forces besieging Smolensk, who then suffered extreme privations. A second relieving force under Suleshov and Prozorovsky similarly failed in its objective, and the Muscovites were obliged to lift the siege of Smolensk. Between 1618 and 1620 Pogozhy was governor of Belgorod, and in 1621 served as an emissary to England. In 1625 he attended the Persian ambassador, and later that year the emigrant Archbishop Joseph Kuntsevich, who later became archbishop of Riazan. In 1626 he was one of the groomsmen at the tsar's second marriage, and in 1628 was one of several Moscow notables receiving a group of Persian merchants. In 1629 he was appointed governor of Voronezh, but returned the following year, and is last attested at a reception for the Swedish ambassador Anton Monier in 1631.

    10.   Prince Nikita Petrovich Boriatinsky (?-1629) is first described in 1598 as a "crown agent with a salary." In 1614, during the younger Odoevsky's military actions against Zarutsky, he guarded Alatyr with his own armed contingent. In 1615 he was commissioned to clear the Riazan lands of rebel cossacks, but was slow to move into action and failed in his task. He was sent with lesser reponsibility in 1616 to be governor of Voronezh but in September of the same year was ordered to Pskov, in anticipation of a Swedish attack. When this proved to be a false alarm, he was ordered to Dorogobuzh, where he was besieged by Gasiewski, until Suleshov came to his relief. Boriatinsky, along with the other commanders, was rewarded with gold pieces for this campaign. In 1619 he and Prince Mikhail Petrovich Katyrev-Rostovsky were put in charge of the defense of Moscow against the forces of Prince Wladyslaw. Subsequently Boriatinsky served in a number of Siberian governorships, including Verkhoturie from 1623 to 1627. From there he was transferred to Viatka, where he died.

    11.   Prince Semeon Ivanovich Prozorovsky (?-1660) was in active service during the reign of Tsar Vasily Shuisky, winning a victory over the forces of False Dmitry II at Khmelniki in 1608. He was in charge of the Chancellery of Posts in 1643.

    12.   Stanislaw Czaplinski (?-1618) first served in the royal army during the early stages of Polish intervention in the Time of Troubles. In 1609 he

led a troop of heavy armed cavalry (piatigortsy) under the overall command of Jozef Budzilo at the Kaliazin monastery near Tver. At Klushino he was in the regiment led by Colonel Chruslinski in Sapieha's army, but in November 1610 led a mutiny and brought his contingent over to False Dmitry II at Kaluga. In December he quarelled with the Tatar prince Peter Urusov, who later murdered the pretender. He then joined Lisowski's irregulars, and took overall command after the leader's death in 1615. In 1617 he took part in skirmishes with the Muscovite forces at Meshchersk and Kaluga. The following year he played a minor part in the action around Mozhaisk and Borisov, and in the assault on Moscow. As related below, Czaplinski was killed at Vokhna, near the Trinity monastery.

13. Prince Peter Ivanovich Pronsky (?-1652) is first mentioned at the marriage celebrations of Tsar Vasily in January 1608. At the coronation of Michael in July 1613 he was one of the ten attendants preceding the tsar from the palace to the Dormition cathedral. From 1613 to 1616 he was governor of Kholmogory, which was being attacked by roving Polish and cossack bands. Pronsky captured a number of informants and sent the results of his interrogations on to Moscow. Apparently also the Kholmogory townsmen were plundering villages and trading settlements belonging to the Archangel monastery. The tsar ordered Pronsky to restore order. In 1616 he was promoted to the court rank of table attendant and was sent to Dorogobuzh, together with Prince Ivan Alexandrovich Koltovskoy, but reported that he could not get into the town, as it was besieged by Poles. They were ordered to Viazma, from there to organize the relief of Dorogobuzh. When Wladyslaw came on campaign in person, the governor of Dorogobuzh, Adodurov, surrendered the town as to his loyal sovereign. Pronsky and Prince Mikhail Vasilievich Beloselsky, who had replaced Koltovskoy, fled in panic from Viazma, which was captured by Wladyslaw without any resistance. Pronsky and Beloselsky were brought in chains to Moscow, knouted and exiled to Siberia. Pronsky was imprisoned in the Turinsk fort. His immoveable property was confiscated and redistributed to other commanders. Some time before 1622 he returned from exile, and in 1625 was appointed governor of Briansk. He was frequently in attendance at the tsar's table, and was one of the attendants at the tsar's second marriage. In 1627 he served as governor of Putivl, in 1628 attended the reception of the Persian ambassador, and from 1629 to 1631 was governor of Tomsk. He served in the Vladimir Judicial Chancellery in 1633 and 1634, then spent two years as governor of Viazma. He was governor of Tobolsk from 1639 to 1643, and was ordered to assist Prince Peter Petrovich Golovin, who was sent to establish Yakutsk and remain there as governor. On April 22, 1647 Pronsky was promoted directly from noble to boyar; apparently his court table attendant rank which had been stripped from him in 1617 was not restored to him on his return from exile. Pronsky was left in charge of the

capital late in 1647 while Tsar Alexis went on pilgrimage, and he was also present at the tsar's marriage to Maria Miloslavskaia in 1648.

14. Ivan Alexandrovich Koltovskoy (dates of birth and death unknown) was a comrade-in-arms of Prince Dmitry Mikhailovich Pozharsky in the fighting around Moscow in Holy Week of 1611. In 1617 he was appointed governor of Viazma, in 1618 of Kaluga and in 1619 of Nizhny Novgorod. In 1625-1626 he was deputy head of the Patriarchal Chancellery.

15. Andrzej Lipski (1572-1631), later chancellor of Poland and bishop of Cracow. He was brought up a Protestant, studied law at Strasbourg and went on to further studies at Heidelberg. He returned to Poland in 1595 and was employed in the office of the chancellor. About that time he was converted to Catholicism and found his vocation to the priesthood. He was in minor orders by 1600, and continued to be a prolific author of legal studies. In 1604-1605 he studied at Rome, where he became a doctor of law *utriusque juris*. He then played a leading role as a jurist at the Polish court, and was sought out as a legal consultant by Emperor Rudolph II. In 1614 he became administrator of the Cracow diocese on the death of Bishop Piotr Tylicki, and in 1616 was consecrated bishop of Lutsk, being confirmed by the pope the following year. He emerged as a vigorous defender of the privileges granted the Ursulines and Jesuits by King Sigismund III, and also of the king's intervention in Russia. In 1618 he was appointed deputy chancellor. On becoming Bishop of Wloclawek in 1623, he consecrated a suffragan bishop of Lutsk. In 1630 be became bishop of Cracow and chancellor of Poland.

16. Konstanty Plichta (?-1631) in his youth served in the Wallachian campaign under the command of Jan Zamoyski in 1601. In 1606 he succeeded his father as castellan of Sochaczew, and in 1607 was in the royal encampment at Ilza, where King Sigismund III raised his standard against the Zebrzydowski rebellion. In 1611 he was appointed to the parliamentary commission to look into the further conduct of the Muscovite wars. Plichta supported the king's policy, and in 1616 was appointed to Prince Wladyslaw's war council. During the campaign he became the personal enemy of Marcin Kazanowksi, and this rivalry erupted into an open feud at Yampolie. Wladyslaw himself had to send back to Warsaw to invoke the king's good offices to reconcile the quarrel. During the assault on Moscow Plichta supported the decisions of Hetman Chodkiewicz, risking the personal displeasure of the prince. In 1619 Plichta accompanied the king on his journey to Wilno. He saw action in 1621 at Khotin with his regiment of 150 hussars under the overall command of Prince Wladyslaw. He then played a leading part in securing the loyalty of the Zaporozhian Cossacks. In 1618 he had witnessed the act investing Johann Sigismund of Brandenburg as duke of Prussia, and in 1626 fought in the Prussian campaign against Gustavus

Adolphus, particularly distinguishing himself at the siege of Gniewa (September 22-December 1). In 1629 he represented the province of Rawa at the Royal Tribunal, and in 1630 was appointed governor of Mazovia.

17. Piotr Opalinski (1587-1624) was educated in the Jesuit academy of Poznan, and went on to study at Ingolstadt, Bavaria, in 1604. In 1605 he was in Padua and accompanied his brother Andrzej, one of the royal secretaries, on a mission to Rome. He was elected to the Sejm in 1606, but later associated himself with the Zebrzydowski rebels. He became reconciled to royal authority by 1611, and was appointed elder of Srem, in succession to his father Lukasz. In 1613 he was sent to Lublin to pacify a confederation of troops mutinous by reason of arrears in pay. By 1616 he was identified closely with the royalist cause, and was one of the most ardent supporters in the Sejm of Wladyslaw's quest for the Muscovite throne. In the campaign which opened in April 1617 Opalinski played a prominent part, commanding a regiment which proceeded by way of Smolensk and Dorogobuzh and established winter quarters in Viazma. But then he deserted the prince's cause and joined a confederation at Srodz, where on January 2, 1618 he argued for a cessation of imposts destined to finance the Moscow campaign. In June he led a contingent of 120 hussars, recruited at his own expense, but became bogged down with Chodkiewicz's contingent at Kaluga. In 1619 he attended the Sejm, and was appointed castellan of Poznan in 1620. He took part in the Khotin campaign of 1621, commanding a regiment of twelve hundred troops. In the 1623 Sejm he sat on a commission investigating the prevention of future anti-royalist confederations. Up to a few days before his death he argued for the establishment of a modern standing army to replace the quasi-feudal levies which constituted the royal army.

18. Jakub Sobieski (1588-1646) was elected four times marshal of the Sejm, and was nicknamed by the Poles "the buckler of our liberty." He took a leading part in the preliminary peace talks on the Presnia near Moscow in October 1618, and later at the successful talks leading to the Truce of Deulino in December. He was one of the two signatories on behalf of the Polish Commonwealth to the Peace of Khotin in 1621. In 1629 he signed the truce of Altmark between Poland and Sweden, and similarly the truce of Stumsdorf (1635) between the same two powers. He inherited great wealth from his father, and also from his wife Sophia Theophila, a granddaughter of Hetman Stanislaw Zolkiewski. This enabled him to indulge his artistic tastes, of which his castle of Villanova, near Warsaw, is the most outstanding testimony. His wealth also led him to entertain royal ambitions for his sons Jakub (1628-1652) and Jan (1629-1696). The latter, of course, became king in 1676, and is best remembered for his relief of Vienna in 1683, which definitively stemmed the Ottoman threat to Europe. The ghost of Jan Sobieski certainly haunted Tsar Nicholas I. In Warsaw for his coronation as

king of Poland in 1828, being mindful of his own costly Turkish wars, he pointed to the statue of Sobieski, saying: "There is the other fool who wasted his time fighting the Turks". Later, bitter at Austria's failure to support Russia during the Crimean War, in return for Nicholas's intervention against the Hungarian patriots in 1849, he is said to have posed the riddle: "Who were the two most foolish kings of Poland?" He answered himself: "The first was Jan Sobieski, the second is myself; we both saved Vienna!"

19. Zolkiewski concluded the treaty with the Moscow boyars on the understanding that Wladyslaw would become ruler of Muscovy, convert to Orthodoxy and come to Moscow soon. He discovered to his chagrin that King Sigismund had no intention of honoring any of these conditions, but instead was intent upon advancing his own claims to the Muscovite tsardom.

20. Prince Yury Nikitich Trubetskoy (dates of birth and death unknown) was cousin to the more famous Prince Dmitry Timofeevich. He was at first loyal to Tsar Vasily Shuisky, but changed sides after being accused unfairly of treasonable dealings during the campaign against the Bolotnikov rebels. Unlike his cousin, who eventually sided with the liberation forces, he remained loyal to False Dmitry II. After the death of the pretender it was Prince Yury who came to Kaluga to urge the inhabitants to swear allegiance to Wladyslaw, while it was Prince Dmitry who successfully urged them to temporize.

21. Bartlomiej Nowodworski (1544-1624), a knight of Malta. In his youth he served at the court of Stefan Bathory, and fought against the Turks and Tatars. Because of disorders in Poland he went into exile and spent some time in France, where he fought on the Catholic side during the religious wars. In 1599 he went to Malta to defend it against the Turks, who were anxious to avenge Lepanto. Returning to Poland in 1609, he served as a colonel in the 1610 and 1618 campaigns against Moscow. He also founded bursaries for needy scholars at the Cracow academy and other educational institutions, and at the end of his life was decorated as knight commander of the Order of St. John of Malta.

22. A certain Ivan Grigorievich Adodurov had been chamberlain to Tsar Vasily Shuisky, but it is uncertain whether he can be identified with this governor of Dorogobuzh.

23. Prince Mikhail Vasilievich Beloselsky (?-1637) is first mentioned in 1610, when he was governor of Viazma. In 1614 he was governor of Torzhok, but was recalled to Moscow and sent to Samara, where he campaigned against cossack bands plundering the Volga basin. In 1616 he was recalled to take part in the defense of Moscow, being entrusted with the defense of the sector from the Arbat to the Tver gates, with forty nobles and 53 court servitors under his command. Later that year he was sent with

Ivan Mikhailovich Karamyshev to forestall an anticipated Swedish attack on Pskov. Karamyshev brought a precedence suit, as a result of which both commanders were removed. Next, as related here, Beloselsky played an inglorious part in the defense of the western front, abandoning Viazma to the enemy. He and his colleague Prince Peter Pronsky were sent in chains to Moscow, knouted and exiled to Siberia (see Note 13, above). Beloselsky returned from exile in 1619 and in 1622 presented a petition for the restoration of some of his confiscated property. In 1627 he was appointed governor of Berezov, where he remained until 1629. On his return to the capital he was ordered to attend the reception of the French ambassador Louis Deshayes de Cormenin, and in 1631 similarly attended the Swedish ambassador Anton Monier. He then was posted to Rzhev Volodimerov, and in the Smolensk war took part in the recapture of Belaia. Then, with his contingent largely composed of newly-baptized Tatars, he proceeded to reinforce Shein but was among those who surrendered on March 1, 1634. On his return to Moscow once again he was exiled to Siberia, his wife and children banished to the provinces, and their estates were confiscated. He was spared the death sentence only because all of his followers testified that he was sick at the time of the surrender. He is last seen back at court in 1637, taking part in the talks with the Polish emissaries Jan Oborski and Samuel Sokolinski.

24. Prince Nikita Nikitich Gagarin (?-1640), nicknamed "Slashed Cheeks" on account of a saber wound he received in a battle with Lisowski's troops in 1615, served in various governorships between 1614 and 1640, including Staritsa, Viazma, Rzhev Volodimerov, Tsaritsyn, Pskov, Solvychegodsk, Putivl, Kazan and Odoev. In June 1617 he was sent to pacify the cossacks beyond the Ugra river, and bring them to aid the beleaguered forces at Viazma. Between almost continuous tours of duty, Gagarin was present at the marriage of Prince Mikhail Kaibulovich to the daughter of Grigory Liapunov. Here he got into a precedence dispute with Ivan Dmitrievich Pleshcheev and ended up being seated forcibly at the table. He brought a suit concerning the incident, but later dropped it. In 1623 and 1626 he was in charge of the arrangements for Tsar Michael's pilgimage to the monastery of St. Nicholas on the Ugresha river. In 1625 and 1627 he was in attendance at the tables of Tsar Michael and Patriarch Filaret. He escorted the imperial ambassador from Viazma to Moscow in 1632, and then went to Archangel to receive a contingent of mercenary soldiers. In mid-June 1633, while serving as governor of Putivl, he and his colleague Andrei Urusov warned Moscow of the approach of fifty thousand Lithuanians and Zaporozhian Cossacks. They withstood the siege of Putivl and were rewarded by the tsar the following year. In 1634 Gagarin was in attendance upon the Holstein and Swedish ambassadors, and in 1635 was sent as head of a commission to inspect and improve the defense works in the

Riazan region. In 1636-1637 he was chief assistant to Ivan Vasilievich Morozov at the head of the Vladimir Judicial Chancellery. On September 8, 1637 he was appointed governor of Kazan, and briefy served at Odoev before being recalled to Moscow in September 1640. From 1626 to 1640 he is listed among the "Moscow nobles."

25. Ignaty (?-1640) was a Greek, originally archbishop of Cyprus. After the Turkish conquest of that island he fled, and lived for a while at Rome. During the reign of Tsar Fedor Ivanovich he appeared in Russia, and under Boris Godunov was appointed administrator of the Riazan archbishopric. When False Dmitry I was advancing on Moscow Ignaty solemnly greeted him at Tula, which lay within his eparchy. He accompanied the pretender, who four days after the surrender of Moscow appointed him patriarch after the deposition of the incumbent Job. In this capacity he officiated at Dmitry's coronation and his marriage to Marina Mniszech. Immediately after the death of the pretender he was deposed from patriarchal and even episcopal rank, and was confined to the Miracles monastery as an ordinary monk. When Patriarch Hermogen was deposed and imprisoned, shortly before Easter 1611, Ignaty was released and proclaimed patriarch in concert with the boyars who were supporting Prince Wladyslaw. Fearing dire consequences for himself after the liberation of Moscow, he fled to Poland, where King Sigismund granted him permission to live in the Uniate monastery at Wilno. When in 1616 Wladyslaw set off on his Moscow campaign it was announced that Ignaty would accompany him, although it is not known whether in fact he did. In any case the Muscovites were not informed that he had joined the Uniate church. Details of the latter part of his life are lacking, except that King Sigismund granted him some estates in the Vitebsk region.

26. It is not indicated either in the chronicles or in the official acts when Sergius became archbishop. When King Sigismund, who was besieging Smolensk between September 1609 and June 1611, called upon the city to surrender, Sergius is said to have replied: "In the shrine of the Virgin we have vowed not to betray our sovereign Vasily Ivanovich, or to be enslaved forever by you, the Lithuanian king and your lords." The archbishop inspired the defenders of the city, sharing hardships and dangers with them. When the city fell, Sergius was wounded and taken prisoner. He died in captivity, since he was not among the prisoners released in 1619, although he is known from this particular passage still to have been alive in 1616-1617.

27. Prince Dmitry Petrovich Lopata-Pozharsky (?-1637) played an important role in the Second Militia Force under the command of his cousin Prince Dmitry Mikhailovich. It was he who secured Yaroslavl for the Militia Force, and then led the advance party for the relief of Moscow. In 1614 Lopata, as governor of Samara, sent two regiments of musketeers to the

relief of Astrakhan. While he was serving at Samara his village of Kozar, in the Riazan district, which had been granted to him "for his humble services, his blood and the liberation of Moscow," was confiscated without cause. In 1615 Prince D.M. Pozharsky, who was fighting Lisowski, was hampered by desertions and dereliction of duty by subordinate commanders, and finally fell sick. Lopata was instructed to intercept the enemy between Viazma and Mozhaisk. Lopata did not reach Mozhaisk, but took up position on the Ugra. He disregarded orders from the tsar to advance, pointing out that his troops were in no fit state to do so, being depleted by scarcity and desertions. Michael ordered Lopata placed under arrest, and then sent for further duty. In 1616 he was ordered to put down peasant rebellions in the Suzdal area and then, as related here, to defend Tver against the Poles. He served as governor of Tver from 1618 to 1620. He then commanded the rearguard regiment at Krapivna, and in 1621 was recalled to Moscow. In 1623, while governor of the Dvina lands, he received a reprimand from the tsar, ordering him not to hinder the brethren of the Archangel monastery from purchasing hemp from the peasants, and also to assist the Dutch merchant De Moline. He received sick leave in 1624-1625, but then was sent as governor to Verkhoturie. He complained to the tsar that there was insufficient artillery, and that the fortifications were in serious disrepair. The tsar ordered artillery and timber to be sent, and later also a missive ordering Lopata to allow Russian traders to do business with the local Voguls. Despite repeated petitions, it was only in 1628 that he received an enlargement of his landed estates. In 1627 and 1628 he was in attendance at the patriarch's table, and in 1628 accompanied the tsar on pilgrimage to the Trinity monastery. Late in 1628 he was appointed governor of Porkhov, but almost immediately was transferred to Pskov. There he and his colleague Prince Dmitry Gagarin were accused of malfeasance and subjected to a seven-month audit, from which they emerged exonerated. In 1631 Lopata appears at the Palace of Facets for the reception of the Swedish ambassador. In 1634 he kept vigil at court while the tsar went on pilgrimage to the monastery of St. Nicholas on the Ugresha river. A petition was presented by Lopata and Prince Dmitry Mikhailovich in 1635 alleging that their cousin, Prince Fedor Ivanovich Pozharsky, was mismanaging some of the family estates near Mozhaisk, and asking the tsar to place the culprit in monastic confinement. Shortly before his death Lopata made a rich bequest of lands and goods to the Spaso-Evfimiev monastery in Suzdal.

28. Fedor Vasilievich Buturlin (?-1665) is first mentioned in January 1608 at the marriage of Vasily Shuisky to Princess Maria Buinosova. In 1617 he took part in the campaign against the Poles and was rewarded for his services with a silver goblet, forty sables and a length of scarlet velvet. In 1627 he was appointed governor of Livny, where he repelled a party of Tatar raiders. For this he was rewarded with a goblet, a sable robe, and his

land entitlement was increased. In 1628 Buturlin was posted to the province of Severia, from whence, during hostilities with the Poles, he was sent to aid Shein, who was besieging Smolensk. In 1637 he was governor of Toropets, and in 1638 was ordered to inspect the southern defenses of the tsardom, with special attention to the Oka bank from Serpukhov to Riazan. Then he was again appointed governor, first in Krapivna, then in Odoev. In 1639 he served at Kazan, and in 1642 at Mtsensk. Between 1643 and 1646 he was second-ranking judge in the Chancellery of the New Quarter, and in 1646 spent five months as governor of Venev. In 1648 he assisted at the marriage of Tsar Alexis to Maria Miloslavskaia. In 1649 he was promoted lord-in-waiting, and served as governor of the Dvina lands from 1650 to 1652. In 1653 he was governor of Yablonov, and in 1654, Putivl. In November 1654, together with Boris Vasilievich Sheremetev, he commanded the tsar's forces at Belaia Tserkov, and in conjunction with Hetman Bogdan Khmelnitsky repelled a combined Polish-Crimean force. In March 1655 he was recalled to Moscow and was richly rewarded by the tsar. When Alexis was absent on campaign Buturlin was the third-ranking commissioner left in charge of the capital. In 1657 he was sent to Chigirin with an important mission to Khmelnitsky, to assure him that the tsar had no intention of handing the Ukraine back to the Poles. In August of the same year Buturlin was appointed governor of Kazan, where he remained until 1660. He also served at Venev 1660-1661, and at Tula from 1662 until his death in 1665.

29.   Danila Yurievich Leontiev (dates of birth and death unknown) later served as majordomo to Patriarch Filaret from 1620 to 1625.

30.   Grigory Leontievich Valuev (dates of birth and death unknown) distinguished himself during the Time of Troubles, being the assassin of False Dmitry I in May 1606. Afterwards he served loyally in the ranks of the army of Prince Mikhail Vasilievich Skopin-Shuisky, but was one of the chief culprits in the Muscovite defeat at Klushino on June 24, 1610. He then concluded a truce with Zolkiewski, which allowed the Poles to advance on Moscow virtually unopposed. He became an ardent supporter of Prince Wladyslaw, but when Michael was elected he was loyal to the Romanov regime. He is last mentioned in 1624 as governor of Astrakhan.

31.   Prince Vasily Petrovich Cherkassky (?-1652) was a lord-in-waiting and served on numerous campaigns under Tsars Michael and Alexis. With his death the Akhemashkov line of the Cherkassky clan became extinct.

32.   Ivan Gavrilovich Kondyrev (dates of birth and death unknown, fl. 1614-1632) was sent by Tsar Michael to the Nogay Horde to reason with Khan Ishterek, and prevent him from joining forces with Zarutsky. The next year he was sent on an embassy to King Louis XIII of France, to inform him of Michael's accession to the throne, and to obtain aid against the Swedes and Poles. The king received the embassy graciously at Bordeaux,

and agreed to inscribe the tsar's name as requested, but refused the proposed aid. In 1618, as related here, Kondyrev was sent to Wladyslaw's encampment near Viazma to explore peace terms, but his mission was unsuccessful. In 1622 Kondyrev was sent with the secretary Bormosov and the Turkish ambassador Thomas Cantacuzene to Constantinople. This was a disastrous journey for Kondyrev. First he was captured by the Don Cossacks, who would not release him until he had paid over the bulk of the treasury he had brought with him. Then the inhabitants of Azov seized the ambassadors, threatening reprisals for recent cossack raids. When they reached Constantinople they encountered great disorders. Sultan Osman had been murdered by his janissaries, who placed his uncle Mustafa on the throne. Once again the ambassadors were threatened with reprisals for the actions of the Don Cossacks. The new grand vizier, Husayn, demanded lavish gifts from the ambassadors, otherwise he would detain them for several years. Eventually Kondyrev reached an agreement, even though by now Turkey had concluded peace with Poland. The sultan agreed to restrain the inhabitants of Azov from attacking the Muscovite borderlands, and promised to attack Poland if the Zaporozhian Cossacks put so much as one raft out to sea. The only concrete result Kondyrev obtained from his mission was the release of some Russian captives, although he recruited some Turkish subjects for Russian service, including a number of newly-baptized Christians. The return journey was equally unpleasant. At Kerch the town authorities imprisoned and physically abused the ambassador, who once again was accused of complicity in cossack raids. In Temriuk the Zaporozhian Cossacks imprisoned him in a tower because of the brigandage of the Don Cossacks on the steppe. Only the intercession of the governor of Azov and the Turkish ambassador prevented him from being sold into Nogay captivity. Doubtless Kondyrev was glad to see Moscow again in September 1623. In 1627 Kondyrev was dispatched to the Nogay Horde with gifts for the murzas. This was the end of his diplomatic career. In August 1632, during the Smolensk war, he was given a military command at Rzhev Volodimerov.

33. Fedor Vasilievich Volynsky (?-1646), lord-in-waiting, headed the Chancellery of Posts in 1636.

34. Yakov Ostafiev Tukhachevsky (?-1639), a nobleman of the Smolensk province, is recorded elsewhere as campaigning against the Kirghiz in 1609.

35. Dmitry Zhedrinsky served as governor of Tsarevo-Sanchursk in 1614.

36. Peter Konashevich Sahaidachny (?-1622) came from a Galician noble family. After serving in command of Ukrainian cossacks in the Muscovite wars, he fought against the Crimeans and Turks, playing a prominent

part in the Polish victory at Khotin in 1621. He was an active member of the Orthodox Brethren, and sent envoys to Moscow requesting the tsar to accept the Ukrainian cossacks as his subjects. Michael's government, however, did not want to upset the recent truce. Sahaidachny died April 20, 1622 of wounds sustained at Khotin, and was buried within the Brotherhood monastery in Kiev.

37. Prince Grigory Konstantinovich Volkonsky (?-1634) served as ambassador to Poland during the reign of Vasily Shuisky. He was promoted lord-in-waiting in 1622.

38. *Chronicle of Many Rebellions*, p. 318

39. Nikita Vasilievich Godunov, lord-in-waiting 1601, died 1616.

40. *Chronicle of Many Rebellions*, p. 322.

41. Prince Grigory Vasilievich Tiufiakin (dates of birth and death unknown) held the rank of table attendant, and served as governor of Belgorod from 1616 to 1623.

42. Pskov, originally itself a bytown (prigorod) of Great Novgorod, had a number of secondary towns dependent upon it, such as Gdov, Izborsk, Ostrov, Pechory, Krasny and others.

43. See Volume 14, pp. 18-22.

44. The four-year-old son of Marina, heir to the claims of Dmitry Ivanovich, was hanged outside the Serpukhov gates of Moscow in 1614. Here the Poles attempt to reactivate the "changeling" legend, alleging that the real Ivan Dmitrievich had been spirited away, and was being educated in the Caves monastery of Kiev.

45. At this time Poland, like other Roman Catholic countries, was on the Gregorian or New Style calendar whereas Russia still adhered to the Julian or Old Style calendar. In the sixteenth and seventeenth centuries the two calendars were ten days apart.

46. Under the terms of the Union of Brest (1595) the Orthodox hierarchy in Poland-Lithuania was abolished, and adherents of the Orthodox church were increasingly under pressure to conform to the Uniate church. The Orthodox Brethren of the Exaltation of the Holy Cross were formed in order to counteract this pressure. They founded schools, patronized churches and monasteries and in 1620, in defiance of royal authority, reestablished the Orthodox hierarchy, which was legalized in 1632.

47. The title "sovereign" or "great sovereign," usually the prerogative of the tsar, also was used when addressing Filaret, for whom the patriarchal throne had been kept vacant. The patriarch enjoyed a status of virtual parity with the tsar until the quarrel between Tsar Alexis and Patriarch Nikon put an end to such theocratic pretensions.

48. Flor Yudich Lugovskoy (sobriquet Tomila, dates of birth and death unknown, fl. 1607-1637). Lugoskoy first appears as a crown secretary in May 1607, when he took part in Tsar Vasily Shuisky's campaign against

Tula. In 1608 he was one of the negotiators with the Polish-Lithuanian ambassadors over the renewal of the truce and the release of Polish internees. In 1610 he was employed in the Chancellery for Novgorod and later in the same year participated in the negotiations concerning the election of Prince Wladyslaw. Later he was included in the high embassy sent to the king's encampment outside Smolensk. The negotiations dragged on but Lugovskoy, despite Leo Sapieha's blandishments, refused either to accept rewards from the king or abandon the embassy. Consequently he was interned in Poland along with Filaret and Golitsyn (see Volume 15, pp. 188-190). As related here, he was released in June 1619. Between then and 1628 he rose steadily in rank. From conciliar secretary he was promoted to Moscow noble, and eventually to conciliar noble. He conveyed proclamations conferring promotion to boyars or lords-in-waiting, and acted as a judge in a number of precedence disputes. In March 1628 he was appointed deputy governor of Kazan, where he served for two years. At the time of the Smolensk campaign of 1632 he contributed a hundred quarters of grain for provisioning the troops. At Easter 1634 he received a personal audience with the tsar, and at Easter 1636 he was a table guest of the tsar and Patriarch Joseph. Later the same year he was sent to Putivl to survey the land boundaries, and he is last mentioned in 1637 when he attended a reception for the Lithuanian embassy. He then entered the monastic life, but the date of his death is unknown.

49. See above, Chapter II, Note 8.

50. Boris Morozov (1590-1661) and his brother Gleb (?-1662) came from a not particularly distinguished boyar family, but rose to prominence under the Romanov dynasty. In 1633 Boris became tutor to the heir apparent, Tsarevich Alexis, and was the all-powerful favorite under the new reign, until forced into exile as a result of the urban riots of 1648. He returned in 1651 and continued to enjoy a prominent position at court, but never regained the full extent of his former power and influence. See entry by Lindsey A.J. Hughes, MERSH, Vol. 23, pp. 71-73. Gleb Ivanovich served for a time as governor of Novgorod.

51. Vasily Korobyin (dates of birth and death unknown, fl. 1619-1634) later, in 1621, was sent along with Afanasy Kuvshinov as ambassador to Persia. The embassy is remarkable in that Shah Abbas announced his intention of sending to Moscow Christ's seamless robe, which he had captured in one of his Georgian campaigns. On the return journey in 1624 they sent news of this from Terka, and on March 11, 1625 the Persian ambassador Rusan Bek presented Michael with the relic, which was enshrined in the Dormition cathedral of the Moscow Kremlin. In 1627 Korobyin was sent to Denmark to take care of various diplomatic matters, and in 1634 he travelled to Constantinople.

52. The throne was reoccupied briefly by Ignaty (see above, Note 25) but when he fled the patriarchal see was administered by Metropolitan Ephraim of Kazan, who died in December 1613. Metropolitan Jonas of Krutitsy formally acted as *locum tenens*, but was ousted quickly after Filaret's return. Filaret seems to have been aware that the patriarchal throne was being reserved for him, since he styled himself metropolitan, not only of Rostov, but also of All Russia.

53. Theophanes IV, patriarch of Jerusalem, was enthroned in 1601. His consecration was attended by his lifelong friend Cyril Lukaris, patriarch of Alexandria. As related here, Theophanes happened to be in Moscow in 1619 for the enthronement of Filaret and in 1620, on his way back to Jerusalem, stayed in Kiev, where he re-established the Orthodox hierarchy in the Polish-held Ukraine by secretly consecrating seven bishops. In 1630 he wrote to the metropolitan of Kiev defending Lukaris against charges of Lutheran heresy, and in 1638 attended a General Council of the Orthodox church at Constantinople. See Steven Runciman, *The Great Church in Captivity*, Cambridge, 1968.

CHAPTER IV

1. Maria Ivanovna Khlopova (?-1633) was selected in 1616 as a prospective bride for Tsar Michael. She, her grandmother and her aunt were installed in the upper story of the tsar's palace, and the tsar showed favor to her relatives, especially her uncle Gavrila Vasilievich. As related here, Mikhail Mikhailovich Saltykov, the court favorite, picked a quarrel with Gavrila and subsequently spread the rumor that the tsar's bride was incurably ill. She was evicted from her quarters in the palace, which she had occupied altogether for six weeks, and with her female relatives was exiled to Tobolsk, while her parents were removed from the capital with the appointment of her father as governor of Vologda. With the return of Filaret, Khlopova was permitted to return as far as Verkhoturie, and then in 1620 was allowed to reside in Nizhny Novgorod. Apparently as late as 1621 Michael had not given up his intention of marrying her but it was only in 1623, after negotiations for a foreign bride had failed, that Filaret reopened the investigation into her alleged infirmity. As a result Saltykov and his brother were disgraced and exiled since Khlopova was given a clean bill of health by the examining physicians Bills and Balthser. This time it was Michael's mother who intervened, saying that if Khlopova were chosen consort, she herself would stay away from court. Michael gave in, but in order partly to compensate Khlopova for her disappointment, she was given a house in Nizhny Novgorod which formerly belonged to Kuzma Minin.

2. Namely Anastasia, the first wife of Ivan IV and mother of Tsar Fedor Ivanovich, the last ruler of the ancient stem.

3. Christian IV (1577-1648), king of Denmark and Norway from 1588. For the first eight years of his reign he was subject to a four-man regency council. In 1596 he came of age officially and was crowned, and in the following year married Anna Catherine of Brandenburg, who became the mother of his sons Christian (died 1647) and his successor Frederick III. After his coronation he endeavored to limit the the role of the state council (Rigsrad), keeping the leading offices vacant and surrounding himself with an entourage of Germans, mostly drawn from his duchy of Holstein. Against the wishes of the Rigsrad, he declared war on Sweden in 1611. The War of Kalmar (1611-1613), although tactically a Danish victory, failed in its objective of reuniting the crowns of Denmark and Sweden. During the succeeding years Christian concentrated on the economic development of his kingdoms, founding new cities and ports, including Kristiana (now Oslo) and Kristiansand in Norway, Kristianstad and Kristianopel in Scania, Christianshavn in Denmark and Glückstadt in Holstein. He also enlarged the royal shipyards, and remodelled his capital of Copenhagen. In 1624, again in the face of protests from the Rigsrad, he entered the Thirty Years' War, largely to prevent Sweden from assuming the role of Protestant champion in Germany. The imperial generals Tilly and Wallenstein invaded Jutland, whereupon Christian was compelled to forge an alliance with Gustavus Adolphus. After Wallenstein abandoned the siege of Stralsund in 1629 Christian forsook the Swedish alliance, concluding a separate peace at Lübeck. In the ensuing years he resorted to raising repeatedly the Sound tolls to secure revenue not subject to Rigsdag control, to the extent that with Dutch backing the Swedes attacked Denmark in 1643. By the end of January 1644 the Swedes had overrun most of Jutland. The king, who led the defense personally, lost an eye at the battle of Kolberger Heide. Although the battle was inconclusive, the Danish fleet later was annihilated and Christian was forced, in August 1645, to conclude a humiliating peace, which cost him the provinces of Halland, Jamtland, Harjedalen and the islands of Gotland and Oesel. His warlike policies, undertaken against the advice of the Rigsdag and nobility, now led to a revolt in which even his sons-in-law turned against him. This revolt, commonly known as Tortensson's war, forced Christian to accept considerable limitations on royal authority. In the last years of his reign Christian grew increasingly sullen and mistrustful, withdrawing from public view. The council demanded and obtained a summons of the estates to ensure the succession of his second son Frederick, who had become heir apparent on the death of Prince Christian. The king died before the estates met, and was spared the ordeal of seeing the powers of the crown severely diminished by the accession charter which Frederick was forced to accept.

4. In November 1620 Gustavus Adolphus married Maria Eleonora, sister of Elector George William of Brandenburg (born 1595, reigned 1619-1640).

5. Mikhail Mikhailovich Saltykov (dates of birth and death unknown) was, as related here, the chief culprit in the Khlopova affair. After the 1623 investigation he and his brother Boris were banished perpetually from court and their service tenures were confiscated. Apparently they were restored to favor after Filaret's death, since they took part in the procession greeting the remains of Tsar Vasily Shuisky in June 1635. In 1641 Mikhail Saltykov was appointed to boyar rank, and some time in the 1650s served as governor of Kazan.

6. The monastery dedicated to the Miracles of St. Michael was founded in 1365 by Metropolitan Alexis, and for more than five hundred years was the most important monastery in the Moscow Kremlin. During the Time of Troubles the monastery played a very important role. Grishka Otrepiev, who later surfaced as False Dmitry I, formerly had been a monk there. His patriarch, Ignaty, was imprisoned there from 1606 to 1611, and within its walls Patriarch Hermogen was starved to death. During the reign of Michael a school for translating works from Greek and Latin was established within the monastery. During the 1930s the Miracles monastery and the adjoining Ascension convent were demolished to make way for the School for Red Commanders. Joseph was archimandrite of the Miracles monastery from 1621 until his death in 1627.

7. See Chapter I, Note 35.

8. Ivan Kirillovich Griaziev, conciliar secretary, appointed head of Chancellery for Foreign Affairs in 1632.

9. Makary, archbishop of Vologda in 1613, metropolitan of Novgorod (the second of that name), 1619, died December 12, 1626.

10. "At the capture of Marienburg there had fallen into his hands a Russian named Rubtsov, and Gustav Adolf had sent him to the Tsar, in the hope of inducing a Muscovite attack on Poland which would give the Swedish forces leisure for a sally to the south-west." Michael Roberts, *Gustavus Adolphus*, Vol. II, p. 329.

11. In 1628 the imperial general Wallenstein, who had been awarded the confiscated domains of the duke of Mecklenburg, obtained also command of the imperial fleets in the North and Baltic seas. He attempted to round out his dominions by capturing the port of Stralsund. His principal subordinate, Hans Georg von Arnim, failed him. This failure proved to be the major factor leading up to Wallenstein's dismissal by Emperor Ferdinand II in 1630.

12. Ferdinand II (1578-1637), Holy Roman emperor from 1619. He was educated at the Jesuit academy of Ingolstadt, Bavaria. In 1596 he assumed the rulership of his hereditary lands, and in 1600 married Maria Anna of

Bavaria. He avoided taking sides in the quarrel between his cousins Rudolph II and Matthias, but in 1617 secretly negotiated with his Spanish relatives for recognition as heir apparent to Matthias, in exchange for Alsace and some imperial fiefs in Italy. The same year he was elected king of Bohemia and in 1618 succeeded also to the Hungarian crown. In 1619, however, the Bohemian Diet deposed him and elected Frederick V, count palatine of the Rhine, thus setting in motion the Thirty Years' War. Ferdinand was able to secure election as Holy Roman emperor and went on to defeat the Bohemian rebels at the White Mountain in 1620, but then entered upon a troubled relationship with his over-powerful generalissimo, Wallenstein.

13. Timofey Arendarenko, hetman of the Ukraine, 1630-1631.

14. Isaac Borisovich-Chernitsky (?-1641). In 1602, at the behest of Konstantin Ostrozski, he founded the Dermany monastery at Ostrog where, with the help of the priest Damian, he published several theological works. He was a prominent member of the Orthodox Brethren in Lutsk, where he taught in the local school. In 1621 he was consecrated bishop of Lutsk and Ostrog, but was driven out in 1623 by the Uniate bishop, Jeremiah Pochapovsky. In 1624 he travelled to Moscow on behalf of Metropolitan Job Boretsky, proposing the unification of the Ukraine to Muscovy. Until he was permitted to return in 1632, Isaac administered the affairs of his diocese from his residence in Kiev.

15. Job, metropolitan of Kiev (?-1631), in secular life Ivan Matveevich Boretsky. A native of Lvov, he was rector of the Lvov Brotherhood school in 1604, and moved on to assume the same position at the Kiev school in 1617. He was one of the prelates illegally consecrated by Patriarch Theophanes of Jerusalem in 1620, becoming in his capacity as metropolitan of Kiev and Galich the head of the Ukrainian Orthodox church. In 1624 he discussed with Moscow, through the intermediacy of Bishop Isaac of Lutsk, the proposed unification of the Ukraine and Muscovy, and possibly was the author of the *Protestations*, a polemical tract denouncing the oppression of the Ukrainian church and people by the Polish government.

16. Constantine Lukaris (1570-1638) was born in Candia, Crete, at that time under Venetian sovereignty. He studied at Venice and Padua, and was

ordained deacon at Constantinople by Patriarch Melitos Pegas of Alexandria. At this time he changed his baptismal name to Cyril, by which he was known for the remainder of his life. In 1594 he was sent to Poland to strengthen Orthodox resistance to Catholic proselytization. When the synod of Brest-Litovsk proclaimed the union of the Catholic and Orthodox churches, Lukaris in a different part of the same town led a counter-synod, which denounced the union. He remained in Poland until 1598, then returned for a second visit in 1600-1601. Returning to Constantinople, he was ordained priest, and later in 1601 was consecrated patriarch of Alexandria in succession to Melitos. He resided for the most part in Constantinople, although he is notable for having transferred the administrative center of his eparchy from the decaying port of Alexandria to the Egyptian capital of Cairo. A staunch opponent of church union, Cyril maintained friendly relations with individual Catholics and even wrote a letter to Pope Paul V, implying recognition of papal supremacy. At the same time he opened contacts with Dutch and English Protestants, and his *Confession of Faith*, published at Geneva in 1609, is considered to be strongly Calvinist in sentiment. In 1620 Cyril was elected patriarch of Constantinople, but was deposed and reinstated by the Ottoman authorities no less than six times. Finally he was arrested on a charge of inciting the Don Cossacks to attack Ottoman territories. He was taken out to sea in an open boat, and there he was strangled. See Runciman, *The Great Church in Captivity*, pp. 259-288.

17. Peter Simeonovich Mogila (1596-1647), who also wrote under the literary psudonym Evsevy Pimin, was the son of a hospodar of Moldavia and Wallachia. He received his education in the Lvov school of the Orthodox Brethren and then attended a number of Western European universities. As a young man he also served in the Polish army. In 1627 he was appointed archimandrite of the Caves monastery in Kiev, and in 1632 became metropolitan of Kiev and Galich. The same year he founded a college which was to expand to become the Kiev Academy. In 1640 he proposed to Tsar Michael the formation of a similar institution in Moscow, but met with little response. Nevertheless, at the unification of the Ukraine and Muscovy, Ukrainian scholars were free to move around Muscovy, where their influence was great, both on the Nikonian reforms and in the eventual establishment of the Slavic-Greek-Latin Academy in Moscow by the Likhud brothers in the 1690s. (See Volume 25 of this series). For a brief biography of Peter Mogila, see Hugh F. Graham, "Peter Mogila—Metropolitan of Kiev," *Russian Review*, Vol. 14, No. 4 (1955), pp. 345-356. On the Kiev Academy, see Alexander Sydorenko, *The Kievan Academy in the Seventeenth Century*, Ottawa, 1977.

18. Mark Ivanovich Pozdeev (dates of birth and death unknown) was serving in the Chancellery for Crown Service and Appointments in 1608. In 1611 he was in Liapunov's camp, and his signature is on the document

conferring plenary powers upon the triumvirate. He later served in the Far-
riers' Court (*Kuznetskii dvor*), and then was town secretary at Kostroma. In
September 1612 he was serving in the Chancellery for Crown Service and
Appointments with the Second Militia Force. In 1613 he signed the
Comfirmatory Charter of Michael's election. He frequently adjudicated precedence disputes and conveyed proclamations of promotion to boyar rank.
In 1615 he accompanied the commission investigating the Cheremiss rebellion in the neighborhood of Kazan. As related here, he was part of the embassy to England in 1617-1618. In 1619 he was among the deputation to
greet Patriarch Theophanes on his visit to Moscow, and assisted at the enthronement of Patriarch Filaret. He took part in 1621 in the interrogation of
Ivan Korensky, accused by the governors of Putivl of treasonable relations
with Poland. In 1632 he accompanied Prince D.T. Trubetskoy to Yaroslavl
with a commission of array addressed to the local gentry. He was sent as
town secretary to Astrakhan in 1623, but was accused of malfeasance. He
was banished from Moscow and his property was confiscated. By 1632 he
had returned to favor and was serving in the Moscow Judicial Chancellery,
and in 1633 took part in the defense of the Trans River quarter of Moscow
in anticipation of a Polish assault. In 1636 he was dismissed from the Moscow Judicial Chancellery for some unspecified offense, but in 1637 was
among those receiving the Polish emissaries, and was among the tsar's
table guests at the Easter celebrations. He then was appointed to the Chancellery for Criminal Affairs, and in 1640 was a member of the commission
to inspect the defenses of Earthen Town and the outer perimeter of Moscow. He probably died in the late 1640s. Two of his sons, Ivan and Fedor,
served in the administration, but did not rise to prominence.

19. King Sigismund had not renounced his claim to the Swedish throne,
neither were his Vasa successors Wladyslaw IV or Jan Kazimierz to do so
until 1660.

20. Christian IV's first wife (died 1612) was Anna Catherine, sister of
Elector George William of Brandenburg.

21. Courland was a duchy created in 1561 for Gotthard Kettler, the last
grand master of the Livonian Order, as a Polish fief. After Kettler's death
in 1587 the duchy was disputed between his two sons Friedrich and Wilhelm. In 1618 the Polish government secured the banishment of Wilhelm,
and Friedrich remained as sole ruler until his death, being succeeded by
Wilhelm's son Jakob, who ruled 1642-1682.

22. See above, Chapter II, Note 54.

23. Sir Dudley Digges (1583-1639) was born at Barham, Kent, and
studied at University College, Oxford, as a gentleman commoner from 1598
to 1601. He travelled to the continent a few years thereafter. In 1607 he
was knighted by King James I and from 1610 to 1614 sat in the House of
Commons as member for Tewkesbury. His participation in parliamentary
debates earned him the displeasure of the king and a brief period of imprisonment. In 1614 Digges was a candidate for the governorship of the

East India Company, of which he had been an early shareholder, and in 1612 he was one of the charter members of a company founded to explore the possibilities of the Northwest Passage. When Tsar Michael approached King James for a war loan, the East India and Muscovy companies were ordered to furnish the funds, sending Digges to Russia to arrange the terms. Digges proceeded upstream a short distance from Archangel but returned in a panic when he observed the lawlessness of the country. He sent ahead his secretary Finch with less than half of the twenty thousand pounds sent from England. The tsar refused to argue over terms, and compelled Finch to hand over the money. Meanwhile Digges returned to England with the other half of the money. An account of the embassy was written by John Tradescant, who accompanied the embassy in the capacity of naturalist. In 1621 Digges was sent to Holland along with Maurice Abbot, governor of the East India Company, to negotiate settlement of outstanding disputes between the English and Dutch companies, but negotiations fell through as a result of what Digges perceived to be Dutch duplicity. Digges again represented Tewkesbury in the House of Commons from 1624 to 1626, thereafter sitting as one of the knights of the shire for Kent. In 1626 he wrote a frank letter to King Charles I counselling him to act with moderation and firmness, and the same year opened the impeachment proceedings against the royal favorite, the duke of Buckingham. As a result he was committed to the Fleet prison but released after three days, following an indignant remonstrance from the Commons. In January 1627 he again was confined to prison for "unfit language," but was released a month later on issuing an apology. In 1633 Digges was placed on the Court of High Commission, and in 1636 he succeeded to the office of Master of the Rolls.

24. Nikofor Vasilievich Trakhaniotov, governor of Perm in 1592, lord-in-waiting and treasurer, 1613-1618.

25. Four altyns per ruble is equivalent to twelve percent.

26. Grigory Ivanovich Tverdikov (dates of birth and death unknown) was among the signatories to the confirmatory charter concerning Boris Godunov's election in 1598. In 1610 he participated in the embassy to Sigismund III relating to the election of Prince Wladyslaw to the Muscovite throne. As related here, his opinion was solicited by the boyar council concerning the granting of trading privileges to the English merchants.

27. Soloviev here probably is referring to the leading merchant Fedot Afanasievich Kotov, who almost alone among the leading merchants whose opinions were asked, was relatively favorable to the English. In 1623 he was sent on a trading mission to Persia on behalf of the tsar's treasury. From Isfahan he travelled also to Turkey and India. His travel diary was printed and published in 1852 in the journal *Vremennik* (Vol. 25).

28. Frederick V (1596-1632) count palatine of the Rhine from 1610, was married to James's daughter Elizabeth in 1613. He had been elected

king of Bohemia in 1619 by the Protestant party in that country, but had been driven out by the forces of Archduke Ferdinand of Styria at the battle of the White Mountain (1620), while shortly afterwards the imperialist forces overran his Rhineland territories. He was thus a king without a country, scornfully dubbed by his opponents the "winter king."

29. This particular name is illustrative of one of the pitfalls of this kind of translation, where it is necessary to back-transliterate from Russian into another language. Soloviev's French translator rendered it "Gué de Cour-menin," but I was unable to corroborate this spelling in any source dealing with French diplomatic history until I stumbled on the monograph by A. Tongas, *L'ambassadeur Louis Deshayes de Cormenin*, Paris, 1937. Louis Deshayes de Cormenin (1600-1632) was the son of a governor of Montargis, and was educated by the Barnabite order in Savoy. In 1621 he travelled as ambassador extraordinary to Jerusalem to obtain reconfirmation of French rights to custodianship of the Holy Places. In 1624 he was sent to Scandinavia, where he persauaded Christian IV of Denmark to intervene in the German conflict, but he was less successful with the Swedish king, Gustavus Adolphus. In 1626 he was charged with a mission to Shah Abbas, to promote direct trade between France and Persia, but was prevented from proceeding further than Aleppo by the French ambassador to Constantinople, Philippe de Harlay, comte de Césy. His fourth embassy, related here, gave him some cause for satisfaction, but on his return to France he was slighted by Cardinal Richelieu, who entrusted the mission to the German princes to Cormenin's rival, Hercule-Girard, baron de Charnacé. Driven by jealousy, Deshayes threw in his lot with Duke Gaston of Orleans, who in 1631 fled in the company of the queen mother to the court of Duke Charles IV of Lorraine. Lorraine was at that time still an imperial fief, and its ruler an ardent supporter of the Habsburgs. In May 1632 Deshayes met Gustavus Adolphus at Munich, attempting to enlist the Swedish king's support for Gaston, and also offering to mediate between him and Emperor Ferdinand II. His biographer (p. 100) also alleges that Deshayes's mission was to invite Gustavus Adolphus to mediate between Louis XIII and Gaston, but as Michael Roberts (*Gustavus Adolphus*, Vol. II, p. 711) points out, "since Tongas also puts the place of the meeting at Magdeburg, he may well be in error about the subject with which it was concerned." In any case, Deshayes returned empty-handed to Gaston, who by reason of the French invasion of Lorraine had been forced to set up his headquarters in Brussels. From there Deshayes was again dispatched to Germany, this time to Mainz, to negotiate a loan from the Hanseatic towns on the security of the queen mother's jewels and to raise a mortgage on Gaston's duchy of Alencon. By a strange coincidence, Charnacé was also in the vicinity of Mainz and was alerted to Deshayes's presence. The unfortunate emissary was arrested on August 14 by Charnacé on imperial soil and conveyed to

Béziers, where the royal court was in session. Since all his papers were seized at the time of his arrest he could present no other defense than that he was acting under the orders of his patron, the Duke of Orleans. Deshayes was sentenced to death on October 12, 1632 and was executed on the town hall square of Béziers on the evening of that same day. Despite speculations to the contrary, there was no connection between the Deshayes affair and the revolt of Henri de Montmerency, who was executed eighteen days later, following the edict suppressing the privileges of the estates of Languedoc.

30. Literally "the mid-day land."

31. Frederick Henry (1584-1647), prince of Orange, count of Nassau, stadholder of the United Provinces of the Netherlands from 1625. A half-brother of Prince Maurice, originally he was destined for service in France, but Maurice insisted he remain in the Netherlands. He was educated at Leiden and was made a member of the Council of State in 1601. In 1624 he married a lady-in-waiting of the exiled queen of Bohemia, and succeeded to the stadholdership of five of the seven Dutch provinces on Maurice's death. As a strategist in the Thirty Years' War his expertise was most evident in the capture of fortified places. "God preserve us from pitched battles" is his best remembered dictum. As a result the present southern frontier of Holland owes much to Frederick Henry's successes or failures. Among his most important conquests were 's Hertogenbosch (Bois-le-Duc) and Breda. Since Charles I's daughter Mary was married to his son William, Frederick Henry tended to favor the royalist side in the English civil war, whereas the States-General naturally tended to support Parliament. The alliance with France against Spain, concluded in 1625, met with mixed success and Frederick Henry did not, of course, live to see the Peace of Westphalia. Soloviev in his text incorrectly names him "Prince Henry," but I have taken the editorial liberty of amending it to the style by which the stadholder generally was known.

32. See Chapter II, Note 52.

33. Prince Johan, duke of Holstein, who was brought to Russia in 1602 as a prospective bridegroom for Xenia, the daughter of Tsar Boris. He died suddenly in October of the same year and was buried in the Lutheran church in the Foreign Quarter of Moscow. His remains were returned to Denmark in 1637.

34. Ivan Ivanovich Baklanovsky previously participated in an embassy to The Hague, where he arrived unannounced in June 1618, and obtained for the tsar military supplies to the value of twenty thousand guilders. The States-General entrusted the ambassador to the care of Isaac Massa, who accompanied both Baklanovsky and the military supplies to Moscow. See Massa, *Short History of the Muscovite Wars*, pp. xvi-xviii and 189-197.

35. Bethlen Gabor (1580-1629) was born into a leading Protestant family in northern Hungary. As a young man he was sent to the court of his compatriot Stefan Bathory, king of Poland. Later he helped Istvan Bocksay

gain the throne of Transylvania, and then supported his successor Gabor Bathory. Differences later arose, and Bethlen was forced to take refuge in Turkey. Sultan Ahmed I provided him with an army which enabled him to seize the princely throne in 1613. During the initial stages of the Thirty Years' War Bethlen seized most of northern Hungary, including Poszony (Bratislava), as well as the actual Crown of St. Stephen which, however, he did not presume to don. He did become briefly titular king of Hungary (1620-1621), but after the defeat of the Bohemian rebels at the White Mountain he renounced his royal pretensions in return for guarantees of religious freedom previously granted by the 1606 Treaty of Vienna. He took up arms once more against Ferdinand II in 1623-1624 and in 1626, but was forced to make peace on much the same terms as in 1621. It appears that Bethlen Gabor was still alive when d'Assedeville and Roussel left on their mission, but had died by the time they reached Moscow.

36. Murad IV (born 1612, reigned 1623-1640) came to the throne at the age of eleven, though for several years the regency was in the hands of his mother Kosem. Effective power rested with the *sipahiyan* (feudal cavalry) and the janissaries. Embittered by the excesses of the troops, Murad determined to re-establish order, especially since in 1632 the sipahiyan invaded the palace and instigated the execution of the grand vizier and sixteen of his ministers. Murad staged a counter-coup, ruthlessly suppressed the mutiny, banned the use of tobacco and closed down the coffee houses and wine-shops. During the balance of his reign he maintained firm rule and straightened out the state finances. In foreign policy he took personal command of the continuing war against Persia, and in 1638 reconquered Baghdad after a siege that ended in the massacre of the garrison and citizenry. In religious affairs, Murad did not adhere strictly to religious law, as can be seen from his execution of the Shaykh-al-Islam (the highest religious dignitary in the empire), and the fact that eventually he drank himself to death.

37. Prince Mikhail Petrovich Boriatinsky (?-1618) was appointed governor of Novgorod Seversk in 1614. He was recalled hastily to Moscow and dispatched to relieve Rzhev, which was besieged by Lisowski's irregulars. Although he relieved the siege he was dilatory in pursuing the enemy, and consequently was relieved of his command and imprisoned at Suzdal. He was released during the following year and was given a command at Toropets. In May 1618 he was recalled and placed at the head of the embassy to Persia. He did not return from this embassy alive, dying at the mission's winter quarters at Kazbin. The remainder of the embassy was detained in Persia until the end of 1620.

38. Grigory Petrovich Chicherin (?-1635) was sent on the embassy in 1618, but returned the following year with an interim report and request for further supplies and instructions. In 1619 he was placed in charge of the firewatching and policing arrangements in the capital. In 1620 he was appointed governor of Odoev, 1621-1625 governor of Litvin. He was transferred in 1625 to Novosil, where he remained until 1631. From 1631 to

1633 he was once again in charge of security arrangements for the city of Moscow. In 1634 he was appointed governor of Galich, but was forced through illness to relinquish his post. He returned to Moscow, where he died in January 1635.

39. The Kumyks inhabit the plains and part of the foothills of Dagestan. They are Sunni Muslims by religious tradition and speak a Turkic language. A small number also reside in the present Chechen-Ingush ASSR and Northern Ossetia.

40. Iberia was the Greco-Latin name for Kartli, the ancient kingdom of eastern Georgia.

41. Georgia was not at this time under formal Muscovite sovereignty, but close relations between Moscow and the Georgian rulers by now were well established. See W.E.D. Allen, *Russian Embassies to the Georgian Kings, 1589-1605*, Cambridge, 1970 (Halkuyt Society, Second Series, No. 188-189).

42. Vasily Korobyin was later, in 1630, sent on an embassy to Denmark, and in 1634 to Constantinople. See also Chapter III, Note 51, above.

43. Fedor Vasilievich Panov was for many years crown secretary of the Chancellery for Kazan. In 1632 he was one of those responsible for obtaining supplies for Shein's army besieging Smolensk. He was governor of Donkov from 1645 to 1647.

CHAPTER V

1. The Soviet editor (p. 365) is unable to identify the version of the *Chronograph* which Soloviev is citing. My own search of the sources has been equally fruitless.

2. Grigory Fedotievich Kireevsky (dates of birth and death unknown), Moscow nobleman, compiled cadastral surveys of Riazan area in 1613, and between 1627 and 1651 of the districts of Donkov, Sapozhok, Riazhsk and Riazan. Served as governor in various locations, 1627-1640.

3. See Chapter I, Note 91 and Chapter III, Note 20.

4. The conference which ended the Russo-Polish war of 1632-1634. See below, p. 229–232.

5. For information on Veliaminov, see Chapter I, Note 81, above.

6. Another reference to Sigismund's claim to be the legitimate ruler of Sweden, rather than Gustavus Adolphus, whose father Karl IX usurped the throne from Sigismund.

7. Henri of Valois (Henryk Walezy) was elected in 1573 and crowned in 1574, but fled precipitately on hearing the news of the death of his brother Charles IX of France. The Polish magnates, convinced that Henri, having inherited the throne of France, had no intention ever of returning to Poland, declared the throne vacant although Henri himself never renounced

the Polish crown. There ensued a double election and civil war, in which Stefan Bathory eventually prevailed. See Davies, *God's Playground*, Vol. I, pp. 413-420.

8. Stefan Bathory ended his life at odds with his subjects, whom in his will he berated for their ingratitude. He died without consolation of the sacraments at Grodno on December 12, 1586. It was rumored widely that he was poisoned.

9. Wladyslaw's mother, Anna of Austria, daughter of Archduke Karl and sister to the future Emperor Ferdinand II, had married Sigismund III in 1592. She died in 1598, and in 1605 Sigismund married her sister Constantia, who died in 1631.

10. The son of Marina, who had been executed outside the Serpukhov gates of Moscow in 1614, at the age of four. Some Poles maintained that he had been rescued, and had been fostered in the Caves monastery of Kiev. See Chapter III, Note 44.

11. Philippe de Harlay, comte de Césy, served as French ambassador at Constantinople from 1618 to 1641. He also derived considerable profit by farming the customs dues of Aleppo. For this reason he did all he could to obstruct the mission of Louis Deshayes de Cormenin to Persia in 1626.

12. Osman II (1603-1622) came to the throne in 1618. He undertook a military campaign against Poland, which had been interfering with his vassal principalities of Moldavia and Wallachia. Despite his victory at Cecora in 1620 his forces were defeated in 1621 at Khotin, largely because of the indiscipline of the janissaries. He cut their pay and closed down their coffee shops, and was about to go ostensibly on a pilgrimage to Mecca, but in reality to Egypt to recruit an army to break the power of the janissaries, when the latter got wind of his plan. They deposed and murdered him in May 1622.

13. An interesting twist to Muscovite protocol. Ivan IV, of course, was no blood relative to Michael, while Fedor Ivanovich was his father's first cousin. Yet the fiction of Michael's direct descent from Ivan IV gradually became commonplace in official documents, and as the Romanov dynasty became established, fewer were tactless enough to point out its inaccuracy.

14. The Glinsky family derives its name from the town of Glinsk, situated in the ancient Severian principality. The family claimed descent from the Tatar khan, Mamay, whose son Mansur Kingat allegedly settled in the Dnieper valley soon after the battle of Kulikovo (1380) and there founded the settlements of Glinsk, Poltava and Glinnitsa. According to an alternative version, another of Mamay's sons, Mansur Ksan, wandered between the estuaries of the Don and Dnieper, and it was his son Leksada who swore allegiance to Grand Prince Vitovt of Lithuania, in return for which he received Glinsk and Poltava. The first Glinsky princes of whom there is any firm historical record are Ivan and Boris, first mentioned in 1437. Prince

Mikhail Lvovich Glinsky fled from Lithuania to Muscovy in 1508, accompanied by his brothers Ivan and Vasily, whose daughter, Elena Vasilievna, became the second wife of Grand Prince Vasily III. Another branch of the Glinsky family remained in Poland-Lithuania, but lost its princely rank.

15. Not to be confused with Alexander Leslie, first earl of Leven (1580-1661), who was indeed active in the wars of Gustavus Adolphus, but returned to Scotland in 1639 to take part in the Bishops' War and the subsequent conflicts between Charles I and his subjects. Michael Roberts (*Gustavus Adolphus*, Vol. II, p. 563) indentifies "Alexander Leslie the Younger" "On 21 June (1631) he (Gustavus Adolphus) wrote to the Tsar giving leave for Alexander Leslie to raise 5000 men in North Germany for Russian service." He does not state whether he was related to the future earl of Leven. It appears that the younger Leslie left Russia after the Smolensk War, but returned in 1647 and was given an estate in the Volga region. "Before long the Russian tenants on Leslie's estates and the Russian servants employed in his home began complaining to the local authorities of the cruelty of their new lord, and especially of his lady, as well as the offenses they committed aginst the Orthodox religion. In one complaint it was stated that Lady Leslie compelled her servants to eat dog meat, and that in Lent. It was reported also that she threw an icon into the fire; and that the colonel and his guest, Lieutenant Thomson, amused themselves by shooting at the cross on the local church. The Leslies were arrested." George Vernadsky, *The Tsardom of Moscow*, p. 422. Despite this incident, rather than be herded into the newly-instituted Foreign Quarter beyond the Yauza river, Leslie and his family converted to Orthodoxy in 1652. Vernadsky, p. 567.

16. Levky, in addition to being archimandrite of the Simonov monastery, was appointed administrator of the Pskov archdiocese in 1631. He was consecrated archbishop in 1634, but in 1649 was deposed for lack of firmness in suppressing the urban riots of that year. He was recalled to Moscow, where he died of the plague August 4, 1654.

17. Glebov was at that time governor of Pskov, later of Novgorod.

18. In other words, the system of *mestnichestvo*, or precedence, was suspended for the duration of the campaign in order that military commands be awarded according to ability rather than pedigree. On the system of *mestnichestvo* see the entry by Hugh F. Graham, MERSH, Vol. 22, pp. 8-13.

19. Albrycht Stanislaw Radziwill (1595-1656), deputy chancellor of Lithuania 1619, chancellor, 1623. He had travelled extensively throughout Western Europe as chamberlain to Prince Wladyslaw on his grand tour of 1624-1625. On the death of Sigismund III, Radziwill supported Wladyslaw's candidature, and he was also an advocate of closer relations with the Habsburgs. An ardent Catholic, he founded a church in his native town of Olyk, and a Jesuit college in Pinsk. He wrote, in Latin, his memoirs,

covering the years from 1632 until shortly before his death. A Polish translation was published in 1839.

20. Joseph I, patriarch of Moscow 1634-1640, came from a gentry family and entered the religious life at the Solovetsk monastery, where Isidore was archimandrite. When Isidore became metropolitan of Novgorod in 1604, he took Joseph with him. In 1621 Joseph was appointed archimandrite of the Pskov Caves monastery and on January 1, 1617 became archbishop of Pskov. In 1632 he presented a petition to the tsar against foreigners being granted commercial concessions in Pskov. The tsar was displeased, and Joseph was suspended briefly from office. He soon returned to favor, and is thought to have been Filaret's nominee for succession to the patriarchal office, although in fact he was chosen from a short list of three candidates presented by a synod of bishops. Joseph did not enjoy the power and prestige of his predecessor, being addressed as "great lord" rather than "great sovereign." His patriarchate is notable for the greater volume of books commissioned by the Printing Office, and also by the tightening of ecclesiastical discipline. He was a generous benefactor to the Solovetsk monastery where he had spent the early years of his religious life.

21. See above, Note 1.

22. Feodosy succeeded Joseph as archimandrite of the Miracles monastery in 1627. He died in 1634.

23. A rather strange assertion, since Ivan IV's principal antagonists in the Livonian war, which lasted 24 years, were a succession of Polish-Lithuanian rulers.

24. The towns of the Volga basin downstream from Nizhny Novgorod.

25. See above, Note 1.

26. Jakub Zadzik (1580-1642), bishop of Chelmno, 1624, chancellor of the kingdom of Poland, 1628-1635, bishop of Cracow, 1635. Apart from being a negotiator at Polianovka in 1634, he was a member of the delegation which negotiated the Truce of Stumsdorf with Sweden in 1635.

27. See Chapter I, Note 111. Vasily was surnamed "the Dark" because he was blinded by his political opponents in 1446.

28. See Chapter I, Note 109.

29. The Orthodox cross does not have upon it the image of the crucified Christ, which is regarded as a "Latin" innovation.

30. The *efimok* (plural efimki) was the Joachimsthaler overstamped with the Muscovite emblem. Thirty altyns are equivalent to 90 copecks whereas 16 altyns are equivalent to 48 copecks. The copeck was originally the Novgorod denga with the spearman (kopeika) on the obverse; the Moscow denga, of less value, had a swordsman on the obverse.

31. A masque based upon the Book of Judith, a deuterocanonical book of the Old Testament, relating how Judith, a beautiful and pious widow, enticed and assassinated Holofernes, the Assyrian general besieging her home city of Bethula.

32. Raphael (Roman Ivanovich Zhuravlev) was archimandrite of the Savior monastery, Riazan, 1613-1618, bishop of Kolomna and Kashira, 1618-1652, and died January 15, 1653.

33. Paul was archimandrite of the Simonov monastery, Moscow, 1612-1613, of the St. Anthony monastery, Novgorod, 1616-1623, archbishop of Pskov and Izborsk, 1623-1626, metropolitan of Krutitsy, the second of that name, from 1626 until his death in 1636.

INDEX

Abbas I, Persian shah, 21 26, 67, 78, 81-82, 85, 115, 192, 195, 198, 265, 267, 319.

Abbot, Maurice, governor of East India Company, 318.

Adodurov, Ivan Grigorievich, 131-132, 301, 304.

Ahmed I, Ottoman sultan, 75, 77-78, 287, 321.

Ahmed Pasha, Ottoman grand vizier, 75, 77-79.

Akkerman, 75.

Aladyin, Denis Grigorievich, emissary to Poland, 34-36, 273.

Alatyr, 275, 300.

Alba Murza, Tatar chieftain, 168.

Aleksin, 39.

Alençon, duchy, 319.

Aleppo, 323.

Alexandria, 312, 315-316.

Alexandrovskaia Sloboda, 255.

Alexis, metropolitan of Moscow, 126, 314.

Alexis Mikhailovich, tsarevich, later tsar, 198, 258, 273, 302, 308, 310-311.

Alferiev, Nikofor, Russian émigré, Anglican parson, 121, 185, 254.

Aliabiev, A.S., governor of Nizhny Novgorod, 254.

Aliabiev, Grigory Andreevich, 272.

Altmark, truce, 303.

Amos, archpriest, 290.

Ananiev, Liubim, 225.

Anastasia, first wife of Ivan IV, 162, 313.

Andreev, Irik, Swedish interpreter, 107.

Andrew, apostle, 289.

Andrewes, Lancelot, English bishop, 289.

Andronov, Fedor, 29, 34-35, 48-52, 57, 59, 63, 141, 268, 276.

Andrusovo, truce, 288.

Anforowicz, Nicholas, Polish emissary, 203.

Anna, archduchess, first wife of Sigismund III of Poland, 273-274, 323.

Anna Catherine of Brandenburg, first wife of Christian IV of Denmark, 313, 317.

Anstruther, Robert, English ambassador to Denmark, 289.

Anthony, abbot of Annunciation monastery, Novgorod, 88.

Antichrist, 298.

Antonov, crown secretary, 139.

Archangel, 66, 114, 117, 120, 123, 179, 183, 189-192, 276, 305.

Ardebil, 198.

Arendarenko, Timofey, cossack hetman, 178, 315.

Aristov, undersecretary, 211.

Armenia, Armenians, 128, 265.

Arnulf, Frankish king, 299.

Arzamas, 19, 272.

Asia, 298.

Assembly of the Land xiii, xviii, 1-5, 7-10, 12, 14, 18-19, 34, 36-37, 47, 95, 206-208, 221, 247, 252-253, 255-256, 259, 263-264, 269, 278, 288, 291.

Aston, Sir Arthur, 116, 297.

Astrakhan, 20-21, 25-28, 80-81, 85, 114, 117, 135, 168, 182-183, 191, 195-196, 254, 265-266, 271, 276-277, 287, 306, 308, 317.

Austria xv, 56, 66-75, 78, 175, 177, 188, 276, 285-287, 304.

Azov, 21-22, 77-79, 287, 309.

Azov, sea of, 288.

Babkin, Nekhoroshy, Tushinite governor of Suzdal, 284.
Baghdad, 198, 321.
Bakhterianov-Rostovsky, Prince Peter Vladimirovich, 256.
Bakhterianov-Rostovsky, Prince Vladimir Ivanovich, 1, 255-256.
Bakin, Gavrila, 225.
Baklanovsky, Ivan Ivanovich, ambassador to Denmark, 193, 320.
Balakhna, 33, 254, 269.
Balash, Ivan, cossack rebel, xviii-xix.
Balchik, island near Astrakhan, 254.
Baloven, cossack ataman, 30, 33.
Balthser, physician, 164, 312.
Baltic sea, 111, 174, 275, 320.
Bannister, Thomas, English merchant adventurer, 298.
Barham, Kent (England), 317.
Barnabite order, 319.
Basmanov, Peter Fedorovich, 289.
Bass, Dirk, Dutch mediator, 99.
Bat, Jacob, Swedish emissary, 122.
Bathory, Stefan, see Stefan Bathory, Polish king.
Baturin, 215.
Bauer, Jakob, Austrian Bailiff, 71.
Bazhenko, steward, 63.
Beast, biblical allegorical figure, 126, 298.
Bekbulatovich, Semeon, 283.
Belaia, 36, 64, 119, 133, 141-142, 150, 215, 228, 278, 281, 305.
Belaia Tserkov, 308.
Belev, 37-38, 210, 276.
Belgorod, 75, 127, 268, 279, 284, 300, 310.
Beloozero, 18, 25, 128, 143, 269.
Belorussia, 173.
Beloselsky, Prince Mikhail Vasilievich, 131-132, 215-216, 225, 301, 304-305.
Belsky, Bogdan Yakovlevich, 264.
Belsky, Prince Ivan Dmitreevich, 258.
Bengart, Georg, Swedish emissary, 172, 174.
Berezov, 305.
Bethlen Gabor, Hungarian ruler, 194-195, 206, 276, 320-321.

Bezhetsky Verkh, 128.
Béziers, 320.
Bezobrazov, Ivan, favorite of False Dmitry I, 48, 52.
Bielsk, 128, 145.
Bills, Valentine, physician, 164, 312.
Birkin, Ivan, 264, 286.
Bishops' War (Scotland), 324.
Black sea, 75, 122, 287.
Blom, Klim, Danish interpreter, 194.
Boborykin, Yakov, Novgorod noble, 88, 95.
Bohemia, 185, 276, 286-287, 315, 319.
Bohemian diet, 315.
Bohuslav XIV, Pomeranian duke, 274.
Boiashev, Fedor Mikhailovich, 32, 127.
Bolkhov, 37-38, 124, 279.
Bolotnikov, crown secretary, 140, 158.
Bolotnikov rebellion, 259-260, 266, 268, 280, 304, 308.
Boretsky, Andrei Matveevich, 178.
Boretsky, Ivan Matveevich, see Job, metropolitan of Kiev.
Boretsky, Porfiry Matveevich, 178.
Boriatinsky, Prince Fedor, emissary to Sweden, 122-123.
Boriatinsky, Prince Ivan, 214.
Boriatinsky, Prince Mikhail Petrovich, 195-196.
Boriatinsky, Prince Nikita Petrovich, 127, 300.
Boris Fedorovich Godunov, tsar, 3-4, 44, 47-48, 52, 54, 84, 118, 120, 145, 179, 185, 232, 242, 253-254, 259-264, 266, 268, 271, 273, 275, 280, 288-290, 296, 306, 318, 320.
Boris Vladimirovich, early Rus prince, martyr, 126, 299.
Borisov, 265.
Borisov Gorodishche, 135.
Borisovich-Chernitsky, Isaac, bishop of Lutsk, 178, 315.
Bormosov, crown secretary, 309.
Borniakov, Muscovite herald, 208-210.
Borovsk, 17, 135-137.
Borzma, 215.
Brabançons, 188.
Brahe, Ebba, wife of Jacob de la Gardie, 293.

Bratislava, see Poszony.

Bratovshchino, village, 14.

Breda (Holland), 320.

Brederode, Reinhold van, Dutch mediator, 99.

Bremen, Adam, Swedish emissary, 172.

Brest-Litovsk, synod and union, 310, 316.

Briansk, 38, 129, 143-144, 207, 210, 255, 269-270, 279, 298, 301.

Bronnitsy, 96, 139, 295, 299.

Brussels, 319.

Bryn, river, 36.

Buckingham, George Villiers, duke of, 318.

Budzilo, Jozef, Polish commander, 301.

Buinosova-Rostovskaia, Princess Maria Petrovna, wife of Tsar Vasily Shuisky, 290, 307.

Bukhara, 25.

Bukharov, undersecretary, emissary to Persia, 81.

Bulat Bek, Persian ambassador, 196-197.

Bulgakov, trader, 119.

Burgh, Albert Conrad de, Dutch ambassador, 189.

Buturlin, Fedor Vasilievich, 97, 133, 158, 217, 307-308.

Buturlin, Mikhail Matveevich, 37, 127, 278-279, 300.

Buturlin, Vasily Ivanovich, 50, 54, 96, 290-291, 295.

Cairo, 316.

Calvinism, 237, 281.

Candia, 315.

Cantacuzene, Thomas, Ottoman ambassador, 205-206, 309.

Casimir IV, Polish king and Lithuanian grand prince, 64, 229, 285.

Caspian sea, 122, 254.

Catherine II, Russian empress, 288.

Catherine, sister of Elector George William of Brandenburg, 164.

Catholics, Catholicism, 232, 237, 293, 297, 302, 304, 310, 316, 324.

Caucasus, 255.

Cecilia Renata, archduchess, first wife of King Wladyslaw IV of Poland, 274.

Cecora, battle, 267, 282, 284, 323.

Césy, Philippe de Harlay, comte de, 205, 319, 323.

Chaadaev, Peter Yakovlevich, nineteenth-century litterateur, 270.

Chancelleries: Apothecary, 262; Artillery, 49, 260; Criminal Affairs, 269, 272, 317; Crown Revenues, 49, 287; Crown Service and Appointments, 316-317; Exchequer, 226; Farriers' Court, 316; Foreign Affairs, 49, 70, 177, 185, 275, 285-286, 314; Investigations, 269, 271-272, 281; Kazan and Siberia, 55, 269, 272, 278, 282, 322; Keeper of the Seal, 49, 275; Military Appointments, 49, 70, 272; Military Recruitment, 258; Monasteries, 269; Moscow Judicial, 258, 281, 317; Musketeers, 49, 262; New Quarter, 308; Nizhny Novgorod, 49; Novgorod, 311; Office of Chancellery Affairs, 272; Patriarchal, 302; Polish Lords, 49; Posts, 269, 300, 309; Printing Office, 325; Royal Household, 273, 287; Service Foreigners, 262; Slavery, 279; Stonework, 279; Treasury, 50; Vladimir Judicial, 258, 265, 279, 301, 306.

Charles IV, duke of Lorraine, 319.

Charles, prince of Wales, later King Charles I of England, 85, 194, 318, 320.

Charles IX, French king, 322.

Charnacé, Hercule-Girard, baron de, 319.

Charon, Gaston de, 194.

Cheboksary, 255, 273.

Chechen-Ingush, 322.

Chelmno, 325.

Chemesov, Stepan Vasilievich, 31, 33, 270.

Cherdyn, 17-18.

Cheremiss, 33-34, 254, 260, 271-272, 317.

Cherkassians, 19, 34, 37, 39-40, 75, 79, 97, 148, 172, 177, 197, 264.

Cherkassky family, 262, 268.

Cherkassky, Prince Boris Kanbulatovich, 261.

Cherkassky, Prince Dmitry Mamstriukovich, xviii, 37, 133, 135-137, 211-213, 216, 220-222, 262, 269, 272, 277-278.

Cherkassky, Prince Ivan Borisovich, 15, 164, 182, 261-262.

Cherkassky, Prince Mamstriuk Temriukovich, 277.

Cherkassky, Prince Mikhail Temriukovich, 277.

Cherkassky, Prince Vasily Akhamashukovich, 217.

Cherkassky, Prince Vasily Kordanukovich, 275.

Cherkassky, Prince Vasily Petrovich, 133, 308.

Cherkassky, Prince Yakov Kudenetovich, 262.

Cherkizovo, 173.

Chernigov, 129, 142, 146, 254, 298-299.

Chernigov miracle-workers, 298-299.

Chernetsky, Smaga, Don ataman, 76.

Cherny, Mikhail, 27.

Chicherin, Grigory Petrovich, 195-197, 321-322.

Chicherin, Ivan, 51.

Chigirin, 308.

China, 115-118.

Chmieliewski, Lithuanian captain in Muscovite service, 297.

Chodkiewicz, Jan Karol, Lithuanian hetman, 47, 49, 129, 131, 134, 137, 140, 267, 277, 282, 302-303.

Christian, Danish prince, 313.

Christian IV, Danish king, 86, 162, 179, 193, 258, 313, 319-320.

Christianshavn, 313.

Christina, Swedish queen, 293, 296.

Christina, Swedish queen mother, 293.

Chronicle of many rebellions, 20, 29, 39, 139, 142, 265, 268, 310.

Chronograph, 199, 220, 227, 322, 325.

Chruslinski, Polish colonel, 301.

Chukhloma, 34.

Churches and Cathedrals: Annunciation (Moscow Kremlin), 48; Archangel (Moscow Kremlin), xx, 242; Brethren Church of the Holy Spirit (Wilno), 152, 280; Dormition (Moscow Kremlin), 14, 173, 242, 301, 311; Dormition (Riazan), 252; Holy Wisdom (Novgorod), 107-108, 113, 171, 290; Nativity (Riazan), 252-253; St. Gregory of Armenia (Khutyn monastery, Novgorod), 294; St; Nicholas on the Arbat (Moscow), 241; St. Nicholas Yavlenny (Moscow), 241; St. Stephen (Vienna), 286.

Chusovaia, river, 264.

Chuvash, 254, 272.

Constantia, archduchess, second wife of King Sigismund III of Poland, 323.

Constantinople, 18, 21, 75-76, 80, 188, 210, 268, 311-312, 316, 322-323.

Copenhagen, 193, 313.

Cossacks, xiii-xiv, xix, 9, 11, 20, 29-34, 84, 142, 150, 177, 181, 197, 202, 207, 246, 248, 253, 265, 275, 299, 301, 304, 309.

Council of Regency (Sweden), 293.

Council of the Whole Land, 263.

Courland, 179, 317.

Court of High Commission (England), 318.

Cracow, 282, 302, 304, 325.

Crete, 315.

Crimea, Crimeans, xv, xviii, xx, 75, 77, 82-83, 110, 123, 153, 166-167, 207-208, 210-211, 232, 254, 258, 264, 270-271, 273, 290, 308-309.

Crimean war, 304.

Cyprian, archimandrite of Khutyn monastery, later metropolitan of Novgorod, 90, 92, 94-95, 291-292, 294.

Cyprus, 306.

Cyril, patriarch of Alexandria, later Constantinople, 178, 205-206, 312, 315-316.

Czaplinski, Stanislaw, Polish colonel, 127-128, 132-133, 140, 147-148, 300-301.

Dagestan, 302.
Daniel, book of, 126, 298.
Danilov, Mikhail, crown secretary, 287.
Danilov, Semeon, crown secretary, 75, 140.
Dantzig, 189.
Darnley, Henry earl of, 289.
Dashkov, crown secretary, 212.
D'Assedeville, Charles Talleyrand, marquis, ambassador from Bethlen Gabor, 194-195, 321.
David, biblical king, 289.
Dead Donets, 76, 288.
Dederino, conference, 99-108.
Dedilov, 20, 210.
De la Gardie, Jacob, Swedish commander and statesman, xvi, 90, 92-94, 96, 98-108, 112, 290-295.
De la Gardie, Magnus, 293.
De la Gardie, Pontus, 292.
De Moline, Dutch merchant, 307.
Denmark, Danes, xvii, xx, 97, 111, 162-163, 174-175, 179, 191-194, 211, 227, 258, 285, 289, 293, 311, 319-320, 322.
Deshayes de Cormenin, Louis, French ambassador, 186-189, 305, 319-320, 323.
Deulino, conference and truce, xvii, 143-152, 199, 231, 260, 271, 274, 277, 279-280, 303.
Digges, Dudley, English ambassador, 179-180, 317-318.
Dmitriev, Mikhail, Muscovite commander, 124.
Dmitrov, 11.
Dmitry, archpriest, 253.
Dmitry Donskoy, grand prince, 259, 267.
Dmitry Ivanovich, tsarevich, xiv, 4, 26, 252, 256.
Dnieper, river, 75, 131, 178, 216, 323.
Dolgoe, village, 277.
Dolgorukova, Princess Maria, first wife of Tsar Michael, xvii, 166.
Domnino, 5, 244.
Domodedovsk, 17.
Don, river, 20, 22-23, 26, 76-78, 323.

Don Cossacks, xv, 21-26, 44, 55, 76, 78-80, 129, 148, 203, 207, 222, 256, 280, 287, 309, 316.
Donau, Abraham, imperial ambassador, 262.
Donkov, 20, 210, 322.
Dormition, miraculous icon, 253.
Dorogobuzh, 37, 64, 101, 122, 127-128, 131, 141-142, 153-154, 200-201, 209, 211, 213, 215, 217, 222-224, 230, 271, 278, 282, 300-301, 303-304.
Dorogomilovo, 241.
Dorohostajski, Krzystof Mikolaj, Lithuanian marshal, 46, 281.
Dorpat, 282-283.
Drevliane, ancient Rus tribe, 251.
Druia, 215.
Duckett, George, English merchant adventurer, 298.
Dunikowski, Polish colonel, 54.
Dutch, 69, 98-108, 117, 153, 183, 188-192, 205, 211, 273, 281, 287, 307, 313, 316.
Dvina, river, 191.
Dvina lands, 307-308.

East India Company, 318.
East Indies, 87, 191.
Efimok, 325.
Egypt, 316, 323.
Elets, 138.
Elizabeth I, English queen, 289.
Elizabeth of Bohemia, daughter of James I of England, 318, 320.
England, English, xv, xx, 70, 83-88, 98-108, 114-116, 118-120, 153, 178-186, 188, 190, 211, 218-219, 265, 279, 286, 288, 297, 300, 316-317.
English civil war, 320.
Ephraim, metropolitan of Kazan, 15, 247, 263, 268, 312.
Epifan, 19-20, 210, 265.
Estonia, 129.
Evdokia, wife of Grand Prince Dmitry Donskoy, 259.
Evdokimov, Muscovite, 130.

False Dmitry I, 3, 36, 47-48, 52-54, 99, 252, 254, 256-257, 259-262, 265-268, 270, 275, 279, 281-283, 288, 290, 295, 306, 308, 314.

False Dmitry II, 21, 52-54, 148, 254-257, 260-261, 266-270, 273-275, 277-279, 281, 283-284, 295, 300-301, 304.

Fedor, boyar of Prince Mikhail of Chernigov, 298-299.

Fedor, martyr, 126, 299.

Fedor Borisovich Godunov, tsar, xiii, 289.

Fedor Ivanovich, prince of Starodub, 299.

Fedor Ivanovich, tsar, 2, 44, 88, 99, 105, 117, 179, 184, 207, 264, 280, 289-290, 306, 313, 323.

Fedotievo, village near Riazan, 253.

Feodorit, archbishop of Riazan, 1, 5, 10, 252-253.

Feodosia Fedorovna, tsarevna, 254.

Feodosy, archimandrite of Miracles monastery, 222, 325.

Feofilatiev, Grigory, ambassador to Persia, 198.

Ferdinand, archduke of Styria, later Emperor Ferdinand II, 176, 199, 205-206, 276, 287, 314-315, 319, 321, 323.

Fifths (piatinnye den'gi), xiv.

Filaret, metropolitan of Rostov, later patriarch of Moscow, xiii-xiv, xvii-xviii, 2, 4, 34, 41-45, 55, 59, 62-63, 134, 150, 152-153, 155-162, 166, 169, 173-174, 180-181, 189, 197-199, 202, 206, 212, 220, 223, 225-227, 229, 249, 255, 261, 268, 272, 274-276, 279-280, 283, 296, 305, 307-308, 310-312, 317, 325.

Filosofov, Ivan, 250.

Finch, Thomas, secretary to English ambassador, 179, 181.

Fioravanti, Aristotle, Italian architect, 261.

First Militia Force, 50, 256-257, 260-262, 266, 271, 277-278, 284, 287, 290, 295, 299.

Fleet prison, London, 318.

Fleming, Klaus, Swedish negotiator, 98.

Florence, 240, 286.

Florence-Ferrara, council, 268.

Fomin, Ivan, translator, 70-74, 285-286.

Foreign mercenaries, xviii-xix, 211-212.

Formosus, pope, 126, 299.

France, French, xx, 111, 153, 186-189, 194, 205, 275, 287, 304-305, 319-320, 322.

Frederick III, Danish king, 313.

Frederick V, count palatine, titular king of Bohemia, 185, 315, 318-319.

Frederick Henry, prince of Orange, Dutch stadholder, 189-190, 194, 320.

Freiburg, 281.

Friedrich, duke of Courland, 317.

Gabor Bathory, ruler of Transylvania, 321.

Gagarin, Prince Dmitry, governor of Pskov, 307.

Gagarin, Prince Nikita Nikitich, 131, 305-306.

Gagarin, Prince Semeon Nikitich, 36-37, 210, 215,276-277.

Galagan, Mikita, Ukrainian peasant, 250-251.

Galich, 34, 143, 315, 322.

Galicia, 309.

Gasiewski, Alexander, 47-52, 55, 58-59, 61-63, 65, 127, 141, 143-145, 148, 150,.153-154, 238, 241, 281-283, 300.

Gasiewski, Krzystof, 238.

Gaston, duke of Orleans, 319-320.

Gavrilov, Afanasy, Don Cossack captain, 129.

Gdov, xvi, 96-97, 103, 108-109, 292, 295, 310.

Geneva, 316.

George William, elector of Brandenburg, 164, 179, 314, 317.

Georgia, 85, 196-197, 268, 311, 322.

Gerasim, archbishop of Suzdal, 30, 268.

Germany, Germans, 56, 70, 101-102, 133, 140-141, 153, 175, 177, 182, 186, 205, 211, 227, 313, 319, 324.

Ghulams, 267.

Gilian, 25.

Girlyan (Novaia Zemlia), 87.

Gizingarski, Malteiul, Danish ambassador, 191, 194.

Gizycki, Albert, 238.

Gladky, Grigory, inhabitant of Putivl, 177-178.

Gleb Vladimirovich, early Rus prince, martyr, 126, 299.

Glebov, Moisey, 214, 222, 324.

Glinka, Mikhail, composer, 245.

Glinnitsa, 323.

Glinsk 323; Glinskaia, Elena Vasilievna, wife of Grand Prince Vasily III, 209, 324.

Glinsky family, 209, 323-324.

Glinsky, Prince Boris, 323.

Glinsky, Prince Ivan, 323.

Glinsky, Prince Ivan Lvovich, 324.

Glinsky, Prince Mikhail Lvovich, 323-324.

Glinsky, Prince Vasily Lvovich, 324.

Glückstadt, 313.

Gniewa, battle, 303.

Godunov family, 3, 361.

Godunov, Boris Fedorovich, see Boris Fedorovich Godunov, tsar.

Godunov, Fedor Borisovich, see Fedor Borisovich Godunov, tsar.

Godunov, Ivan Ivanovich, 278.

Godunov, Ivan Vasilievich, 48.

Godunov, Nikita Vasilievich, 139, 180, 310.

Goeteeris, Anthonis, Dutch emissary and memoirist, xv, 99, 296.

Golden Horde, 287, 299.

Golitsyn, Prince Andrei Vasilievich, 48-49, 54.

Golitsyn, Prince Ivan Vasilievich, 41.

Golitsyn, Prince Vasily Vasilievich, 41, 43-44, 52, 54, 59, 63, 129, 134, 150, 152, 274-275, 279-280, 311.

Golovin, crown secretary, 140.

Golovin, Fedor Vasilievich, 1, 256.

Golovin, Peter, commander of Terek Cossacks, 27.

Golovin, Prince Peter Petrovich, 301.

Golovin, Stepan Vasilievich, boyar, 270.

Gorodishche Monastyrskoe (Muromsk), 142.

Gotikon, old man, 129.

Gotland, 313.

Gramotin, Ivan Tarasievich, crown secretary, 35, 51, 173, 182, 275, 284.

Great Britain, 111.

Greater Nogay Horde, 115, 264.

Greeks, 80, 205, 306.

Griaziev, Ivan Kirillovich, conciliar secretary, 121, 168, 193, 314.

Grigoriev, Grigory, 84.

Grigoriev, Joseph, Austrian, 67-68.

Grodno, 152, 280, 282, 323.

Grot, imperial ambassador, 67.

Gruszecki, Polish lord, 56.

Grydycz, Jan, secretary to King Sigismund III of Poland, 46, 52, 57, 133, 142, 147.

Gustav, Swedish prince, 262, 268.

Gustav Vasa, Swedish king, 293.

Gustavus II Adolphus, Swedish king, xvi, xviii, 9, 76, 84, 87, 90, 92-93, 96-98, 100, 104, 110, 112, 122-123, 164, 171, 173-174, 176-177, 179, 193, 207-208, 229, 291, 293, 295-296, 298, 302-303, 313-314, 319-320, 322.

Guy, duke of Spoleto, 299.

Guzow, battle, 282.

Habsburgs, 174, 319.

Hague, The, 83, 320.

Halland, 313.

Halycz, 267.

Hamburg, 70.

Handelius, Erasmus, imperial ambassador, xv, 56-57, 59-60, 63-66, 72-73.

Hanseatic League, 297, 319.

Harjedalen, 313.

Heidelberg, 302.

Henry of Valois, Polish king, later King Henri III of France, 202, 322-323.

Hermogen, patriarch, 53, 55, 59, 158, 252-253, 256, 260, 262-263, 266, 283, 306, 314.

Holland, xv, xviii, xx, 69-70, 83-84, 111, 211, 273, 318, 320.

Holofernes, Assyrian commander, 240, 326.
Holstein xx, 191, 285, 305, 313.
Holy Roman empire, emperor, 76, 83, 111, 174-176, 179, 188-189, 205.
Holy synod, 2, 16, 35, 206, 208, 256.
Horn, Evert, Swedish commander, xvi, 92-93, 95, 97, 101-102, 291, 294.
Horn, Henrik, Swedish negotiator, 98, 172.
House of Commons (England), 317-318.
Husayn, Ottoman grand vizier, 205, 309.
Hussein Bek, Persian bailiff, 197.
Hungary, 194-195, 205, 276, 286, 315, 321.
Iberia, 114, 196.
Ignaty, patriarch, 132, 252, 306, 312, 324.
Ilyin, crown secretary, 30.
Ilza, 302.
India, 87, 115-116, 118, 185, 318.
Ingolstadt, Bavaria, 282, 303, 314.
Ingria, 292.
Irina Fedorovna, tsaritsa, wife of Tsar Fedor Ivanovich, 10, 12.
Irina Mikhailovna, tsarevna, 258.
Isfahan, 267, 318.
Ishterek, khan, 21, 25, 28, 254, 264, 308.
Isidore, metropolitan of Kiev, 268.
Isidore, metropolitan of Novgorod, 88, 113, 168, 263, 289-290, 294, 325.
Istlenev, Stepan Ivanovich, 38, 279.
Istvan Bocksay, Transylvanian ruler, 320-321.
Ivan IV, tsar, xix, 10, 72, 117, 207, 209, 258, 260, 263-264, 277, 290, 313, 323, 325.
Ivan V, tsar, 244.
Ivan Dmitreevich, son of Marina Mniszech, xiv, 25-28, 42, 82, 148-150, 203.
Ivan Ivanovich, tsarevich, 254.
Ivan Kalita, grand prince, 253.
Ivan Mikhailovich, tsarevich, 269.
Ivangorod, 103, 105, 107-108, 292.
Ivangorodishche, 215.
Ivanov, crown secretary, 12.

Izborsk, 310, 326.
Izhora, 109, 123, 175
Izmailov, Artemy Vasilievich, xviii-xix, 33, 36-37, 47, 140, 157, 213, 215, 223-225, 228, 230, 269-271.
Izmailov, Semeon Artemich, 225.
Izmailov, Semeon Vasilievich, 271.
Izmailov, Timofey Vasilievich, 226.
Izmailov, Vasily Artemich, 225, 228, 271.
Jacob, duke of Courland, 317.
James I, English king, 84-87, 98, 109, 114, 116, 118, 120-121, 179, 191, 289, 318.
Jamtland, 313.
Jan Arslan, Nogay pretender, 21.
Jan Kazimierz, Polish king, 275, 293, 317.
Jan Sobieski, Polish king, 128, 303-304.
Janibek Girey, Crimean khan, xv, 82-83.
Janissaries, xviii, 210, 321, 323.
Jerusalem, 240, 312, 319.
Jesuits, 177, 302-303, 314, 324.
Jews, 76, 166.
Joachim, Albrecht, Dutch mediator, 99.
Job, metropolitan of Kiev, 178, 315.
Job, patriarch, 252, 288, 306.
Johan, Danish prince, 192, 258, 268, 320.
Johan, duke of Ostergötland, 99, 298.
Johann Sigismund, elector of Branden-burg, 302.
John, evangelist, 126.
John VIII, pope, 299.
John IX, pope, 299.
Jonas, metropolitan of Krutitsy, 263, 312.
Jonas, metropolitan of Moscow, 126, 267-268.
Joseph, archbishop of Pskov, later patri-arch, 220, 272, 311, 325.
Joseph, archbishop of Riazan, 158, 300.
Joseph, archimandrite of Miracles mon-astery, 165, 314.
Joseph, archimandrite of New Savior monastery, 242.
Judith, biblical heroine, 240, 326.
Jutland, 313.

Kabardia, 27, 268, 277.
Kaffa, 76.
Kaibulovich, Prince Mikhail, 305.
Kalmar, war of, 289, 293, 313.
Kalmyks, 276.
Kaluga, 36-37, 132-135, 137, 143, 257, 259, 277-278, 301, 303-304.
Kaluga brigand, see False Dmitry II.
Kama, river, 264.
Kamieniec, 140-142.
Kanay Murza (baptismal name Mikhail), 140, 298.
Kara straits, 276.
Karachev, 38, 126.
Karamyshev, Ivan Mikhailovich, 305.
Karelia, 292.
Kargopol, 288.
Karl, Austrian archduke, 323.
Karl IX, Swedish king, 88, 90, 101, 291, 293, 295, 322.
Karl Philipp, Swedish prince, xvi, 90, 92-93, 95, 102-104, 257, 290-294, 298.
Karpovich, Leonty, archimandrite, 152.
Kartli, 322.
Kashin, 30, 39, 128.
Kashira, 19, 284, 326.
Kashkin, crown secretary, 122.
Kasimov, 255.
Katyrev-Rostovsky, Prince Mikhail Petrovich, 300.
Kazan, 18-19, 25, 29, 33-34, 39, 55, 80-81, 88, 116, 182, 195-197, 226, 252, 256, 258, 260, 264-265, 268-269, 271-272, 276, 286, 305-306, 308, 311, 314, 317.
Kazanowski, Marcin, 23, 267, 302.
Kazbin, 321.
Kazimierski, Prince, bishop of Kiev, 58.
Kent, 317-318.
Kerch, 309.
Kettler, Gotthard, grand master, 317.
Khalid Pasha, Ottoman grand vizier, 79-81.
Khariton, priest, 49.
Khilkov, Prince Andrei Vasilievich, 212, 258.
Khimka, river, 147.

Khitrovo, governor of Mozhaisk, 202.
Khlopov, Gavrila Vasilievich, 164-165, 312.
Khlopov, Ivan Vasilievich, 164-165.
Khlopova, Maria Ivanovna, xvii, 161-162, 164-166, 314.
Khmelniki, battle, 300.
Khmelnitsky, Bogdan, hetman, 250-251, 275, 286, 308.
Khodynka, river, 158, 261, 277.
Khokhlov, Vasily, musketeer commander, 27-29.
Kholmogory, 85, 116, 123, 179, 301.
Khorosan, province, 267.
Khotin, 302-303, 310, 323.
Khovansky, Prince Andrei Andreevich, 36-37, 272, 276.
Khovansky, Prince Ivan Andreevich, 37, 124, 126, 278-279.
Khovansky, Prince Ivan Fedorovich, 95, 295.
Khvorostinin, Prince Ivan Andreevich, 36-37, 261, 277.
Khvorostinin, Prince Ivan Dmitrevich, 21, 27, 254, 265-266.
Khvorostinin, Prince Yury Dmitreevich, 49, 283.
Khvostov estate, Dederino 99.
Kiev, 177-178, 284, 310, 312, 315.
Kiev Academy, 316.
Kineshma, 257, 284.
Kirchholm, battle, 267, 282.
Kireevsky, Grigory Fedotievich, 200, 322.
Kirghiz, 309.
Kizilbash, 267.
Klesl, Melchior, cardinal, 73-74, 276, 286-287.
Kliazma, river, 11.
Klin, 133, 262.
Kliuchevsky, Vasily Osipovich, historian, 270.
Klushino, battle, xvi, 100, 102, 106, 274, 292, 295-296, 301, 308.
Knäred, peace, 289.
Knudsen, Anna, wife of Vasily Ivanovich Buturlin, 295.
Kochanowski, Jan, Polish emissary, 79.

Koet, Dutch master craftsman, 211.
Kokenhausen, 282.
Kola, 123, 192, 292, 297.
Kolberger Heide, battle, 313.
Kolomna, xiv, 17-18, 39, 56, 138-139, 242, 279, 326.
Koltovskoy, Prince Ivan Alexandrovich, 128, 301-302.
Kolychev, Novgorod noble, 88.
Kondyrev, Ivan Gavrilovich, 134, 186-187, 308-309.
Konev, 178.
Koniecpolski, Stanislaw, Polish hetman, 178, 267.
Konshin, Novgorod crown secretary, 88.
Koporie, 103, 105-108, 292.
Kopyczewski, Polish colonel, 133.
Korela, 100, 106, 169, 296-297.
Korensky, Ivan, 317.
Korobovskoe, 283.
Korobyin, Vasily, 156, 193, 197, 222, 311, 322.
Korsakov, Larka, 201.
Kosem, mother of Sultan Murad IV, 321.
Kostomarov, N.I., historian, 243-250.
Kostroma, xiii, 3, 5, 39, 143, 182, 194, 243-245, 249, 253, 256-257, 262, 285, 316.
Kotov, Fedot Afanasiev, trader, 318.
Kotov, Rodion, leading merchant, 119, 183, 318.
Kozakowski, Polish captain, 56.
Kozar, village, 307.
Kozelsk, 36-37, 132, 141, 262, 271.
Kozlovsky, Prince, 245.
Krapivna, 20, 258, 307-308.
Krasinski, Polish emissary, 142.
Krasny, 142, 144, 215, 310.
Krichev, 215.
Kristiana, 313.
Kristianopel, 313.
Kristiansand, 313.
Kristianstad, 313.
Kriuk-Kolychev, Ivan, 255.
Kromy, 38, 126, 254, 289.
Krutitsy, metropolitan, 158, 206, 214, 242, 263, 294, 326.

Krzycki, Polish chancellor, 46.
Kuchuk Kainardji, treaty, 287.
Kulikovo, battle, 323.
Kumyks, 196-198, 322.
Kuntsevich, Joseph, see Joseph, archbishop of Riazan.
Kurakin, Prince Ivan Semeonovich, 39, 41, 51, 86-87, 261, 279.
Kursk, 126, 129.
Kuvshinov, Afanasy, ambassador to Persia, 197, 311.
Kvashin, Ivan Rodionovich, 283.

Ladoga, 103, 106-111, 284.
Ladoga, lake, 110-111, 122, 270, 292.
Ladyzhensky, Amvrosy, Muscovite emissary, 166.
Lambert, duke of Spoleto, 299.
Lappland, Lapps, 87, 116, 123.
Lavuia, river, 110-111, 122.
Leading merchants (gosti), 17, 118, 298.
Lebedian, 20, 138.
Leiden, 320.
Leksada, Tatar ancestor of Glinsky family, 323.
Leontiev, Danila Yurievich, emissary to Persia, 82, 133, 139, 308.
Lepanto, battle, 304.
Leslie, Alexander "the Younger", Scottish colonel in Muscovite service, 211-212, 215, 217, 219, 324.
Leslie, Alexander, earl of Leven, 324.
Leslie, Lady, wife of Alexander Leslie "the Younger", 324.
Lesser Nogay Tatars, 82, 264.
Letter of Majesty, 286.
Levky, archimandrite of Simonov monastery, 214, 324.
Liapunov, Grigory, 305.
Liapunov, Prokopy Petrovich, leader of First Militia Force, 23, 50, 54-56, 63, 253, 257, 260, 266, 276, 284, 292-293, 295, 316.
Liapunov, Zakhar Petrovich, 253, 266, 296.
Likharev, Nikita Paramonovich, 124, 298.
Likhud brothers, 316.

Likhvin, 37-39.

Lipski, Abdrzej, bishop of Lutsk, 128, 302.

Lisishnikov, Don Cossack ataman, 76.

Lisowski, Alexander Jozef, leader of Polish irregulars, 32, 34, 38-39, 105, 147-148, 255, 269, 278-279, 284, 295, 301, 305, 307, 321.

Lithuania, Lithuanians, 1-4, 8-9, 16-17, 20-21, 23, 30, 34-38, 45-46, 48, 51-52, 54, 56-58, 60-61, 63-66, 75, 82-84, 92, 94, 100, 107, 124, 127-129, 134-137, 141-147, 150-156, 166-167, 173, 188, 197, 202, 206-209, 213-214, 216, 219, 222, 224, 227, 230, 235, 237-238, 244, 246, 270, 276, 281-282, 285, 297, 305, 311, 324.

Litvin, 321.

Liubtimovo, village near Moscow, 10.

Livny, 20, 82, 138, 270, 307.

Livonia, Livonian war, 99, 104-105, 110, 122-123, 129, 177, 210, 233, 254, 282, 285, 291-293, 297, 325.

Lombards, 299.

Lopata-Pozharsky, Prince Dmitry Petrovich, 33, 133, 271, 287, 306-307.

Lorraine, 319.

Louis XIII, French king, 118, 186, 195, 308, 319.

Lower towns, 225, 325.

Lübeck, 313.

Lublin, 128.

Lugovskoy, Tomila, 128, 155-158, 250, 310-311.

Lukaris, Constantione, see Cyril, patriarch.

Lukh, 284.

Lutherans, 169, 171, 205, 237, 312.

Lutsk, 128, 130, 302, 315.

Lützen, battle, xviii, 296.

Luzha, 215.

Lvov, 315-316.

Lvov, Prince Alexis Mikhailovich, 34, 162, 164, 168, 238, 240, 272-273.

Lykov, Prince F.I., 284.

Lykov-Obolensky, Prince Boris Mikhailovich, xiv, xviii, 30-33, 54, 88, 133, 135-137, 211-213, 222, 268 270.

Lykov-Yaroslavsky, Prince Alexis Mikhailovich, 229, 237.

Madalinski, Lithuanian, 148, 225.

Magdeburg 297, 319.

Mahmet Shah Murza, see Suleskov, Vasily Yansheevich.

Mahomet Pasha, Ottoman grand vizier, 80, 1.

Mainz, 319.

Makary, metropolitan of Novgorod, 168-169, 174, 314.

Malagoszcz, 281.

Malmyzh, 261.

Maloyaroslavets, 33.

Malta, 304.

Mamay, Tatar khan, 323.

Mangazeia, 276.

Mansur Ringat, son of Mamay, 323.

Mansur Ksan, son of Mamay, 323.

Mansurov, Peter, ambassador to Constantinople, 75-76.

Manuel, deacon, 79.

Maria Anna of Bavaria, wife of Emperor Ferdinand II, 314-315.

Maria Eleonora of Brandenburg, wife of King Gustavus Adolphus of Sweden, 314.

Maria Grigorievna, tsaritsa, wife of Tsar Boris Fedorovich Godunov, 288.

Maria of Spain, wife of Emperor Maximilian II, 286.

Maria Temriukovna, second wife of Ivan IV, 277.

Marie Louise of Gonzaga, second wife of King Wladyslaw IV of Poland, 275.

Marienburg, xiii, 44, 150, 173, 256, 281, 314; illustration, 149.

Marina Mniszech, wife to pretenders, xiv, 19-21, 25-28, 42, 82, 85, 265, 267, 270, 278, 281, 290, 306, 310.

Marinus I, pope, 299.

Maritime towns, 30, 39.

Mark, English trader, 84.

Marshalsea prison, London, 297.

Martensson, Mons, Swedish emissary, 98, 101, 122.

Martha, nun (Xenia Ivanovna Romanova), mother of Tsar Michael, xiii, xvii, 3-4, 10-11, 42, 157, 247-248, 259, 263, 271, 312.

Martha, nun (Maria Fedorovna Nagaia), widow of Tsar Ivan IV, 10, 12, 259.

Mary, daughter of King Charles I of England, 320.

Mary Stuart, Scottish queen, 289.

Maslov Stav, 177.

Massa, Isaac Abrahamszoon, 116-117, 297, 320.

Master of the Rolls (England), 318.

Matthias, Holy Roman emperor, xiv, 36, 40, 66-69, 71, 74-75, 276, 285-286, 315.

Mattison, foreign colonel in Russian service, 215.

Maurice, prince of Orange, Dutch stadholder, 292, 320.

Maximilian, archduke of Tyrol, 67-68, 287.

Maximilian II, Holy Roman emperor, 286.

Mazovia, 303.

Mecca, 323.

Mecklenburg, 174, 314.

Medveditsa, 20.

Melitos Pagas, patriarch of Alexandria, 316.

Meller, Johann, Swedish agent, 176.

Mena, 215.

Mencinski, Andrzej, 123.

Merchants' Hundred, 57, 285.

Merrick, John, English agent, xv, 85-88, 98, 100-108, 110, 114-121, 180-186, 287-289, 297.

Meshchera, 271.

Meshcherinov, Yushka, renegade Muscovite, Polish governor of Nevel, 201, 225.

Meshchersk, 301.

Meshchersky, Prince Fedor Andreevich, 49, 283.

Meshchersky, Prince Nikofor Fedorovich, 94-95, 291, 295.

Meshchovsk, 36-37, 132.

Mestnichestvo (precedence), 324.

Mezetsky, Prince Danilo Ivanovich, 12, 96, 99, 101-102, 104, 113-114, 139-140, 142, 157, 260.

Miasnoy, Lukian, 72-75, 264, 285-286.

Michael, Prince of Chernigov, 126, 298-299.

Michael Fedorovich Romanov, tsar, xiii-xiv, xvi-xxii, 1-16, 18-19, 21-22, 24-26, 29, 34, 41, 43, 45-46, 60, 62-63, 65-69, 71, 73, 77-78, 80-82, 86-87, 90, 95, 98, 103-104, 110, 117, 124, 126, 137-138, 140, 150-151, 155, 157, 161-162, 166, 174, 179-181, 186, 189, 194-195, 199-201, 203, 209, 212, 216, 220-221, 223, 227, 229-231, 236, 239-240, 242-243, 245-248, 253-262, 264, 269-270, 272, 274-281, 284-285, 287-292, 294, 299, 301, 305, 307-308, 311-312, 314, 316-318, 323; illustration, 13.

Michael Malein, patron saint of Tsar Michael, 15, 263.

Mikhailov 19-20, 138.

Mikhna, governor of Wallachia, 206.

Mikulin, Timofey, governor of Mozhaisk, 277.

Miloslavskaia, Maria, wife of Tsar Alexis, 302, 308.

Minin, Kuzma, 15, 41, 57, 202, 247, 250, 257, 259, 261, 268, 275, 278, 292, 312.

Mirgorodok, 215.

Mitau, 285.

Mitrofan, archbishop of Riazan, 252.

Mius, river, 76, 288.

Mogila, Peter, archimandrite of Caves monastery, Kiev, 178, 316.

Molchanov, Mikhail, favorite of False Dmitry I, 48-49, 283.

Moldavia, Moldavians, 75, 206, 316, 323.

Monasteries and Convents: Annunciation (Moscow), 88; Antonov (Moscow), 277; Archangel (Dvina lands), 307; Archangel (Kholmogory), 301; Archangel (Yuriev-Polsky), 268; Ascension (Moscow Kremlin), 10, 12, 253,

259, 314; Brotherhood (Kiev), 310; Caves (Kiev), 150, 178, 310, 316, 323; Caves (Pskov), 325; Danilov (Moscow), 253; Dermany (Ostrog), 315; Donskoy (Moscow), 32, 139, 270; Georgenburg (Schwaz, Austria), 287; Kaliazin (Tver), 301; Khutyn (Novgorod), 90, 94-95, 113, 288, 291, 294; Kolmov (Novgorod), 291; Luzhetsk (Mozhaisk), 135; Mikhailovsk (Belaia), 228; Miracles (Moscow Kremlin), 165, 222, 306, 314, 325; Mother of God (Tikhvin), 270; New Savior (Moscow), 1, 242, 253; St. Anthony (Novgorod), 326; St. Cyril (Beloozero), 255; St. George (Novgorod), 88; St. Hypatius (Kostroma), xiii, 3, 249, 256; St. Joseph (Volokolamsk), 277; St. Nicholas (Ugresha river), 305, 307; St. Paphnutius (Borovsk), 270; St. Savva (Zvenigorod), 158; Savior (Riazan), 252, 326; Simonov (Moscow), 1, 33, 214, 253, 272, 324, 326; Solovetsk, 254, 279, 289-290, 292, 325; Spaso-Evfimiev (Suzdal), 268, 307; Transfiguration (Moscow), 259; Trinity-St. Sergius (Zagorsk), xvii, 7, 11, 14, 27, 32, 142-144, 148, 254-255, 258, 267, 272, 275, 277, 280, 283, 288, 299, 301, 307; Yakimansk (Mozhaisk), 136.

Monastyrev, Vasily, 140.

Monastyrevsky, 48.

Monier, Anton, Swedish emissary, 174, 176, 273, 300, 305.

Montargis, France, 319.

Montmorency, Henri de, 320.

Moravia, 276, 286.

Mordvin, 254.

Morozov family, 156.

Morozov, Boris Ivanovich, xvii, 156, 311.

Morozov, Gleb Ivanovich, 156, 311.

Morozov, Ivan Vasilievich, 306.

Morozov, Vasily Petrovich, 12, 97, 158, 260-261, 296.

Mosalsky, Prince Vasily, 51.

Moscow, Muscovites, xiii, xv, xvii, 2, 5, 7, 9, 12, 14-15, 19-20, 23-24, 27, 30-32, 34, 45-46, 49, 52, 54, 56-57, 59, 63, 65-67, 74-75, 81-82, 84-85, 88, 90, 93, 97, 109-111, 116, 122-123, 127, 129, 131-139, 141-144, 146, 148, 150, 152, 154-156, 158, 161, 166, 168, 178-179, 182, 187, 190-191, 193, 195, 197, 201-202, 210-211, 214, 220, 226, 228, 230-233, 235-236, 238, 244, 253-255, 258-260, 262, 264-265, 269, 271, 273-274, 277-279, 282-283, 287-288, 294-296, 300-302, 304-307, 311-312, 314-315, 317, 321-322, 324; Arbat, 304; Arbat gates, 139, 272, 290; Deposition of the Robe gates, 242; English compound, 84; Exaltation of the Cross street, 242; Foreign quarter, 320, 324; Frolov gates, 53, 56, 284; Kitai quarter, 23, 53, 56, 84; Kolomna highway, 56; Kulishki street, 56; Nikita gates, 139-140; Pereiaslavl road, 142; Petrov gates, 139; the Pipe, 139; Presentation gates, 139, 142; Presentation street, 270; St. Nicholas gates, 53; Serpukhov gates, xiv, 257, 310, 323; State Historical Museum, 283; Stone bridge, 242; Taganka, 253 Trans river quarter, 317; Trinity road, 142; Tver gates, 139, 270, 304; Tver street, 270; Water gate, 56; White quarter, 55-56; Wooden city, 55-56, 242; Zhivoy bridge, 56.

Moscow Kremlin, 5, 12, 23, 34, 242, 255, 259, 261, 267, 273, 282, 314; Golden Chamber, 10, 12; Golden Scriptorium, 14; Palace of Facets, 10, 206, 254, 259, 307; Savior tower, 259; School of Red Commanders, 259, 314; Treasury Court, 242.

Moscow miracle-workers, 27, 126, 267-268, 298.

Moscow river, 270.

Mozhaia, river, 136.

Mozhaisk, 39, 102, 128, 133-137, 147, 158, 222-223, 225, 230, 269, 273, 277, 282, 301, 307.

Mozyr, 128.
Mstislavl, 215.
Mstislavsky, Prince Fedor Ivanovich, 9, 15, 19-20, 41, 51, 53, 101, 105, 138, 157, 206, 255, 258-259, 262, 279-280.
Mstislavsky, Prince Ivan Fedorovich, 258.
Mtsensk, 36, 258, 270, 308.
Mufti, Turkish religious leader, 80-81.
Munich, 319.
Murad IV, Ottoman sultan, 188, 195, 321.
Muraviev, Matvey, 95.
Murom, 33, 255, 271.
Muromsk, 142.
Muscovy, Muscovite realm, 22-23, 36, 42, 49, 67-68, 73, 77, 84, 88, 103, 129, 131-132, 141, 143, 145-147, 151-152, 157, 166, 172, 177, 185, 188, 200-203, 205-208, 213, 221, 232, 234-235, 238-239, 280, 290, 292, 304, 316.
Muscovy Company, xv, 288-289, 318.
Muslims, 67, 166, 322.
Mustafa, Ottoman sultan, 309.
Myshetsky, Prince Efim, 217.
Myshkino, 102.
Mytishi, village near Moscow, 11.

Nagaia, Maria Fedorovna, see Martha, nun.
Nagaia, Yevlampia Mikhailovna, 273.
Nalivaiko, cossack rebel leader, 284.
Narva, 105, 175, 292-293.
Nashchokin, Prince Boris Ivanovich, 37, 277.
Nazarov chronicle, 245.
Neglinnaia, river, 242, 284.
Netherlands, 111, 179, 276, 281, 320.
Neva, river, 107.
Nevel, 129, 142, 215, 276.
Neverov, crown secretary, 186.
New Chronicler, 265.
New Style (Gregorian) calendar, 310.
Nicholas I, pope 299.
Nicholas I, Russian emperor, 303-304.
Nikandor, archimandrite of St. George monastery, Novgorod, 88.

Nikitnikov, leading merchant, 183.
Nikolaev, David, Dutchman, 192.
Nikolskoe, village, 158.
Nikon, patriarch, 265, 310, 316.
Nikon chronicle, 246.
Nizhny Novgorod, 33-34, 49, 57, 88, 162, 164-166, 182-183, 197, 254-256, 261-263, 269, 271-272, 276-277, 287, 302, 312, 325.
Nogat, river, 281.
Nogay Tatars, 17, 21, 25, 27, 79, 168, 254, 258, 264, 284, 308-309.
North sea, 314.
Northern Ossetia, 322.
Northwest passage, 318.
Nosenichi, 215.
Novaia Zemlia, 87, 116.
Novgorod, Great Novgorod, xvi, 24, 39, 86, 88-96, 98-99, 101, 103-104, 107-114, 121, 123, 168-172, 186, 206, 217, 254-255, 261, 270, 272, 276, 279, 283-284, 287, 290, 292, 294, 296, 310, 314, 324-325.
Novgorod miracle workers, 171.
Novgorod Seversk, 129, 142, 215, 231, 259-260, 271, 285, 321.
Novgorodok, 230.
Novikov, N.I., 265.
Novosil, 321.
Nowodworski, Chevalier Bartlomiej, 131, 139-140, 142, 304.

Ob, river, 87, 115-116, 118.
Obolensky-Lykov, see Lykov-Obolensky.
Obonezh "fifth", Novgorod lands, 270.
Oborski, Jan, Polish emissary, 305.
Ododurov, Ivan Grigorievich, ambassador to Turkey, 287.
Odoev, 305-306, 308, 321.
Odoevsk, 210.
Odoevsky, Prince Ivan Nikitich "the Elder", 88, 102, 290-292, 294-295.
Odoevsky, Prince Ivan Nikitich "the Younger", 20, 25, 28-29, 264-265, 271, 300.
Odoevsky, Prince Nikita Ivanovich, 258.
Odoevsky, Prince Nikita Romanovich, 264.

Oesel, 313.
Ogarev, Ivan, 214.
Oka, river, 17, 138, 290, 308.
Okunev, bailiff, 186-187.
Old Style (Julian) calendar, 310.
Olesnicki Mikolaj, Polish diplomat, xv, 44-45, 281.
Oliwa, treaty, 275.
Olonets, 40, 110.
Olyk, 324.
Onega, river, 40.
Onega, lake, 123.
Onuchin, musketeer captain, 29.
Opalinski, Andrzej, 303.
Opalinski, Lukasz, 303.
Opalinski, Peter, elder of Srem, 128, 303.
Opulchin, tsar's emissary to Don Cossacks, 22.
Orel, 38, 254, 269.
Oreshek, 107-108, 110-111, 175, 292.
Orsha, 46, 152, 154, 203.
Orthodox Brethren, 152, 274, 280, 310, 315-316.
Osipovich, crown secretary, 129.
Oskol, 127, 273.
Oslo, 313.
Osman II, Ottoman sultan, xvii, 205-208, 210, 309, 323.
Ostashkovo, 98.
Ostergötland, duchy, 298.
Ostrog, 315.
Ostrov, 310.
Ostrozski, Prince Konstantin, 315.
Otrepiev, Grishka, renegade monk, 4, 36, 52, 54, 77, 314.
Ottoman empire, 267, 303.
Our Lady of Riazan, miraculous icon, 253.
Our Lady of Vladimir, miraculous icon, 53.
Ovsey, 215.
Oxenstierna, Count Axel, Swedish chancellor, 97, 293, 295-296.
Oxford, 317.
Ozerishche, 215.

Padua, 315.
Palchikov, musketeer captain, 29.

Pafnuty, metropolitan of Krutitsy, 263.
Pagaliewski, Lithuanian captain in Muscovite service, 297.
Pakhra, river, 283.
Palitsyn, Avraamy, chronicler, cellarer of Trinity monastery, 1, 253-254, 295.
Panov, Fedor Vasilievich, crown secretary, 198.
Papal nuncio, 240.
Paris, 293.
Parliament (England), 320.
Passau, 286.
Paul, metropolitan of Krutitsy, 242, 326.
Paul V, pope, 316.
Pavlovo, village, 255.
Pechory, 310.
Peipus, lake, 122.
Pereiaslavl-in-Riazan, 3, 18, 39, 142, 253, 264, 278.
Pereiaslavl-Khmelnitsky, 264.
Pereiaslavl-Zalessky, 19, 256, 264.
Peremyshl, 37, 39.
Perm, 318.
Pernau, 282.
Persia, Persians, xv, 19, 21, 26, 78-79, 81-83, 85, 87, 110, 114, 115, 117-118, 123, 153, 181-184, 186, 191, 195-198, 265, 267, 272-273, 276, 283, 286-288, 300-301, 318-319, 321, 323.
Peski, 99.
Pesochna, hermitage, 153.
Peter I, Russian emperor, 244, 287, 296.
Peter, bogus tsarevich, 259.
Peter, metropolitan of Moscow, 126, 253.
Petrizhitsky-Kulaga, Ivan, cossack hetman, 178.
Petrov, Osip, cossack ataman, 280.
Philip III, Spanish king, 195.
Phillips, Ernest, Dutch merchant, 191.
Piliusz, cousin of Emperor Matthias, 67.
Pimin, Evsevy, pseudonym of Peter Mogila, 316.
Pinsk, 324.
Pivov, Levka, cossack, 148.
Plemiannikov, table attendant, 211.

Pleshcheev, Fedor Kirillovich, 56, 96, 255, 280, 284-285, 295, 299.
Pleshcheev, Ivan Dmitrevich, 305.
Plichta, Konstanty, castellan of Sochaczew, 128, 140, 302-303.
Pochapovsky, Jeremiah, Uniate bishop of Lutsk, 315.
Pochep, 129, 142, 210, 215.
Podolia, 267.
Pogoreloe Gorodishche, 298.
Pogozhy, Fedor, 55.
Pogozhy, Ivan Semeonovich, 127, 297, 299-300.
Poland, Poles, xiii-xiv, xx, 1, 3, 5, 8-9, 14, 16, 23, 34-36, 40, 43, 45-48, 51, 57, 59-60, 63, 65, 72, 77, 83-84, 92, 101, 106, 121, 123-124, 127, 129, 133-134, 137, 139-143, 145-146, 148, 150, 152-153, 155, 158, 166-167, 174, 176-180, 186, 195, 197, 199-244, 246, 248, 253-254, 256-257, 265, 270-271, 273, 275, 277-278, 284, 288-289, 293, 295, 297, 300-304, 306-311, 314, 316-317, 322, 323.
Polev, governor of Elets, 138.
Poliane, ancient Rus tribe, 251.
Polianovka, river, xix, 153, 156.
Polianovka, conference and truce, xiii, xix, 201, 229, 231, 238, 274, 325.
Polish Commonwealth, 45, 61-62, 128, 130, 134, 239, 303.
Polish Senate, 40-41, 46.
Polotsk, 215.
Polovtsians, 287.
Poltava, 323.
Pomerania, 174, 274.
Pope, 75, 175, 179, 189, 221, 287, 302.
Popova Gora, 142-144.
Porkhov, 103, 108-109, 292, 307.
Porto, episcopal, 299.
Poshekhonie, 25, 143.
Posnikov, undersecretary, 75.
Poszony, 321.
Potemkin, Yushka, renegade Muscovite, Polish governor of Serpeisk, 201, 225.
Potocki brothers, 282.
Pozdeev, Fedor, 317.

Pozdeev, Ivan, 317.
Pozdeev, Ivan, crown secretary, 178, 316-317.
Pozharsky, Prince Fedor Ivanovich, 307.
Pozharsky, Prince Dmitry Mikhailovich, 7, 14-15, 23, 38-39, 41, 67-68, 88, 132-138, 154, 158, 214, 216, 220, 222, 247, 249-250, 253, 257, 259, 261, 263, 268, 272, 275, 278, 291-292, 302, 306-307.
Prague, xviii, 74.
Presnia, river, 140, 142, 147, 158, 303.
Pronchishchev, Osip, emissary to Sweden, 122.
Pronsk, 131.
Pronsky, Prince Peter Ivanovich, 128, 131-132, 301-302, 305.
Propoisk, 215.
Pristaltsov, Tomitka, 107.
Prosovetsky, Andrei, 255, 284.
Protasiev, Solovoy, ambassador to Constantinople, 75, 79, 143, 148, 287.
Protestants, Protestantism, 174, 177, 302, 313, 316, 319-320.
Protopopov, governor of Briansk, 270.
Prozorovsky, Prince Semeon Ivanovich, 96, 127, 215-216, 225, 300.
Prussia, 173-174, 274-275, 302.
Pskov, 24, 39, 95-98, 107, 110, 119, 123, 144, 187, 217, 254, 270, 275, 283-284, 292, 294 305, 307, 324-326.
Pushkin, Gavrilo, conciliar noble, 15.
Pushkin, Ivan, Muscovite commander, 38, 279.
Pushkin, lord-in-waiting, 158.
Pustozersk, 192.
Putivl, 129, 138, 148, 207, 270, 301, 305, 308, 311, 317.

Radilov, Epikha, cossack ataman, 22.
Radimichi, ancient Rus tribe, 251.
Radom, 281.
Radziwill, Albrycht Stanislaw, Lithuanian chancellor, 215, 228, 238, 240, 324-325.
Radziwill, Krzystof, Lithuanian hetman, 58, 146, 230-231, 235, 285.
Rakhmantsevo, battle, 280.

Raphael, bishop of Kolomna, 242, 326.

Rawa, 303.

Razmysl, privy councillor to Emperor Matthias, 67.

Reformation Commission (Austria), 286.

Repnin, A.A., governor of Nizhny Novgorod, 254.

Reval, 99, 110, 112, 293.

Revelation, book of, 298.

Riazan, 18, 50, 54, 158, 245, 252, 254, 258, 266, 269, 271, 300, 306-308, 322.

Richelieu, cardinal, 319.

Riga, 282, 293.

Rigsrad (Danish parliament), 313.

Riksdag, (Swedish parliament), 122, 293.

Rizzio, David, 289.

Rogachevo, village, 143.

Roman empire, 298.

Romanchukov, Savva, crown secretary, 117.

Romanov, 25.

Romanov family, 254, 261-262, 269, 311.

Romanov, Alexander Nikitich, 256.

Romanov, Fedor Nikitich, see Filaret, patriarch.

Romanov, Ivan Nikitich, 15, 41, 44, 164, 256, 261-263, 269.

Romanov, Nikita Ivanovich, 263.

Romanov, Vasily Nikitich, 256, 262, 288.

Romanova, Anastasia Nikitichna, 268.

Romanova, Uliana Fedorovna, 263.

Romanova, Xenia Ivanovna, see Martha, nun.

Rome, 287, 299, 302-303, 306.

Romen, 215.

Romodanovsky, Prince Grigory Petrovich, 54.

Roslavl, 141-142, 215.

Rostock, 295.

Rostokino, village near Moscow, 32.

Rostov, 10, 19, 206, 256, 258, 278, 312.

Rostov-on-Don, 287.

Roussel, Jacques, ambassador from Hungary, 194-195, 321.

Royal Tribunal (Polish), 303.

Rozverman, foreign colonel in Russian service, 219.

Rozynski, Roman, 295.

Rubtsov, Alexander-Liubim Dementievich, Swedish emissary, 172-174, 270, 314.

Rudolph II, Holy Roman emperor, 72, 74, 276, 286, 302, 315.

Ruffo, Marco, Italian achitect, 259.

Rurik, early Rus prince, 88, 105, 132.

Rusan Bek, Persian ambassador, 197-198, 311.

Russian empire, 287.

Ruza, 135.

Rylsk, 129, 272.

Rzhev, 127-128, 145, 278, 300, 321.

Rzhev Volodimerov, 39, 305, 309.

Rzhevsky, 250.

Safavid dynasty, 267.

Sahaidachny, Peter Konashevich, 138-139, 143, 148, 309-310.

Salis, battle, 282.

Saltykov family, 156.

Saltykov, Boris Mikhailovich, 164-166, 242, 314.

Saltykov, Ivan Mikhailovich, 49, 269, 283-284, 287, 290.

Saltykov, Mikhail Glebovich, 35, 48, 51, 152, 261, 273, 275-276, 283.

Saltykov, Mikhail Mikhailovich, 164-166, 242, 312.

Saltykova, Martha Mikhailovna, 271.

Samara, 25-26, 304, 306-307.

Samsonov, Semeon, crown secretary, 75-76.

Sanchursk, Tsarevosanchursk, 273, 309.

Sanderson, English colonel in Russian service, 218-219.

Sandomir, 281.

Sanguszko, Samuel, Polish emissary, 211.

Sapieha, Jan-Piotr, 23, 267, 280-281, 284, 301.

Sapieha, Krzystof, 142-143.

Sapieha, Leo, Lithuanian chancellor, xiv, 43-47, 50, 58, 128-129, 137, 140-141, 143-145, 147, 232, 238-239, 280-282, 311.

Sapozhok, 322.
Saratov, 270.
Saray, 298.
Satin, Muscovite noble, 222.
Scandinavia, 319.
Schwaz, Austria, 287.
Scotland, 289.
Sebezh, 129, 142, 215.
Second Militia Force, 40, 88, 257, 261-265, 271, 278, 286-287, 291, 295, 297, 306, 317.
Sejm (Polish parliament), 46, 61, 128, 134, 147, 153, 212, 275, 281-282, 303.
Sekerin, Perfily, 272.
Selishchi, 99.
Semlevo, 230.
Sergius, archbishop of Smolensk, 132, 146, 306.
Serpeisk, xix, 37, 142, 144, 203, 207, 215, 230-231.
Serpukhov, 17, 33, 39, 143, 262, 268, 284, 290, 308.
Severia, 21, 32, 38, 64, 129, 143, 217, 279, 308, 323.
Sevsk, 285.
Shaykh-al-Islam, 321.
Shchekatov, geographer, 244.
Shcherbatov, Luke Osipovich, 255.
Shcherbatov, Vasily Petrovich, 277.
Shein, Ivan Mikhailovich, 225.
Shein, Mikhail Borisovich, xix, 43-44, 46, 131, 152, 156-157, 213, 215-217, 219-222, 224, 226-230, 235, 256, 269, 280, 305, 308, 322.
Sheremetev family, 252, 262.
Sheremetev, Boris Vasilievich, 308.
Sheremetev, Fedor Ivanovich, xvii, 1, 39, 41, 114, 140, 142-143, 146, 148, 155-157, 165, 229-230, 236, 238, 254-255, 262, 265.
Sheremetev, Ivan Petrovich, 8, 10, 23, 257-258.
Sheremetev, Vasily Petrovich, 257.
Sheremeteva, Elena Ivanovna, widow of Tsarevich Ivan Ivanovich, 254.
's Hertogenbosch, 320.
Shipov, crown secretary, 162.

Shuia, 33, 284.
Shuiskaia, Princess Catherine Grigorievna, xix, 241-242, 296.
Shuisky family, 253, 261, 273.
Shuisky, Prince Dmitry Ivanovich, xix, 36, 43, 47-48, 52, 101-102, 240-242, 266, 273, 279-280, 296.
Shuisky, Prince Ivan Ivanovich, 36, 43, 47, 143, 151, 200-201, 262, 266, 280-281.
Shuisky, Prince Vasily Ivanovich, see Vasily Ivanovich Shuisky, tsar.
Shulgin, Nikanor, 18-19, 264.
Siberia, 19, 88, 115, 119, 132, 197, 225-226, 261, 264, 272, 276-277, 294, 300-301, 305.
Sidorka, Pskov pretender, 299.
Sigismund III, Polish king, xv, xix, 34, 36, 40-42, 44, 46, 50-52, 57-59, 62, 64, 68, 73-75, 78-81, 84, 97, 99, 109, 115, 120, 123, 132, 140-141, 152, 172-173, 175-177, 183, 186, 188, 190, 206, 208-209, 212-213, 224, 228, 238, 240-241, 253-254, 256-257, 261, 267-270, 273-275, 279-281, 284, 293, 302, 304, 306, 311, 317-318, 322-324; illustration, 204.
Silesia, 274.
Singel, imperial herald, 41, 71.
Siniawski, Polish herald, 23.
Sinope, 77.
Sipahiyan, 321.
Sitsky, Alexis Yurievich, 47, 282.
Skopin-Shuisky, Prince Mikhail Vasilievich, 100-101, 255, 262, 266, 279-280, 290, 292, 296, 308.
Skorobovitsky, Kirilka, cloth merchant, 63.
Skowronski, Polish artillery commander, 226.
Skuratov, Dmitry, Muscovite commander, 124, 126.
Skuratov, Maliuta, Ivan IV's henchman, xix.
Slavic-Greek-Latin Academy, 316.
Sliezen, Alexander, Polish emissary, 156-157.
Slonim, 44.

Smith, Fabian, English agent, 179, 181.
Smith, Sir Thomas, English ambassador, 289.
Smolensk, xiv-xvi, 20, 24, 35, 37, 46-47, 52, 54-55, 61-62, 64-66, 73, 101, 119, 124, 127, 129, 131-132, 135, 141-142, 146, 176, 205, 211, 213, 215-217, 221-224, 226-229, 235, 238, 254, 256, 260, 263, 269, 274-276, 278-283, 300, 303, 306, 308-309, 311; Bogdanov pathway, 217; Borova stream, 215; Intercession hill, 215-217; Skervonkaia hill, 217; Zapresk side, 216.
Smolensk war, xvii-xix, 263, 269, 273, 305, 309, 322, 324.
Sobakin, Grishka, 107.
Sobieska, Sophia Theophila, 303.
Sobieski, Jakub, governor of Lublin, 128, 140, 303.
Sobieski, Jakub, the younger, 303.
Sobieski, Jan, see Jan Sobieski, Polish king.
Sobinin, Bogdashka, Ivan Susanin's son-in-law, 243, 247, 249.
Sochaczew, 128, 302.
Söderköping, 293.
Soissons, duke of, 194.
Sokolinski, Polish emissary, 238-239, 305.
Sokolowski, Polish lord, 133.
Solario, Pietro, Italian architect, 259.
Sol Galitskaia, 34.
Solomensk, trading settlement, 110.
Solomon, biblical king, 289.
Solovetsky, Stepan, 49, 51, 63.
Solvychegodsk, 263, 305.
Somov, crown secretary, 140.
Spain, Spanish, 111, 153, 177, 188-189, 281, 315, 320.
Spens, James, English ambassador to Sweden, 289.
Spoleto, duchy, 299.
Srem, 128, 303.
Srodz, 303.
Staraia Rusa, 99-100, 103, 108-109, 255, 292.
Staritsa, 128, 278, 305.

Starodub, 124, 129, 142, 215, 270.
States-General (Netherlands), 69, 83-84, 189-190, 320.
Stefan Bathory, Polish king, 202, 281, 304, 320, 323.
Steinbock, Gustav, Swedish emissary, 122.
Stempkowski, Polish ambassador, 258.
Stephen VI, pope, 299.
Stockholm, 88, 92, 110-111, 121-123, 291.
Stolbovo, peace treaty, xvi, 108-113, 121, 124, 178, 292.
Stralsund, 174, 313-314.
Strasbourg, 281, 302.
Strawinski, Balthsar, elder of Mozyr, 128.
Streshneva, Evdokia Lukianova, second wife of Tsar Michael, xvii, 166, 272.
Stroganov family, 15-16, 263-264.
Struys, Nicholas, Dutch colonel in Polish service, 34, 41, 45, 154, 156-157, 256.
Stumsdorf, truce, 274, 303, 325.
Sudermania, duchy, 293.
Sukhona, river, 87.
Sukhotin, Muscovite captain, 215, 219.
Suleshov, Akhmat Pasha, Crimean ambassador, 82-83.
Suleshov, Ibrahim Pasha, 83.
Suleshov, Prince Vasily Yansheevich, 271-272.
Suleshov, Prince Yury Yansheevich, 34, 127-128, 242, 271-272, 300.
Suma, fort and district, 39, 106-109, 279, 292.
Sumbulov, Grigory, 266.
Sumbulov, Isaac, 96.
Surgut, 295.
Surozh, 124, 215.
Susanin, Ivan, xiii, 5, 243-244, 247-250, 257; illustration, 6.
Suzdal, 20, 33, 148, 255, 273, 284, 307, 321.
Svatkovo, village, 11, 143-144, 148.
Sviatopolk Vladimirovich "the Damned", early Rus prince, 299.
Sviyazhsk, 19, 255.

Sweden, Swedes, xiii-xiv, xvii-xviii, xx, 5, 9, 30-31, 64, 66, 72, 74, 83, 87-114, 121-122, 124, 168-179, 186, 191, 193, 202, 208, 210-211, 226, 232, 255, 261, 263-264, 267, 270, 273-275, 278, 281-282, 284-285, 288-290, 292-294, 296-297, 299-300, 303, 305, 307-308, 313, 317, 322, 325.

Taininskoe, village near Moscow, 14, 159.
Tara, 276, 294.
Tarakanov, Muscovite captain, 127.
Tarnowiecki, Polish officer, 53.
Tatars, 18, 26, 33-34, 77, 105, 123, 135, 155, 166-168, 198, 208, 210, 254, 258, 262, 265-266, 269, 271-272, 277-278, 283, 286, 288, 301, 304-305, 307.
Telepnev, crown secretary, 102.
Teliatevsky, Prince Peter Ivanovich, 283.
Temriuk, town, 309.
Terek, river, 24-25, 27, 29.
Terek Cossacks, 24-25, 265.
Terka, 25, 27, 255, 311.
Teusen, treaty, 296-297.
Teutonic knights, 281, 297.
Tewkesbury, 317-318.
Theodosius II, pope, 299.
Theophanes IV, patriarch of Jerusalem, 158, 312, 315, 317.
Thirty Years' War, xvii, 276, 293, 295, 313, 320-321, 324.
Tiber, river, 299.
Tilly, imperial general, 313.
Tikhonov, Muscovite noble, ambassador to Persia, 81.
Tikhvin, xvi, 30, 95-96, 106, 284, 292, 299.
Time of Troubles, xv, 18, 28, 124, 168, 181, 238, 246, 250, 255, 264, 267, 273, 275, 284, 300, 308, 314.
Timothy, patriarch of Constantinople, 79-80.
Tinbaev, Prince Mikhail Konaevich, 124, 298.

Tiufiakin, Prince Grigory Vasilievich, 143, 198, 310.
Tiukhin, crown secretary, 195-197.
Tiumen, 255.
Tmutorokan, 287.
Tobolsk, 162, 254, 261, 271, 276-277, 279, 285, 301, 312.
Tolochanov, Mikhail, favorite of False Dmitry I, 48-49, 283.
Tomsk, 301.
Toropets, 9, 64, 145, 150, 207, 217, 276, 308, 321.
Tortensson's war, 313.
Torun, treaty, 281.
Torzhok, 96, 128, 295, 304.
Totma, 39.
Tovarkov, 133.
Tradescant, John, geographer, 318.
Trakhoniotov, Nikofor Vasilievich, treasurer, 180, 318.
Transylvania, 206, 321.
Trebizond, 77.
Tretiakov, Peter, crown secretary, 15, 66.
Troekurov, Prince Ivan Fedorovich, 7-8, 37, 257.
Trubchevsk, 142, 215, 230-231.
Trubetskoy princes, 129.
Trubetskoy, Prince Andrei Vasilievich, 260.
Trubetskoy, Prince Dmitry Timofeevich, 14-15, 23, 41, 96, 142, 158, 247, 260-262, 271, 277-278, 295, 297, 299, 304, 317.
Trubetskoy, Prince Yury Nikitich, 49, 129, 132, 143, 152, 200, 260, 271, 276, 278, 304, 322.
Tsarev-gorod, 276.
Tsarevo-Sanchursk, Sanchursk, 273, 309.
Tsarevo-Zaimishche, 260.
Tsaritsyn, 305.
Tukhachevsky, Yakov Ovstafiev, native of Smolensk, 136, 309.
Tula, 20, 260, 266, 273, 278, 306, 308, 311.
Turgenev, Bogdan, native of Yaroslavl, 136.
Turinsk, 294, 301.

Turkey, Turks, xv, xviii, xx, 18, 21, 24, 45-46, 59, 67, 74, 75-81, 110, 115, 117, 129, 131, 186, 188, 205-206, 208, 228, 235, 258, 267, 275-276, 284, 287-288, 304, 306, 309, 318, 321.

Tushino, Tushinites, 48, 100, 139, 142, 255-256, 267, 269, 275, 277-278, 283-284, 295.

Tver, 133, 174, 301, 307.

Tverdikov, Grigory, leading merchant, 182, 318.

Tverdilishchi, 127, 300.

Tylicki, Piotr, bishop of Cracow, 302.

Ufa, 262.

Uglich, 25, 39, 128, 278.

Ugra, river, 305, 307.

Ukraine, Ukrainians, 19, 34, 37, 131, 134, 250, 275, 284, 286, 308-309, 315-316.

Uniates, 306, 315.

Unzha, 34.

Uppsala, 123.

Ural steppes, 257.

Uraz Mohammed, Tatar khan, 278.

Ursuline order, 302.

Urusov, Andrei, governor of Putivl, 305.

Urusov, Ivan, 139.

Urusov, Kurmash Murza, 135.

Urusov, Peter, Tatar prince, 301.

Us, cossack ataman, 29.

Ushakov, Stepan Mikhailovich, 33, 66-72, 75, 83, 285.

Usov, Andrei, 152-153.

Ustiug, 39, 288.

Ustiuzhna-Zhelezopolskaia, 32, 96, 117, 128, 284.

Uswiat, 215, 267.

Uzbek, Mongol khan, 299.

Uzbeks, 267.

Vaga, river, lands, 39, 261, 271.

Valuev, Grigory Leontievich, 133, 308.

Valuiki, 271.

Van Damme, Dutch officer in Muscovite service, 211.

Varangians, 88.

Vasiliev, Sydavny, crown secretary, 41.

Vasily II, grand prince of Moscow, 64, 229, 267-268, 285, 325.

Vasily III, grand prince of Moscow, 324.

Vasily Ivanovich Shuisky, tsar, xiii, xvi, xix, 10, 12, 36, 43, 45, 47, 52, 54, 99-100, 102, 106, 135, 145, 240-242, 252-253, 255-256, 259-262, 265-266, 268-269, 271-272, 274-282, 285, 290-292, 296, 299-301, 304, 306-307, 310, 314.

Vasily Mikhailovich, tsarevich, 269, 273.

Veliaminov, governor of Pskov, 95.

Veliaminov, Andrei Ignatievich, 16.

Veliaminov, Ivan, 210.

Veliaminov, Miron, governor of Kaluga, 37, 202, 279.

Velikaia, river, 97.

Velikie Luki, 201, 207, 217.

Velizh, 124, 129, 142-145, 150, 215.

Veltdril, Johann, Dutch ambassador, 189.

Venev, 308.

Venice, Venetians, 287, 315.

Verkhoturie, 162, 276, 296, 300, 307, 312.

Viatichi, ancient Rus tribe, 251.

Viatka, 300.

Viazma, xix, 37, 39, 47, 128, 131-134, 141, 147, 152-154, 200, 222-223, 241, 276, 278, 282, 301-305, 307, 309.

Viazma, river, 230.

Vienna, xv, 66, 72, 285-287, 303-304, 321.

Villanova, castle, 303.

Vilna, Vilnius, see Wilno.

Vitebsk, 124, 306.

Vitovt, grand prince of Lithuania, 323.

Vitovtov, Evdokim, 49, 51, 130.

Vladimir, 1, 20, 33, 90, 138, 148, 255, 261, 271, 279, 284, 295.

Vladimir-in-Volhynia, 130.

Vladimir Sviatoslavich, early Rus prince, 245, 299.

Vladimir Yaroslavich, early Rus prince, 297.

348   INDEX

Vnukov, Pozdney, 156.
Voguls, 307.
Vokhna, battle, 140, 301.
Volga, river, 22—25, 85, 87, 114—115, 117, 181—182, 254, 304, 324—325.
Volga Cossacks, 21.
Volkhov, river, 291, 294.
Volkonsky princes, 253.
Volkonsky, Prince Grigory Konstantinovich, 83, 138-139, 158, 222, 310.
Volkonsky, Prince Mikhail, 253.
Volkonsky, Prince Nikita, 31, 33.
Vologda, 39, 88, 119, 128, 158, 264, 269, 312, 314.
Volok, 298.
Volokolamsk, 45, 133, 135, 147, 270, 274.
Volynsky, Fedor Vasilievich, 136, 309.
Volynsky, Stepan Ivanovich, 38, 178, 279.
Voronets, Lithuanian, 156-157.
Voronezh, 20, 277, 297, 300.
Vorontsov-Veliaminov, Leonty, governor of Tikhvin, 96.
Vorotynsky, Prince Alexis Ivanovich, 263.
Vorotynsky, Prince Ivan Mikhailovich, 12, 14, 47-49, 51-52, 57-61, 63-66, 260.
Vorsma, river, 255, 266.
Vygovsky, cossack grand notary, 286.
Vyborg, 90, 92, 110, 291.
Vyborg, treaty, 290 291.

Waldemar, Danish prince, 258, 272, 286.
Waljawski, Eustace, Polish officer, 23.
Wallachia, Wallachians, 75, 206, 267, 282, 302, 316, 323.
Wallenstein, imperial general, 313-315.
War Council (Poland), 281.
Warsaw, 43-44, 128, 131, 134, 137, 147, 275, 302.
Weiger, Polish colonel, 228.
Weissenstein, 282.
West Indies, 191.
Westphalia, peace, 320.
White Mountain, battle, 315, 319, 321.
White Sea, 123, 279.

Wiener-Neustadt, 286.
Wilhelm, claimant to duchy of Courland, 179, 317.
William, son of Frederick Henry of Orange, 320.
Wilno (Vilna, Vilnius), 35, 152, 276, 282, 285, 302, 306.
Wisniowieck, 177.
Wiszel, Polish colonel, 127.
Wladyslaw, Polish prince, later King Wladyslaw IV of Poland, xvi, xix, 35-36, 40, 42, 44-45, 52, 54-55, 59, 60-62, 64-65, 122, 128-134, 137, 139, 141-143, 151-153, 199-200, 202-203, 205, 207, 209-210, 215, 219-221, 224, 226-232, 236-239, 254-257, 261-262, 266-267, 269, 273-276, 279, 281, 283-284, 288, 293, 295, 300-304, 306, 308-309, 311, 317-318, 314; illustration, 216.
Wloclawek,302.
Wojewodski, Stanislaw, Polish governor of Smolensk, 215.
Wojtkowski, Polish lieutenant, 54.
Wolmar, 292.

Xenia Borisovna Godunova, tsarevna, 259, 268, 320.

Yablonov, 308.
Yaik, river, 22, 24-25, 29.
Yaik Cossacks, 24-25.
Yakutsk, 301.
Yama, 103, 106-108, 292.
Yampolie, 302.
Yanov, Vasily, crown secretary, 35, 49, 151-152, 275-276.
Yaropolch, 261.
Yaroslav Vladimirovich "the Wise", early Rus prince, 105, 297.
Yaroslavl, 1, 9-10, 25, 30, 32, 39, 55, 67, 117, 136, 143, 182-183, 249, 255-257, 259, 261-264, 272-273, 278, 286-288, 291, 297, 299, 306, 317.
Yasenichi, 215.
Yauza, river, 142, 269, 324.
Yenisei, river, 117.

Yeremeev, Yeremey, translator, 40, 68.
Yermak, cossack leader, 264.
Yudin, trader 119.
Yumin, Boris, Don Cossack ataman, 129.
Yuriev, Ivan, leading merchant, 182.
Yuriev, Klim, foreigner, 192.
Yuriev, Vaska, priest's son, 63.
Yuriev-in-Livonia (Dorpat, Tartu), 105, 186, 297.
Yurkaevo, 134.
Yury, baptismal name of Yaroslav the Wise, 105.

Zaborovsky, Semeon, ambassador to Austria, 66-72, 75, 83.
Zadzik, Jakub, bishop of Chelmno, 229-231, 238, 241, 325.
Zamoyski, Jan, chancellor, 281-282, 302.
Zaporozhian Cossacks, 79, 83, 147-148, 172, 177-178, 203, 205, 234-235, 288, 302, 305, 309.
Zaporozhian Sech, 288.
Zaporozhie, 173, 288.
Zaraisk, 20, 278.
Zarutsky, Ivan Martynovich, 5, 18-22, 24-29, 42, 82, 85, 256-257, 261-262, 265-266, 269, 271, 278, 283, 297, 300, 308.
Zarutsky, Zakhar, Lithuanian, 225.
Zasekin, Prince Alexander Petrovich, 48-49, 283.
Zebrzydowski rebellion, 267, 282, 302-303.
Zhedrinsky, Dmitry, native of Nizhny Novgorod, 136, 309.
Zheliabuzhsky, Afanasy Petrovich, xiv, 41-47.
Zheltye Vody, battle, 275.
Zhuravlev, Roman Ivanovich, see Raphael, bishop of Kolomna.
Ziuzin, Alexis Ivanovich, 84, 86, 99, 113-114, 120, 288.
Zmud, 282.
Zolkiewski, Stanislaw, Polish hetman, xix, 50, 54, 102, 129, 131, 134, 238, 260, 267, 274, 282, 284-285, 296, 303-304, 308.
Zolkwa, 238.
Zubov, native of Smolensk, 131-132.
Zurawinski, castellan of Bielsk, 128.
Zvenigorod, 139, 158.

THE EDITOR AND TRANSLATOR

George Edward Orchard was born at London, England in 1935 and grew up in Hampshire, where he received his primary and secondary education. At the age of eighteen he was conscripted into the British armed forces, where he learned Russian at the Joint Services's School for Linguists, Bodmin, Cornwall, and then served with the 755 Signal Unit of the British Army of the Rhine. Having completed his military service he read Modern History at St. John's College, Oxford, receiving his Bachelor of Arts degree in 1959. After a year of teaching at Bemrose School, Derby, he studied at St. Mary's College, Strawberry Hill, for the Postgraduate Certificate in Education as an external student of the University of London. The subsequent two years were spent teaching at Owerri Grammar School, Imerienwe, Nigeria. Having migrated to Canada in 1963, he studied at McGill University, Montreal, from 1964 to 1966, receiving his Ph.D. in history in 1967. Since 1966 he has taught at the University of Lethbridge, as well as the occasional summer course at Nipissing University College, North Bay, Ontario. He has visited the Soviet Union three times, and was one of the first participants in the Canada-USSR Academic Exchange. During the academic year 1984–1985 he was a Visiting Fellow at the University of London School of Slavonic and East European Studies, and was the keynote speaker at the Annual Conference on Russian Studies at the University of Wales. His publications include a scholarly translation of Isaac Massa's *Short History of the Muscovite Wars* (Toronto, 1982), and he has contributed numerous entries to the *Modern Encyclopedia of Russian and Soviet History*, as well as articles and reviews on early Russian themes to numerous learned journals. He has recently completed a scholarly translation and edition of the memoirs of the early seventeenth-century soldier of fortune Konrad Bussow. Professor Orchard lives with his wife Ellen Claire and his daughter Catherine Jane in Lethbridge, Alberta.

FROM ACADEMIC INTERNATIONAL PRESS*

THE RUSSIAN SERIES

1 S.F. Platonov **History of Russia** (OP)**
2 **The Nicky-Sunny Letters, Correspondence of Nicholas and Alexandra, 1914-1917**
3 Ken Shen Weigh **Russo-Chinese Diplomacy,** 1689-1924 (OP)
4 Gaston Cahen **Relations of Russia with China...1689-1730** (OP)
5 M.N. Pokrovsky **Brief History of Russia** (OP)
6 M.N. Pokrovsky **History of Russia from Earliest Times** (OP)
7 Robert J. Kerner **Bohemia in the Eighteenth Century**
8 **Memoirs of Prince Adam Czartoryski and His Correspondence with Alexander I** (OP)
9 S.F. Platonov **Moscow and the West.**
10 S.F. Platonov **Boris Godunov**
11 Boris Nikolajewsky **Aseff the Spy**
12 Francis Dvornik **Les Legendes de Constantin et de Methode vues de Byzance**
13 Francis Dvornik **Les Slaves, Byzance et Rome au XIᵉ Siecle** (OP)
14 A. Leroy-Beaulieu **Un Homme d'Etat Russe (Nicholas Miliutine)...**
15 Nicolas Berdyaev **Leontiev** (In English)
16 V.O. Kliuchevskii **Istoriia soslovii v Rossii**
17 **Tehran Yalta Potsdam. The Soviet Protocols**
18 **The Chronicle of Novgorod**
19 Paul N. Miliukov **Outlines of Russian Culture** Vol. III Pt. 1. The Origins of Ideology
20 P.A. Zaionchkovskii **The Abolition of Serfdom in Russia**
21 V.V. Vinogradov **Russkii iazyk. Grammaticheskoe uchenie o slove**
22 P.A. Zaionchkovsky **The Russian Autocracy under Alexander III**
23 A.E. Presniakov **Emperor Nicholas I of Russia. The Apogee of Autocracy**
24 V.I. Semevskii **Krestianskii vopros v Rossii v XVIII i pervoi polovine XIX veka** (OP)
25 S.S. Oldenburg **Last Tsar! Nicholas II, His Reign and His Russia** (OP)
26 Carl von Clausewitz **The Campaign of 1812 in Russia**
27 M.K. Liubavskii **Obrazovanie osnovnoi gosudarstvennoi territorii velikorusskoi narodnosti. Zaselenie i obedinenie tsentra** (OP)
28 S.F. Platonov **Ivan the Terrible** Paper
29 Paul N. Miliukov **Iz istorii russkoi intelligentsii. Sbornik statei i etiudov** (OP)
30 A.E. Presniakov **The Tsardom of Muscovy**
31 M. Gorky, J. Stalin et al., **History of the Civil War in Russia** (Revolution) (OP)
32 R.G. Skrynnikov **Ivan the Terrible**
33 P.A. Zaionchkovsky **The Russian Autocracy in Crisis, 1878-1882**

34 Joseph T. Fuhrmann **Tsar Alexis. His Reign and His Russia**
35 R.G. Skrynnikov **Boris Godunov**
38 V.V. Shulgin **Days of the Russian Revolutions. Memoirs From the Right, 1905-1907.** Cloth and Paper
43 Nicholas Zernov **Three Russian Prophets. Khomiakov, Dostoevsky, Soloviev** (OP)
44 Paul N. Miliukov **The Russian Revolution** 3 vols.
45 Anton I. Denikin **The White Army** (OP)
55 M.V. Rodzianko **The Reign of Rasputin—An Empire's Collapse. Memoirs** (OP)
56 **The Memoirs of Alexander Iswolsky**

THE CENTRAL AND EAST EUROPEAN SERIES
1 Louis Eisenmann **Le Compromis Austro-Hongrois de 1867**
3 Francis Dvornik **The Making of Central and Eastern Europe** 2nd edition (OP)
4 Feodor F. Zigel **Lectures on Slavonic Law**
10 Doros Alastos **Venizelos—Patriot, Statesman, Revolutionary** (OP)
20 Paul Teleki **The Evolution of Hungary and its Place in European History**

FORUM ASIATICA
1 M.I. Sladkovsky **China and Japan—Past and Present**

THE ACADEMIC INTERNATIONAL REFERENCE SERIES
The Modern Encyclopedia of Russian and Soviet History 50 vols.
The Modern Encyclopedia of Russian and Soviet Literatures 50 vols.
The Modern Encyclopedia of Religions in Russia and the Soviet Union 30 vols.
Soviet Armed Forces Review Annual
USSR Facts & Figures Annual
USSR Documents (1987-) Annual
USSR Calendar of Events (1987-) Annual
USSR Congress of Peoples's Deputies 1989. A Stenographic Record 2 vols.
Documents of Soviet History 12 vols.
Gorbachev's Reforms. An Annotated Bibliography of Soviet Writings. Part 1 1985-1987
Military-Naval Encyclopedia of Russia and the Soviet Union 50 vols.
China Facts & Figures Annual
Encyclopedia USA. The Encyclopedia of the United States of America Past & Present 50 vols.
Sports Encyclopedia North America 50 vols.
Sports in North America. A Documentary History
Religious Documents North America Annual
The International Military Encyclopedia 50 vols.

SPECIAL WORKS
S.M. Soloviev **History of Russia** 50 vols.
SAFRA Papers 1985-

*Request catalogs **OP—out of print